POLICE ANALYSIS AND PLANNING
FOR VEHICULAR BOMBINGS

ABOUT THE AUTHOR

John W. Ellis is an enlisted veteran of Vietnam who has both bachelor's and masters degrees in administration of justice. He has seven years active military duty, seven years of law enforcement duty as a local police officer and Deputy U.S. Marshal, seven years as a private security officer, and four years as a licensed private detective. He is certified as a firearms instructor and currently serves as the secretary for the Kansas Association of Private Investigators (www.kapi.org).

In 1991, he was activated as an Army Reserve officer and deployed to Saudi Arabia for the cease-fire phase of Desert Storm. During the one-year tour, he served as the Provost Marshal, Khobar Towers and as an Operations Officer for Headquarters, Army Forces Central Command (Forward).

POLICE ANALYSIS AND PLANNING FOR VEHICULAR BOMBINGS

Prevention, Defense, and Response

By

JOHN W. ELLIS

CHARLES C THOMAS • PUBLISHER, LTD.
Springfield • Illinois • U.S.A.

Published and Distributed Throughout the World by

CHARLES C THOMAS • PUBLISHER, LTD.
2600 South First Street
Springfield, Illinois 62704

© *1999 by* CHARLES C THOMAS • PUBLISHER, LTD.
ISBN 0-398-06938-7 (cloth)
ISBN 0-398-06939-5 (paper)

Library of Congress Catalog Card Number: 98-50863

Printed in the United States of America
CR-R-3

Library of Congress Cataloging-in-Publication Data

Ellis, John W.
   Police analysis and planning for vehicular bombings : preven-
tion, defense, and response / by John W. Ellis
      p.   cm.
   Includes bibliographical references and index.
   ISBN 0-398-06938-7 (cloth) ISBN 0-398-06939-5 (pbk.).
   1. Bombing investigation--Case studies. 2. Vehicle bombs--
Prevention--Case studies. 3. Police--Special weapons and tactics
units--Case studies. I. Title.
HV8079.B62E55   1999
363.25'964--dc21
                                                        98-50863
                                                           CIP

On June 25, 1996, Building 131, Khobar Towers, Al-Khubar,
Kingdom of Saudi Arabia partially disintegrated in a truck bomb blast.
I felt it half a world away.

This text is dedicated to those who stand guard and to those who stand behind them.

PREFACE

This text is oriented toward planning police operations in the public sector, but will be usable by other public officials as well as some military and private sector police operations. It addresses police threat assessment of, vulnerability assessment to, defense against, and response to attacks by weapons of mass destruction. It begins with an essay on the distinctions between military and police operations and includes an examination of the U.S. counterterrorist policy, assessment of the various types of weapons of mass destruction and the terrorist ability to make and use them, the legal limitations of police response operations in the United States, and defensive response to this form of attack. It concludes with commentary on actions that may be needed if this threat continues to develop in the United States.

In preparing this text, I am attempting to provide the local police official the basic considerations in these areas. This will enable those officers to provide the best level of protection that they can with the resources they have available and will provide indications of the possible response to such situations or the threat of such situations. The included essay is a short review of historical and related topics but is not based on extensive research which is documented and footnoted to clearly demonstrate its validity. While containing references and notations, the text is mostly based on personal experience, study, and reading over a number of years. Consequently, it is primarily opinion but clearly an educated one. I include this essay to lay the foundation for statements and comments in the following chapters, and for the final conclusions which point to social changes that are needed to confront this threat.

INTRODUCTION

In 1991, I was activated in my capacity as an Army Reserve Officer during the cease-fire phase of Desert Storm. One of many reservists sent to the Persian Gulf to assist in the closeout of the war effort, I drew two assignments that lasted nearly a year. First, I was assigned as the Army Provost Marshal to the largest troop billeting facility in the area at the time. I held this position during the October peace talks. I brought to this assignment 6 years of active and 12 years of reserve military duty, 7 years civilian law enforcement experience at local and federal levels, and 7 years of private security experience in large hotels as well as a lengthy list of educational and training schools. I needed all of this background.

It is hard to accurately describe the transition from the American civilian security setting to the Mideast security setting, and even tougher to describe the impact of being placed in charge of a military police force whose primary duty is to protect several thousand people from possible terrorist or commando attack. Calling it a "reality check" does not even begin to address the feeling. As I performed the various functions required of a Provost Marshal in this setting, I slowly grew the uncanny feeling that virtually everything I had ever done or learned had been preparing me for this assignment. I applied knowledge and experience that ran the gamut from my enlisted experience in Vietnam through personal security assignments performed as a Deputy U.S. Marshal to attendance at weekly staff meetings of a large hotel. In spite of all this background, I found that the assignment was simply more than one person could effectively handle. Had it not been for the assignment of an excellent Deputy Provost Marshal, John R. Murphy, the job could not have been accomplished with the level of proficiency that we attained. Some of the knowledge I include in this text was gained by reviewing "Murph's" work and the work of several Air Force Security Police officers, and comparing it to what I would have done myself. I also benefitted quite strongly from contact with a Saudi Arabian Military Police Officer with some direct experience in counterterrorist operations.

At the completion of this duty, which disappeared due to planned downsizing of the military operations, I drew a second assignment as an Operations Officer with the forward headquarters element of ARCENT (Army Forces Central Command). In this position, I found myself drafting a set of Rules of Engagement for an infantry unit placed into Kuwait for a short time period for security duties. This required review of and blending of the Rules of Engagement for Desert Storm and the Army's regulations on the Use of Force and Counterterrorism. When the draft was complete, I watched the review process by various high-level headquarters and embassies. It was an informative experience. This was followed by drafting the initial rear security plan for Army forces remaining in country for a limited time.

On return to the United States, I continued in the private security sector, conducting research for a publication and attempting to start a business. Unexplained illnesses of mine and the terminal illness of my father slowed this process significantly. I became certified as a firearms instructor for private detectives and security personnel and began to study more closely the issues in this area. Out of long habit, I continued reading about and watching world events relating to military operations and terrorism, analyzing them as I did so. I found the events in Somalia and Haiti interesting, particularly as they related to Rules of Engagement and Use of Force, an area becoming more and more sensitive in the public view.

As the summer of 1995 neared, I was working at my computer one morning on some of my research. I had the television on in the background when the show was interrupted for a news bulletin concerning what the announcer said was "a natural gas explosion" in Oklahoma City. I looked at the rather poor, initial aerial shots of the federal building and was immediately skeptical. The destruction appeared to be too great for a natural gas explosion. As the event unfolded, the pictures improved in quality and the report changed to "a bomb of possibly 1,000 pounds." Having seen the damage much better, I felt that this was probably incorrect. Subsequent reports in the media confirmed this. Like most other Americans, I watched the reports from and the actions occurring in Oklahoma City. Unlike most others, I had a much different response.

It took me nearly two days to realize that I was having virtually no emotional response to the situation, a result of the many years of training and several months of planning for this exact possibility. I found myself simply comparing the planning that I had done in the Persian Gulf to the actual requirements occurring at the scene, mentally noting what we had done well and what we had not. My sole emotional response was to attempt to contact Murph; he had come from Oklahoma when he was activated. Also, unlike many others, I did not immediately suspect Mideast terrorists as the prime possibility. I considered them as one of three likely possibilities, and not the most probable. When I noticed the emotional response of the people around me, it started me thinking about why I wasn't responding and others were. I realized that the difference was my psychological preparation for battle. With me, the intended effect had not been obtained. I had defeated the enemy in advance of his attack; I was not "terrorized" by the incident.

As I thought about the significance of this, the uncanny feeling that I had during my Desert Storm service came back. I recalled the articles I had written for a military publication on rear battle and the tremendous response that I had received to them. I realized that I had exactly the right educational and experience background to write a planning text for police and other emergency services dealing with this topic. At the current time my career path is almost perfectly balanced between military service, civilian law enforcement duty, and private security operations. I understand the problems, limitations, and resources of all three to address attacks by vehicular bombs, recently defined in the United States Code as "weapons of mass destruction." Hopefully, this text will be of benefit to those officers and officials who have never had to confront this type of problem, and will help build the psychological preparation for battle that prevents the attack and enables effective response.

CONTENTS

POLICE ANALYSIS AND PLANNING
FOR VEHICULAR BOMBINGS

Chapter 1

POLICE OPERATIONS NEAR THE BORDER OF WARFARE

I have served in both active and reserve status as a Military Police Officer. The significance of this statement becomes obvious when you examine the role contrast inherent in the designation. The term "military police officer" is both a contraction and a contradiction of terms. This evolves from the duality of roles and missions that they are expected to perform. In a wartime setting, they serve as military officers in a police structure to wage and win a conflict, and in a peacetime setting, they serve as police officers in a military structure to prevent and rectify conflict. In both settings, they are required to do so for the defense of the people of the United States. It is, perhaps, this dualistic role undertaken for the same purpose which prompts this essay. The flexibility required to perform such changes of duty creates the opportunity for possible insights into the problems which occur for police operations as the internal conflicts in a society approach, but do not cross, the border to open warfare among the civil populace of a country. Since I intend to address some police operations within the United States during such a situation, it will be of value to review some historical background prior to examining the requirements for conducting such operations.

Since the inception of the United States, the government has operated "...to form a more perfect union, establish justice, insure domestic tranquility, provide the common defense, promote the general welfare, and ensure the blessings of liberty..."[1] to the people as its basic purpose. The founding documents laid out basic guidelines and structures which affect the provision of these common goals and the development of the services necessary to provide them to the American society. The provision of the included common defense goals (justice, tranquility, common defense) occurs, primarily, through the military services, the civilian public sector emergency services, and the private sector security services. Each of these services has limited, different authority and a consequent limited, different scope of activity with all generally working to fulfill the same purpose. These different limitations have influenced the development of each service and its primary components: organizational structure (personnel and equipment), operational patterns, and support requirements; simultaneously, the common purpose has worked to produce similarities among the three services. This dual-influence process has created a more refined set of parameters within which each service operates, but has also confused when, how, where, and why the three services operate, overlap, and interact in support of the common purpose. In order to understand their interrelationship and its impact, let us examine the pertinent basic authority structures, historical development, and current parameters. The result can be used as a basis for projecting the limitations and capabilities for each of these services in furtherance of justice, domestic tranquility, and common defense.

THE LEGAL FOUNDATIONS OF THE COMMON DEFENSE SERVICES

The authority and structure of the military services is founded clearly in the U.S. Constitution. The President is delegated the responsibility to command the army and navy as well as to appoint its officers.[2] The Congress is delegated the responsibility to raise and support armies, to provide and maintain a navy, to regulate the land and naval forces, to declare war, to finance the common defense, to define offenses against the laws of nations, and to make laws necessary to carry out these powers.[3] This basic structure has been furthered in the United States Code by the creation of the Department of Defense with its various military departments, personnel regulations, acquisitions regulations, and so forth. The only other significant limitation of the military services is that contained in the Posse Comitatus Act[4] which prohibits members of the Army and Air Forces from being used for civilian law enforcement. Its initial purpose is presumed to have been to prevent local sheriffs from summoning soldiers as a posse, but it is used and interpreted differently in this era. Now it is widely presumed by the average person that military personnel are totally prohibited from enforcing civilian law, a presumption which is not accurate. There are circumstances where it is appropriate and legal for them to do so.

The second group to examine is the militia. The U.S. Constitution does not directly authorize or establish a militia; it simply assumes that the militia already exists. It authorizes Congress to provide for calling the militia forth; organizing, arming, and disciplining it; and for governing such part of it as is in federal service (as happens when the militia is called forth).[5] The Constitution reserves the appointment of militia officers and the actual training of the militia to the States, but specifies that the Congress shall prescribe the discipline for the militia.[6] The actual legal foundation of the militia structure is in the United States Code.[7] This legal foundation is repeated, and, in some cases, amplified in the Constitutions and Statutes of the various states within the union. Basically, the legally-defined militia of the United States consists of an organized militia (National Guard and Naval Militia) and an unorganized militia (all other able-bodied males aged 17-45 except those specially exempted).[8] Most states retain this structure in their individual constitutions and statutes with some adding other classifications such as a military reserve (retired members of the Armed Services, etc). The organized militia is included in the definition of the Reserve Components of the Armed Forces,[9] but the unorganized militia is not. This distinction is important when examining other portions of the United States Code or state statutes.

The basic constitutional authority to call forth the militia is delineated in the United States Code[10] and supplemental federal regulations. The organization, location, and command of the organized militia is basically established within the United States Code.[11] The training of the organized militia is also addressed[12] by the United States Code as is the provision of uniforms, arms, and supplies.[13] Various Department of Defense regulations elaborate further upon these guidelines which form the basis for the state statutes and regulations of the various state national guard units. The final portion of the discipline of the organized militia is provided by Congress through the Uniform Code of Military Justice enacted under Executive Order.[14] The final constitutional limitation concerning the militia is to recall that the 2nd Amendment guarantees the right of the people to keep and bear arms to preserve a well-regulated militia.

The basic framework for the militia is, then: Congress provides for the discipline, regulation, etc., but it is the States that actually control the discipline, training, etc. according to the standards established by Congress. The standards are established primarily through the United States Code; the militia is not a direct Constitutional structure. The unorganized militia is not part of the Armed Forces and its discipline, arming, equipping, etc is not directly provided for in the United States Code. Both the organized and unorganized militia may, under the Constitution, be called forth "... to execute the laws of the Union, suppress Insurrections, and repel Invasions."[15] When called forth to federal service, it becomes part of the Armed Forces and is commanded by the President.

Public sector emergency agencies and officers have no direct legal foundation in the United States Constitution; their existence and authority is established in the United States Code. It is derived from the Constitutional powers granted to the Executive and Legislative branches of government under Articles I and II. Congress uses its authority to make all laws necessary and proper to establish the agencies, and the President utilizes the executive powers to appoint and commission officers. This direct constitutional authority is supplemented by authority delegated through the United States Code to various subordinate executive agencies, department heads, or independent agencies which also establish regulations as needed. No federal law enforcement, state law enforcement, or municipal law enforcement agency or officer can demonstrate direct constitutional authority, only derived authority.[16]

Private sector security agencies have no clear legal foundation in the U.S. Constitution and virtually no mention in the United States Code. The only portions of the Constitution which somewhat pertain to the private sector are the Ninth and Tenth Amendments. This reservation of rights to the people and the states is only a background foundation. Examination of the United States Code finds no direct reference to private sector security agencies, but does contain some sections which control activities typically performed by them as well as others. Examples would include United States Codes pertaining to Fair Credit Reporting,[17] Debt Collection,[18] Employee Polygraph Protection,[19] or information privacy restrictions found in the Social Security Act and various other statutes. The most direct reference is found in a section[20] which restricts private sector security use of certain names, badges, identification, etc. that might indicate a federal government connection. In the final analysis, almost all authority for private security is actually based upon the personal rights enjoyed by a private citizen under common law. The two common law concepts which are usually relied upon are: the right of personal self-defense and the right of the personally accountable owner to control either property or employees. The various states have developed statutes which define and elaborate upon these rights. Some states and local jurisdictions have also developed statutes and ordinances which regulate private sector security operations.

Having established the basic framework under which the military, the public sector, and the private sector operate, a short review of trends in the development and use of these services is the next step. The order in which these trends are addressed is not of any particular significance.

PROFESSIONALIZATION

The first easily identifiable trend over the last several decades is a conscious attempt to professionalize the people providing the core of the emergency services. This has taken various forms depending upon the type of emergency services. The military services had recognized this problem over a century ago and developed the service academies, Reserve Officer Training Corps programs at land grant colleges, and various subordinate training schools within the various branches of the armed forces. This professional training and education approach continues very strongly inside the armed services but has fallen off in its general application among people who would constitute the unorganized militia. The virtual end of the military draft and nearly simultaneous reduction in the mandatory R.O.T.C. training requirement at many colleges has reduced the existing numbers of people with introductory military training. Since this is the population base from which the unorganized militia is drawn, this reduction in turn lowers the overall capability of the general population to perform or assess the common defense. Their unfamiliarity and lack of experience with actual technical requirements and capability makes it more difficult to recognize the appropriate need for common defense forces or to recognize appropriate performance by those forces, and generally weakens both the recruiting base and the community support for those forces.

The emergency services have responded to this generalized problem, the need for professionalization, and specific problems noticed during many incidents, by undertaking both educational and organizational changes. Over the last four decades, every emergency service (police, fire, ambulance, etc.) has experienced a tremendous increase in the educational requirements for the positions. In the 1960s, police officers with college degrees were rare. In the 1990s, police officers with advanced degrees are rather common in many places. The same statement can be made with equal validity about firefighters, nurses, emergency medical technicians, communications dispatchers, and many other emergency services workers. Due partly to this influx of educated people, but also due to outside pressures for improvement, the organizations have changed as well.

The first evidence of organizational change can be seen in the creation of positions which did not exist four decades ago. Three are easy to cite: SWAT Team Police Officer, Paramedic, and HAZMAT Team Firefighter. All three of the positions were developed over the last three to four decades as responses to recurring specific problems and widespread recognition that improvement required actually changing the nature of the job in order to improve performance. All three of these examples have in common the fact that each is a development which is based upon new organizational structures that contain positions requiring skill, training and equipment which differs from similar positions within the same organization. SWAT Officers receive advanced tactical training, and significantly different firearms than other police officers; paramedics receive advanced life support training and carry defibrillator, drugs, etc; HAZMAT Teams undergo extensive training in effects of various chemicals and other substances and carry unusual equipment such as nonporous suits, absorbent materials, impermeable drums, etc. for which the average firefighter has little use. These organizational changes are not only signs of professionalization within the emergency services but are also clearly, at times, intermingled with societal changes as well. The easiest citations of the latter being the introduction of 911-centralized emergency dispatching and Worker Right-to-Know programs which identify all hazardous materials in the workplace. These tie right in with the organizational changes in the emergency services but have enormous impact on the general population at large. Actually, these last two show how close the interrelationship between the community-at-large and its emergency services really is. The societal context must always be considered when evaluating change.

Professionalization has also been pursued by detailed analysis of events and incidents with consequent development of procedures and techniques to better deal with those events and incidents. Volumes of examples could be cited easily, but I wish to focus on one particular area to assist later explanations. In the 1950s and early 1960s, several individual police incidents involving the lawful use of force, particularly firearms, came to attention in various ways. Sometimes the attention was public and sometimes the attention was mostly within the profession and virtually unnoticed by the public. Both the public attention and the rather dramatic failures noticed within the profession caused the members of the police profession to begin analyzing the use of force, especially armed encounters (gunfights, to use the old term which is avoided these days). Driven by the desire to professionalize, the desire to avoid lawsuits, and the strong desire to survive the encounter, the profession underwent many changes.

In most agencies, the use of force policy changed significantly as the body of civil law became more clearly developed. Firing at fleeing felons was slowly narrowed and then virtually eliminated in most agencies (Now limited authority is appearing in state statutes). Agency policies were brought into line with state laws so that the language of the law was reflected in the use of force policy. State legislatures began to tighten the requirement for use of force which had widely been left to officer discretionary judgment. Officers began to receive more extensive training in the meaning of the statutes and policies. This was followed by improvements in the judgment portion of the firearm training. Filmstrips, slide shows, live scenarios with blanks, etc. were developed to teach the officer how to make the shooting decision under stress in realistic situations and were then widely implemented. Equipment, ammunition, and tactics changed as each event was analyzed, its meaning assessed, and the answers added to the database.

The predominance of revolvers slowly gave way to the predominance of pistols as shotguns are now slowly giving way to carbines or submachineguns. Ball ammunition gave way to hollow points (to prevent overpenetration and protect the innocent). Slow velocity rounds gave way first to high velocity rounds with light grain bullets and now to slightly lesser velocity rounds with medium grain bullets. Protective vests appeared, adopted first by individual officers convinced of their need and not by administrators; now completely accepted by administrators who, sometimes, have to *order* their usage. Now officers have available ballistic helmets, shields, and panels to protect them from opposing fire and allow capture in incidents where gunfire was previously the only reasonable alternative. Target-style shooting for handgun qualification gave way to practical-style shooting for qualification. More rounds were fired at closer ranges as the analysis proved that ranges were typically short in armed encounters. Speed loaders were developed for revolvers and timed exercises for reloading and target engagement became prevalent. New stances were tried, night-firing began, and frequency of training increased. All this to better approximate the armed encounter. The changes in police firearms training over the last forty years in the United States are probably not matched by any other period of training on weapons anywhere in history. In spite of this, two observations are clear:

1. The outcome of the armed encounter still depends upon the individual officer's judgment and skill applied in a split-second time frame;
2. The public examination of, attention to, and expectations about such situations have not lessened, but actually seem to have increased.

Consequently, one has to question whether professionalization of the officer contains the final answer. Maybe professionalization of the public is part of the answer. It is clear that the public has strong influence; sometimes the influence does not make sense. Take for example, the limitations placed upon police officers in simple ways as a result of perceived problems.

The availability of personal information versus personal privacy presents some interesting examples. Based upon what was perceived as intrusiveness by businesses and government, a number of privacy provisions were enacted by various legislatures over the last twenty or thirty years with interesting results. Fair Credit provisions make it illegal for a police officer to access your credit record without a court order. This means that a police officer (whose background is investigated, who is fingerprinted and photographed, who is polygraphed and psychologically-tested, who is interviewed by a board of public officials, and must present references) cannot see what the 17-year-old-cashier *can* see when he runs your credit card at the point of purchase. This is obviously in your best interest, right? How ridiculous can these provisions become? Here are two examples:

> A military officer who clipped a copy of a newspaper article and photograph of his neighbor, a civilian, and retained it would be committing an illegal act. This constitutes maintaining a file on civilians and is illegal for the military without special permission, given only for terrorists and other dangerous people.
>
> One police department was confronted with the need to distribute a photograph of a convicted murderer who had escaped from prison and was returning to the area where the homicides (convicted of two, suspected of more) had occurred. His mug shot had been destroyed by the department that arrested him in accordance with state law that prohibited keeping the photo more than a certain number of years as a violation of *privacy*. How do you violate the privacy of a convicted murderer by maintaining a picture of him in a police file while he is still in prison?

At this point, you may be wondering what this obvious tirade has to do with professionalism of the common defense forces. The answer is: Response, both by the Public and for the Public.

The military has "professionalized", becoming an all-volunteer force in response to public pressure in the 1960s and 1970s due to its perceived misuse in VietNam. The emphasis has been on the volunteer force, trained to deal with problems overseas. The organized militia has become mostly focused on performance as a Reserve Component of the Armed Forces, and lessened its emphasis on domestic actions. This trend has begun to reverse in the last five years as the volunteer force has downsized and the frequency or extent of peacekeeping and domestic problems has increased. The unorganized militia effectively exists only on paper. This deterioration has helped feed the justification for unofficial militias which began moving into the vacuum.

Police and other emergency services have "professionalized" due to changing requirements, expectations, civil rights demands, civil liability, and so forth. As the trend emerged, the same forces driving it also drove out those who were viewed as the "least" professional. The volunteers, the auxiliaries, the reserves or the sheriff's posses of various emergency services dwindled and virtually disappeared. Recently, they have begun to reappear, supplemented by neighborhood watches, citizen patrols, and increases in private security functions. Sparked by changes in the types, intensity, and rates of crime, adjustments have slowly occurred as the professionalization trend grew. Yet, what is the public impact? Has this professionalization served the public interest? The change was not deliberately planned, it came as a response to several factors. It has left clear impact on both the capability of the military and the police.

PUBLIC STIMULUS: RIGHTS ASSERTION

Professionalization has actually been a response to a Public Stimulus, the assertion of individual rights. Such a statement requires a broad view of the civil rights movement, not one that confines it simply to the racial aspect. This rights assertion has taken two primary forms which are intertwined. The first form is the deliberate advancement of individual rights by the various elements of the civil rights movement; the second form is the primary enforcement tool of civil rights, civil liability. A strong emphasis on individual civil rights began in the 1950s and grew into many areas. Racial equality, gender equality, physically-disabled equality, privacy issues, consumer rights, freedom of speech and expression, protestor rights, and myriad criminal defendant issues received attention. As the rights were asserted to advance both personal or group agendas, the opposition frequently was directed at the police and military or simply crunched them between the two opponents. This led to an identification of the police and the military as the opponent by many societal subgroups. Eventually, this generalized to the government and its operatives, the politicians and the bureaucrats. The extent of this generalization has left long-term effects upon the social interaction between the government and its citizens. One could speculate whether this was a continuation of *The Manufacture of Madness* theorized by Thomas Szasz in his book,[21] but such speculation is mostly immaterial to this discussion.

The point is to recognize that the civil rights advancements and the accompanying gigantic increase in civil liability risk has had enormous impact. The perceptional change that has been created in the conduct of police and military operations affects both public expectations and actual procedures.

The shift in the public attitude has been one of increasing expectations; a demand for error-free, perfect operations by everyone involved. Stated in this fashion, it is easily recognizable as an unrealistic expectation, but that is seldom recognized by the public. The really interesting portion of this change in expectations is its accompanying decline in acceptable conduct by the others involved. The public expectation has simultaneously grown much more tolerant of actions by those who are opposing the police or military. In some cases, the acceptable conduct grows to unbelievable proportions. Physical struggles, shots fired through doors, hour-long car pursuits, 80-day stand-offs, fugitive flight from justice lasting decades, killing of law enforcement officers, etc. have all occurred, and have all recently been justified as "appropriate" by some segment of the public. The explanation for the expectations defy logic. Why does a high-speed police pursuit that lasts over an hour become an example of police brutality and not an example of excessive risk to several hundred citizens by fleeing criminals? How does firing blindly through a front door become an appropriate use of force by a citizen when it is a law enforcement officer on the other side of the door? Where do such concepts originate? Why are these views accepted so widely in some segments of the population? An examination of the development of police operational tactics may help explain it.

POLICE TACTICAL RESPONSE DEVELOPMENT

Since the 1960s, there are three sources of conflict which have strongly influenced police tactical response, and, to a lesser extent, military response as well. The first is the growth of nonviolent confrontation techniques, the second is the growth of low-intensity conflict (insurgency, terrorism, and other undeclared forms of warfare), and the third is the increase in the rate of, with concurrent changes in the intensity of, violent crimes within the United States. All of these have contributed to the application of current tactical response, and have generally affected other areas of operations. As the three types of conflict became more predominant, police and military techniques were adapted.

Nonviolent confrontation in the United States is linked primarily to the civil rights movement in the southern states in the 1960s. The initial reaction by police officials included use of police dogs, fire hoses, tear gas, riot batons, and similar techniques. As these techniques were repeatedly applied, their effectiveness diminished quickly due to many factors. First, the nonviolent confrontation techniques were intended to overload the judicial system by simply providing more people than could be arrested by the officers present, by filling jails, by overloading the courts' calendars, and by slowing the system with extensive legal wrangling in every form. Second, arrest incidents were increasingly filmed, bringing the conflict into the home of most Americans. Many had never witnessed a violent confrontation in any form, and were appalled by what they saw. In some cases, those being arrested engaged in deliberate provocation to increase the response. Sometimes the provocation was done in a carefully disguised fashion so that it would not show on camera. As the confrontations spread into other areas of the political spectrum, police agencies were encouraged to utilize other techniques.

Since the purpose of nonviolent confrontation was, to some extent, to provoke a response, agencies could defeat the purpose by changing the response. In some cases, this involved avoiding arresting persons during the confrontation. This freed the court to address the usual criminal activity. Crowd control and management techniques were revised. Fire hoses, police dogs, and shotguns disappeared from riot usage. Tear gas use was limited, and carefully planned. The psychological aspects of crowd response were studied, and then taught to police officers. Formal announcements of "Unlawful Assembly" appeared in procedure manuals. Emergency information (crisis) centers were formed and activated on demand. Police departments acquired helmets with face shields, long riot batons, bullhorns, barricades, and similar control devices. The impedimenta of riot control and the training to use them were mandatory in every department. Procedures had changed in response to the nonviolent confrontation. What had also changed was the strategic theory behind the procedures.

The strategy behind police response to nonviolent confrontation was to defeat the *purpose* of the confrontation, not the actual individual activity, however unlawful it might be. This meant, on occasion, backing off, avoiding arrest, etc. *if standing firm meant that the confrontational purpose would be achieved.* Slowly, however, this departure from the norm became accepted and began to spread, becoming the new norm. The idea was to be nonconfrontational. An easy concept to apply, it was favored ("naturally selected") if the officer was in a hurry due to a call overload, was tired of being called names, was new (and, therefore, familiar with *modern* techniques), etc. It didn't take long for the officers or other groups, including bandits, to catch on. Expenses could be kept down, and the crime rate lowered statistically, an administrator's dream. *Real* police officers could concentrate on *real* crime, a *real* self-image builder. There were all kinds of advantages. Actually standing firm against criminal offenses, particularly minor ones, became unpopular in many sectors. Since civil rights confrontation had made public affairs a hot issue, and affirmative action had made agencies conscious of their "image", being seen as enlightened helped the agencies with both. If there were differences in the long-term vs short-term benefits or narrow vs broad application issues of the approach, so what? The officer and administrator performance review period is always short-term. By the time anyone notices, I have already advanced, right? Okay, you say that I am oversimplifying. That only applies to minor crimes, not serious crimes. Well, let's examine response to violent crimes during the same time period.

As professionalization spread in departments and confrontations created a loss of confidence which lead to serious questions about police performance, violent crime became the most important measure for many departments. Beset with confrontations, including instances of deliberate ambushes of officers with political ramifications, departments began to respond. The major case squad was developed as a means to increase the solution rate of cases that were widely publicized for a variety of reasons. The analysis and theory was simple. Murder and other serious cases created a lot of work which could be addressed by a small number of investigators for a long time or be addressed by concentrating a large team of investigators for a short time. The second approach frequently produced a statistically higher arrest rate due to the nature of evidence needed to prove the case in court. It had to be demonstrated, but it was accepted and met the public test as an improvement.

Some improvements in serious crime response were more internally-oriented, and the significance of the change was not immediately clear to the public. Two examples which are related were an emphasis on officer survival and the development of special weapons and tactics teams. In the early 1960s, several incidents focused attention on officer performance during armed encounters. As the loss rate of officers and uninvolved citizens during armed encounters increased, various agencies began to analyze the causes. Individual officers began to receive more extensive training in firearms. As previously mentioned, the changes went through a variety of stages which continue as the data collected on officer-involved shootings increases. Use of cover, body armor and emphasis on weapons retention techniques also were added to operational procedures. At about the same time, analysis of call response helped identify that certain types of emergency calls were more likely to result in situations prone to shootings. This led to a differentiation in the standard response to those situations, and served as the impetus for the formation of the first SWAT organization.

Operating under a variety of names (Special Weapons and Tactics Team, Special Response Teams, Emergency Service Units, etc.), the concept of the operation is basically the same. Analysis showed that two problem areas existed in the high-risk situations where shootings were most likely to occur:

1. Most patrol officers lacked the type of equipment and training that were needed to handle many of the most severe situations;
2. Both officers and uninvolved citizens were placed at risk by this deficiency;

The original function, then, was to provide increased training and better equipment to individual officers, form them into a special unit, and then utilize them in selected situations in order to reduce the risk to both officers and citizens. In short, management of the risk to reduce the potential loss to the public. Originally fielded in the 1960s, the SWAT concept has continued to evolve as the nature of the situations changed, and the results of various operations were analyzed.

Hostage negotiators were added as the result of several incidents of extended capture of citizens by various bandits and terrorists. Weapons changed and related equipment changed to meet the fast, close combat situation or the precision long-range shot.

Communications equipment underwent miniaturization and was eventually molded to free the hands and match the command and control structure established to make the teams functional. Specialized, mobile command and control centers appeared at the scenes and some teams began using excess military armored vehicles in order to evacuate personnel under fire. Add specialized ballistic equipment (helmets, vests, portable shields), gas masks, prybars, bolt cutters, the occasional battering ram, fire extinguishers, tear gas dispersers, etc., and you have an unbelievable collection of equipment. If you ask, everyone can explain why everything is needed: "Well, once down in ... (you name it) a ... (DEA Agent, State Trooper, Fugitive Squad Detective, etc.) was raiding this ...(meth lab, biker gang bar, serial murderer lair), and ..." The explanation will be factual, rational, long-winded and make complete sense. It is probably only a coincidence that "Once down in ..." sounds so much like "Once upon a time ...". Have you noticed just how much change there has been in 30 years? Look at a picture of a 1960s SWAT member. He is obviously a police officer, but has some extra or unusual equipment. Now look at a photo of a 1990s SWAT member. They come in two versions: ragamuffin and ninja space soldier. Neither is very identifiable as a police officer.

The first type shows up in whatever he is wearing, has scrounged, etc. and looks it. When confronted with him, your first reaction is confusion. Is he a dumpster-diver from behind the local Salvation Army Store, an actor doing "Patton's Nightmare" (Willie and Joe's 1990s video), or an escapee from the local funny farm (you were able to rule out juve-gang-wanna-be tryout on the basis of age)? Police Officer? Really? Could I see some identification, please? Wait, Wait, I want to get my camera. The second version shows up in a completely color-coordinated matching outfit (black preferred). Helmet on, balaclava on, heavy vest (covering the subdued police identification sewn on the black fatigues), equipment carrier over the vest, wired for sound, carrying a pistol, and another firearm (shotgun, submachine gun, rifle), with several extra magazines, naturally, at least one set of handcuffs, rappelling belt attached, gas mask hanging on one side, night vision equipment in the fanny pack, and heavens only knows what else inside the variety of pockets. Your first reaction is amazement (You didn't know they were making another kungfu/star wars film). After the initial shock of such a bizarre sight, the average citizen will ask, "What's going on?" It simply never occurs to them that this could be a policeman. This is part of the current problem. The public image has been overlooked during outfitting consideration; the image is now affecting the public response to the police response. The problem is aggravated by the natural progression of events in a social setting. A successful concept has spread from selected situations to many situations. The exception has become the routine. Fugitive arrest squads have adopted the SWAT model, Drug squads have adopted the SWAT model, Juvenile Gang Officers have partially adopted the SWAT Model, etc. The SWAT Teams themselves have adopted the Counterterrorist Model. This is both a natural, sensible reaction, and an unnatural one.

Counterterrorist Teams began developing worldwide in the 1960s and expanded dramatically in the 1970s. This was the era of the modern terrorist, the glamorous guerilla fighter, wars of liberation, and the beginning of the military strategic concept of conflicts in varying intensity: Low, Medium, and High. The strongest emphasis in the United States on developing Counterterrorist Teams to respond to low-intensity conflict occurred in the 1980s. Under U.S. policy, terrorism is treated as criminal conduct and primary enforcement is left to the local police. Since that mission is tasked to them, local officials have responded by upgrading, losing sight of some of the original reasons for SWAT organization. The military services underwent several steps in reaching the current organization, Navy Seal Team development, Army DELTA Team development, Air Force Paracommando development, which all eventually led to the formation of the Special Operations Command encompassing the complete range of the mission. The federal civilian agencies, given the stated policy and limitation on using soldiers to enforce law, had to develop police forces to handle the terrorism problem on federal property. They did so, the two primary units being the FBI Hostage Rescue Team, and the US Marshal Service Special Operations Group. Other federal organizations can be found, based on the federal requirement, flowing from the terrorism policies, to task organizations in certain settings to form a Special Response Team and a Crisis Management Team. The concepts and procedures spread in response to this basic policy on Terrorism which is the primary point of this portion of the discussion.

The next area of police tactics in response to serious crime is to examine some operational techniques in social context. Police response patterns have a tendency to recur in a cyclic pattern, rising or falling with social expectations of the community. A cursory examination of some current techniques can illustrate the point.

DARE (Drug Abuse Resistance Education) is a hot social topic right now. Many departments are training officers to teach in local school systems using this approach. Parents, teachers, and public affairs officers (and the assigned officers) love it. While there is some dispute concerning its effectiveness in some quarters, it is basically a program which brings police officers into direct contact with children in a friendly setting with a prevention goal. In this respect, the program is simply a resurgence of the popular Police Athletic League concept found in many department in the 1950s. The concept faded in the 1960s as the police agencies came under attack and the society was in upheaval over a variety of issues. When studies into police-community relations began, to correct the perceived problems, specific studies began to appear which directly influenced current trends. The best example here is the Cincinnati Youth Attitude Project[22] which dealt with a child's view of a police officer as basically either good or bad. This provided part of the foundational information upon which prevention programs like DARE are based. The result, however, bears a strong resemblance to the types of programs run by various police departments and churches years before the study and decades before DARE. These programs came under attack in the 1960s from various sectors. This affected their social support, and the programs slowly disappeared. It may be important to remember that the late 1940s and 1950s were a time period of pronounced juvenile gang activity in many cities and in much of the social science literature as well. The same recurring concept of social acceptability and credibility can be seen in one of the latest "hot" investigative techniques, profiling.

Profiling is an analysis technique developed by college-educated police officers who applied a combination of statistics, behavioral sciences, scientific information, and police investigative experience to develop it. The basic idea is that you can forecast a "profile" of the criminal involved in a crime including basic information such as age, sex, race, occupation, likes, dislikes, hobbies, experiences, etc. which can be used to help locate him. Sounds really modern, exciting, and slightly mystic. Call me a skeptic, if you will, but I am not razzle-dazzled. I recognize this technique from my first year in police science in 1970, twenty years before it appeared.

I had enrolled as a student in a university which was just developing an Administration of Justice major, a fairly common occurrence on universities at that time. Since the curriculum was just forming in a new major area, the university was short of professors and instructors. Consequently, they recruited many experienced local police officers to teach. The texts in use were standard police texts that were widely recognized in the police field, but beginning to age. These instructors and texts made references to the "criminal personality." During this time period, this "criminal personality" concept had come under severe attack from the highly-educated segment of society. Professors, especially psychiatrists, psychologists, sociologists, and educators, openly ridiculed the entire concept, and began to produce studies, essays, etc which debunked it. Insisting that the concept was antiquated, wrong, etc., the texts and instructors were slowly forced out by the "properly" educated and "properly" written texts. The problem was that the educated segment was applying their own concept of personality and not using the police officer's concept of the term. The police officers had experience but usually did not have advanced education. The police could not explain the concept in educated terms, and the educated could not translate the "practical" term into educated terms. The educated segment had insufficient practical experience or contact with officers and offenders to recognize the rose by another name. In some cases, the highly-educated also lacked the desire to treat police officers and their conduct as socially acceptable. It was a classic skilled craftsman vs designer/engineer confrontation: step-by-step procedure vs operations analysis flow chart. Criminal profiling is simply criminal personality, repackaged, renamed, and supported by the appropriate scientific analysis to satisfy the educated. The same repackaging has occurred in other areas.

Community Policing with its bicycle patrols, strategic planners, and town hall or neighborhood meetings and similar current terminology is just a repackaged concept. It evolved from Neighborhood Watches, Storefront Outreach Programs, Operation Identification Programs, etc. The operational content of Community Policing can actually be traced in various forms back to the best foot patrolmen operating on beats from precincts in various large cities. There is nothing new here, only repackaging of the same concepts to meet the variations in social acceptance that ebbs and flows with social issues of the day. Don't believe it? Ask yourself two basic questions:

1. Why does the death penalty disappear from usage, only to reappear at a later date? Does its effectiveness change, or only its social acceptance? Why does the societal response to criminal conduct keep changing from exile to cure, punishment to salvation?

2. Is the 1990s person and his criminal conduct really different from the 1980s person, the 1890s person, the 1790s person, etc.? Or is the social acceptance of the person's conduct just vacillating? After all, there are only so many basic ways to stay alive, to interact with the people around you. Does life really vary that much over the centuries in its basic interaction patterns, its stimulus and response?

The essential point, of course, is that police response varies as a reaction to community stimulus. In that context, it is a mirror image of the community, and subject to the same social actions, reactions, ills, benefits, and even something as simple as social fads or fascinations.

Police fad? Hey, look at police hypnosis of witnesses; came and went. Police fascination? Well, look at police car emergency lights. In the 1960s, the average patrol car had one rotating light on the roof and possibly a spotlight. In the 1990s, the average police car has light bars with multiple lights on the roof and may have supplementary lights in the grills, rear windows, etc. Does this make the car *that* much easier to see? This appears to be a fascination with technology advancement, a typically American response to a problem. The same trend can be seen in other equipment. Police equipment and operations, including tactics, respond to the community stimulus, reflecting its trends and its evolution of problems and solutions. Having reached this point, pause for a minute and ask yourself how these observations currently apply to serious criminal activity (drug sales, juvenile gangs, homicide rate, etc). Then go one step further and ask yourself how these observations currently apply to right-wing protest activities (antiabortion, tax protests, and informal militias) and international terrorists operating in the United States. What are the response patterns, both tactically and judicially, by both the public and the common defense forces?

The final area to examine in tactical response pattern development is to look at the basic difference between the public sector and the private sector. As a military officer exposed to the theories of strategy in warfare, I have noticed one clear difference between the basic response capability of public sector versus private sector operations. Public sector response is typically based upon mobile defense theory while private sector response is typically based upon static defense theory. The difference is significant; it gives clear indication of the response capability of both.

A mobile defense is conducted by a force that has a large area to defend, somewhat limited numbers of troops, and both movement and communications capability. It is normally conducted in an area where the threat of attack is low, and where movement is relatively easy. The defensive response by the mobile force follows a simple pattern: detection of the attack, communication of that detection to the defense force, movement of the defense force to the attack, and engagement of the attacker. Engagement is conducted, preferably, by first isolating (surrounding) the attacker. A mobile defense orients upon the attacker, and not upon locations. The response pattern and usual conditions demonstrate how the mobile force is defeated. It is easy to defeat at a given location since its forces are spread thin. It is easy to defeat whenever the attack cannot be readily identified or whenever the communication capability is lacking. It is also easy to defeat in areas or at times when movement is hindered. In the case of a public sector agency, you can see that detection and notification are primarily performed by the public. This is why areas with high crime rates also coincide with areas that have poor police-community relationships. The mobile defense force has to depend upon the static forces (the public and the private sector agency) to detect and notify; the defense force itself is weak in these areas.

A static defense is conducted by a force that has a limited area to defend and has larger numbers of troops (larger ratio of troops per area). It orients on a particular asset, usually a specific location, although it can be a specific person or group of people. The static defense is defeated primarily by movement. This can be staging movement (concentrating sufficient attackers at the attack point) prior to the attack or maneuvering movements (outrunning the defender) either during or after the attack. A static defense depends upon reinforcement either by other static defenders nearby or by mobile defense forces that respond to assist. The static defense may have a lot of resistance capability or very little resistance capability depending upon their personal assets and preparation, but that capability can only be used within a limited area. Static defenders usually have limited movement capability, but a lot of personal motivation to hold the position. In this discussion, the static defense force is the private security agency and the general public. Since their personal possessions, their livelihood, and their lives are on the line, their personal motivation to defend is high or low depending upon their concern for possessions, livelihood, and lives. From this observation, we can deduce that static defense capability will vary widely from place-to-place with similar private places having different crime rates and victim profiles. We can also deduce that the areas with high crime rates will be typified by places that are difficult to prepare or reinforce or by people who lack the motivation to prepare or reinforce those around them. In short, community or neighborhood cohesion and resources affect the response and the crime rate. That is why we see communities and neighborhoods with low crime rates that typically have high participation in programs like Neighborhood Watches, DARE, etc. or simply have strong social connections like family, friends, or nosy neighbors. The level of social concern goes hand-in-hand with willingness to accept attack. Those who are concerned dedicate their resources and thereby raise their preparation and reinforcement capability (increase their static defense), and the attack (criminal activity) becomes harder to successfully complete.

This comparison of public sector to private sector capability in terms of strategic warfare as applied to response to crime is a valid means of examining the other civilian public-private sector operations as well. If you define a life-threatening emergency as an attack, the rest falls into place. A medical emergency such as a heart attack is most likely to occur while you are present at a location other than a hospital. Simple probability tells us that the highly trained medical defense force (doctors, nurses, etc.) is going to be elsewhere when the attack occurs. This means that the attack will be addressed initially by the static defense force (the private security agency and general public) using the training and equipment immediately available. The structure that has been created to do this is extensive: EMTs (Emergency Medical Technicians), first responders, CPR instructors, CPR certification courses, basic and advanced first aid courses, job-related first aid equipment (OHSA requirements), etc. This structure operates at specific sites and initiates the critical treatment. They then activate the immediate mobile defense force consisting of paramedics, EMICTs (Emergency Medical Intensive Care Technicians), EMTs (Emergency

Medical Technicians), etc. which utilize an equally staggering array of equipment: helicopters, primary and secondary care ambulances, rescue squads, and so forth. All of this works to isolate the attack (medical condition of victim) and apply the mobile defense forces (doctors, hospitals, etc.) to stop it. In the medical sector, we actually move the attack to the defense forces instead of moving the defense forces to the attack, but the concept is the same. The same pattern applies also to firefighting. We have developed these mobile defense forces (fire stations with firefighters) and provided a wide array of equipment (fire trucks of many types, tanker aircraft, hoses, pumps, foam units, etc.) which move to the attack (fire), isolate it, and defeat it. These mobile forces depend upon the static force for the usual detection and notification of the attack. We have also provided static defense against fires. Look at all of the preparation and equipment typically found in our society for use by the general population against fires: fire hoses and extinguishers in buildings for occupant use, fire stand pipes or hydrants in buildings and neighborhoods, fire alarm systems, smoke detectors, carbon monoxide detectors, fire doors, fire walls in the buildings, marked evacuation routes and exits, marked fire lanes around buildings, OSHA requirements for worker training and fire teams, fire drills for school kids, fire prevention weeks, building codes, etc. The list seems endless when you start thinking about it. A thorough preparation by the society to address the life-threatening event of fire by use of both mobile and static defense forces.

In this regard, then, private security agencies, as a specialized segment of the general public, can be viewed as static defense forces which fight the various life-threatening attacks of violent crime, medical emergencies, fires, and other disasters. The development of private security agencies is a specialization of static defense at locations where the mobile defense force is not or cannot be deployed for some reason. There are two interesting points within this observation. First, notice that private security officers tend to be more generalist in their duty performance (addressing all life-threatening actions) while public agencies are much more specialized. The private officers' duties vary widely according to the needs of the particular location. Second, look at the resistance to arming private officers in many sections of the country. This point hits upon the basis of the current political wrangling in the country over gun control which is actually an argument over self-defense rights. Basic mobile and static defense force capability demonstrates clearly that the mobile defense force (police) cannot be expected to be present at the time of a deadly attack. Their response depends upon the usual detection and notification which will, of course, be followed by a delay. The deadly attack must be dealt with by the static defense force (private security and general public) during the police response time. This principle is unequivocally clear, and widely accepted by the society for medical and fire response. Yet, it is rejected by large segments of the same society when the attack becomes a self-defense situation rather than a medical, fire or disaster life-threatening situation. This defies both reason and military strategic experience. One can only assume that part of the problem is the decrease in the general public's direct experience with warfare or other self-defense situations, the decrease in the use of firearms in any daily context, and the decline in unorganized militia training. The arguments currently raging over gun control and the rise of informal militias are intertwined; both are part of the self-defense issue and how society will tactically address or not address it, as the case may be. In any case, personal self-defense of an individual is simply beyond the tactical capability of a mobile defense force in most circumstances, and clearly falls to the static defense force consisting of the general public and its specialized members (the private security agency). The study of warfare tactics and strategy makes this clear. Having examined police-community interaction in terms of warfare, let us now go to the next step and examine how warfare and crime interact, that is, compare their similarities and differences. I will do this by examining the legal considerations that basically apply to both and then compare and contrast the various common defense force capability to deal with them.

BASIC LEGAL CONSIDERATIONS FOR EMPLOYMENT OF COMMON DEFENSE FORCES

The terrorist, as we currently view him, is a person not understood by many people. Terrorists display some traits usually ascribed to soldiers and some traits usually ascribed to criminals. You could, in colloquial terms, define a terrorist as a felon on steroids playing war or as a soldier with a criminal personality. The terrorist engages in actions that are so severe that the actions seem beyond criminal conduct but do not seem as severe as a war might be. The terrorist attempts to operate in the gap between crime and war. He does so to avoid the legal consequences of unlawful conduct and the survival consequences of conducting a war. The point is to socially justify the conduct to such an extent that people hesitate to call it crime but to minimize the actions to such an extent that people hesitate to call it an act of war. In short, the point is to avoid all consequences. This is imperative for both success and survival. When the judicial system or the war system activates to engage him, the terrorist begins to lose. Therefore, defeat of the terrorist can be attained by applying either the public sector agencies or the military services, the judicial and the defense systems. The private sector agencies have limited direct impact on terrorism since they are not directly part of either the judicial or the defense system. The private sector, including the general public, can only counter terrorism by activating the other agencies.

Based on this observation and the previous discussion, we can conclude that terrorism will be able to operate in locations or conditions that are unfavorable to the mobile defense. Terrorism will be influenced by the static defense only where the static defense is prepared and reinforced. Conditions that are favorable to high crime rates will also be favorable to terrorism; conditions favorable to low crime rates may be favorable or unfavorable to terrorists depending on the type of community cohesion and how it relates to the justification advanced by the terrorist for his actions. The community may counteract the terrorist by using one of two basic options, arrest or use of force. However, both require *locating* the terrorist, and location requires identification. Therefore, the common critical task is identification which is best addressed by the static defense force since it possesses the most knowledge of the community at its static location (the personal motivation based on possessions, livelihood, and life). The breakdown of responsibilities then is the static defense force (the public and the private sector agency) prepares defense at specific locations, communicates identification information, recognizes the attack, and activates the mobile defense force. The mobile defense force (the military services and the public sector agencies) react to communications of identification and recognition of the terrorist and the attack, move to the terrorist to arrest or to use force against him, and to respond to the consequences of the attack. When and where these two responses can be used is dependent upon the status of the opponents.

Opponent status is primarily a legal concept, so it is determined by examining and summarizing the appropriate legal codes. In this case, that will primarily be the United States laws, but it will also include the Law of Warfare[23] as it controls conduct between nations or acts of war, generally. It may seem strange to include the Law of Warfare inside the United States, but it is applicable. Portions of the Law of Warfare overlap the United States laws so that either opponent may claim to be acting under either system as it is convenient to do so. The areas of overlap which will be most illustrative of the potential ramifications are the definition of the terms "belligerent" or "partisan" and "aggression" or "act of war," the United Nations stance on the "right to self determination" by the disenfranchised, and the limitations on utilization of various weapons. A quick summary of the pertinent points follows:

> ***Belligerent*** - A combatant; a person involved in the fighting. May include irregular forces or those who rise up in defense of their home on approach of an attack (partisans). A four-fold test is used to determine status:[24]
>> Commanded by a person responsible for his subordinates;
>> Fixed distinctive emblem recognizable at a distance;
>> Carry arms openly;
>> Conduct their operations in accordance with the laws and customs of war.
>
> ***Aggression***–The basis of an act of war. The definition normally depends upon action by armed forces (invasion, armed attack, etc.) of a nation and prohibits political, economic, or military justification. However, provision is made for persons "forcibly deprived" of the right to self-determination, freedom, and independence. The clause contains not only the right for such persons to use aggression, but the right of other nations to assist them.

Opponent status, then, is determined primarily by two factors: the "official" nature of the opponent (open action, assumption of responsibility, governmental support) and the "intent" of the opponent.

The terrorist may openly make general declarations, but seldom does so formally and recognizably. He is seldom identifiable by uniform, has no commander (name a terrorist general), and specializes in hiding the attack to prevent its interception. Notice that nations that wish to support a terrorist must only rely on the provision in the UN resolution and simply avoid openly declaring their support. The really interesting part, however, is to apply the issue the other way around. What is a partisan?

A terrorist may easily qualify as a belligerent by simply assuming command responsibility, carrying arms openly during the attack, by displaying some recognizable insignia, and by conducting operations in accordance with the Law of Warfare. So may others. A uniformed officer of a police agency easily passes the test to qualify as a partisan but so can a private security officer. Given the recognized right to self-defense under both the Law of Warfare and the United States legal system, this means that either the public sector or the private sector may legitimately use force to stop terrorists by organizing, carrying arms openly, and establishing a command authority. However, they must do so in accordance with the law of whichever legal system applies during the attack. Both sectors are accustomed to applying the United States law, but have not really considered the possibility of applying the Law of Warfare to the situation. If the terrorist stages the attack as a "belligerent", the response will have to meet the Law of Warfare. This provides the terrorist the opportunity to exploit an opening, attaining a propaganda victory by forcing the defending forces to commit a war crime. How? By use of current equipment by the defenders inside the United States. Under the Law of Warfare, use of hollow point bullets, buckshot, pepper spray, or tear gas would all violate various provisions thereby subjecting the defender to legitimate charges of a war crime before an international tribunal, a clear propaganda victory in the international sphere. Notice that the controlling factor is the *manner* in which the terrorist stages the attack, not the defender's response. The defender can only avoid this trap by ceasing use of this equipment prior to the attack or by claiming emergency circumstances as a defense to the charge.

Applying these considerations to the current situation in the United States raises some interesting points. Consider the informal militias that have appeared around the nation. First, let me make it clear that I do not refer to the legally-defined militias (organized, unorganized, or military reserves). These informal militias may qualify as partisans under the Law of Warfare if they meet the four-fold test; many do. However, none (of which I'm aware) meet the legal test for militias within the United States. This test, based on Constitutional provisions mentioned earlier, consists of state governmental recognition and submission to the regulation and discipline specified by the United States Congress. The informal militias may legitimately rise up to defend against attack or invasion under provisions of the Law of Warfare, or may claim to be persons "forcibly deprived" of self-determination, etc. as provided for in the United Nations resolution quoted above. If they do so, they achieve status as a legitimate opponent under international law and response to them must meet the Law of Warfare. The informal militia, under such circumstances, would also be required to conduct themselves under the Law of Warfare as well. As you can see, the dividing line between patriot and survivalist whacko is legally thin. To completely understand the implications, apply the considerations to three situations: the standoffs at Waco, Texas; Jordan, Montana and El Paso, Texas.

At Waco, the Branch Davidian group:

• Was obviously controlled by Koresh (command by a person assuming responsibility)
• Collectively displayed religious insignia; some individual display (Fixed distinctive sign, a borderline call based on facts)
• Used firearms to oppose arrest (carrying arms openly)
• Allowed evacuation of wounded under cease-fire arrangement (demonstrated some compliance with the Laws of War)
• Opposed the federal government with arms inside the United States (seizure of a portion of a nation while under arms is the legal definition of an invasion, an act of war)
• Stated they were being oppressed by antireligious forces (disenfranchised test of UN Resolution)

At Jordan, the Freemen:

• Were represented in negotiations by one or more persons (Command by a person assuming responsibility)
• Displayed a flag of their own choosing (fixed distinctive insignia, a borderline call based on the facts)
• Carried firearms within perimeter on sentry duty (carried arms openly)
• Opposed the federal government by force (declared portion of United States no longer under U.S. control while armed; meets definition of invasion, an act of war)
• Stated that they were not part of the United States and refused to recognize the U.S. government as legitimate; further stated they

were being economically oppressed by a discriminatory government (disenfranchised test of UN Resolution; may also meet test of independent nation eligible for membership in the United Nations)

At Fort Davis, The Independent Republic of Texas:

• Was represented in negotiations by one person claiming to be a diplomat of a separate nation (command by a person assuming responsibility)
• Displayed a flag of their own choosing (fixed distinctive insignia)
• Carried firearms within perimeter on sentry duty; used firearms during an actual operation, the "raid" on the "spy"; and used firearms to resist apprehension (carried arms openly)
• Opposed the federal government by force: declared portion of United States no longer under U.S. control while armed; attacked U.S. citizens within boundaries of United States while armed; resisted Texas government officials while armed (meets definition of invasion, an act of war)
• Stated that they were not part of the United States and refused to recognize the State of Texas government as legitimate; further stated they were being deprived of their liberty and oppressed by a "foreign" government, the State of Texas (disenfranchised test of UN Resolution; may also meet test of independent nation eligible for membership in the United Nations)

Were they criminals being arrested, partisans rising up to defend their homes from attack and tyranny, or terrorists stopped before launching attack? The answer is found by a combination of factors, and is debatable. First, all ultimately submitted to arrest (one forcibly, one not, one mixed on resistance) and did not pursue the disenfranchised test of the UN resolution at the time of arrest (the Freemen actually reject the UN since it's the proponent of the New World Order). Second, the federal governmental forces initiated the actions in the first two situations, and did so as an arrest, not a defense against invasion. In the third situation, the state government dealt with it as an arrest, not an invasion, even though the final confrontation resulted from the act that constituted an invasion. Third, neither the Branch Davidians or the Freemen met the test of partisans or oppressed persons at the beginning of the incident, only attained that status (possibly) during the course of the standoff. The Republic of Texas, on the other hand, claimed to be partisans at the outset of the confrontation and took their action on that basis. Fourth, the evidence available indicates that all apparently committed the illegal acts involved for economic gain, not to "throw off the governmental oppression." This indicates criminal intent rather than political intent rather clearly in the first two situations, but less clearly in the third situation. The legal status of each group in these three situations is absolutely clear, right? There is no legal question whether response to these groups is enforcement of the law or defense against invasion, right? Now you understand why this chapter is entitled "Police Operations Near the Border of Open Warfare." All three incidents are near that boundary; some may say that they were over the line into warfare with the groups attaining belligerent status. Had the federal government chosen to, it might legally have been able to define each incident as an act of war and respond to each as such, particularly in the case of The Republic of Texas. Such a response would have been lawful since the federal government is the only entity in the United States that can, constitutionally, conduct war, and since proving that they were *not* acts of war would have been difficult or impossible. Trying to operate in the gap between acts of criminality versus acts of war has risks as well as benefits for these groups. All of which leads to the formulation of response and which portion of the common defense forces makes it.

PREPARATION AND RESPONSE BY THE COMMON DEFENSE FORCES

As seen in the previous section, the opponents in a conflict within the United States have some ability to mold the legal status of the conflict to put it either within the laws of the United States or the Law of Warfare. More simply, it may be molded to be either a criminal act or an act of war by either opponent, but only at certain points in the conflict. This, of course, leads to the conclusion that the nature of the threat determines the nature of the response. But, the reverse is also true. The nature of response preparation determines the nature of the threat evolution. Since preparation affects threat, a quick look at the societal preparation is in order.

The military services clearly prepare to deal with terrorism, but basically employ that preparation overseas. The organized militia (national guard) has been tasked in some states to prepare for terrorism but are not currently deployed to do so. The unorganized militia has received no specific training to defend against terrorist attack; some obviously attain it through personal experience or resources. The public sector agencies do receive some training for this specific task. This is, generally, simply an extension of standard law enforcement training unless the agency maintains a tactical response team. Occasionally, you will find some private sector agencies that have specifically prepared for terrorist attack, but this is unusual. When it does occur, it is normally in response to some governmental requirement placed on a particular type of business such as airlines or nuclear power facilities. Having established the usual preparation, next evaluate the various common defense forces on the two basic types of responses, arrest or use of force.

The military services have virtually no right to arrest under the United States legal system, although the organized militia does have some right-to-arrest under state laws. When arrest is the purpose, the military services should not be utilized. The public sector agencies have clear arrest rights which vary by jurisdiction. The private sector has some right to arrest but is not as proficient at it as the public sector. This right to arrest varies somewhat from jurisdiction to jurisdiction and place to place within the jurisdiction. Under international law, including the Law of Warfare, the right to arrest is virtually nonexistent for all of the common defense forces.[26]

The military services have tremendous capability to use force, but strong limitations on when it can do so. These limitations exist under both the United States legal system and the Law of Warfare, although they are much less restrictive under the latter. The key is which legal system is in force. The public sector agencies have a strong right to use force under the United States legal system while the private sector has, basically, only a right of self-defense under this system. The private sector may exercise use of force for arrest under some limited circumstances under United States law. Both the public sector and private sector may qualify as partisans under the Law of Warfare in some circumstances. This allows them to use force in self-defense as an informal part of the military services in these limited circumstances. The amount and type of force that may be used is determined by which legal system applies, the laws of the United States or the Law of Warfare. The final portion of response is the determination of instant response capability at the time and place of attack.

Instant capability is determined by the defensive preparations overall, but primarily by the deployment and equipment of the defender at the attack site. The military services will not be present at the attack site unless the specific target is a military installation. This is due to the counterterrorist policy of the United States and the fact that the military services are deployed internally only for war, not for law enforcement.[27] Deployment only occurs inside the United States when an emergency has been declared by civilian officials. This limitation applies equally to the organized militia (national guard) who are also not deployed unless an emergency has been declared. While the organized militia may enforce state laws, it will not do so until an emergency has been declared by the state. Consequently, the most prepared and equipped forces *will not be present at the attack site.* This leaves the unorganized militia, the public sector agencies, and the private sector.

The unorganized militia has no equipment, no organization, and virtually no training. It basically exists as a legal, paper entity in the laws of the federal and the various state governments. Its potential is extremely limited since it is envisioned to be called forth only after resources of the military services and organized militia have been exhausted. The public sector agencies are present for duty, but, if you will recall, they operate primarily as a mobile defense force. This means they *will probably not be present at the attack site,* only called as the first reinforcement response to the event. The instant capability at the attack site will be provided by the private sector. This may be a private citizen using whatever resources are available. However, given the nature of the usual terrorist attack profile and current local ordinances in most places, it is more likely to be a private sector security agency. In short, the attack will be directed against the least trained, least prepared, and least equipped portion of the common defense forces. This vulnerability is magnified by current social policies and trends.

Any private security agency that initiates an arrest risks civil suit and intense pressure. Currently, intense public pressure is applied against any private security officer (or police officer for that matter) who actually uses deadly force. The possibility of civil suit is almost 100 percent if the private security agency uses deadly force. Now look at the equipment policy. Many site security officers work unarmed due to the civil liability risk. Where the private security officer is armed, it will probably be with a handgun only. Some shotguns can be found in use, but they are rare. Use of rifles is virtually nonexistent. Under current gun laws, a private security officer cannot own the type of weapon that would actually halt a vehicular attack. How bad is this situation? Look at the current public policy.

There is extreme pressure on gun ownership, ostensibly as a crime control device. Whether this is a good or bad idea or whether such control is effective or not, is, quite frankly, totally immaterial to the assessment that I am about to make. Under the federal gun provisions passed in 1968, the private ownership of machineguns, rocket launchers, or similar weapons was prohibited to the private sector[28] This includes that portion of the private sector that meets the legal definition of the unorganized militia. Yes, there is a legitimate question of whether this violates the 2nd, 9th or 10th Amendments, but the provisions of this gun act were adopted by all the states and are currently in force. This law actually contradicts the provisions for equipment specified for the militia under the federal code[29] which requires the use of the same type equipment currently issued to the military services. In talking about individual weapons for troops, this would currently mean that the militia would be required to use the M249 Squad Automatic Weapon,[30] M16A2 Rifle,[31] or the M9 Pistol,[32] the currently specified individual weapons in appropriate Department of Defense acquisition regulations. The M249 is a light machinegun and prohibited under the 1968 federal gun act and the equivalent state laws; it is not manufactured in a semiautomatic version. The M16A2 Rifle and the M9 Pistol were both affected by the federal gun act implemented in 1995, the Brady Bill. The semiautomatic version of the M16A2 is called the AR15 on the civilian gun market. It is specifically defined as an "assault weapon" (this is technologically incorrect) and specifically prohibited for sale to private citizens. The M9 Pistol is known as the Model 92 Beretta on the civilian gun market. While it can be legally purchased, if you meet the various gun laws and ordinances applicable to the specific location and purchase, its magazine capacity of 15 in the military version is reduced to 10 in the civilian version. This means that the 1995 provisions of the Brady Bill directly conflict with the federal code requirement for the legally defined militia as well as raising issues of constitutionality under the 2nd, 9th, and 10th Amendments, issues already advanced in many sections of the country. Constitutional issues aside, both the unorganized militia and the private security agencies (in fact, all private citizens) do not have access to the weapons specified by the federal government for defense use against attack. They can only access a reduced capability handgun. Yes, I have considered whether they can be provided by the various governments.

At the current time, neither the federal or state governments are stocking these weapons for issue to the unorganized militia. The Department of Defense used to maintain an individual weapon for each member of the military services including the organized and unorganized militias. This practice was discontinued within the last few years as a budgetary cutback of the Department of Defense. The states only stock weapons for the organized militia (national guard). In short, *there is no actual, legal way for the unorganized militia to obtain these weapons.* Consequently, the unorganized militia cannot possibly be called forth to defend against terrorist attack on short notice. This effectively eliminates it as a common defense force, leaving only the private citizen as an individual or as a private security officer to provide defense at a site. When you add in the lack of training caused by the end of the draft, you have the final step of the instant capability determination. The cumulative effect of these social policies and trends is to invalidate the expressed usage of the militia found in the Constitution of the United States, Article I, Section 8: "To provide for calling forth the militia to execute the laws of the Union, suppress insurrections, and repel invasions." We have, by a cumulative effect, actually amended this portion of the Constitution without ever formally considering such an amendment. The militia was intended by the framers of the Constitution to address widespread "lawlessness, insurrections, and invasions," locally. We have created a system which completely prohibits them from doing so. To place this in perspective, we have succeeded in decreasing the capability of the private citizen to perform the essential task of common defense of the local community. This is the cumulative effect of removing the responsibility to help defend the nation (ending the draft), eliminating the access to the individual equipment to do so (by various gun laws), and strongly regulating or restricting the use of private security officers. We have done so at a time when warfare has changed to favor attack by forces which orient against the local community or individual citizens in order to evade the inherent danger of actually conducting war by a nation with another nation. What have we created to offset this threat? A mobile defense consisting of military forces and public sector police agencies.

The military forces are prohibited from being used, and the public sector agencies are prohibited from routinely defending private sites. In fact, the police agencies seldom defend even public sites using static defense techniques. What, then, can we expect for a static defense force? What is the snapshot of the common defense of the private or public site within the United States at the current time? When a potential attack occurs at a site within the United States, the statistics and analysis show us that the site will either *not be defended at all or will be defended by a private security officer who is* a male, in his early twenties; a high school graduate; without military training or experience; without police training or experience; with about three days security training; actually armed with a handgun only about half the time; whose firearms proficiency is average to below average; and is being paid about $6.00 - $10.00 per hour.

This security officer will have approximately three seconds to decide whether to repel the invasion (the truck that just turned into the driveway) which is being driven by either "Davey the Dependable Deliveryman," "Carl the Crazy Criminal," or "Teddy the Terrible Terrorist."

After this decision, but still within the three second time frame, he will have to consider the legalities involved and decide his response. Is the approaching truck a routine delivery of no apparent danger making any use of force grounds for firing from his job and a valid civil lawsuit, a criminal attack under the Laws of the United States which can be met with deadly force only when a deadly threat is clearly present and imminent, or an act of war which can be met by an instantaneous high level of deadly force with minimum legal consequences and less restrictive rules of when and how to engage?

Should he run; hide behind something solid; sound the alarm; fire his handgun at a potential truck bomb, that is, use a weapon unlikely to halt a vehicular attack but which may detonate the bomb while he is inside the killing zone of the bomb?

Should he worry more about losing his job; a possible civil suit; his own death; or the potential death of others?

What does all of this mean? It means that we have arrived at the final point of this long-winded essay; you now are psychologically prepared to confront the reality of my evaluation of this situation. If a terrorist group actually launches an attack against a site within the United States, its probability of achieving some level of success exceeds .99 (99% plus). The exact level of success attained will depend primarily upon the skill level of the terrorist group, and, to a lesser extent, upon the physical characteristics of the attack site.

If you are a public official, business owner, police officer, or private security officer tasked to provide security to such a site, the impact of this evaluation is now beginning to crawl up your spine. If you are a private citizen, the possibility that the military forces, police forces, and private security forces cannot defend you is making you uncomfortable, and you probably want to reject it.

WELCOME TO REALITY!

The feelings that you have are very familiar to mine; I experienced them strongly, for a prolonged period in 1991 as an Army Reserve Officer in Saudi Arabia serving as the Provost Marshal for a place called "Khobar Towers." Had the bombing attack of 1996, which produced over 200 U.S. casualties, occurred in 1991, the casualty count could easily have been much higher. Khobar Towers was a much more lucrative target during that time period. You may, at this point, be inclined to disbelieve my evaluation or simply fail to see the significance of the various issues introduced in the essay. As a free citizen, you are entitled to your opinion or your lack of concern as the case may be. You are even entitled to bet your life on your opinion. In fact, you already have.

In the following chapters, I will walk you through the detailed considerations that must be made while planning the defense against truck bombs and similar weapons of mass destruction, and then conclude with some recommendations of actions that may need to be taken by the society. I can tell you from personal experience that the feeling and consequent pressure does not go away. You can only lessen it slightly, and adjust to it. In short, live with it, or die from it.

Notes

1. Preamble, Constitution of the United States of America.
2. Article II, Section 2, Paragraphs 1 & 3 and Section 3, Constitution of the United States.

3. Article I, Section 8, Paragraphs 1, 11-14, & 18, Constitution of the United States.

4. 18 USC 1385.

5. Article I, Section 8 Paragraphs 15 & 16, Constitution of the United States.

6. Article I, Section 8, Paragraph 16, Constitution of the United States.

7. 10 USC 311.

8. 10 USC 332.

9. 10 USC 261.

10. 32 USC 102.

11. 32 USC 103-104.

12. 32 USC 501.

13. 32 USC 701-706.

14. Executive Order 12960, Office of the President of the United States, dated 12 May 1995 which amends several previous Executive Orders citing authority derived from provisions of Title 10 United States Code Chapter 47.

15. Article I, Section 8, Paragraph 15, Constitution of the United States.

16. It is possible to interpret Article I, Section 8, Paragraph 15 in such a way to "classify" law enforcement agencies as part of the militia since they actually perform a function specified by this paragraph as a militia function. Such an interpretation may be legitimate and has enormous impact.

17. 15 USC 1581.

18. 15 USC 1692.

19. 29 USC 2001-2009.

20. 18 USC 712.

21. *The Manufacture of Madness* by Thomas S. Szasz, M.D., 1970, Dell Publishing Co, Inc., New York.

22. An LEAA-funded project. It examined how children formed opinions of police officers as either helpful or harmful, and the age at which that opinion seems to become basically fixed. Its results were published by the Police Foundation in the early 1970s.

23. The term "Law of Warfare" will be utilized here in a generic sense to encompass generally the United Nations Charter and Resolutions as well as all the international conventions, treaties, agreements, etc. that are recognized to control how war is conducted between nations.

24. Articles 1 and 2, "Hague Convention (IV) Respecting the Laws and Customs of War on Land, Annex to the Convention," the Hague, 1907; Page 41, "The Laws of War" by W. Michael Reisman and Chris T. Antoniou, 1994, Vintage Books, New York.

25. Article 7, United Nations Resolution 3314, 1974; Page 10, *The Laws of War* by W. Michael Reisman and Chris T. Antoniou, 1994, Vintage Books, New York.

26. Note that arrest is different from detention which typically occurs on battlefields. Prisoners of war, refugees, etc. may be taken into custody by military forces on a battlefield, but they are not charged with an offense. The purpose of the detention is to remove them from the battlefield to either prevent them from fighting or to ensure their safety. The only arrests which occur in a battlefield setting are those made under the Uniform Code of Military Justice or those made under the authority of some military tribunal established under various treaties.

27. It is informative to notice how this separation of power is blurred internationally with the deployment of military forces in "peacekeeping" status or to locations such as Panama where the primary point seems to be to enforce law.

28. It is instructive to note that the items prohibited were those that met the Law of Warfare designation as anti-equipment weapons rather than anti-personnel weapons. This demonstrates the interrelationship of the United States Laws with the Law of Warfare. It also demonstrates the probable intent at the time of the passage of the act and shows how part of the vulnerability to terrorist attack developed.

29. 32 USC 701.

30. A light machinegun available only with automatic fire capability.

31. The M16A2 has a 3-shot burst capability which qualifies it as a machinegun under the gun laws. The earlier versions, M16 and M16A1 have full automatic capability.

32. A semiautomatic pistol which is known as the Beretta Model 92 in the civilian gun sector. The military version is furnished with 15 round magazines.

Chapter 2

POLICY REVIEW

The counterterrorism policy of the United States has been structured by a combination of three spheres of influence: the United Nations, various international agreements, and the Constitutional structure of the United States. The three spheres of influence worked, from the United States perspective, to create a conscious decision to address international terrorism as criminal conduct rather than a form of warfare. This viewpoint of terrorism as criminal action rather than a form of warfare is not universally accepted. In some quarters, terrorism is viewed as a legitimate form of warfare practiced by the relatively powerless, those with limited access to power or resources, against the powerful tyrant who is engaging in some form of oppression. The development of this policy formation, based upon a particular viewpoint, requires a cursory examination to help establish the operating parameters of police operations in this area.

UNITED NATIONS AND INTERNATIONAL AGREEMENTS

The initial point of examination is the formation and role of the United Nations, and its relationship to the nation. The United Nations was formed by adoption of mutual agreements between many nations which were formalized in the Charter of the United Nations in 1945. The Charter was then adopted by the various nations using their own governmental procedures for ratification as required within the Charter. In the United States, this meant that the President signed the treaty with the advice and consent of Congress as provided in the Constitution of the United States.[1] Having ratified it, the United States became voluntarily bound to comply with its provisions. This concept of voluntary compliance is the basis of most international agreements, functioning, in this respect, similar to the simple contracts with which most people are familiar in their daily lives. The Charter of the United Nations is simply a social contract on a vast scale. This social agreement establishes certain limitations on the international actions and responses of the United States. The simplest way to define these limitations is to review the structure and selected provisions of the Charter of the United Nations.

The Charter bears some similarity in structure to the Constitution of the United States. It begins with a preamble of similar structure and content, and contains 111 articles divided into chapters. There are portions of three chapters which have some bearing on the topic:

Chapter I Purposes
Article 1–The purposes of the United Nations are:

1. To maintain international peace and security, and to that end: to take effective collective measures for the prevention and removal of threats to the peace and for the suppression of acts of aggression or other breaches of the peace, and to bring about by peaceful means, and in conformity with the principles of justice and international law, adjustment or settlement of international disputes or situations which might lead to a breach of the peace;

2. To develop friendly relations among nations based on respect for the principle of equal rights and self-determination of peoples, and to take other appropriate measures to strengthen universal peace; ...

Chapter II Principles
Article 2–The organization and its members, in pursuit of the purposes stated in Article 1, shall act in accordance with the following principles:

1. The organization is based on the principle of the sovereign equality of all its members.

2. All members, in order to insure to all of them the rights and benefits resulting from membership shall fulfill in good faith the obligations assumed by them in accordance with the present Charter.

3. All members shall settle their international disputes by peaceful means in such a manner that international peace and security, and justice, are not endangered.

4. All members shall refrain in their international relations from the threat or use of force against the territorial integrity or political independence of any member or state, or in any other manner inconsistent with the purposes of the United Nations.

5. All members shall give the United Nations every assistance in any action it takes in accordance with the provisions of the present Charter, and shall

refrain from giving assistance to any state against which the United Nations is taking preventive or enforcement action.

6. The organization shall insure that states not members act in accordance with these principles so far as may be necessary for the maintenance of international peace and security.

7. Nothing contained in the present Charter shall authorize the United Nations to intervene in matters which are essentially within the domestic jurisdiction of any state or shall require the members to submit such matters to settlement under the present Charter; but this principle shall not prejudice the application of enforcement measures under Chapter VII.

Chapter VII Action with Respect to Threats to the Peace, Breaches of the Peace and Acts of Aggression

Article 51. Nothing in the present Charter shall impair the inherent right of individual or collective self-defense, if an armed attack occurs against a member of the organization, until the Security Council has taken the measures necessary to maintain international peace and security. Measures taken by members in the exercise of this right of self-defense shall be immediately reported to the Security Council and shall not in any way affect the authority and responsibility of the Security Council under the present Charter to take at any time such action as it may deem necessary in order to maintain or restore international peace and security.   ...

To focus on the essentials, the important points are summarized. Article 1 orients on peaceful settlement of disputes by compliance with international law, but recognizes self-determination. Article 2 orients on equality among sovereign nations, responsibility of those nations, and limits the use of force by nations. Article 51 recognizes the right to self-defense as applied to a nation. These Charter articles are clearly binding upon member nations. Resolutions of the General Assembly, on the other hand, only state a general policy, but do not absolutely bind the member nations to comply with the content of the resolution.[2] Six such resolutions will be examined, initially.

The first, the "Declaration on Principles of International Law Concerning Friendly Relations and Cooperation Among States in Accordance with the Charter of the United Nations"[3] says, in part:

> ... by virtue of the principle of equal rights and self-determination of peoples enshrined in the Charter of the United Nations, all peoples have the right freely to determine, without external interference, their political status and to pursue their economic, social and cultural development, and every State has the duty to respect this right in accordance with the provisions of the Charter.

Notice that the resolution opens the door for small groups or individuals to oppose member nations on the basis of self-determination while binding the member nation to comply with the provisions of the Charter and other pertinent international agreements.

The second resolution spells out the difference between self-defense and a prohibited act of war, the "Definition of Aggression."[4] The pertinent issues are contained within Articles 1, 3, 5 and 7 of this resolution. Article 1 defines aggression as action between member nations and binds the nations to the Charter:

> Aggression is the use of armed force by a State against the sovereignty, territorial integrity or political independence of another State, or in any other manner inconsistent with the Charter ...

Article 3 specifies seven actions which constitute aggression even if war has not been declared:

> The invasion or attack ... of the territory of another State ...
> Bombardment ... or the use of weapons ... against the territory...
> The blockade of ports or coasts ...
> An attack ... on the land, sea or air forces, or marine and air fleets...
> The use of armed forces ... within the territory of another ... in contravention of the conditions provided for ...
> The action of a State in allowing its territory ... to be used ... for perpetrating an act of aggression ...
> The sending by or on behalf of a State of armed bands, groups, irregulars or mercenaries, which carry out acts of armed force ...

This article repeatedly expresses the definitions in terms of actions between member nations; it does not address actions by individuals or groups. Article 5 does not differentiate between member nations and lesser groups, but article 7 does in a significant manner.

> A war of aggression is a crime against international peace. Aggression gives rise to international responsibility. [Article 5]

> Nothing in this Definition ... could in any way prejudice the right to self-determination, freedom and independence, as derived from the Charter, of peoples forcibly deprived of that right ... particularly peoples under colonial and racist regimes or other forms of alien domination; nor the right of these peoples to struggle to that end and to seek and receive support ... [Article 7]

Article 7 clearly opens the door for acts by individuals and small groups, that are not member nations, to pursue self-determination by force against a nation that is forcibly depriving them of that right. This is the door utilized by the terrorists; the same door opened during the "wars of liberation" occurring worldwide in the 1960s and 1970s. The next four resolutions pertain specifically to terrorism; the response by the United Nations to problems occurring throughout the world.

The four United Nations resolutions of the General Assembly pertaining specifically to terrorism were passed over a twelve-year period in response to incidents. The first, for Prevention and Punishment of Crimes Against Internationally Protected Persons, Including Diplomatic Agents,[5] dealt with the attacks against diplomatic personnel (murder, kidnaping, and embassies) and the response to them by the member nations. The most significant part, for policy purposes, was the requirement for member nations to implement laws internally to protect the diplomats, prosecute offenses, and extradite the offenders. The second resolution addressed the protection of innocent citizens used as pawns to pressure their governments. The "International Convention Against the Taking of Hostages"[6] prohibits member nations from allowing unofficial groups to seize, detain or threaten individual citizens within their boundaries in order to compel a third party to act or abstain from a certain action. Again, the resolution contained a requirement for member nations to implement laws within their jurisdiction to protect hostages, prosecute the offenders, and to extradite as appropriate. The third and fourth resolutions basically reaffirm the United Nations stance against terrorism, and strongly encourage member nations to assume the previously specified responsibilities.[7] They contain no additional information that affects policy formation, merely restates it.

Moving away from the United Nations, there are other international agreements pertaining to terrorism which are binding upon the United States. Each is a voluntary compliance situation and was subject to the U.S. Constitutional ratification process. The first three were responses to the tactic of aircraft hijacking initiated in the 1960s. The Tokyo convention, signed in 1963,[8] designated that aircraft offenses have concurrent jurisdiction, prosecutable in both the place of occurrence and the territory "flagging" the aircraft, and directed returning control of the aircraft to the commander. The next agreement was signed at The Hague.[9] This agreement required the parties to make the offense unlawful, prosecute the offense (included arbitration provisions to resolve concurrent jurisdiction), and to extradite according to treaties in effect. Montreal was the site for the third agreement in 1971.[10] The provisions in this convention simply clarified the details of the existing policies, expanding them slightly.

Two additional conventions pertaining to terrorism dealt with more expanded topics. In Tokyo, the G7 nations issued a joint statement[11] which affirmed their willingness to act jointly against terrorism. It specifically condemned support for international terrorism and addressed six areas of cooperative action:

> Refusal to export arms
> Limits on the size and activities of consular and diplomatic
>   missions
> Denial of entry to persons with terrorist connections
> Improved extradition procedures
> Stricter immigration and visa procedures
> Close cooperation between police and security organizations

While rather general in the nature of its provisions, the content focused the policy on the areas that were seen as problems at the time, and left the details to the specific governments and agencies involved in the specific incidents. The final agreement pertaining to terrorism was much more specific. Signed in Montreal, it dealt with plastic explosives.[12] In detailed text, it provides for the signatories to control the transfer, movement, manufacture, and tracing of high-grade explosives. It establishes an International Explosives Technical Commission which provides technical expertise and maintains a registry of trace elements placed in explosives during the manufacturing process. These trace elements assist in identification of the source of explosives by analysis of residue at the scene of an explosion. The source, then, helps identify the terrorists involved. Introduction of such chemical evidence is very effective in the legal process, and leads into the final international agreements affecting counteterrorism policy.

UNITED STATES POLICY

Using these agreements as guidelines, the counterterrorism policy of the United States was formed. Among the considerations that were made are two that need to be mentioned. First was the possible use of INTERPOL, an international police organization developed by cooperation among many countries to deal with criminal activity on an international scale. Use of INTERPOL for counterterrorism was ruled out due to two factors. The agreement establishing INTERPOL prohibits it from becoming involved in any political matter. Since terrorism is frequently justified by its users and acknowledged by some as a political act, INTERPOL cannot become involved. Additionally, all INTERPOL files are accessible to any member nation, including a nation that might be sponsoring the terrorist activity. Consequently, use of INTERPOL would be against its charter and might actually alert the terrorist that had state support. Use of the United Nations was considered as a second possibility, and rejected. The primary reason is in the Charter which indicates that the UN deals with problems between member nations. Since terrorist groups are not member nations, although they may be supported by a member nation, the United Nations has no legitimate authority to deal directly with terrorism. Consequently, the Security Council can not be used. All that the UN can do is to coordinate agreements and actions of its member nations as they undertake the counteractions to terrorism. The United States then adopted the criminal model of terrorism and applied what has been called a trilevel concept, implementing this organizational structure in the late 1970s.[13]

The term "trilevel concept", is derived from the primary organizational structure developed by the federal government to respond to terrorist incidents. It has three basic organizational components which are formed out of existing agencies with recognition of the authority and responsibilities tasked to each agency by the Constitution and various executive orders, statutes, or regulations. At the first level, a special coordination committee was formed in the National Security Agency dealing with national policy and command in regard to terrorist incidents. At the second level, existing federal agencies were tasked to perform certain functions in response to possible terrorist actions. An executive committee of major federal agencies was formed, and interagency coordination and operational responsibilities were sorted out. The scope of each possible agency involvement resulted in the Lead Agency Concept based on whether the terrorist action was geographically internal or external to the territory of the United States. This led to the designation of the Federal Bureau of Investigation as the lead agency for internal actions and the Department of State as the lead agency for external actions. These agencies serve as the coordinating and control point for all counterterrorist actions taken by the various agencies with some role in combating terrorism. This approach developed the third level of the organizational response which focused on the operations. A working group on terrorism was identified and responsibilities tasked to individual agencies in four general operational areas that focused on four goals: diplomacy (prevention goal), protection and security (deterrence goal), incident response (reaction goal), and intelligence (prediction goal). This basic structure has remained in place with some redesignations and reassignment of responsibilities since its formalization in the 1970s.

The primary policy guidance for dealing with terrorism was established by the Department of State in these seven statements of policy:[14]

All terrorist actions, regardless of their motivation, are condemned as criminal.

All lawful measures are to be taken to prevent terrorist acts and to bring to justice those who commit them.

The United States will not accede to terrorist blackmail; to grant concessions only invites further demands.

When Americans are abducted overseas, host governments are expected to exercise their responsibility under international law to protect all persons within their territories, and to ensure the safe release of hostages.

During terrorist incidents, the United States will maintain close and continuous contact with the host government and support the host government with all practical intelligence and technical services.

The United States understands the extreme difficulty of the decisions governments are often called upon to make. For example, how to reconcile objectives of saving lives of hostages with making sure that terrorists can gain no benefit from their lawless action.

The importance of international cooperation to combat terrorism is recognized. The United States intends to pursue all avenues to strengthen such cooperation.

Similar guidelines have been developed for internal incidents with much of the actual response to an incident tasked to local or state agencies rather than to federal agencies.

In summation, national policy evolved from the United States' voluntary participation in and acceptance of various international organizations or agreements which define the international goals regarding the maintenance of peace and the permissible boundaries of warfare or other conflict. These agreements establish the parameters for and place limitations upon the national response to terrorism. The national policy continues to evolve as each terrorist action is reviewed and the response requirement is formulated or revised as necessary. The country has already implemented most of the legal requirements of the international agreements by passing various laws which enact their provisions. A short review of the legal situation within the United States will show how these provisions are being implemented, and help define the internal parameters within which a local agency operates to perform its part in the response to terrorist actions.

Notes

1. Article II, Section 2, Paragraph 2, Constitution of the United States. Article I, Section 8, Paragraphs 3, 10 and 18.

2. A resolution may be referred to as customary law taking on, in the international sphere, the same role that common law has within the United States.

3. Resolution 2625, General Assembly, 1970.

4. General Assembly Resolution 3314, 29th Session, 1974; page 10, "The Laws of War" by W. Michael Reisman and Chris T. Antoniou, 1994, Vintage Books, New York.

5. General Assembly Resolution 3166, 1973; page 299, *The Laws of War* by W. Michael Reisman and Chris T. Antoniou, 1994, Vintage Books, New York.

6. General Assembly Resolution 146, 1979; page 300, *The Laws of War* by W. Michael Reisman and Chris T. Antoniou, 1994, Vintage Books, New York.

7. "Resolution Adopted by the United Nations General Assembly to Prevent International Terrorism", Resolution 61, 40th Session, 1985; "Resolution Adopted by the United Nations Security Council Condemning Hostage-Taking and Abduction", Resolution 579, 40th Session, 1985; pages 303-304, *The Laws of War* by W. Michael Reisman and Chris T. Antoniou, 1994, Vintage Books, New York.

8. "Aviation: Offences and Certain Other Acts Committed on Board Aircraft," 1963; page 294, "The Laws of War" by W. Michael Reisman and Chris T. Antoniou, 1994, Vintage Books, New York.

9. "Suppression of Unlawful Seizure of Aircraft (Hijacking)," 1970; page 294, *The Laws of War* by W. Michael Reisman and Chris T. Antoniou, 1994, Vintage Books, New York.

10. "Convention for the Suppression of Unlawful Acts Against the Safety of Civil Aviation," 1971; page 296, *The Laws of War* by W. Michael Reisman and Chris T. Antoniou, 1994, Vintage Books, New York.

11. "Texts of the Statements Adopted by Leaders of Seven Industrial Democracies (At the Tokyo Summit Meeting, Concerning Terrorism," 1986; page 304, *The Laws of War* by W. Michael Reisman and Chris T. Antoniou, 1994, Vintage Books, New York.

12. "Convention on the Marking of Plastic Explosives for the Purpose of Detection," 1991; page 306, *The Laws of War* by W. Michael Reisman and Chris T. Antoniou, 1994, Vintage Books, New York.

13. Chapter 3, *US Strategy to Counter Domestic Political Terrorism* by James B. Motley, 1983, National Defense University Press, Washington, DC.

14. Chapter 3, *US Strategy to Counter Domestic Political Terrorism* by James B. Motley, 1983, National Defense University Press, Washington, DC.

Chapter 3

LEGAL REVIEW

A review of the current legal considerations which affect the ability to prevent or react to attacks by weapons of mass destruction must cover a broad range from international agreements to local ordinances and encompasses all levels of government and all types of controlling guidelines. Such an examination will show that planning parameters are established by laws, agreements, regulations, administrative orders, and, occasionally, simple social customs. Frequently, considerations which appear to have no immediate connection to this overall topic will affect the ability to deal with it. The complexity of this particular area should not be minimized, and it is important to remember that this is a planning overview, not a legal brief. The entire point of the examination is to gain some knowledge of the limitations imposed by various sources and how they may affect assessment, prevention, defense and response. The topical areas which require some examination are:

1. Selected portions of the United States Code which enact various provisions of the voluntary international treaties, conventions, or agreements or establish United States policy;

2. Federal laws or regulations which control materials usable for explosives or special weapons;

3. Federal or local codes pertaining to structural access or physical materials used in the structures;

4. Federal, state, and local emergency government powers provisions;

5. Federal, state, and local use-of-force provisions including the use of military forces.

While it is not initially obvious to most people how these topical areas may pertain, each of them has an effect upon the preparation for defense, and prevention of and response to attacks by weapons of mass destruction. The application of the various areas will become more apparent as the subject is examined and then applied in later chapters.

The first area to examine is the response by the federal government to the various agreements, resolutions, and treaties mentioned in the policy review section. This response appears primarily in the form of statutes enacted by the government and made part of the United States Code. The primary sections of the code which apply are discussed in the following paragraphs.

UNITED STATES CODE: TERRORISM AND DANGEROUS MATERIALS

The first codified response to modern international terrorism came in the early 1960s with the onset of aircraft hijacking worldwide. The United States passed legislation against aircraft piracy.[1] This led to the establishment of the Sky Marshal program and airport security provisions both eventually taken over by the FAA. As efforts against aircraft hijacking became more organized and more effective worldwide, terrorists began to direct their attacks increasingly against the diplomatic community both the individual diplomats and the consular or embassy buildings. Initially, the various countries developed their individual approaches based upon some common beliefs concerning the propriety and effectiveness of various responses. As international terrorist events became more complicated, international agreements were developed. This led to the passage of the Diplomatic Security and Antiterrorism Act of 1986[2] which was eventually amended twice[3] as world events showed that changes were needed. The breadth of the initial act was quite large; here is a partial listing of the areas addressed by the original act and its later amendments:

    a. Congress made a statement of its Findings and Purposes.[4]

    b. Tasked overseas responsibility for countering terrorism to the Secretary of State[5] and antiterrorism enforcement to the Attorney General[6] (the "Lead Agency" concept).

c. Mandated the cooperation of other federal agencies in support of the Secretary of State.[7]

d. Established (some would say expanded) the diplomatic security service, specifically giving it authority to provide security to lesser foreign diplomats within the United States, and United States diplomats overseas.[8]

e. Centralized and strengthened embassy security provisions via the diplomatic security program.[9]

f. Granted broad, but focused, general authority to provide or restrict terrorism in the international sphere through a variety of means including:[10]

(1) Providing antiterrorism assistance of a variety of forms to other countries.

(2) Banning the importing of goods and services from countries supporting terrorism.

(3) Restricting certain munitions and weapons.

(4) Designating some countries as terrorist sponsors and some groups as terrorists.

(5) Altering the restrictions on assistance to United States law enforcement agencies by intelligence agencies, and placed some restrictions on law enforcement training outside the United States.

(6) Altering the authority statements of various executive offices, departments, and agencies to perform the related tasks.

(7) Making provision for the necessary appropriations.

g. Provided for rewards for information pertaining to international terrorism and espionage, protection of informant identity, and eligibility for the witness protection program.[11]

h. Legally defined terrorism, established extraterritorial jurisdiction, provided for civil remedies, and asserted the primacy of federal jurisdiction.[12]

i. Made adjustments to the espionage-related statutes to cover terrorist activities.[13]

j. Adjusted federal personnel regulations to provide benefits during captivity for both civilian employees and military personnel.[14]

k. Revised the definition of protected personnel under the law enforcement, government official, and diplomatic personnel statutes.[15]

l. Addressed the possible cooperation between or possible financing of terrorist activity by drug running.[16]

m. Prevented immigration of individuals with backgrounds related to terrorism, providing for exclusion for certain acts.

The next really significant antiterrorism legal actions came in 1994 in response to continuing problems with vehicle bombs and a growing hard line position toward terrorists by both government officials and the general populace. It was contained in the Violent Crime Control and Law Enforcement Act.[18] The primary features were the definition of weapons of mass destruction[19] and adjustments to the death penalty to include most terrorist acts,[20] but it also contained provisions for:

a. Extending United States jurisdiction to maritime targets.[21]

b. Returned special consideration to aviation resources by extending jurisdiction to international airports.[22]

c. Extended the statute of limitations for some offenses.

A variety of additional measures which indirectly deal with terrorism can be found in the federal code. These provisions have been passed at various times in response to various actions. Some were in response to domestic problems, and some to international problems. Many address the same issue in either arena. The first of these additional areas to address is the control of materials usable for terrorist actions.

The theory behind materials control is quite simple. First, you identify those materials needed to make various terrorist weapons; then you formulate and implement regulations to control access to the materials. This has been done within the United States. The interesting point is that these controls began as responses to other problems, but are now applicable to terrorist actions pertaining to weapons of mass destruction.

ACCESS CODES

The federal government has defined a large number of materials as hazardous.[23] The primary means of federal regulation is control of the material during transportation[24] and secondarily through its storage, handling or other exposure in the workplace and community.[25]

Included are a wide variety of chemicals or other materials with four subcategories that are of some significance to a discussion of the full range of weapons of mass destruction. The four subcategories are radioactive materials, biological/medical materials, explosives, and selected chemicals used to produce chemical agents. Radioactive material is generally controlled as part of a larger regulation of all materials defined as hazardous,[26] and specifically controlled by limiting its transactions,[27] its transportation,[28] and its disposal.[29] Biological and medical materials tend to cross over the lines of regulations with some areas being subject to controls by one agency while others are controlled by others.[30] Explosives are subject to the general controls for transportation of hazardous materials but are also subject to specific controls in virtually every area of storage, manufacture, etc.[31] Chemicals are controlled, as previously mentioned, by DOT and OSHA, but are also subject to usage and disposal requirements instituted by the EPA.[32] There are even controls placed upon mailing of many of these items.[33] The basic approach is to control the access to materials during transportation, storage, and use in order to reduce the hazards in normal daily usage. In some cases, the regulatory measures are intended to prevent or at least identify inappropriate diversion or use as a secondary benefit. Few of these measures were written with the intention to halt any terrorist action, let alone their use in a weapon of mass destruction.

The next area considered is codes affecting design or access to structures. These are usually found in municipal ordinances or state statutes, and may be quite varied. Regional Development Plans, Zoning or Commercial Usage Codes, Building Construction Codes, Fire Codes, and Traffic Codes are the most important and most typical of these. There is some attempt to establish nationwide standards, but this is incomplete and has only been partially implemented where such nationwide standards have been established. The only nationwide code which clearly applies is the Americans with Disabilities Act[34] which establishes access requirements in publicly-used buildings and transportation. The codes which do apply have not been written with defense of either the structures or the transportation means as the primary requirement nor even as one of the range of requirements. Where safety is the issue for the codes, the safety risk is presumed to be a natural disaster or routine technology risk such as fire, pressure container eruption, ease of evacuation, etc. Consequently, the codes do not necessarily meet even simple defense requirements in the event of any attack by a weapon of mass destruction.

EMERGENCY POWERS

Governmental Emergency Powers are the next legal consideration. These are the provisions of the federal, state, and local governments to deal with unusual or widespread problems affecting the general population which are beyond the scope of daily activities. Among the problems that might fit this category are natural disasters, nuclear reactor problems, failure of dams, electrical blackouts, pipeline explosions, riots and civil disturbances, or deliberate attacks of various types. At the federal level, the primary consideration is whether or when federal resources will be used. The basic theory is that local and state governments will respond first. Consequently, the procedure for using federal assets is a little cumbersome, and there are strong limitations, particularly upon the use of military assets, especially for law enforcement actions.[35] The basic procedure requires that assistance be requested by local or state officials, certified by a federal representative, and then provided based upon an executive order of the president.[36] This is reinforced by the federal requirement to establish state planning commissions.[37] States have implemented these requirements establishing procedures for use by the municipalities as needed. A typical state might implement emergency provisions with statutes on the following:

Commander in chief, chief of staff, rank, qualifications, aides-de-camp.
Adjutant general, powers and duties
Ordering militia into active service
Call for aid by local officials
Disaster or drought
Powers of governor during state of disaster emergency
State disaster emergency plan
County and city disaster agencies
Interjurisdictional disaster agencies
Emergency declaration

Duty of individuals
Force and effect on municipal ordinances
Immunity from liability
Emergency preparedness for disasters
Emergency interim executive and judicial succession acts
Emergency interim legislative succession act
Emergency location of governments for state political subdivisions
Emergency location of state government
Nuclear energy development and radiation control
National guard mutual assistance compact
Interstate civil defense and disaster compact
Department of civil air patrol

Local governments, depending on size or governmental structure, will further implement these emergency provisions with ordinances that pertain. A typical listing of municipal ordinances would include the following:

Authority to declare emergency
Authority to request assistance
Curfews
Suspension of ordinances
Suspension sales of selected items

Cities will prepare their ordinances as needed to fit their own situation, the projected emergencies based on past experience and simple area or terrain analysis, and the state and federal requirements that pertain to their area. Moving from emergency powers, we must next review the legal situation pertaining to use of force. In examining this area, a broad viewpoint must be taken. This will include not only the use of force by law enforcement officers, but also the use of military forces including the militia. An understanding of the exact limitations is critical to defense against weapons of mass destruction. Consequently, this area will be examined in more detail.

USE OF FORCE AND COMMON DEFENSE FORCES

The United States Constitution states the basic purpose of the union in the Preamble. This can be viewed as the mission statement for the country: "...in order to form a more perfect union, establish justice, insure domestic tranquility, provide for the common defense, promote the general welfare, and secure the blessings of liberty to ourselves and our posterity ..." Justice, domestic tranquility, the common defense, and the general welfare are the stated purposes of the union. The inclusion of the common defense implies that use of force is acceptable in furtherance of the other purposes. The other articles of the Constitution go on to outline the basic framework of responsibilities for the common defense (the use of force):

In Article I, Section 8 (Powers of Congress), Congress is specifically tasked to provide and pay for the common defense; to define offenses against the laws of nations; to declare war; to raise and support armies; to maintain a navy; to make rules for regulation of the land and naval forces; to provide for calling forth the militia; to organize, arm, and discipline the militia; and to make all necessary laws to execute the powers of the Constitution.

In Article I, Section 10 (States Prohibited from the Exercise of Certain Powers), the States are prohibited from keeping troops in time of peace or engaging in war unless actually invaded or in such imminent danger as will not admit of delay.

In Article II, Section 2 (President to be Commander-in-Chief...Nomination of Certain Officers), the President is designated the Commander-in-Chief of the Army and Navy of the United States and of the militia of the several states when called into actual service of the United States. The President is also given authority to make treaties and appoint officers of the United States with the advice and consent of the Senate.

The organization for war or use of force is this: Congress raises and regulates the forces, declares the wars, and enacts the laws relating to these actions; the president commands the war-fighting forces and appoints the military officers; and the states are prohibited from engaging in war unless invaded or in imminent danger. War is a federal responsibility, but the militia, though it must follow the discipline specified by Congress, is a state responsibility. This is clear when you examine both the Second and Tenth Amendments. The Second Amendment begins, "A well-regulated militia being necessary to a free state, ..." Notice that the terms "Union" or "United States" used in other places throughout the Constitution are not used in reference to the necessity for the militia. In the Tenth Amendment, powers not delegated to the United States are reserved to the states. Since the Constitution also only allows the militia to be commanded by the president when it has been called forth into federal service, it is clear that the militia is under state control on a daily basis. Having established this, the critical question is what constitutes the militia.

The militia has been defined by Congress in the United States Code[38] as all able-bodied males at least 17 years of age and under 45 years of age who are citizens of the United States. A recent modification was to add female members of the National Guard. Some exemptions from service are permitted. The same section further specifies the classes of militia as the organized militia (the National Guard and the Naval Militia) and the unorganized militia (all others who meet the definition). Congress has further regulated the militia by identifying its structure and organization,[39] its purpose,[40] its training,[41] its equipment and arms,[42] and its purchase and issuance of supplies.[43] Basically, these sections require the militia to use the same equipment as the Army and Air Forces, and obtain its equipment and supplies from the same sources. The section on training also includes a statement that the training is conducted by the states, clearly implementing the intent seen in the basic constitutional structure. The states have enacted their own legislation based on this structure.

The various state constitutions and statutes basically follow these general guidelines for the militia. Most have similar provisions in their constitutions, bills of rights, and statutes which define the classes and composition of the militia, the manner in which they are called forth, and their authority when called forth. The states reserve their command of the militia to the governor of the state through an adjutant general, the state militia commander. The state statutes usually define the emergency powers of the governor both in regard to the militia and to the other citizens as well.[44] In most states, the organized militia is accorded the status of law enforcement officers when deployed in a disaster role rather than in a war fighting role.[45] Their situation becomes a little less clear when deployed in an internal peacekeeping role such as a riot, political action such as a takeover of a building, or a hostage situation. In such cases over the last several decades, the organized militia has been deployed in a law enforcement role in these situations, but their deployment and use of force instructions run up against the boundary line between civilian law enforcement and military war fighting. The problem is that the same stimulus actions can themselves potentially be either a criminal act or an act of war. This means that the response actions can potentially be either as well. In recent United States history, the boundary has not been crossed, or at least has not been *acknowledged* as being crossed by either of the opponents. This leads us to two interwoven areas of legal consideration, the law on use of force and the internal application of the Laws of Warfare.

The use-of-force statutes found within the United States are based on the common law of self-defense with slight modification to cover the use-of-force during arrest. Most significant is the fact that all use-of-force statutes are state laws;[46] there are no federal codes on use-of-force. Federal use-of-force policy is derived by executive authority from the basic Constitutional purposes found in the preamble. Consequently, it has the same legal basis as the use of military force during war-fighting. This is an important distinction to notice: *State officials provide the common defense of the population as a self-defense action based upon the common law of self-defense; Federal officials provide the common defense of the population with the* **option** *to provide it as a self-defense action based on the common law of self-defense* **or** *to provide it as a war-fighting action based on the Laws of Warfare.* This means that **all** federal officials have a much broader latitude in the formulation of use-of-force instructions. The United States Constitution does not delegate war-fighting *only* to the Department of Defense. It delegates it to the federal government. There is nothing that prevents the federal government from issuing war-fighting instructions to the Justice Department, the Treasury Department, or the State Department rather than just issuing them to the Department of Defense. An examination of the statutory mission statements of executive agencies and the military departments reinforces this viewpoint.[47] This means that the federal authorities must consider the impact of responding to an incident as an act of war rather than as a criminal act. The difference affects both the purpose of the response and the means or methods of the response. Here is how.

The first area to examine is the use-of-force specification. Under state use-of-force statutes and federal executive use-of-force policy, deadly force can be used *only in exceptional circumstances.* This would apply to federal, state, or local law enforcement officers; private security officers; and private citizens. In war, use-of-force can be used in *all but exceptional circumstances.* This would apply to military forces, the militia, and, under some circumstances, to federal law enforcement officers and any private citizens acting as partisans. Which legal standard applies may not be easy to determine at the instant of confrontation or to sort out afterwards. The second area that becomes important are the procedures or restrictions within the Laws of Warfare that affect typical police operations within the United States. There are five such considerations that are immediately obvious:

1. Differentiating between "An Act of War" and "An Act of Criminality" which determines the legal status of the participants.

2. The definition and role of the Partisan.

3. The identification and restrictions pertaining to protected personnel and structures.

4. The requirements for bombardment notifications to civilians and neutrals.

5. The equipment currently used by police forces.

These five considerations will be addressed in more detail, separately.

The primary difference between an act of war and a criminal act is one of declaration or of intent on the part of the participants. Consequently, either opponent has the option of declaring the action as an act of war. There are advantages and disadvantages to doing so. The Law of Warfare assumes that opponents will declare war prior to attack. When the opponent attacks without first declaring war, a state of war does not "automatically" exist. The opponents have the option of calling it something else. To help sort out this gap out, the situation was addressed by the United Nations which produced the following tests to determine whether an act of war has occurred. The tests[48] are:

> General test for act of war:
>> Armed action by a State (nation) against the sovereignty, territorial integrity or independence of another State (nation).
> Specific tests for act of war against a State (nation):
>> Invasion or attack of its territory.
>> Bombardment or the use of weapons against its territory.
>> Blockade of its ports or coasts.
>> Attack on its land, sea or air forces or marine and air fleets.
>> The use of armed forces within its territory in contravention of an agreement.

Allowing its territory to be used for perpetrating an attack against another.
Sending of armed bands, groups, irregulars or mercenaries which carry out
    acts of armed forces on behalf of a state.

Notice that these tests rely upon action by an established nation. If the
group involved is not an established nation, then the test for an act of
war relies more heavily upon intent. The test advanced is two-fold:

The group is seeking the right of self-determination, freedom and indepen-
    dence having been forcibly deprived of that right.
The group is complying or attempting to comply with the Laws of Warfare.

The first test is difficult to assess at the time and point of attack. The
second test for groups, in the context of a weapon of mass destruction,
relies upon evaluation of three of the other considerations: partisans,
respect for protected status, and notification. Other evaluations can be
used but are of less immediate application.

A partisan is, technically, a person who rises up in defense of himself or his land upon the approach of an armed force. Partisans, also
called militia or volunteers, can be found on either side of a conflict.
The test of whether an individual is a partisan is fourfold:[49]

Commanded by a person responsible for his subordinates.
Fixed distinctive emblem recognizable at a distance.
Carries arms openly.
Conducts operations in accordance with the laws and customs of war.

It is important to notice that virtually all police officers and all armed
private security officers would meet this criteria as would the legally-
defined militia of the United States. A similar test for a civil war can
be applied. The standard for the conduct of a civil war under international law is this basic orientation:

Persons taking no active part in the hostilities, ... shall in all circumstances be
treated humanely, without any adverse distinction founded on race, colour,
religion or faith, sex, birth or wealth, or any other similar criteria.[50]

These tests are relatively easy to assess at the scene of an incident.
Respect for protected status is also relatively easy to assess at the scene
of an incident.

Protected status as a concept is based upon the theory that wars are fought between military forces of two or more nations and are intended to be somewhat respectful of an opponent's right to differ. In holding to this chivalrous view of war, the Laws of Warfare have identified certain categories of people and structures that may not normally be included in the war effort. Generally, the categories of noncombatants are civilians not directly involved in the war effort,[51] neutral parties and their diplomats or citizens,[52] medical personnel or the sick and wounded,[53] chaplains or similar religious personnel,[54] and prisoners-of-war or detainees.[55] These people may not be deliberately taken under fire, but they lose this status if they voluntarily participate in the opposition or if, after notification and opportunity, they choose to assume the risks of battle. The list of protected structures is lengthy and a little unclear at times. Hospitals and churches are clearly included[56] and easily identifiable, but other buildings are not necessarily identifiable. Buildings which are culturally important or irreplaceable are also mentioned; this would include educational, artistic, scientific, charitable or historic buildings.[57] The problem is that they would lose their protected status if involved in supporting the war effort. How to determine this is not obvious. There are two other considerations for these structures. Any protected structure which is deliberately defended by the opponent loses its protected status, and these structures are required to be marked in such a manner as to be obvious to the air or ground forces involved. This requirement is why military ambulances are typically marked with a Red Cross on a white background. The critical factors, then, are the identification or marking of the person or structure and the action being taken by the person or by the people at the structure. This brings us to the bombardment notification requirement.

When a military force is attacking a target where there are known to be or are very likely to be civilians or other protected persons, the Laws of Warfare require that notice of the attack be given and those persons be afforded the opportunity to depart to safety.[58] Once this notice and opportunity have occurred, there is no requirement to refrain from attacking the target. Any person of protected status who stays after notice, loses the protected status. While they may not be deliberately attacked as individuals, their presence at the scene does not "legally" prevent the war action. They have "assumed the risk"; this is the same "assumed risk" standard applied inside the United

States under existing civil liability law. This brings up the topic of civil liability and how it may affect police actions or response. This will be considered in more depth after a look at equipment considerations under the Laws of Warfare.

We are all generally aware that equipment for war is subject to some limitations. Existing police agencies and civilians inside the United States typically use some equipment that might be a problem under the Laws of Warfare. Bullets used in firearms during warfare are limited.[59] The first limitation is size; bullets used against personnel must be of .50 caliber or less.[60] The bullets must be single projectiles, fully-jacketed, visible on x-ray inside a person's body, and not be explosive on contact. This effectively prohibits the use of buckshot shells and may prohibit the use of some shotgun slugs, depending on their diameter. It also prohibits hollow-point, soft-point, and lead, unjacketed rounds. Their use would be a war crime under the Laws of Warfare. Of similar concern are the various nondeadly sprays used by police officers.

Mace or tear gas is, technically, a chemical warfare agent under international law, even though classified as a noncasualty producing agent.[61] The same problem surfaces with OC (Oleoresin Capsicum) spray. Its active ingredient is a plant extract which technically classifies as a toxin and makes OC spray a biological warfare agent under international law.[62] While both are classified as noncasualty producing agents, there is disagreement in the international sphere about the use of such agents. The United States and many other nations assert that the international agreements pertaining to chemical and biological warfare only cover casualty producing agents. Other nations do not agree with this viewpoint. This raises the possibility that their use inside the United States against any group claiming their action as an act of war could be viewed as a war crime prosecutable under an international tribunal. The United States has signed treaties renouncing the use of chemical agents and biological agents in hostilities.[63] Consequently, the ramifications of their use must be considered. Their use poses both criminal and civil liability questions.

Civil liability considerations will arise for both the public and the private sector during assessment of, defense against and response to weapons of mass destruction. The first problem that will arise is that some insurance policies may have an exclusion for "Acts of War". This means that any loss may not be covered by the insurance in place for anyone involved. Even if the insurance covers it, the possible loss may be greater than the policy coverage or greater than the assets of either the insurance company or the reinsurance pool of the state. This exclusion possibility also arises in the emergency provisions of many states which prevent civil liability of the state militia, and sometimes other public officials under emergency circumstances. This could prevent a party from recovering damages against the officials involved, even when the individual had no way to prevent the officials from taking the options which created the loss. Emergency provisions under state laws are quite broad and frequently allow seizure or control of private assets for the public good. This is an area of civil liability that is not well-developed in the United States.

The third problem for businesses, and public agencies to a lesser extent, is the "Reasonable Care Doctrine" which is typically applied to businesses. The theory behind this doctrine is that a business can predict its possible risks and appropriately address them; therefore, a customer has a right to expect the business to take "Reasonable Care" in the conduct of its business to protect the customer from harm. Aside from the obvious problems arising from trying to protect customers from a weapon of mass destruction, the nature of these weapons raises a secondary problem area. A business could effectively defend itself against an attack only to be confronted with the reality that its defensive measures actually displaced or increased the damage to neighboring businesses. This raises the possibility that effective defense could be the basis for civil liability under the reasonable care doctrine since the effects of the defense itself are "reasonably foreseeable circumstances," the test used in this civil liability doctrine. Whether this test could or would be applied is not clear.

The final civil liability area present is the assumption of civil liability risk for the person involved in the defense. Some military officials are exempt from civil liability during the performance of their official duties, and some state officials are as well under the state statutes. Whether "civil rights" liability provisions could be applied to assess liability individually is not clear, but it is clear that a private individual would not have this protection. Consequently, a private security officer or other private person might have civil liability for acting or for failing to act against an attack by a weapon of mass destruction. The entire area of civil liability in these situations is not developed. It is just beginning to surface as the attacks against the buildings in New York and Oklahoma are being sorted out. This legal issue is, essentially, an unknown quantity in the considerations, and even it is affected by the differing legal status and consequent differing owner responsibilities between public and private property. The overall outcome may be very different for the two incidents cited based on the property ownership difference alone.

WEAPONS OF MASS DESTRUCTION

The final legal consideration pertaining to weapons of mass destruction is to identify the specific legal meaning of the term. The sections of the federal code that directly apply are:

18 U.S.C. 2332a.(b)(2) the term "weapon of mass destruction" means
(A) any destructive device as defined in section 921 of this title;
(B) poison gas;
(C) any weapon involving a disease organism; or
(D) any weapon that is designed to release radiation or radioactivity at a level dangerous to human life.
18 U.S.C. 921(a)(4) The term "destructive device" means
(A) Any explosive, incendiary, or poison gas
    (i) bomb
    (ii) grenade
    (iii) rocket having a propellant charge of more than four ounces,
    (iv) missile having an explosive or incendiary charge of more than one-quarter ounce,
    (v) mine, or
    (vi) device similar to any of the devices described in the preceding clauses;
(B) any type of weapon (other than a shotgun or shotgun shell which the Secretary finds is generally recognized as particularly suitable for sporting purposes) by whatever name known which will, or which may be readily converted to, expel a projectile by the action of an explosive or other propellant, and which has any barrel with a bore of more than one-half inch in diameter; and
(C) any combination of parts either designed or intended for use in converting any device into any destructive device described in subparagraph (A) or (B) and from which a destructive device may be readily assembled. ...

Basically, a weapon of mass destruction is a large bomb and\or a chemical, biological or radiological weapon, but can include other, modified military weapons. Based on this legal definition and its criteria, the following classification system for weapons of mass destruction can be created for further discussion:

• Conventional Weapon of Mass Destruction (CWMD): A destructive device that contains only explosives or incendiary material. This category can be subdivided based on the material into the following categories:

  • Explosive Weapon of Mass Destruction (EWMD): A destructive device that contains only explosives.
  • Incendiary Weapon of Mass Destruction (IWMD): A destructive device that contains only incendiary material; May be called a fire bomb or flame weapon.
  • Enhanced Weapon of Mass Destruction (EnWMD): A destructive device that contains both explosives and incendiaries.

• Special Weapon of Mass Destruction (SWMD): A destructive device that contains poison gas, a disease organism or radioactive materials. This category can be subdivided into the following subclassifications:

  • Chemical Weapon of Mass Destruction (ChWMD): A destructive device which contains a poison gas (chemical agent).
  • Biological Weapon of Mass Destruction (BWMD): A destructive device which contains a disease organism or toxin (biological agents).
  • Radiological Weapon of Mass Destruction (RWMD): A destructive device which contains a radioactive material. This category is itself subdivided into two parts:
    • Radiation Weapon of Mass Destruction (RdWMD): A destructive device which is designed to scatter a radioactive material.
    • Nuclear Weapon of Mass Destruction (NWMD): A destructive device which is designed to create a nuclear detonation.

To wrap up the classification based on legal criteria, the following terms should be made clear:

Rocket: A destructive device which relies on unguided, powered flight to reach its point of detonation.
Missile: A destructive device which relies upon guided, powered flight to reach its point of detonation.

Mine: A destructive device which is emplaced at a specific point for detonation. The emplacement is traditionally burying, but could be concealment of another type. Several subcategories of this type could be constructed, but only one will be included here.

Vehicular bomb: A destructive device which can be driven to its point of emplacement/detonation.

Projectile bomb: A destructive device which is thrown, hurled, dropped or otherwise launched to its point of detonation. This would include grenades or satchel charges and mortar rounds, aerial bombs, or other explosive projectiles.

Classification of devices and other technical points pertaining to the destructive devices will be discussed further in Chapter 5.

Summation of the legal issues involved in the police assessment of and defense or response to weapons of mass destruction is not easy. The complete impact of some of the legal issues mentioned will not become completely clear until the assessment, prevention, defense or response actions are discussed in more detail. The critical points are understanding what a "weapon of mass destruction" is, and recognition that its nature seriously raises the issue of whether its use is an act of war or an act of criminality. All assessment, prevention, defense, or response to such weapons is complicated by this dualistic possibility. It affects what level of government can act; what type of forces can be deployed; what authority, jurisdiction, or rights the force has; what type of force can be used in defense; and the legal consequences for all people involved at the scene of any attack. The true measure of the impact will become clearer in the following chapters.

Notes

1. Initially listed as Aircraft Piracy in Title 18 of the federal code, it was modified in the 1980s in favor of offenses which covered other forms of terrorist action as well. It consequently disappeared as a separate offense and is now covered by the hostage and various assault sections of Title 18. The most direct coverage is found in 18 U.S.C. 1201 and 1203.

2. Public Law 99-399, 1986.

3. Public Law 100-204, 1987 and Public Law 101-246, 1990.

4. 22 U.S.C. 4801.

5. 22 U.S.C. 4802.

6. 22 U.S.C. 5203.

7. 22 U.S.C. 4805.

8. 22 U.S.C. 4821 and 4822. Security for visiting foreign heads of state was retained by the United States Secret Service as previously directed in its authority statements established by various statutes and executive orders.

9. 22 U.S.C. 4851 to 4864.

10. 22 U.S.C. 2349aa.

11. 18 U.S.C. 3071 to 3077 and 22 U.S.C. 2708.

12. Title 18 Chapter 113B Terrorism; 18 U.S.C. 1116, 18 U.S.C. 1203, 18 U.S.C. 2331, 18 U.S.C. 2332, 18 U.S.C. 2333 and 18 U.S.C. 2338.

13. 18 U.S.C. 793 to 798 and 18 U.S.C. 3077.

14. 5 U.S.C. 5569, 5 U.S.C. 5570, 5 U.S.C. 5928, 5 U.S.C. 6325, 10 U.S.C. 1032, 22 U.S.C. 2349aa-2, 26 U.S.C. 104; 37 U.S.C. 310, and 50 U.S.C. 403k.

15. 18 U.S.C. 970, 18 U.S.C. 1114, 18 U.S.C. 1116, 18 U.S.C. 1119, and 18 U.S.C. 2336.

16. 10 U.S.C. 124, 19 U.S.C. 2491 to 2492, 22 U.S.C. 2708, 22 U.S.C. 2714, 22 U.S.C. 2291, and 22 U.S.C. 2321k.

17. 8 U.S.C. 1101, 8 U.S.C. 1181, 8 U.S.C. 1251, 22 U.S.C. 2714, and 22 U.S.C. 5202.

18. PL 103-322, 1994.

19. 18 U.S.C. 2332.

20. 18 U.S.C. 34 [Aircraft and Motor Vehicles], 18 U.S.C. 794a [Espionage], 18 U.S.C. 844(d) [Explosives], 18 U.S.C. 1116(a) [Foreign Officials], 18 U.S.C. 1201(a) [Kidnaping], 18 U.S.C. 1716 [Letter Bombs], 18 U.S.C. 1992 [Trains], 18 U.S.C. 1203 [Hostage Taking], 18 U.S.C. 1091(b)(1), and 18 U.S.C. 2332(a) [Weapons of Mass Destruction].

21. 18 U.S.C. 2280 and 18 U.S.C. 2281.

22. 18 U.S.C. 37.

23. 40 C.F.R. 302 Designation of hazardous substances; reportable quantities and 40 C.F.R. 707-796 Toxic substances control.

24. Chapter 51--Transportation of Hazardous Material. 49 U.S.C. 5101 Purpose; 49 U.S.C. 5104 representation and tampering; 49 U.S.C. 5108 registration; 49 U.S.C. 5110 shipping papers and disclosure; 49 U.S.C. 5112 Highway routing of hazardous material; 49 C.F.R. DOT HAZMAT regulations.

25. Employee Right-to-Know Program mandated and monitored by OSHA; Community Right-to Know Program mandated and monitored by E.P.A. (40 C.F.R. 370).

26. 40 C.F.R. 302 Designation of hazardous substances, reportable quantities; 40 C.F.R. 370 Hazardous chemical reporting; community right-to-know.

27. 18 U.S.C. 831 Prohibited transactions involving nuclear materials and 22 U.S.C. 2371. Enacted by PL 97-351, 1982; PL 100-960, 1988; PL 103-272, 1994; PL 103-322, 1994. Also, Executive Order 12930 Measures to Restrict the Participation by US Persons in Weapons Proliferation Acts

28. Controlled generally as a hazardous material, there are two sections that directly pertain: 49 U.S.C. 5105 Transporting certain highly radioactive material; 49

U.S.C. 5114 air transportation of ionizing radiation material. E.P.A. regulations also apply: 40 C.F.R. 190-195.

29. Chapter 108--Nuclear waste policy. 42 U.S.C. 10101.

30. Medicines would be subject to controls from the Drug Enforcement Administration; biological material to controls from DOT, FDA, OSHA, NIOSH, and CDC; chemicals to controls by DOT and OSHA. In addition to 49 C.F.R. already cited, 21 C.F.R. 1240 Communicable diseases control; 42 C.F.R. 71 Foreign quarantine.

31. Chapter 40, Importation, manufacture, distribution and storage of explosive materials. 18 U.S.C. 842. Unlawful Acts (Explosives); 18 U.S.C. 843 Licenses and User permits; 18 U.S.C. 921(a)(4) [destructive devices definition], and 41 C.F.R. 101-20.303 Explosives.

32. Multiple E.P.A. regulations are under Chapter 40 C.F.R.

33. 18 U.S.C. 1716 Injurious articles as nonmailable.

34. PL 101-336, 1990; PL 102-166, 1991. Chapter 126--Equal opportunity for individuals with disabilities. 42 U.S.C. 12101.

35. 10 U.S.C. 124 Detection and monitoring of illegal drugs, 10 U.S.C. 331 Federal aid for state governments, 10 U.S.C. 332 Use of militia and armed forces to enforce federal authority, 10 U.S.C. 333 Interference with state and federal law, 10 U.S.C. 334 Proclamation to disperse, 10 U.S.C. 371-381 Military support for civilian law enforcement, 10 U.S.C. 401-404 Humanitarian assistance, 18 U.S.C. 1385 Posse Comitatus, 22 U.S.C. 2292 International disaster assistance, 22 U.S.C. 2348 Peacekeeping operations, 32 C.F.R. 185 Military Support of Civil Defense, 32 C.F.R. 501 Employment of Troops in Aid of Civil Authority, 32 C.F.R. 502 Relief Assistance, and 32 C.F.R. 632 Use of Force in Law Enforcement and Security Duties.

36. Executive Order 12656 Assignment of Emergency Preparedness Responsibilities.

37. Subchapter I - Emergency Planning and Notification. 42 U.S.C. 11001. Establishment of State commissions, planning districts, and local committees.

38. 10 U.S.C. 311. Militia: composition and classes.

39. 32 U.S.C. 103 Branches and Organization; 32 U.S.C. 104 Units, Location, Organization and Command; 32 U.S.C. 261 Reserve Components.

40. 32 U.S.C. 261 Purpose.

41. 32 U.S.C. 501 Training generally.

42. 32 U.S.C. 701. Uniforms, arms and equipment to be same as Army or Air Force.

43. 32 U.S.C. 702 Issue of supplies and 32 U.S.C. 703 Purchase of Supplies.

44. As an example, here are the militia portions of the Kansas Constitution and state statutes:

KANSAS CONSTITUTION and BILL OF RIGHTS

4. Bear arms; armies. The people have the right to bear arms for their defense and security; but standing armies in time of peace, are dangerous to liberty, and shall not be tolerated, and the military shall be in strict subordination to the civil power.

ARTICLE 8. MILITIA.

1. Composition; exemption. The militia shall be composed of all able-bodied male citizens between the ages of 21 and 45, except such as are exempted by the laws of the United States or of this state; but all citizens of any religious denomination whatever who from scruples of conscience may be adverse to bearing arms shall be exempted therefrom, upon such conditions as may be prescribed by law.

2. Organization. The legislature shall provide for organizing, equipping and disciplining the militia in such manner as it shall deem expedient, not incompatible with the laws of the United States.

This structure is expanded in the Kansas Statutes.

K.S.A. 48-101 Persons subject to military duty; classes.

All persons subject to military duty under the constitution of this state and not exempt therefrom by the provisions of this act, and such other persons as shall voluntarily enroll themselves, shall be divided into three (3) classes, to wit: One consisting of the federally recognized national guard, which shall be known as the "Kansas army and air national guard"; one consisting of those able-bodied male citizens prescribed and contemplated in article 8 of the constitution of this state not in the "Kansas army and air national guard" which shall be known as "the militia"; and one to consist of all those subject to military duty, but not included in the "Kansas army and air national guard" or "the militia" to be known as the "Kansas military reserve".

K.S.A. 48-102. Persons exempt from military duty.

The following persons are exempt from military duty:

First, all persons in the army or navy or volunteers force of the United States and those who have been honorably discharged therefrom; all persons who have served in the Kansas national guard for the term of four years and have been honorably discharged; all the judges and clerks of the several courts of the state and the county treasurers.

Second, incapacitated persons, mentally ill persons, and persons convicted of infamous crimes.

Third, all persons who are members of any well recognized religious sect or organization at present organized and existing whose creed forbids its members to participate in war in any form, and whose religious convictions are against war or participation therein, in accordance with the creed of said religious organization: Provided, That the aforesaid exempted persons included in the first subdivision of this section shall be liable to military duty in case of war, insurrection or invasion, or imminent danger thereof.

45. An example is this statute from Kansas: **K.S.A. 48-934. Duties and immunities of law enforcement, military and other authorized personnel.** Law enforcement officers, military personnel, or other persons authorized to assist them, while engaged in maintaining or restoring the public peace or safety or in the protection of life or property during a state of disaster emergency proclaimed under K.S.A. 48-924, shall have all powers, duties and immunities of peace officers of the

state of Kansas in addition to all powers, duties and immunities now otherwise provided by law and shall be immune from civil and criminal liability for acts reasonably done by them in the performance of their duties so long as they act without malice and without the use of excessive or unreasonable force. All such personnel shall have the authority to enforce any and all ordinances of any municipality within an area affected by disaster as indicated in the proclamation of a state disaster emergency under K.S.A. 48-924, and for such purpose, all such personnel shall be considered to be authorized officers of said municipality.

46. The Kansas statutes are listed for review as needed.

K.S.A. 21-3211. Use of force in defense of a person. A person is justified in the use of force against an aggressor when and to the extent it appears to him and he reasonably believes that such conduct is necessary to defend himself or another against such aggressor's imminent use of unlawful force.

K.S.A. 21-3212. Use of force in defense of dwelling. A person is justified in the use of force against another when and to the extent that it appears to him and he reasonably believes that such conduct is necessary to prevent or terminate such other's unlawful entry into or attack upon his dwelling.

K.S.A. 21-3213. Use of force in defense of property other than a dwelling. A person who is lawfully in possession of property other than a dwelling is justified in the threat or use of force against another for the purpose of preventing or terminating an unlawful interference with such property. Only such degree of force or threat thereof as a reasonable man would deem necessary to prevent or terminate the interference may intentionally be used.

K.S.A. 21-3214. Use of force by an aggressor. The justification described in sections 21-3211, 21-3212, and 21-3213, is not available to a person who:

(1) Is attempting to commit, committing, or escaping from the commission of a forcible felony; or

(2) Initially provokes the use of force against himself or another, with intent to use such force as an excuse to inflict bodily hard upon the assailant; or

(3) Otherwise initially provokes the use of force against himself or another, unless:

(a) He has reasonable ground to believe that he is in imminent danger of death or great bodily harm, and he has exhausted every reasonable means to escape such danger other than the use of force which is likely to cause death or great bodily harm to the assailant; or

(b) In good faith, he withdraws from physical contact with the assailant and indicates clearly to the assailant that he desires to withdraw and terminate the use of force, but the assailant continues or resumes the use of force.

K.S.A. 21-3215. Law enforcement officer's use of force in making arrest.

(1) A law enforcement officer, or any person whom he has summoned or directed to assist him, need not retreat or desist from efforts to make a lawful arrest because of resistance or threatened resistance to the arrest. He is justified in the use of any force which he reasonably believes to be necessary to effect the

arrest and of any force which he reasonably believes to be necessary to defend himself or another from bodily harm while making the arrest. However, he is justified in using force likely to cause death or great bodily harm only when he reasonably believes that such force is necessary to prevent death or great bodily harm only when he reasonably believes that such force is necessary to prevent death or great bodily harm to himself or another person, or when he reasonably believes that such force is necessary to prevent the arrest from being defeated by resistance or escape and the person to be arrested has committed or attempted to commit a felony or is attempting to escape by use of a deadly weapon, or otherwise indicates that he will endanger human life or inflict great bodily harm unless arrested without delay.

 (2) A law enforcement officer making an arrest pursuant to an invalid warrant is justified in the use of any force which he would be justified in using if the warrant were valid, unless he knows that the warrant is invalid.

K.S.A. 21-3216. Private person's use of force in making arrest.

 (1) A private person who makes, or assists another private person in making a lawful arrest is justified in the use of any force which he would be justified in using if he were summoned or directed by a law enforcement officer to make such arrest, except that he is justified in the use of force likely to cause death or great bodily harm only when he reasonably believes that such force is necessary to prevent death or great bodily harm to himself or another.

 (2) A private person who is summoned or directed by a law enforcement officer to assist in making an arrest which is unlawful is justified in the use of any force which he would be justified in using if the arrest were lawful.

47. While such an action might be viewed as unusual, it is within the legal and constitutional limitations. The basic authority of any cabinet level department is the same. 5 U.S.C. 101 designates the executive departments and establishes their basic authority. 5 U.S.C. 301 gives the executive departments authority to establish regulations and 5 U.S.C. 302 gives the executive departments authority to delegate responsibility. All executive departments have basically the same authority. Under 5 U.S.C. 901, the President has the authority to reorganize the executive branch to better fulfill policy (within certain limitations). Finally, examination of the basic mission statements for the military departments shows that other departments are not excluded from performing any of the functions. 10 U.S.C. 121 gives the President the authority to prescribe regulations and 10 U.S.C. 133 appoints the Secretary of Defense and his duties and powers. The four uniform service mission statements are found at 10 U.S.C. 3062 (Army), 10 U.S.C. 5012 (Navy), 10 U.S.C. 5013 (Marines), and 10 U.S.C. 8062 (Air Force).

48. Definition of Aggression, General Assembly Resolution 3314, 29th Session, 1974; Page 10, *The Laws of War* by W. Michael Reisman and Chris T. Antoniou, 1994, Vintage Books, New York.

49. Field Manual 27-10 The Law of Land Warfare, Department of the Army, July 1956, Chapter 3 paragraph 64.

50. Field Manual 27-10 The Law of Land Warfare, Department of the Army, July 1956, Chapter 1 paragraph 11. The text specifically cites the following as evidence of non-compliance: murder of all kinds, mutilation, cruel treatment, torture, taking

of hostages, outrages on the personal dignity, the passing of sentences without previous judgment pronounced by a regularly constituted court.

51. Field Manual 27-10 The Law of Land Warfare, Department of the Army, July 1956, Chapter 5.

52. Field Manual 27-10 The Law of Land Warfare, Department of the Army, July 1956, Chapter 9.

53. Field Manual 27-10 The Law of Land Warfare, Department of the Army, July 1956, Chapter 3 paragraphs 66-67 and Chapter 4.

54. Field Manual 27-10 The Law of Land Warfare, Department of the Army, July 1956, Chapter 3 paragraph 67.

55. Field Manual 27-10 The Law of Land Warfare, Department of the Army, July 1956, Chapter 3.

56. Field Manual 27-10 The Law of Land Warfare, Department of the Army, July 1956, Chapter 2 paragraph 45 and Chapter 4.

57. Field Manual 27-10 The Law of Land Warfare, Department of the Army, July 1956, Chapter 2 paragraph 45 and 57.

58. Field Manual 27-10 The Law of Land Warfare, Department of the Army, July 1956, Chapter 2 paragraph 43.

59. Field Manual 27-10 The Law of Land Warfare, Department of the Army, July 1956, Chapter 2 paragraph 34.

60. The requirement here is based on the design or intent of the weapon design. Those weapons which are designed for use against vehicles, aircraft, etc are not to be directed specifically against people under routine circumstances since they are exceptionally destructive against a person. This portion of the requirement is frequently hard to meet; there is an emergency exception to it.

61. Field Manual 3-9 Potential Military Chemical/Biological Agents and Compounds, HQ, Departments of the Army, Navy and Air Force 12 December 1990, Chapter 3.

62. Field Manual 27-10 The Law of Land Warfare, Department of the Army, July 1956, Chapter 2 paragraph 37 and Field Manual 3-9 Potential Military Chemical/Biological Agents and Compounds, HQ, Departments of the Army, Navy and Air Force 12 December 1990, Chapter 4.

63. *The Laws of Warfare* by W. Michael Reisman and Chris T. Antoniou, Vintage Books, New York, 1994, pages 57-65.

Chapter 4

ASSESSMENT OF TERRORIST GROUPS

Risk assessment is a concept developed in many settings to analyze the possibilities or probabilities of future events and circumstances, and then forecast the impact this would have on the organization conducting the assessment and on its goals. The purpose of the evaluation is to assist decision-makers in taking a course of action that is most favorable to its goals. There are a number of common approaches. Military forces evaluate the future battle by use of the Intelligence Estimate which orients on the opposing force organization (size, structure, equipment, etc.) and includes an analysis of the possible battlefield by a process called Intelligence Preparation of the Battlefield (IPB). A police agency typically monitors the historical data on crime, compares its fluctuations, and builds a database of information. Analysts then study the data to forecast crime rates, and determine department operational requirements such as manpower, equipment, or budgets. Police departments frequently conduct crime prevention surveys of specific neighborhoods or buildings, traffic studies of vehicular roadways or similar surveys which are actually miniature forms of the IPB process used by the military. Businesses also conduct similar surveys under the banner of loss prevention, loss-risk assessment or cost-benefit analysis, and usually engage in a lot of information gathering in the demographic sphere under the title Marketing Research. Regardless of which of these settings one is most familiar, the process is quite similar. The primary differences among the three approaches are the purpose for which the assessment is conducted and the exact factors which are included as significant. In conducting a risk assessment for possible use of vehicular bombs (conventional weapons of mass destruction), it is actually beneficial to interweave or move between the three approaches just described. This broadens the usefulness of this text but also orients on the reality of terrorist use of such weapons which is usually a political action oriented primarily on civilian targets. Consequently, each of these three approaches has peculiar advantages and disadvantages when assessing this type of risk. I will begin the review by examining the basic assessment procedure and then apply it to terrorist groups and conventional weapons of mass destruction (CWMD) in order to develop the responses.

BASIC ASSESSMENT MODEL

The military or governmental model of basic assessment contains six parts: Information, Threat Analysis, Prevention, Authority and Jurisdiction, Planning for Crisis Management, and Performing Crisis Management. Gathering information has an identifiable cycle. It starts with the collection of information by a variety of techniques. It may be historical data, personal experience, professional research studies, surveys, or many other methods. Some information may be immediately available and some may not be. The initial step is to simply determine what information you will need, the sources for it, and then gather it from those sources. The second step in the information cycle is to analyze the available information. Research methods are varied and do not need to be elaborated here. The final step in the information cycle is to disseminate the findings either in their raw data state or as conclusions for action by the organization.

The military model projects the three basic sources of information as people, communications, and imagery. These basic categories hold up well in the civilian environment but are usually known under different titles. Police departments tend to refer to various types of informants, criminal association patterns (a form of communication traffic analysis or sociometric diagraming for those with a sociology background), and electronic surveillance, while businesses term the same actions as customer requests or complaints, sales demand patterns (of goods or services), and demographic analysis. All are really talking about the same sources or events. The basic concept is that you can obtain information directly from people with whom you deal, from analysis of both the patterns and content of their communications, and by actual images produced by a variety of technical hardware (photos, videos, electronic tabulations, etc.). The primary difference is that the military has greater imagery capability and tends to rely upon imagery to a much greater extent than either police agencies or businesses. Once you have completed the initial information cycle from whatever sources, you are ready to undertake the threat analysis.

Threat analysis in the governmental model consists of both risk assessment and vulnerability analysis. This differs slightly from the meaning of risk assessment as it is typically used in businesses. Business people tend to use the term risk analysis for the entire process of threat analysis rather than for just the first part. Police agencies use both terms, depending upon the type of agency and operation involved. The essential point is that you first determine what you are facing, and then determine how it will affect you. That is the meaning usually attached to the terms of risk assessment and vulnerability analysis. Once you have completed these two steps, you move into the operational area, orienting first on prevention, the deterrence of the risk, and second on response, the management of the actual risk when it occurs. This is termed, generally, prevention in the government operational model, but it will be broken down into three parts in this text: prevention, defense, and response.

Operations security, personnel security, and physical security are the three general categories of prevention used in the governmental model of threat analysis (risk assessment). Operations security includes various subcategories such as information security (is it available, to whom, and how?), communications security (how do you send and protect your information both internally and externally?), computer security, which overlaps the other subcategories, and operational procedures (how do you do business?). Blending of these subcategories is common as they clearly overlap. Police agencies stick pretty close to these subcategories of operations security, but not strictly so. Businesses, however, tend to talk about confidential or private business information (what they do and how they do it), privileged information (legally restricted), or proprietary information (the product of their internal operations) while not clearly separating the categories. Only governmental contractors seem to utilize the same terminology.

Personnel security is implemented by almost everyone. Governments, police agencies, and businesses all screen the people they hire; they just have different methods and purposes in doing so. Basically, personnel security is a determination of the honesty or integrity of the people, and also an assessment of their performance capability. The latter is the view predominate in businesses while the former is the primary focus in the governmental model which also covers police agencies in this instance. For the purposes of this text, the term personnel security will cover four subcategories: Integrity checking, performance capability screening, criticality to the organization, and personal vulnerability. More details on this in a later chapter.

Physical security is a term that is found almost exclusively in the governmental model with the term being primarily applied and used by the military. Most police and business people tend to talk about this area as crime prevention or loss prevention. The term covers what is actually present at a given location in a variety of subcategories. The actual assets examined will include the physical (geographical or spatial) layout, the equipment present (such as alarm systems, locks, and so forth), the people present (police, security officer, managers, employees, etc.), and the procedures being used by those people. To phrase it in the common computer language of the day, think of physical security as an evaluation of the hardware and the software. This brings us to the fourth basic assessment procedural step.

Authority and jurisdiction are commonly recognized terms which need little comment. In this area, we examine the social organizations (government, police, business) to determine their social purpose. What exactly have we said they can do and where are the boundaries; who's in charge and how far can they go? The previous chapters on policy and legal issues were the basics of the authority and jurisdiction examination for this assessment. This leads to the planning step of the assessment.

The governmental terminology for handling nasty events is crisis management. In this step of the assessment one identifies what resources are needed to handle the event, what resources are available, and how must they be organized to deal with the situation. The terminology is widely understood and there is little difference in the terms, concepts, or implementation in the military, police, or business sphere. This is not surprising as this is basically management activity, and the concepts of management are quite similar in all three spheres, although the implementation or terminology is sometimes different. Once the organization is established, it may be tested or put to actual use. This constitutes the sixth and final step of the basic assessment procedure, performing crisis management. With that as background, here is a synthesized outline of the application to a terrorist attack.

ELEMENTS OF TERRORIST GROUP OPERATIONS

Start by examining the type of opponents, individual or group. You may classify them, generally, according to their intentions (political, criminal, crazy, etc.), according to their location of operations (international, transnational, local, etc.), or according to their method of operation (suicide bomber, hijacker, kidnapper, demonstrator, etc.). Once you have generally established their purpose as background, begin examining the specific elements of the terrorist group operation: purpose, structure, organizational skills, and support resources. Here are the details:

• Purpose, intention, or cause; evaluate the following:

The dedication or commitment to the cause.

The level of ruthlessness, willingness to kill or injure.

Their level of personal disregard; how much risk will they accept as a group or as individuals?

• Structure; determine the following:

How do they organize for their operations?

What is their network? Do they have international, interstate, or only local connections?

How likely are they to receive assistance from someone inside your operation; or how likely are they to attempt to place someone inside your operation?

How many of them are there?

How and who do they recruit for their personnel?

• Operational Skills; evaluate the following:

What are their personal, individual skills?

What type of preparatory activities must occur for an operation of the type you are forecasting?

What are the technical skills needed for such an operation? Do they have those skills?

When is such an attack likely to occur; does the group time attacks by current events, by "infamous" anniversaries, or by the time most favorable for success?

How will the attack occur; what is the specific technique used by the group in the past?

• Support Resources; evaluate the following:

How are their finances; how much do they have, where is it, where does it come from, etc?

What is their mobility in two aspects; can they blend easily with the society around you? Do they have access to transportation; what and how do they obtain it?

Do they have safe houses; people who will hide them or established locations where they can hide?

Do they train or practice before an attack? Where?

Do they have critical supplies such as weapons, explosives, or nuclear, biological, or chemical materials? What type? How much? How do they get these materials; buy, steal, manufacture, issued by government?

When you have completed the detailed analysis, you will utilize the data to compile the operational patterns for the group. The intention is to answer the six basic questions: Who, What, When, Where, Why, and How. This forms the basis of your prediction and serves as the basis for response formulation. An example of a completed evaluation can be found in the government publication, *Terrorist Group Profiles* compiled and published in the 1980s. Based on unclassified information, it is a very good basic work. It utilized the following headings for the profile of each group:

Date Formed
Estimated Membership
Headquarters
Area of Operations
Leadership
Other Names
Sponsors
Political Objective/Target Audience
Background
Selected Incident Chronology

In the formation of the operational response, you determine the requirements to counter an attack of the type or types that you have just developed. Again, you are attempting to answer the six basic questions (Who, What, When, Where, Why and How) in detail. The following chapters will step through this in more detail. In reaching these decisions, you may examine significant historical incidents looking for both operational techniques of the attackers and of the defenders. Thoroughness of the risk portion of the threat analysis will directly establish the validity of the vulnerability analysis that follows. The two are directly related; their relationship must constantly be reviewed and reevaluated as necessary.

Chapter 5

ASSESSMENT OF VEHICULAR BOMBS
(CWMD)

A complete risk assessment for terrorist use of vehicular bombs (conventional weapons of mass destruction) includes a review of the classification and technical capability of destructive devices, orienting primarily on car and truck bombs, and secondarily upon what the military calls special weapons (chemical, biological, and nuclear devices). A recently enacted section of the federal code[1] puts both vehicle bombs and special weapons together, defining them as "weapons of mass destruction" for legal purposes under the criminal titles of the code. That definition will be retained throughout this work when the reference is meant to be all-inclusive. When the intent is to separate the two basic categories, they will be designated as conventional weapons of mass destruction or special weapons of mass destruction. In this portion of the risk assessment, the purpose is to identify the technical capability of the various conventional weapons of mass destruction in order to forecast their destructive effects upon a location during the vulnerability analysis. In order to simplify the understanding, this text is devoted strictly to conventional weapons of mass destruction (CWMD) which are, typically, bombs in vehicles. Special weapons of mass destruction (SWMD) will not be included in this threat analysis for vehicular bombs.

DESTRUCTIVE DEVICE CLASSIFICATION

Bombs or destructive devices,[2] as they are labeled in the criminal sections of the federal code, can be classified by general explosive

81

type, by type composition, by activation means, by usage, by operational technique, or by delivery means. Some of these classifications are more important than others for defense purposes while others matter primarily to the bomb experts who must dispose of them. There are four general types of bombs based on the materials used to construct them and the basic manner in which they function to create an explosion.

A low-order explosive, the first explosive type, is composed of a flammable liquid, gas, or powder that is confined in an enclosed space with an oxygen source and ignited. Some representative low-order explosions are gasoline, natural gas, or coal dust. low-order explosions usually just require a spark or simple flame to ignite them. The results of a low-order explosion are typified by a low rumbling boom, pushing damage outward throughout the confined space with rupture at one weak point being common, and scorching of debris throughout the area of confinement. The heat produced is usually relatively low with consequent low pressures at the time of explosion. Most low-order explosions result when chemicals used for purposes other than deliberate explosion are mishandled or equipment fails creating an explosive chemical mixture. While it is possible to build devices for low-order explosions, it is usually not done for bombing purposes, but rather to create a fire (arson).

High-order explosions are the second type. A high-order explosion is usually a mixture of chemicals in either liquid or solid form which is intended to be an explosive and to detonate quickly. The primary differences are the speed at which it burns, the amount of heat it produces for its relative size, and the fact that most, but not all, require a triggering explosion in order to detonate them. Examples of high order explosives are plastic explosives such as composition four (C4), nitroglycerin, or dynamite. High-order explosions are typified by a sharp cracking sound, breaking damage, missile (fragmentation) impact damage, and scorching limited to the area where the explosive was at the time of detonation. High-order explosives are also more likely to produce a crater than low-order explosives.

The third type is an enhanced explosive. This is a term for the deliberate combining of large volumes of low-order explosives around a central high-order explosive to "enhance " the effects. An enhanced explosive (as used in recent vehicle bombs) has typically been compressed gas bottles around the high order explosive, the central bomb component. Enhanced explosives are most likely to have a distinct cracking sound during the initial detonation which is partially masked by the more prolonged low-order booming (The opposite sequence is also possible). This is caused by a sequential rather than simultaneous detonation of the two components. Enhanced explosives will have both types of damage seen in the low and high order explosions. A central crater will be identifiable where the breaking or pulverizing damage occurs with a much larger zone of pushing damage that has scorching. The scorching of the low-order explosion will probably not be as consistent throughout the area of damage due to the design of the bomb which prevents spread of the explosive throughout the area prior to detonation. There may be identifiable differences in the scorching damage around the crater versus the scorching throughout the area due to the differences in the temperature attained by the different explosives. Enhanced explosives typically leave fires burning throughout the damage area, if the material in the area is flammable.

The final type of explosive is the most complicated, and is usually not seen outside of a military setting. The fuel-air bomb is composed of a flammable material, usually a thickened liquid, which is projected into the target area and then ignited after maximum dispersal. The flamethrowers used in World War II and Korea or the napalm bombs used in Vietnam would be the best known examples. Research since then has produced bombs which burn at much higher temperatures and could actually project the material directly into a bunker or building to turn the inside into a giant exploding container. Such weapons make an incoming rocket or projectile noise, a small cracking and whooshing noise as the fuel is released and then a low-order ignition boom. The area would be heavily scorched and the use of such a weapon (dependent on design and detonation manner) would leave projectile parts in the vicinity of the initial burn and may leave projectile impact damage where the device struck the target. Fuel/air weapons are very uncommon and have now been prohibited by international treaty for use in warfare.[3] All four of these explosive types have in common the basic structure of all bombs: a triggering device (fuse), explosive material, oxygen access either as air or as an additional component, and confinement to limited space. The last is what makes an explosion rather than a simple fire, and assists in classifying the composition.

Aside from considering the general explosive type, the composition of the bomb can be classified by the chemicals used and the techniques of assembling, mixing or producing the explosive. The explosive used can be stated as the classification of the bomb. Examples would be an ammonium nitrate bomb, a dynamite bomb, a plastic explosive bomb, etc. Once the explosive has been named, the form in which it is present can also define the classification. Sticks, blocks, barrels, molded, shaped, plastic, liquid, gel, gas, etc. are all appropriate descriptions for classification as is an indication of its origin. Military, commercial, or homemade help define the composition as do terms that identify the containers in which it is present. These can include letter, package, satchel, briefcase, backpack, trash can, car, etc. The form of combining the explosive prior to or during the operation can also be important: solitary (homogenous) versus binary (the explosive is in two components, usually stable, which must be combined to become an explosive). Finally, the composition can be described as simultaneous or sequential, depending on how the explosives present are intended to or will react when triggered. This is a separate consideration from triggering action which, by itself, makes any detonation part of a sequence.

The third area of classification deals with the means by which the explosion is activated or triggered. There are basically four subcategories: Command, boobytrap, delay, and accidental. Notice that these subcategories refer to the intended timing of the blast and not to the manner of operation of the triggering device or fuse. Various types of fuses can be used for any of the techniques. Command activation is the first subcategory. This technique is not typical in terrorist bombings; it requires the presence of a person who decides the exact moment to trigger it, instantaneously (on command). This obviously increases the risk to the bomber of both injury or detection. Suicide bombing is a specialized form of command detonation. Boobytrap activation, the second subcategory, is a stealth technique which can be implemented in a vast number of ways. The triggering is caused by some routine action of a person with security personnel or bomb squad members being the primary targets. It can be implemented in many forms; the four basic forms are pressure, pressure release, electrical circuit completion, or circuit interruption. The final type, delay triggering, is the most common form of activation with delay occurring in one of two ways: detonation at a predetermined time or predetermined event or detonation after a selected time period. The final activation method is by accident which can be the pure accident (no explosion intended) or where the intended explosion occurs at the wrong time (during assembly or emplacement by the bomber). These subcategories are not clearly differentiated and it is relatively common for more than one fusing device to be found on one bomb.

The fourth means of classification is the usage for which the bomb is intended. This is usually described as strategic or tactical. The difference is a combination of both intent and effect. A strategic bomb use is one which simply demonstrates the ability to bomb or terrorize; it is primarily a political usage. Consequently, virtually any target is acceptable. The vehicle bombing of the World Trade Center is an example of a strategic use of a bomb. Tactical usage of a bomb tends to be more precise in selection, and gives an immediate benefit to the user. The target selected is usually the direct opposition. An example would be vehicle bombs detonated next to buses filled with civil police such as has been done by a terrorist group located in Spain. The group reduces the ability of their opponent directly while still attaining some political or terror value. Some targets are not clearly in either sphere and may be classified both ways. The best example of this is the bombing of the Marine Headquarters in Beirut. Oriented directly against an opponent, it was probably intended to force withdrawal of the forces making it both a tactical and strategic use.

The operational techniques used in conducting the bombing can also be used as classification. The first is a comparison of techniques, precision versus proximity. A precision bombing attack typically uses a small quantity of explosive that are emplaced at rather exacting locations to achieve the effect. The explosive charges may be precisely molded into certain shapes and may be detonated in a specific, timed sequence to create stresses or weaknesses in the structure being attacked. Such an attack requires some analysis of the structure being attacked, requires access to the interior or specific points of the structure, and takes a relatively long time to emplace properly. Once detonation occurs, the damage inflicted creates a weakness and the natural pull of gravity or similar physical forces causes the structure to collapse. The best examples of this in the United States are demolition crews that collapse old buildings into a pile of rubble for removal. They typically analyze the structure closely, emplace small charges precisely, and then detonate them in a specific order and time sequence to cause the building to fall in a certain direction. Obviously, this type of attack requires a lot of skill. A proximity attack, by contrast, does not. A proximity attack overcomes, to a large extent, the technical analysis requirement, the structural access requirement, and the high skill requirement. It substitutes large explosive quantity for them. While it may be extremely destructive, use of a proximity bomb is a tip-off that you are probably either dealing with low-skill bombers (amateurs) rather than professionals or that the security provisions of the site are being effective. The Oklahoma City bombing would be classified as a proximity attack since the bomb was large in size and was detonated outside of the building.

The second operational technique of classification is also a comparison. It deals with how the attack was delivered: overtly or covertly. An overt attack is one that is obvious, while the covert attack is stealthy. The Beirut bombing of the Marine Headquarters would classify as an overt attack since the bomber drove the truck through the perimeter, into the restricted area, and past guards attempting to halt him in order to accomplish the attack. The intent was obvious to the guards. The World Trade Center bombing would classify as a covert attack since the truck was driven into the building and parked while appearing to be routine business. One manner of distinguishing the overt from the covert is whether the bomber escaped the scene.

Four other forms of operational techniques should be mentioned, but they are not comparative in nature. The first is the suicide bomber. The person delivering the bomb is willing to die while doing so rather than desiring to inflict damage while escaping detection. He is focused on the success of the attack and not on survival. Suicide bombers may use either overt or covert methods of attack to reach the target. The second form, simultaneous bombing attack, refers to the planned detonation of more than one bomb at the same location or within the same general area at approximately the same time. The purpose here is usually to overload the response forces causing a breakdown in the ability to respond properly. It may also be intended to create general panic for either the first purpose mentioned or to significantly raise the level of terror inflicted. A sequential bombing attack may also overload the response forces or may target them. Sequential attack refers to a series of detonations in a planned order to achieve some specific purpose. Sequential detonation was already cited as a means of weakening a structure during precision attack. The order of attack may have other purposes. It may be intended to draw response forces to a site to weaken the defense elsewhere or may simply draw the response forces to a particular location to target them with a second or third device. A further possibility is the intended penetration of a perimeter by one explosion which allows a second bomb to be moved through the devastated area immediately without security check. The fourth noncomparative form is the segmented attack. This also relies upon sequential activity, but in this case, the sequence is in the introduction of the bomb. At locations where security is tight, a segmented attack may be used to first smuggle the bomb components into the location, stage them at a selected place, and then assemble the bomb on the spot when all components are present, and emplace them in the interior of the target. This type of attack is both difficult for the bomber to perform and difficult for the security force to detect.

Delivery means is the sixth classification category. This deals with how the bomb arrives at its intended target. A laid charge or emplaced bomb is the initial category. This means that the bomber personally puts the bomb on the target and sets it for detonation. A projected charge is the second. This is a bomb prepared for use and then hurled like a projectile onto the intended target. Common forms of projected charges are hand grenades, satchel charges, or improvised mortar rounds. Terrorists have improvised mortars by fusing the bomb to detonate on impact or by a short delay after firing, placing it into a pipe or tube built in an apartment or on the bed of a truck, and then firing the prepared bomb through the air toward its target by use of a separate charge of explosives. Other hurling devices can be improvised. Examples would be catapults or large slingshots. The courier delivery technique comes in two forms, intentional or unintentional, and is the third category. A courier bomb is worn or carried by a person. In the intentional courier bomb, the person is aware that the bomb is there and may either simply be delivering it for the bomber to the target or may intend to command detonate it. A third possibility is that the courier may be extorted to deliver it with command detonation controlled by another party as occurred during an assassination in India. An unintentional courier is one who is unaware that he is carrying a bomb. Letter and package bombs sent through a delivery service such as the U.S. Postal Service or United Parcel Service fall into this category. The deliveryman is simply performing a routine function with no destructive intent. Occasionally, the unintentional courier may believe that he is carrying something else as occurred in one aircraft bomb incident. The courier apparently believed that she was smuggling currency or similar items for the terrorist group in the suitcase, but a bomb had been substituted.

VEHICLE ASSESSMENT

The final delivery means for classification is the vehicle bomb. Actually a form of courier bomb, the classification is separated for convenience due to the special characteristic of self-movement, the usual quantity of the explosive involved, and the need to thoroughly analyze vehicle capability in order to prevent or defend against the attack. Here are the specific factors to evaluate about vehicles:

Stealth or deception capability–How conspicuous or inconspicuous will the vehicle be at the attack site? This will affect the amount of attention given to it by the security forces present and, consequently, the possibilities of detection.

Load rating–How much can the vehicle carry? The primary concern is weight-carrying capability, not number of passengers or overall spatial volume. This statement is based on actual density of typical explosives, and calculations which show that vehicles larger than a motorcycle have more space to store explosives than the vehicle is capable of carrying in terms of the weight of the typical explosive that occupies that amount of space. The vehicle can be completely packed with explosives, but this affects its performance and makes the vehicle obvious. It also risks failure by broken springs, blown engine, etc.

Maneuverability–How well can the vehicle maneuver around, over, or through obstacles to reach the target? The specific mobility factors are as follows:

Approach angle–The steepest angle of slope the front of the vehicle can drive over without digging in.

Breakover angle–The sharpest angle the vehicle can drive over without hanging-up on the frame (frequently called "high-centering").

Departure angle–The steepest angle of slope the rear of the vehicle can drive over without digging in.

Tracking–The track is the distance that the wheels are apart across the vehicle while tracking is the term used for whether the rear wheels travel over the same ground as the front wheels.

Turning Radius–The smallest distance needed by the vehicle to execute a turn, usually expressed as a constant distance of the steering wheels from a selected point.

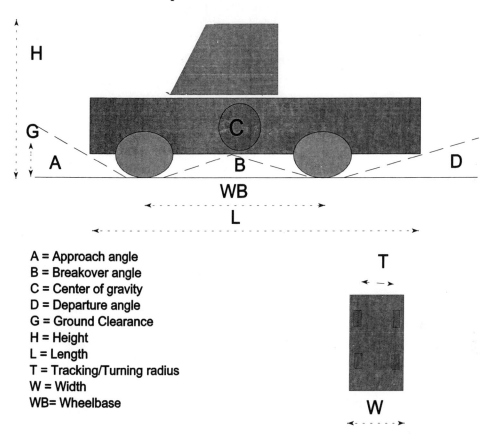

A = Approach angle
B = Breakover angle
C = Center of gravity
D = Departure angle
G = Ground Clearance
H = Height
L = Length
T = Tracking/Turning radius
W = Width
WB= Wheelbase

Figure 1. Vehicle assessment factors. Load rating of vehicle is its weight-carrying capability.

Center of gravity–the notional point where the physical forces affect the vehicle; this helps determine whether the vehicle will roll over or flip over during maneuvering.

Size–Overall height, width, and length.

Wheelbase–The distance the wheels are apart from front to rear.

Wheel size (axle midline)–The diameter of the wheel which helps determine the clearance level of the axle.

Ground clearance–The distance from the ground that the frame, axle or similar component is when the vehicle is on level ground.

Weight–Total weight; usually called gross vehicle weight rating.

These are the factors which must be assessed to determine the suitability of a given vehicle for use as a bomb. The analysis of the data provides the information necessary to develop prevention and defense actions at specific sites. The real problem in assessing vehicle bombs is the large number of vehicle designs. This creates a virtually endless number of possibilities. Consequently, the analysis must focus rather generally on classes of similar vehicles. Having reviewed the types of bombs, usage, techniques, activation, composition, and delivery means, it is now time to review the technical effects of bombs as the first step in assessing the possible effect on the target.

BASIC PHYSICAL PROPERTIES AND EFFECTS OF EXPLOSIONS

The effects of a bomb are best understood by recalling the basic chemistry and physics principles involved, and projecting the analysis from them. An explosion is, by definition, a rapid combustion or burning, usually in an enclosed space. Like the simple flame, an explosion needs heat, fuel, and oxygen. Most explosions occur within the atmosphere which is composed primarily of gases, the most significant being oxygen.[4] Since this is a combustion occurring in a gas, the relationship between temperature-pressure-volume in that gas is the important mechanism. The basic principles are:

(1) Pressure in a gas is always equal throughout the volume of the gas.

(2) Temperature and pressure are directly related in a constant volume of gas; an increase in temperature causes an increase in pressure when the volume of gas remains constant.

TEMPERATURE - PRESSURE

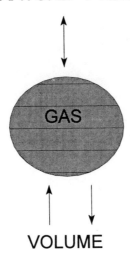

VOLUME

Figure 2. Natural relationships in gas. Temperature and pressure change which
equalizes in all directions producing a pressure wave.

Consequently, when the temperature rises at one point, the gas
expands creating a higher pressure area. If the volume is confined, the
pressure builds until it ruptures the container. If unconfined, the pressure equalizes by moving outward from the point of increase in a theoretically perfect sphere (Figure 3). From this we can deduce that the
mechanism of damage in a bombing is the pressure wave moving outward from the blast point. Studies confirm that the pressure wave is
the most important mechanism of damage with the heat of the explosion being a secondary means, but it is the temperature *rise* which creates the pressure wave. Consequently, we can make three important
statements in rating the effectiveness of an explosive:

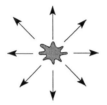

PRESSURE EQUAL IN ALL DIRECTIONS

PRODUCES PRESSURE WAVE

Figure 3. Pressure equalization. A sudden rise in heat produces a pressure change which equalizes in all directions producing a pressure wave.

1. The greater the temperature rise, the more effective the explosive is in creating a pressure wave.

2. The faster the temperature rise occurs, the more effective the explosive is in creating a pressure wave.

3. The smaller the volume of initial displaced gas in which the temperature rises, the more effective the explosive is in creating a pressure wave.

The effectiveness of an explosion is measured by the amount of pressure in the wave produced, and the effectiveness of an explosive is measured by its ability to produce that pressure per unit of weight. This has lead to two relative effectiveness scales to measure explosives. The scale used for conventional explosives is based on one pound of TNT as 1 on the scale with other explosives assigned a number equivalent to the amount of pressure one pound (by weight) of that explosive produces compared to the pressure created by TNT. This is referred to as the RE factor (relative effectiveness) of the explosive. The basic idea is that one pound of relative explosive power may require (by actual weight) one pound of TNT, two pounds of ammonium nitrate, or a half pound of a plastic explosive. The RE factor is multiplied times the weight of the actual explosive present to give the explosive power of the actual detonation. The answer (the product of the equation) is stated in pounds of TNT relative effect. The second scale is that used for nuclear explosions which compares the pressure in terms of tons of TNT producing ratings as kilotons (KT), 1000 tons, or megatons (MT), 1000 KT. Having established pressure as the primary force in conventional explosions, let us look at the pressure wave and its interaction upon the target.

BASIC PHYSICAL PROPERTIES AND EFFECTS
OF PRESSURE WAVES

Studies conducted during nuclear explosions reveal that a pressure wave has five factors that are significant, but only two are of primary concern for the vehicle bomb. The pressure wave moving out is actually a wall of compressed air that has a greater pressure than normal atmosphere. The differential between this greater pressure and normal atmospheric pressure at the blast site is referred to as "overpressure." Of the five factors in the pressure wave (Figure 4), this is the most significant, the most damaging, but it does not act alone. The second significant factor for vehicle bombs is called the "shock velocity" and is basically the speed at which the wall of compressed air is traveling outward from the blast at any given point. The two combine to produce the damage (mass x velocity = force). Naturally, the amount of overpressure and the shock velocity increase as the size of the explosion increases. As this increase occurs, the pressure wave becomes strong enough to bring into consideration another damaging force, the wind following the pressure wave. This is called the "dynamic pressure." Not as strong as the original pressure wave, it does extend the period of damaging force. It only becomes significant when the explosion is very large. In very large explosions, the pressure wave is large enough to actually completely engulf smaller structures with damaging pressures at high shock velocity. When this condition exists, then even another component is added, the "drag factor." This condition occurs behind or above the structure as the pressure wave passes. For a short period, the structure has a partial vacuum above or behind it which tends to pull the structure in the direction of the pressure wave that is passing.

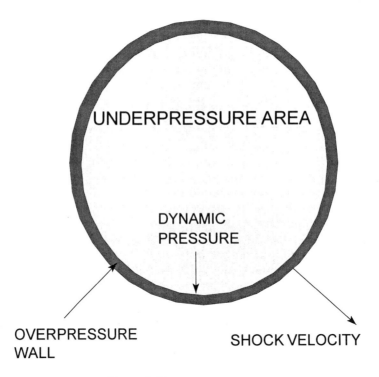

Figure 4. Pressure wave components.

At some point, the temperature increase in the center of the explosion stops and conditions begin to revert to normal. When this occurs, a partial vacuum occurs, the fifth factor, creating an area that is less than normal atmospheric pressure (underpressure) which works to reverse the pressure wave. This temperature drop takes place over a longer period of time than the temperature rise. Consequently, this inward suction is not as strong as the outward blast, but the effect becomes much more pronounced as the size of the explosion increases. At the nuclear level, films taken during testing show that the under-pressure occurs so quickly that debris blown away by the overpressure wall (blast effect) actually can be seen to stop in mid-air and reverse direction before falling back to ground. As the size increases, this reversal is itself actually reversed somewhat so that there is an out-ward, inward, outward wind of sequentially decreasing velocity, a back-and-forth effect as the equilibrium of the air pressure returns to normal. This points us to the next step which is an understanding of how the pressure wave interacts with the surroundings.

Interaction of the pressure wave with the surroundings is simply an application of basic physics principles regarding wave phenomenon and collisions. The pressure wave collides with various structures, both manmade and natural, with predictable results since a moving force always rebounds from a fixed object at an equivalent angle (Figure 5). The areas to examine first are the natural elements, the weather, the atmosphere, and the terrain on which the explosion

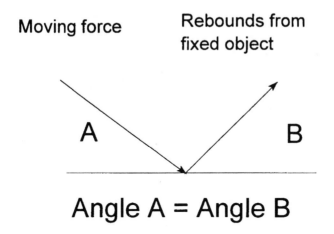

Figure 5. Collision angle. Force rebounds at equivalent angles; an elastic pressure wave will rebound from a rigid object at a predictable angle.

occurs. The weather affects the explosion and resulting pressure wave by four physical factors: temperature, air density, air movement, and environmental impact. Temperature first affects the explosion itself. Since an explosion is basically a fast combustion, the temperature at which the combustible material starts has some effect upon the speed of the combustion and the overall temperature rise. This in turn affects the air pressure rise and consequent shock velocity and overpressure of the resulting blast wave of air. The temperature also affects the surrounding environment and its elasticity-rigidity or combustibility in response to the explosion. The air itself is affected by the temperature helping to determine the air density in two ways. Since the air molecules are further apart at different temperatures, the pressure wave formation and its movement action are affected. Air temperature also affects the ability of the air to hold water and other suspended material, thereby increasing the density even more. In denser air, the pressure wave will not move as far or as fast as it would in "drier" air. The overpressure, however, would tend to be slightly higher in denser air.

The final air factor is the movement of the air, both its direction and speed. Air movement has some impact upon the initial combustion of the explosion by affecting the amount of oxygen present for combustion over a period of time. Once the pressure wave is produced by the explosion, the wind direction and speed will have some impact upon the distance that the blast wave travels, a lesser distance upwind and a greater distance downwind. The wind movement will also have some affect upon the air pressure since the velocity of a gas may raise or lower its pressure at a given point as it interacts with the terrain or structures present. The combinations of the three air factors produces part of the environmental impact. The combination of air density (basically water) and temperature obviously affects whether it is raining, hailing, snowing, etc., which in turn has some impact upon both the combustibility and elasticity-rigidity of the surrounding environment. The presence of such weather will also affect the reaction in other ways.

Storms produce conditions which can either assist the blast effects or resist them. High winds might actually serve to temporarily shield some areas from a pressure wave while the presence of hail in the air during the creation of a pressure wave could conceivably increase its casualty effects upon any people present since the hail could act as airborne fragmentation thereby producing wounds. Obviously, the presence of adverse conditions will affect the mobility factors of the vehicle attack, the defense against it and the response to it, but of more importance will be the effect upon the surfaces at the blast site. Adverse weather, such as the presence of ice, will have some impact upon the deflection, reflection, or reduction of the pressure wave as it passes the various terrain or structures. This brings us to a discussion of the terrain factors.

PRESSURE WAVE INTERACTION WITH TERRAIN

First are altitude considerations. We are aware that the atmosphere is thinner (lower pressure) at higher altitudes, and that the temperature is usually cooler. This influences the formation of the pressure wave since the temperature rise for the same relative explosive size is the same. The maximum temperature produced during the explosion at higher altitudes will be lower, which means the maximum pressure produced will also be lower. The overpressure will be approximately the same, but the terminal effect will be different since the air in the wave started at a lower pressure. As the wave moves outward, it meets less resistance in expansion, which means that it takes a longer distance to equalize the pressure. The summation of all that is an explosion at low altitude is more destructive but over a smaller area than the same relative size of explosion at a higher altitude.

The second terrain consideration is the shape of the ground that is present. Pressure waves traveling uphill tend to compress, increasing the overpressure, while pressure waves traveling downhill will tend to expand, decreasing the overpressure faster (Figure 6). Slopes or hills may work to deflect or reflect the pressure wave causing a shielding, protective effect for structures at some places or a magnified, negative effect for structures at other places, the result of the collision interaction between the pressure wave sphere and the terrain shape. The terrain shape has a very pronounced effect on the horizontal movement of the pressure wave, and strongly affects the results on the intended target. The vertical movement of the pressure wave is always basically the same in the open. The atmosphere above the explosion always allows unrestricted expansion, while the area below the explosion always has a ground level which restricts expansion. This always results in wave reflection from the ground unless the explosion is high enough in the air to equalize pressure before reaching the ground. This will not occur in a vehicular bomb. This wave reflection from the ground back into the high pressure area enhances the pressure and is

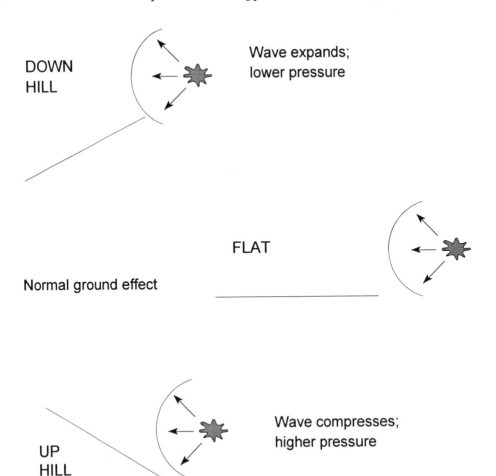

Figure 6. Slope Effects on pressure.

referred to as the "ground effect" (Figure 7). The nature of the terrain at the point of the blast, called "ground zero," determines the amount of the ground effect as seen by simply comparing hills versus valleys at the blast site (Figure 8). There will also be some ground shock (seismic effect–wave transmission through geologic strata) that spreads from ground zero outward, but this is unlikely to be of much significance in the vehicle bomb. Any damage that the ground shock produces will probably be in the immediate area of the blast site due to the relative size of the explosion involved.

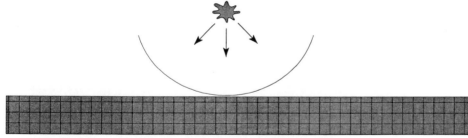

Pressure wave strikes ground.

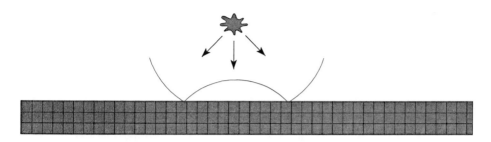

Wave reflects upward,
increasing internal pressure.

Figure 7. Ground effect. Overpressure wall strikes ground and reflects into the high pressure area increasing the internal pressure.

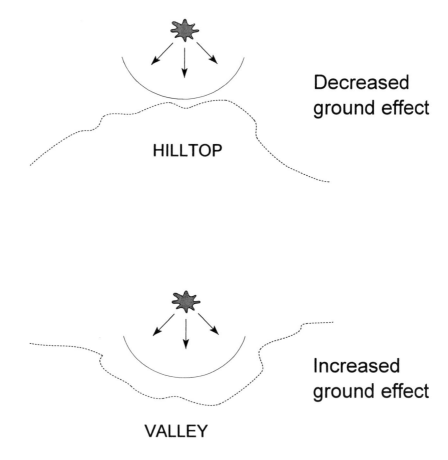

Figure 8. Modified ground effect. Hilltops and valleys modify the ground effect observed on flat terrain.

The presence of large bodies of water near ground zero will affect the air density (reducing the pressure buildup as previously explained), but also alters the effects of the pressure wave. The elasticity of the water compared to the relative rigidity of dirt, rock, etc. means that the pressure wave will not be affected in the same way as it reflects from or passes over the body of water. This is caused by the relative elasticity of water compared to ground. The water tends to create a temporary cavity by compressing the water in response to the pressure wave (Figure 9). As the pressure wave passes, the water pressure returns to normal, returning the absorbed pressure back into the air. The overpressure and shock velocity are both affected; the former decreases faster while extending its duration, and the latter decreases at a slower rate than it would over ground. The difference in the "ground effect" wave reflection is the cause of this.

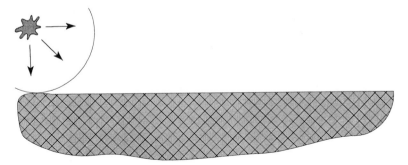

Compresses temporary crater

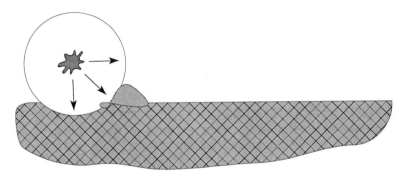

Produces surface wave action.

Figure 9. Water suface interaction with pressure wave. Temporary cavity in water produces initial surface wave action. Water restores its equilibrium returning force of overpressure into the air.

The presence or absence of vegetation, as the third terrain consideration, will affect the rate of reduction of the overpressure, the possibility of fires both during the initial blast and as a secondary effect, and may increase the quantity of debris in the pressure wave. The simple difference between coniferous and deciduous trees will affect both the amount of airborne debris, its type, and its lethality (Figure 10). Large, hard branches typical of deciduous trees will increase the level of impact damage upon structures and people while the smaller branches with needles typical of coniferous trees are less likely to do so. There is a significant difference in the height of branches and foliage

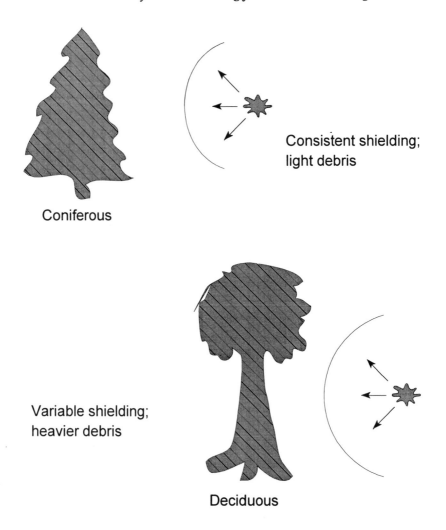

Coniferous

Consistent shielding;
light debris

Variable shielding;
heavier debris

Deciduous

Figure 10. Tree type shielding effects.

on the trees which affects the reduction of the pressure wave at ground level. Even the landscaping layout of the tree planting will affect the manner in which the blast is reduced (Figure 11). This focuses us on the second half of the basic interaction equation, the collision with either the natural environment or the man-made structure. Closer examination of this interaction is needed for a more complete understanding.

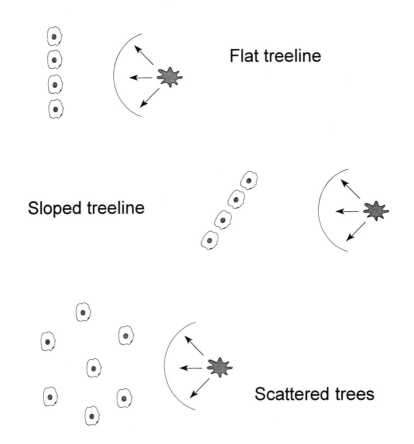

Flat treeline

Sloped treeline

Scattered trees

Figure 11. Tree placement affects shielding.

A collision is defined as two physical objects striking each other. It results from a combination of movement and physical mass. The results, as we know from basic physics, are predictable. In this case, the collision is between a pressure wave of compressed air and whatever terrain or structures are inside the affected area. There are several factors which are of importance in assessing the effect of this collision; many are the same as those for any collision. First is the direction of the movement of the pressure wave in relation to the static position of the structure or terrain. This will affect how the pressure wave reacts during the collision, and how the structure will respond to that directional force or pressure variation. It is important to understand the results at each major collision point in order to predict the overall effect at a site.

The second consideration is the force being exerted on the structure or terrain. The two forceful components during the collision will be the shock velocity and the overpressure of the pressure wave (In a vehicle bomb, neither the dynamic pressure nor the drag factor are likely to be strong enough to produce damage). When the collision occurs, the pressure wave will be deformed since it is composed of a gas and is basically elastic in physical nature. The wave deformation will include deflection, reflection or destruction of the various wave shapes as the pressure wave interacts with the structure or terrain shape. The overpressure will also be affected with both some compression and expansion occurring during the interaction. One final result will *always* be a loss of overall force as damage occurs to the structure or the ground which is basically rigid in physical nature. The exact type of damage that occurs to the terrain is primarily dependent upon its composition while the exact type of damage that occurs to a structure is dependent to large extent upon both the physical factors of the structure, its design, and its composition as well as the shape and strength of the pressure wave. Basically, the terrain will mold the pressure wave by reflecting, deflecting, or absorbing it while receiving relatively little damage. Structures, however, will be damaged by the same pressure wave *while* reflecting, deflecting or absorbing it.

PRESSURE WAVE INTERACTION WITH STRUCTURES

The basics of structure interaction with the pressure wave will be determined by their relative basic locations, the physical properties of the pressure wave previously described, and the overall building shape, its materials composition, and its internal design or construction techniques. In analyzing the interaction, it is important to visualize the explosion as an elastic, expanding sphere which collides with the rigid structure shape (a sphere is the basic theoretical shape of the wave, although other shapes are possible and more probable). The result will be deformation of the pressure wave, initially by compression, followed by reflection, deflection or reduction, and damage to the structure. In larger explosions, a partial vacuum may form behind the structure (drag factor) as the pressure wave passes, creating an additional strain on the structure during the dynamic pressure period. The structural damage will vary from insignificant to total destruction depending on many factors. Whether the explosion is an interior or exterior one is the first determination to make in the interaction relationship. Interior explosions (Figure 12) will be significantly different from exterior explosions. Interior explosions tend to spread damage

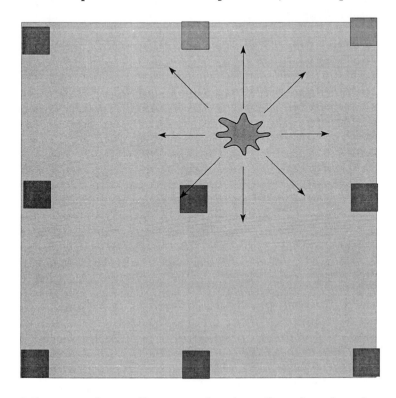

Figure 12. Interior explosions. Damage tends to be uniform throughout the structure. Walls and supports are pushed outward from blast site.

more uniformly throughout the building with somewhat higher relative pressures due to the confinement, and tend to blow windows, walls, and structural supports outward. Exterior explosions (Figure 13) tend to localize damage on one side or in one area; the windows, walls, and structural supports are blown inward on that one side and outward on the opposite side. With those general observations, examination of the direction and distance relationship in more detail can begin.

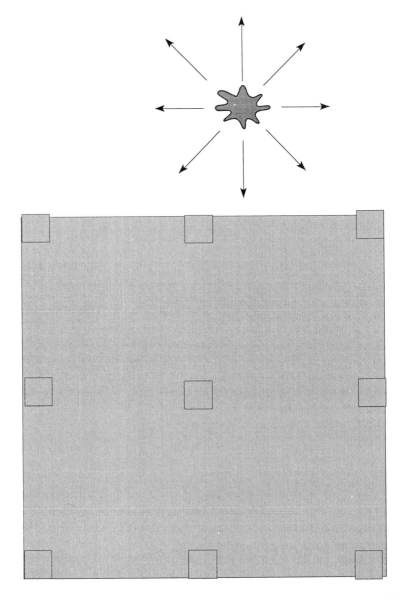

Figure 13. Exterior explosions. Damage tends to be localized in one area. Walls and supports are pushed inward near blast site and outward on other walls of structure.

As the orientation of the expanding spherical pressure wave to the structure varies, it will produce varying results. The basic relationships of distance and direction are critical. Distance must be determined in direct linear measurement from the center of the explosion to the structure (slant range), while direction must be determined in both the horizontal and vertical axis in order to effectively analyze results (Figure 14). Once this has been done, you begin the analysis by forecasting the interaction of shapes first, then determining the pressure

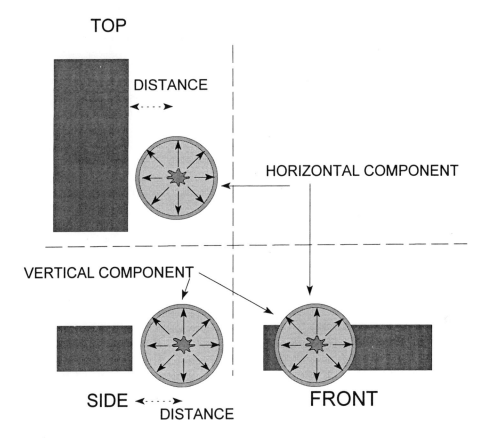

Figure 14. Pressure wave relative position to a building. The horizontal and vertical components of the detonation position from two sides of a right triangle. The hypotenuse of that triangle is then called "the slant range."

effects on the building material at that distance. Buildings with complicated exteriors will, of course, have complicated interaction. It is important to focus on the general or overall shape of the surfaces. Considering the horizontal component of the structure first, a pressure wave moving directly into a flat surface will tend to reflect directly back creating very high pressures near the flat surface and increasing the internal pressures behind the existing pressure wave (Figure 15) while a pressure wave striking the surface at an angle tends to apply a rolling effect of increased pressure along the wall (Figure 16). The

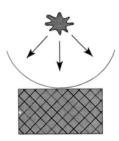

Directly rebounds

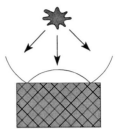

Figure 15. Flat surface interaction. Pressure wave directly rebounds;
tends to affect whole surface at once.

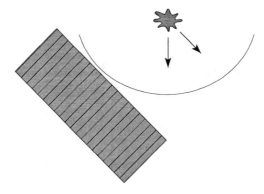

Collision at angle produces
sequential force on wall.

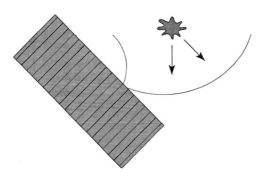

Figure 16. Rolling effect. Pressure wave collides with angular surface. Rebound gives area of increased pressure which moves sequential along surface. This produces a rolling pressure effect.

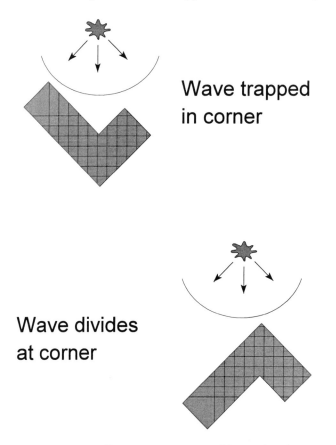

Figure 17. Corner interaction. Pressure wave trapped by an interior corner increases its pressure. Pressure wave divided by an exterior corner decreases its pressure.

same wave striking an exterior corner would tend to simply divide along the walls with little change in the wave, only a minor increase in pressure. However, if it strikes an interior corner, such as that of an L-shaped building, the pressure wave will be trapped by the shape creating an exceptionally high pressure point at the corner (Figure 17). Similar effects would occur with convex structure shapes shedding the wave and concave shapes matching the general wave shape to allow maximum destructive capability (Figure 18). It would, in fact, actually be possible to site the explosive device at the focal point of the convex surface as part of the targeting process.

In the vertical component, structures tend to be found in three basic shapes: block (Figure 19), staircase, and cantilever (Figure 20). Large commercial and governmental buildings built in the first part of this

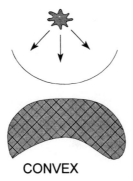

CONVEX

Wave difuses around curve

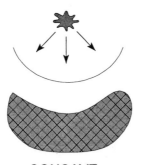

CONCAVE

Wave trapped in curve

Figure 18. Curved surface interaction.

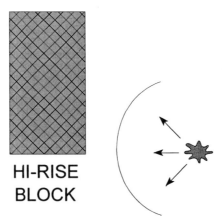

HI-RISE
BLOCK

Basically a flat surface

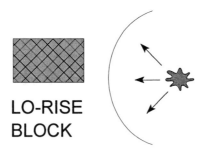

LO-RISE
BLOCK

Figure 19. Block-shaped building interaction with pressure wave.
The overpressure wall encounters a flat surface. Notice that part of the pressure
wave passes over the lo-rise building without colliding.

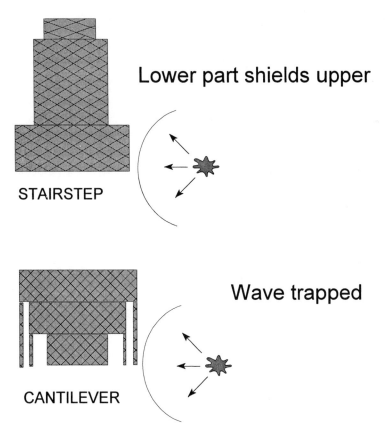

Figure 20. Stair step and cantilever-shaped building interaction with pressure wave. The lower stair step shields the upper part while the cantilever overhang traps the wave.

century tend to be of the staircase design. This shape of building is the best overall shape for surviving a ground-level explosion. The lower floors actually tend to shield the upper portion of the structure from a pressure wave during an exterior blast, and to resist penetration to the center for an interior explosion under the hi-rise portion of the structure. Buildings erected during the middle part of the 1900s tend to be block in shape. They present mostly flat surfaces to the pressure wave with either exterior or interior explosions being likely to affect the upper stories. In the last two or three decades, cantilever buildings have become very frequent for both business and government buildings. They appear stylish and have entry or ground space advantages in crowded urban terrain. Unfortunately, the design tends to trap a ground-level pressure wave, which will magnify its effect. This building shape is exceptionally dangerous during ground-level bombing attack, and is usually rather easy to penetrate for an interior explosion. This brings us to the second consideration, the composition of materials used in the building.

The primary concern for the material used is its strength, the point at which the pressure wave will cause it to bend, twist, crush, shatter, break, pulverize, or whatever. A secondary consideration will be its combustibility as well. This is a determination that can become quite technical, but simple observation will usually suffice for a planning analysis. The everyday knowledge that glass breaks easily, wood snaps and burns, bricks may crumble, siding or tiles may loosen, steel may bend or twist rather than break, and so forth will usually provide a good planning analysis. These observations will allow you to estimate how much fragmentation will be produced when the pressure wave strikes or how much of the building surface area will actually give resistance to the pressure wave. The latter is important since it indicates the peak load that may be put on the building framework. A building with large glass areas, for example, will produce a lot of fragmentation during an explosion but will actually tend to withstand larger explosions better. With large glass surface areas, the pressure wave tends to blow through the building rather than transfer its force to the frame as it would if the building had solid walls. This reduces the peak amount of force exerted on the structure while extending the duration of the force. Finally, the composition of the materials determines which support structures will fail when struck or crushed by the pressure wave. This, in turn, sets up the final analysis of the structure, its construction technique.

Basically, this is an examination of the framework of the structure and how other materials are fastened to it. It is the area where technical assistance from an engineer or architect would be of most value. Here is a simple view, based upon application of simple physics principles, that is useful for planning analysis by a police or government official. There are common styles of construction that are typically found in business buildings. The first is a beam and girder frame (Figure 21). It is usually of steel and joined by rivets and welds. This type of structure holds up well during an explosion, usually bending or twisting rather than breaking. This reduces the possibility of immediate structure collapse. If the force of the pressure wave is transmitted

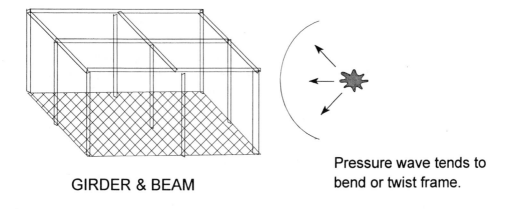

GIRDER & BEAM

Pressure wave tends to
bend or twist frame.

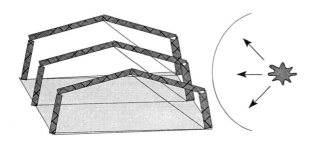

Pressure wave strips
siding and roofing.

FREE STANDING BEAM

Figure 21. Beam-style construction interaction with pressure wave. Girder frames
tend to bend or twist, but remain intact. Siding and roofing strips off or wraps
around the frame. Free standing beam is strong from the side, by may topple if
struck by a pressure wave from the front or back.

in a manner that causes joint separation, then the chances of collapse
increase, but this type of framework serves to limit the scope of the collapse to just the area supported by that joint. Similar approaches are
used in wooden buildings which obviously have less strength due to
the material and the usual manner of joining wood. Newer wood-
frame structures are using joining techniques that may resist joint separation better but still have the inherent strength problem of wood.
The second type of common structural style is the free-standing beam
(Figure 21). This type utilizes the inherent strength of an arc, anchor-
ing the footings, and relying on other materials to connect the free-
standing beams. While providing great strength to the top and sides,
some of these buildings are weaker when attacked from the end. These

buildings usually rely upon a lightweight covering for the roof or walls. A pressure wave striking these buildings tends to strip the siding and roofing off the beams or to wrap it around the existing beams, dependent upon the direction of the force in relation to the material. The beams themselves are unlikely to collapse unless the end-to-end support is weak and the force works against this weakness. If beams are pushed over by the pressure wave, this design has the advantage that the free-standing nature tends to limit the area of collapse since the beams are lightly connected.

A similar construction approach is taken in trestle-style structures (Figure 22). This style of structure relies upon pillars or beams along the sides which are joined by prefabricated trestles to support a lightweight roof covering. Typically used for warehouses and factories, these buildings have large interior open spaces not common to office buildings. The result, when struck by a pressure wave, is similar in

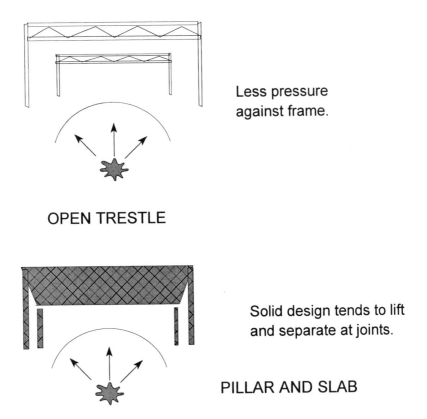

Less pressure
against frame.

OPEN TRESTLE

Solid design tends to lift
and separate at joints.

PILLAR AND SLAB

Figure 22. Trestle and pillar and slab-style construction interaction with pressure wave. Open trestle receives less overall pressure on frame as pressure waves flows through openings. Solid designs tend to lift and separate at the joints; greater pressure against the frame.

regard to the siding and roofing, it tends to strip off or wrap around the supports. The pillars and trestles are not as inherently strong from the side as free-standing beams and consequently are more prone to structural collapse. This collapse is likely to affect large areas since the trestles usually span large open spaces and are interconnected. An advantage of an open trestle design is that the frame presents less surface area for the pressure wave to directly affect than some other designs.

The next general type is the concrete slab and pillars (Figure 22). This is a preformed construction technique. The pillar and slabs are made at a different location and then assembled at the construction site relying on interlocking joints which may be reinforced. A cost effective construction technique, this design has a number of limitations when struck by a pressure wave. The joints are more prone to separate since large surface areas are presented to the pressure wave, and some designs utilize balancing forces to help retain the structure in place. When a joint separates, the balance is gone and the force of gravity may spread the effect more widely. Additionally, the material itself cracks, breaks, or pulverizes much more easily than steel frames. Consequently, this design is much more prone to collapse than the previously cited structures.

The final style of structure is the masonry structure. Masonry structures (rock, brick or concrete block) have a very high number of joints. This simple fact makes them more likely to break when pressure is applied. Most commercial buildings use masonry construction only for walls or facings, relying upon some type of frame to actually support the structure. Reinforced concrete block is less susceptible to complete failure, but still retains the inherent weakness of the material strength of the concrete.

The final design characteristic to examine is the interior construction or layout. This is important for either interior or exterior explosions. An interior explosion tends to "lift" the building ceiling or frame structure while also pushing the vertical support structures aside giving a much greater probability of joint separation or damage. An exterior explosion tends to push inward against the entire framework at one location causing a greater probability of bending or twisting the frame. This gives less probability of immediate collapse of the structure. Exterior explosions can, however, be of sufficient strength to cause interior lifting similar to that seen during interior explosions. This lifting effect will be more localized than a completely interior explosion which tends to work more uniformly throughout the structure. That raises the point that the interior layout will have some effect. A structure with large interior open spaces tends to vent or allow the pressure wave to move through better, producing less pressure buildup, but it also tends to allow the damage level to spread farther and more uniformly throughout the building. Interior layouts with small open spaces will resist the pressure wave causing the damage to be more confined but also more destructive in the confined area since the pressures will be greater there. This effect can either shield the structure and occupants or actually increase the risk to both depending upon the combination of several other factors. Whatever occurs inside the structure and to the frame will clearly be affected by the result of the pressure wave on the walls of the structure.

Most walls are built with a frame of some type to which is fastened a covering such as siding, sheetrock, paneling, etc. There are some

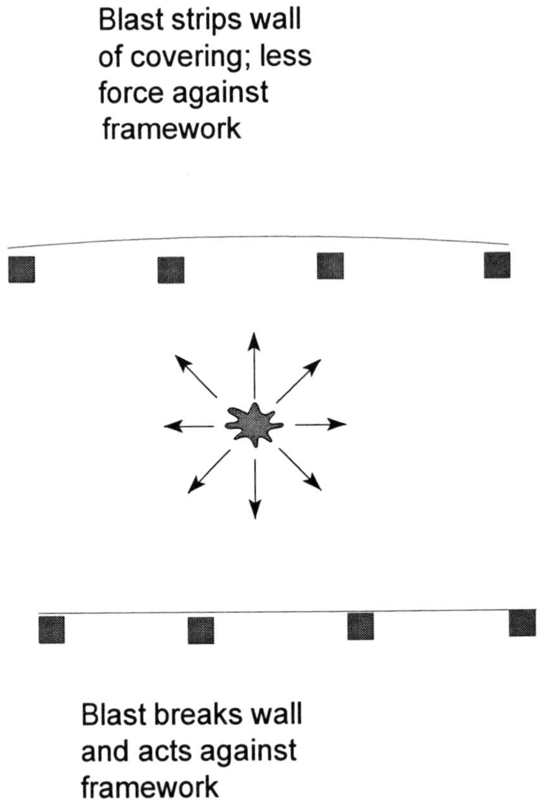

Blast strips wall of covering; less force against framework

Blast breaks wall and acts against framework

Figure 23. Wall-frame interaction effects. Blast may strip wall from frame with less overall pressure or may break wall against frame increasing overall pressure on frame.

basic principles to apply (Figure 23). When the explosion occurs on the side opposite the wall covering, as occurs in an interior explosion, the pressure wave tends to strip the wall covering off the frame. When the opposite occurs, the pressure wave tends to apply force across the entire covering on the wall which increases the force upon the framework of the wall. This is the usual case in an exterior wall. The material composition of the wall is significant in this transference of force. The stronger the siding material, the greater the force transferred to the frame before failure occurs. Consequently, the stronger walls will tend to have the same effect across the entire surface which favors displacing the wall rather than breaking it. Low pressure waves tend to have this effect with increasing pressures tending to break the wall rather than displace it. Increasing pressure levels also affect the manner in which a siding failure occurs. Siding between two supports will tend to bend and break in the center at low pressures, shear at both ends at medium pressures, and disintegrate at high pressures (Figure 24). This is due in part to the "reaction time" of the material; the time needed for the structure to flex and absorb the strain rather than be damaged. It should be clear that predicting the result accurately is complicated by many factors; this analysis is intended as a general guide to point the analysis in the direction needed for serious considerations. Before summarizing the interaction analysis, it is important to point out that the vehicle bomb can be designed not as just a large quantity of simultaneous explosive producing a single theoretically spherical pressure wave, but can be specifically designed for different results.

The vehicle bomb can actually be designed to focus the blast in a manner similar to the shaped charges of a standard military antitank round. In this approach, the explosive is specifically intended to begin detonation from a specified point within the explosive material, usually the back of the shape, and move the wave forward to actually "push" the explosion outward. The container and explosive are shaped to "focus" the pressure wave at a specific point outside of the shaped charge (Figure 25). This design takes advantage of the natural locus or loci of the geometric shape; the focal point of the shape is the point which will have the maximum pressure exerted during the explosion. This increases the destructive power of the relative explosion when the focal point coincides with a particularly critical point of the structure under attack. This is a precision technique which requires

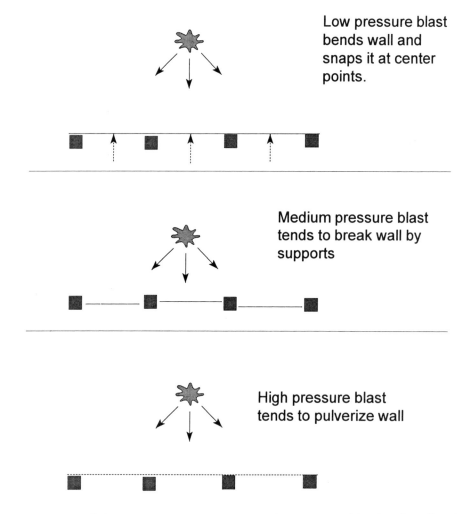

Figure 24. Wall destruction at varying pressures. Low pressure blast bends wall and snaps it a center points between frame supports; strong tendancy to displace will intact. Medium pressure blast tends to break wall by supports, separating at or near joints. High pressure tends to pulverize the wall. Effect is partly dependent upon the strength of the joints and support.

much more skill to produce than the simple large quantity of explosive.

A similar precision technique can also be applied by designing the large destructive device as a sequential detonation. The best immediate example is the enhanced explosion truck bomb. This bomb detonates with a central core of explosives that then triggers an immediate secondary explosion of gas or liquid canisters. This may actually cause

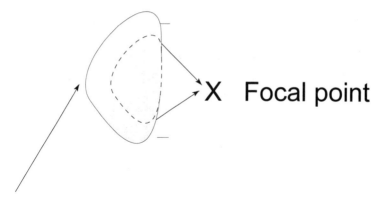

Detonation at rear spreads blast outward and
uses geometric shape to focus pressure at one point

Figure 25. Explosion Focusing. Shaping the explosive charge and detonating it from
the rear focuses the explosion and drastically increases pressure at the focal point.

the canisters to disperse before rupturing or just simply immediately
increase the heat output of the explosion which, of course, increases
the pressure rise. These two techniques could even be combined to
penetrate and then project the enhancement into an area of the structure causing greater destruction. These approaches require greater
skill, greater emplacement precision, and precise information of the
structure being attacked. They are mentioned primarily to point out
that the analysis envisioned to this point has been the simple variety,
the large simultaneous explosion which produces a generally spherical
pressure wave. At this point, a short summation of the structure analysis process is obviously of benefit:

• Determine the type and relative explosive power of the weapon
of mass destruction likely to be detonated near the structure.
• Determine the overall shape and orientation of surface structures
presented to the blast site.
• Determine the distance from the blast site to the structure and the
consequent predicted shock velocity and overpressure.
• Determine the surface area of the structure presented to the pressure wave at various pressures (the surface area will lessen at higher pressures as various parts fail without transmitting significant
force to the frame).
• Determine the style of frame construction.
• Predict the extent of fragmentation and structure collapse.

The forecast developed is intended to estimate not only the extent of damage to the building but also the number, type, and extent of casualties. This is the final area of analysis in the assessment of the conventional weapon of mass destruction.

PRESSURE WAVE EFFECTS ON PEOPLE

There are several means by which people are injured during explosions: impact by fragments or debris in the pressure wave, impact with solid objects when the person is displaced by the pressure wave, impact by debris from structure collapse, burns from fire in low-order or enhanced-effect weapons, and direct damage from atmospheric overpressure. Fragmentation injury can vary in number from a single injury to multiple penetrations while simultaneously varying in severity from a minor cut to large penetrations which go completely through the body. Injuries received by displacement usually involve broken bones and ruptured internal organs. Similar injuries occur immediately during structure collapse but may be increased by secondary fires, lack of oxygen in confined places, and similar difficulties. Burn injuries will be typical in low-order or enhanced explosions and may be quite severe. In other types of explosions, burns will be unusual among survivors. Persons close enough to the blast site to be burned will probably sustain a high level of fragmentation and pressure damage.

The parts of the body that are most susceptible to pressure damage are the eyes, ears, and lungs. Eyes can sustain capillary rupture damage which is usually minor. Eardrums can rupture from the pressure variation. This is usually a relatively minor injury but can increase to a moderate severity level. The lungs are the area of most potential problems. The air pressure variation causes damage by rupturing the air sacs in the lungs where the oxygen-carbon dioxide exchange occurs. This damage can be minor, but it can also be so severe that a fatality results. The key to forecasting the casualties is the determination of the pressure at the point where the person is located. This will forecast not only the direct pressure injuries but will also indicate the fragmentation level, debris and structure collapse occurring in the same area. The easy way to do this is by overlaying templates of the expected pressure wave over the structure diagram. This requires the production of analysis materials to use during assessment.

PRODUCTION OF PLANNING AND DECISION MATERIALS

It is possible to produce planning and analysis materials that can be used during assessment to simplify the process for making estimates. While this can be accomplished in detail by an actual computation of the various factors involved in both the explosive device and the structure being assessed, this is quite involved. The detailed process would include the following general steps:

• Determine the design, quantity, and chemical composition of the explosive device.
• Compute the heat produced during the chemical reactions involved and the speed at which the reaction occurs.
• Based on the temperature rise in air, compute the pressure rise during the explosion.
• Compute the equalization rate in air of the expected temperature and density typical at the site being assessed.
• Determine the pressure wave shock velocity and overpressure at the time it strikes the structure, the shape of the wave and the angle of incidence at which the wave strikes the structure surfaces.
• Compute the resulting vectors of force that result on the structure and on the pressure wave.
• Compute the tensile strength, ductility, etc. of the materials and design of the structure.
• Compute the loading factors on the various structure parts at the force levels shown by earlier computation.
• Compute whether the structure joints or materials displace or break and the result on the structural design.
• Compute the effect of gravity and the continuing pressure wave components on the damaged structure.
• Determine the probable location of people in or near the structure at the time of the incident and the effect of both the pressure wave and the structure reaction upon them.

As you can see, the process would be quite complicated and probably beyond the capability of most people. The information produced would still be somewhat of an estimate since many of the factors can vary over quite a vast range making prediction of the exact combination hard to isolate. There really is no need to go into this detail for initial planning analysis since an estimate is all that is needed to work out the various defensive or response solutions, which is the ultimate goal here. The planner can rely upon existing material on the topics and use it to develop planning analysis tools.

Various reference sources from the military, chemical, architectural, engineering, and medical fields can be used for this purpose. Manufacturers of explosives produce guidelines that detail usage, storage, and safety information for the user. Similar reference books on building materials are in daily use by architects or engineers who are designing structures. The best reference, however, comes from the military studies of nuclear blasts. An unclassified source available through the government printing office[6] has chapters on air blast phenomenon, air blast loading, structural damage, and biological effects which are directly applicable to vehicle bombs such as presented below from the source:

> Theoretically, a given pressure will occur at a distance from an explosion that is proportional to the cube root of the energy yield. Full-scale tests have shown this relationship between distance and energy yield to hold for yields up to (and including) the megaton range. Thus, cube root scaling may be applied with confidence over a wide range of explosion energies. According to this law, if D_1 is the distance (or slant range) from a reference explosion of W_1 kilotons at which a certain overpressure or dynamic pressure is attained, then for any explosion of W kilotons energy these same pressures will occur at a distance D given by

$$(D \ / \ D_1) = (W \ / \ W_1)^{1/3} \qquad (3.61.1)$$

> As stated above, the reference explosion is conveniently chosen as having an energy yield of 1 kiloton, so that $W_1 = 1$. It follows that

$$D = D_1 \ x \ W^{1/3} \qquad (3.61.2)$$

where D1 refers to the slant range from a 1-kiloton explosion. Consequently, if the distance D is specified, then the value of the explosion energy, W, required to produce a certain effect, e.g., a given peak overpressure, can be calculated. Alternatively, if the energy, W, is specified, the appropriate range, D, can be evaluated from equation (3.61.2).

... For explosions of different energies having the same scaled height of burst, the cube root scaling law may be applied to distances from ground zero, as well as to distances from the explosion. Thus, if d1 is the distance from ground zero at which a particular overpressure or dynamic pressure occurs for a 1-kiloton explosion, then for an explosion of W kilotons energy the same pressures will be observed at a distance d determined by the relationship

$$d = d_1 \times W^{1/3} \qquad (3.62.1)$$

This expression can be used for calculations of the type referred to in the preceding paragraph, except that the distances involved are from ground zero instead of from the explosion (slant ranges)."[7]

In short, it is possible to predict the overpressure of a relative explosion size by simple computations using the known pressures of a 1-kiloton explosion and the equations given. The next question, then, is whether there are other differences between nuclear and conventional blasts that are significant.

The primary differences between nuclear blasts as opposed to conventional blasts are that the nuclear blast does not rely upon combustion to produce heat, the nuclear blast produces radiation and consequent immediate interference in the electromagnetic spectrum, and the nuclear blast is simply larger due to the amount of heat produced in such a small space in such a short time. The blast effects can be directly compared since the pressure wave will react the same in the same medium, the atmosphere. All that must be done is to simply reduce the relative size of the explosion to the range being examined. This can be done by simple interpolation of the various charts, tables, and texts in this book. Some don't even require changes to be used, the data is directly applicable. Using such material, chart data can be produced for the expected range of vehicle bombs (see Appendix B), and templates developed to use on scale drawings. The templates are simply circles drawn at various distances at which certain events are known to occur. The important events are the pressures at which structural failures or injuries to people occur. With each relative blast size, the pressure can be translated to specific distances and the distances used to determine the size of the circular template on the drawings being used. This provides quick estimates of the areas of any structure that will be affected. By estimating the typical number of people working within the various areas, an estimate of type and number of casualties can be made. The same approach can be used on the actual site by applying data from charts or tables and actually measuring the distance from the probable attack sites to the various parts of the structure or work areas. This identifies the areas that will be affected by the blast and provides the same estimate for the overall effects on a given site.

The assessment of the conventional weapon of mass destruction, typically a vehicle bomb, begins by evaluating its general explosive type, explosive composition, means of activation, typical usage, operational employment techniques, and means of delivery. This leads directly to an in-depth analysis of the various factors affecting the mobility of vehicles as the primary means of delivery of the conventional weapon of mass destruction. Reviewing and understanding the basic principles of chemistry and physics that are at work in the development of the pressure wave from a large explosion is critical for appropriate planning. Visualization of the pressure wave and its interaction with the environmental factors, both weather and terrain, allows the planner to forecast its impact upon the structures present at the blast site. Using the basic shapes, materials and construction design factors, assessment of the potential attack site produces a forecast of the damage and casualties which together indicate the planning which must occur to effectively prevent, defend or respond to such an attack. The analysis process applies the understanding of these factors by the use of available information prepared into templates and charts for easy reference during assessment. The result of this assessment is the production of the information and materials necessary to conduct a site vulnerability analysis, the next step in the overall process.

Notes

1. 18 U.S.C. 2332a.(b)(2).
2. 18 U.S.C. 941(a)(4).
3. "Convention on Prohibitions or Restrictions on the Use of Certain Conventional Weapons Which May be Deemed to be Excessively Injurious or to Have Indiscriminate Effects," 10 October 1980, Geneva. Fuel/air weapons are covered under Protocol III, "Protocol on Prohibitions or Restrictions on the Use of Incendiary Weapons." Page 54, *The Laws of War* by W. Michael Reisman and Chris T. Antoniou, 1994, Vintage Books, New York.
4. Explosions can occur both underground or underwater, but the subject is truck bombs so we will concentrate on atmospheric blasts. The wave phenomenon is similar in all three anyway.
5. The studies done for low yield nuclear weapons in the atmosphere are valid when applied to conventional explosions. You only need to ignore the radiation effects. As the nuclear yield gets higher or the medium in which the explosion occurs changes to high-altitude, underground, or underwater, the applicability to conventional explosions changes.
6. *The Effects of Nuclear Weapons* compiled by Samuel Glasston and Phillip J. Dolan, 3rd edition published 1977 by the Department of Defense and the Energy Research and Development Administration, U.S. Government Printing Office, Washington, D.C.
7. Paragraphs 3.61 and 3.62, Chapter III, "Air Blast Phenomena in Air and Surface Bursts," *The Effects of Nuclear Weapons* compiled and edited by Samuel Glasstone and Philip J. Dolan, published by the United States Department of Defense and the Energy Research and Development Administration, third edition, 1977, U.S. Government Printing Office, Washington, D.C.

Chapter 6

VULNERABILITY ASSESSMENT

Vulnerability assessment, the defensive term for target analysis, is the examination of a particular site or situation to determine how lucrative it is as a potential target, and how complex it would be to actually attack the location. The vulnerability assessment applies both the terrorist operational profile with vehicle bombs (CWMD) developed during the threat analysis, and the operational effectiveness factors of the vehicle bombs (CWMD) determined during its assessment. The knowledge obtained during these two stages of planning is compared against the site of a potential attack to develop the specific prevention, defense, and response actions that will be needed for that particular location. In short, a site specific (tailored) emergency plan is prepared for the location being assessed as a possible target.

The site vulnerability assessment examines six general areas with the goal of developing a list of critical tasks for prevention, defense, and response. It begins by rating the location's vulnerability to attack, examines the personal security features present at the site, evaluates the preparations already in place, identifies the physical systems that are present, looks at the environmental factors (weather and terrain), and reviews the building design factors. When it is complete, the assessment identifies the critical areas of the structure that need protection, the probable effects of any attack by a vehicle bomb (CWMD), and lists the critical tasks for prevention, defense, or response.

Vulnerability of the site begins by determining how critical the overall site or a specific portion of the site is. Criticality is a somewhat subjective evaluation of the importance of the role that the location plays in fulfilling the purpose of the government or business involved.

Common tests of criticality involve determining its redundancy (how easily it is replaced), the geographical area or population base that it serves, the type of service that it provides, or the impact that its loss will have on the operation involved. Consultation with the people in charge is frequent during this portion of vulnerability assessment. In many cases, those officials have made a determination in advance which prompted the further study.

The physical features of the site will be examined as will the personnel capability both within the site and within the area immediately surrounding the site. During the personnel assessment, examination is made of the ability of the people normally present to deal with any problem identified. Their background, education, training, and current job assignments all become important to the evaluation. Personnel in the surrounding area are assessed in terms of emergency response capability with both strengths and weaknesses identified. Communications capability, both within the site and to the area emergency forces, is examined. Speed of the communications and its redundancy may both be critical factors seriously affecting the security capability of the site. This capability to prevent, defend, or respond to any incident must be determined by analyzing the personnel skills of those present at the site. In some instances, this security presence is due to deliberate planning and assignment of security forces. In other instances, it is a secondary assignment that naturally occurs due to the nature of the facility and the type of personnel normally present. Whoever is present will deal with whatever activity occurs, even if it is simply the activation of area emergency response forces. The availability of assistance in the surrounding area is measured in terms of all types of emergency forces. Police, fire, medical, civil defense units, etc. will all be part of this portion of the evaluation. The composition of these forces varies and is determined, in part, by the setting in which the site is located.

The terrorist operational profile differs in various settings. Consequently, the general location will have significant impact on the vulnerability rating. The first consideration of the setting is the geographic region of the country. This will establish certain access factors and regional social considerations. This helps determine the proximity of the terrorist group operational area and the ease with which they may cross or strike from a protected zone across international or other controlled borders. The third factor is whether the site is located in a rural, a suburban, or an urban setting. The variation in the type build-ings, transportation access, and similar considerations change the risk factor at the site. This leads to the terrain features around the site. As discussed in the preceding chapter, these general environmental fac-tors affect the performance of the vehicle bomb (CWMD) and must, therefore, be part of the vulnerability assessment. These in turn help determine the access to the site, usually referred to as "avenues of approach" in a military setting. This is simply the direction from which an attack might be mounted, and, to some extent, the specific area of the site at which it might be directed. The latter may be determined by the personnel density within that specific area while the former con-siders the same density overall as well as the maneuverability of the terrain on the approaches. The last consideration for rating the site's vulnerability to attack is an examination of its historical record of inci-dents. These will help determine whether the terrorist operational pro-file seems to be favored at the site.

The second general area of assessment is the site personal security features. This is an examination of those factors which directly deal with the safety of the people working at the site. First will be identifi-cation of critical areas of the site and consideration of the access to them. Criticality will be defined and determined by the same criteria used for the site itself. This will lead to complete access review for con-trol of staff, service contractors, and visitors. Personnel screening for access, escort considerations, or other control measures will be identi-fied as will the skill necessary to bypass or overcome them. Next will be a consideration of the personal alarms and duress procedures that are in use by various individuals or staff members. In some cases, this will include a rating of the site's customers, visitors, or general public's ability to summon assistance immediately. Key personnel will be iden-tified and specific information on them will be designated as sensitive. This will include the storage and release of personal data which might allow impersonation by various methods to overcome or alter securi-ty procedures. The itineraries of key personnel or even the site sched-ule of activities might be of importance for various reasons, if only to determine the time of most or least exposure to attack. As security pro-cedures advance, key personnel will be provided training to lower their exposure profile by increasing their countersurveillance skill and to raise their survival chances by increasing their counteraction skills.

Access to specific areas of the site will then be assessed for a variety of reasons. The first area will be office access during off-duty hours.

Access during this time period provides the opportunity for tampering, information access, or other security compromise. Utilities access, both interior and exterior, can be important since the utilities may control other security features. Additionally, a utility such as natural gas can be used to enhance an actual attack or even diverted as a direct attack on the personnel within the site. Following this line of reasoning, access to maintenance or janitorial areas must be included. These areas typically have gas lines and valves, electrical breaker boxes, and water or fire suppression system controls which can be manipulated to an attacker's advantage. They also will have storage areas that contain a variety of cleaning materials or other servicing materials that may serve to initiate or enhance any attack. Restrooms and other public areas will be evaluated as their accessibility affords easy emplacement of small explosive devices. Restrooms are popular targets since they also provide a certain level of privacy during use which allows concealment of the emplacement activity. The last of the specific areas within the site to be assessed are the safe areas or routes. This involves identification of protected areas or exits that will be used in the event of any attack or disaster. In this case, a safe area is one which is likely to shield personnel from any explosion and retain its structural shape. In short, identify likely survival zones in the structure. The location of survival stocks or emergency supplies is included during this survival zone identification. The final areas of site personal security features leads off of the actual site. Transportation routes and means will be evaluated for their impact on personnel safety. Mass transportation collection points create attractive concentrations of people for an attacker intent on casualties. This consideration must go off-site, particularly for key personnel. Complete off-site surveys may be required for these personnel. This is actually a vulnerability assessment for other sites, and begins to cross over into the next general area of site assessment.

Preparation for emergency action is usually present in some form at most sites. Evaluation of it during the vulnerability assessment begins with a determination of its identification as a potential target. What are the factors that cause it to be a target? It may be its affiliation with government, the service provided, or specific people who work there, etc. This gives a tip-off as to its attractiveness as a target. Next examine the alarm response capability. This is simply what happens initially when any alarm sounds. What are the mechanics or electronics involved in transmitting it, and what is the preplanned response to the alarm? This is followed by the current allocation of security resources. What does the facility have and how do they use it? Both equipment and personnel should be included. Now go through the personnel background review procedures. How are employees or service contract personnel screened for security risks? What restrictions are put on their entry into critical areas? What criteria is used to reduce employment of high-risk personnel? This ties closely to a review of the exact capability of the personnel present, and their personal skills. Begin with a listing of the position currently occupied and then look at secondary skills such as previous assignments or jobs, education, volunteer service, hobbies, etc. Seek personnel who have skills that can be utilized during emergency situations. Identify them and plan on their use. Assess the ability of the personnel to conduct countersurveillance at the site or individually when away from the site. This ability reduces the risk profile. Review existing emergency plans such as those for natural disasters; these may have important information on emergency teams for the site. The plans should also include any specific emergency systems that have been installed. Review their capability in detail. This is the preliminary step to a complete physical systems evaluation, the next general assessment area.

A detailed study of the physical systems will be similar to those of standard crime prevention studies; the application is simply oriented toward a slightly different risk. A complete review of any blueprints and floor plans is critical at this point, if not already undertaken. Begin by examining the movement controls that are in place for both personnel and vehicles. These may be control procedures as well as the actual equipment. Typically, gates, turnstiles, checkpoints, identification badges, etc. are already in use as screening techniques. Look at any protective barriers. The location and rating must be determined in detail in order to match their effectiveness against the terrorist operational profile and the weapon capability profile. Next examine the protective lighting to determine how well it deters or assists surveillance of the facility, and how well it assists identification of any attack. This ties in closely with an examination of electronic monitoring in various forms. Alarms, detectors, imaging systems, and recording systems must all be reviewed and tested against the operational profiles. While examining both the protective barriers and electronic monitoring, specifically isolate the locks and keys or other access devices. The control of these access devices is usually an exceptionally important indicator for vulnerability. The ability to repeatedly penetrate a facility makes surveillance easy and sequential, segmented or covert attack much easier. Any physical feature is reviewed, and then response forces are considered. The exact locations, assignments, procedures, and so forth are considered as they may either assist or defeat existing other physical systems. When this is complete, this general area of consideration is expanded to the environment surrounding the site.

The environmental features surrounding the site are basically the natural elements of weather and terrain. This portion of the assessment looks at the impact of weather upon both the site and the potential attack. Its influence upon the tactical aspects is of primary importance. The general climate type and temperature range establish many of the other parameters. Identify the areas most likely to be affected by major weather phenomenon such as hurricanes, tornados, floods, or other natural disasters such as earthquakes. Existing emergency plans probably address these and may have pertinent planning for the assessment. Typical weather events such as fog may make a lot of difference. The reduced observation may affect electronic sensors or imaging, assigned security forces, and even area response forces. Type, frequency, and duration of storms or even wind direction and speed are considerations which must be included. These influence observation, reducing detection of any attack, but also affect movement capability. This has implications for both an attacker and the defender. Do not overlook typical humidity and inversion conditions. Of some importance for vehicle bombs, these considerations become much more important in special weapons assessment.

Terrain considerations during the site vulnerability assessment concentrate upon five tactical concepts affecting the specific engagement envisioned, a vehicle bomb attack. Since the vehicle bomb relies upon movement, maneuverability will be examined first. The presence of slopes will influence the speed of attack and also the overall weapon effect. The exact terrain structure determines the basic avenues of approach, and the points where channeling of the attack occurs. Both the surface composition and its drainage should be considered. The combination affects movement very strongly and influences observation and concealment. The fields of observation affect both visual and electronic surveillance and counter surveillance, and the ability to disguise either the attack or the defense. Tied closely to concealment is the evaluation of cover. This is anything that not only stops observation, but also shields, deflects, or vents any attack. These three factors blend together and help identify key terrain. These are points that may be decisive for either opponent during the tactical engagement. Analysis of the key terrain and avenues of approach produces decision points, places where either opponent must take a specific action or reaction (make a tactical decision). Having identified the probable influences of the terrain upon the attacker and defender, the next step is applying the structural factors discussed in the weapon effectiveness assessment.

Concentrate on the basic building design factors; detailed analysis is not needed at this point. The basic shape of the structure will be determined and the surface areas presented to the likely avenues of approach. Their relative aspect and the ratio of solid to vented surface areas in that aspect determine the basis of weapon and structure interaction. Of course, the materials used must be considered both in the structural framework and in the surfaces presented to the approach. Examine the relative locations of streets or parking lots, the locations and design of building entry points, the location of security/emergency resources, the location of building maintenance support, the location of utilities and the locations and design of personnel spaces. Each identifies vulnerable or critical areas of the structure that seriously affect the overall outcome before, during, and after any attack. Finally, determine the location of any building blueprints or plans and what local codes apply to the situation. Once these considerations have been completed, the goals of the assessment should be complete and now should be specifically stated:

- What are the critical areas of the structure?
- What are the probable effects of an attack against the structure?
- What are the critical tasks which must be accomplished to prevent an attack?
- What are the critical tasks which must be accomplished to defend against an attack?
- What are the critical tasks which must be accomplished to respond to an attack?

Identify the areas, effects, and tasks in detail for each site assessed. If more than one structure exists on the site, each individual structure should be assessed and then an overall assessment made. This completes the site vulnerability assessment.

The overall process of risk analysis identifies the tasks for further action. The vulnerability analysis portion accomplishes this by examining the site criticality, its physical characteristics, its personal security features, its internal access, its emergency preparation, its physical systems, and its environment. By combining the vulnerability assessment findings with the operational profile of a terrorist group developed during the threat assessment, the risk analysis forecasts the probable attacks and their effects to an extent that allows the development of site specific planning to prevent, defend, or respond to the vehicle bomb (CWMD). At this point, an examination of historical incidents will provide some observations that will be applicable to the following chapters on prevention, defense, and response.

Chapter 7

TACTICAL ASSESSMENT AND HISTORICAL REVIEW OF SELECTED INCIDENTS PERTAINING TO VEHICLE BOMBS (CWMD)

Having reviewed the assessment of both terrorist groups and conventional weapons of mass destruction and their application during a site vulnerability assessment, the next step is to review selected historical usage of conventional weapons of mass destruction to develop a generic tactical operational profile. The generic profile will be used as the basis for discussion during the chapters on prevention, defense, and response. The incidents which will be reviewed are selected primarily due to the size of the blasts, but also to illustrate others factors. The selected incidents are the following:

1. Attack on American Embassy in Beirut, Lebanon.
2. Attack on American Embassy Annex in Beirut, Lebanon.
3. Attack on Marine BLT Headquarters in Beirut, Lebanon.
4. Attack on World Trade Center in New York City, NY.
5. Attack on Murrah Federal Building in Oklahoma City, OK.
6. Attack on Khobar Towers Complex in Dhahran, Kingdom of Saudi Arabia.
7. Attacks on American Embassies in Africa.
8. Detonation of semitrailer during fire at construction site in Kansas City, MO.
9. Detonation of tractortrailer during labor incident on interstate Highway.
10. Review of significant operational techniques for vehicle bombs.

In all cases, unless otherwise noted, source material will be open media reports of the incidents. No attempt to dispute or prove the source material will be offered, just observations and analysis of the facts presented in the open sources available.

CASE 1: AMERICAN EMBASSY, BEIRUT, LEBANON, APRIL 18, 1983[1]

The American Embassy building, based on photo analysis, was an eight-story office block-style structure of reinforced concrete using a pillar-and-slab style of construction. The approach to the building was a circular driveway with no perimeter wall or fence. The approach was secured by local security personnel with U.S. Marines controlling entry to the building itself. At approximately 1300 hours on a clear day, a pickup truck with an estimated 2,000 pounds of explosives was driven past the local security personnel and emplaced near the front of the building. The reports contain no clear indication of whether the emplacement was overt or covert or what actions were taken by the security personnel. When the explosion occurred, it resulted in the collapse of seven stories of the first stack of offices within the structure (approximately fifteen feet in depth from the front wall). Sixty-three people were killed, seventeen of whom were Americans. Included in the dead were seven CIA employees, one marine guard, several army training personnel, several U.S. State Department personnel, and local employees. It was not determined whether the bomber escaped or self-detonated with the truck. The American ambassador was initially trapped in his office with minor injuries. Reports indicate that the CIA employees were in a meeting room at the time of the blast.

Initial response was made by French Marines who were on patrol in the area with local militia personnel setting up an additional perimeter. U.S. Marines deployed at the Beirut airport responded, but had to proceed slowly due to the possibility of an ambush enroute. Initial security requirements included protecting personnel from further attack, and also protecting classified documents and items that were exposed and present in the area. Medical response was made immediately by local paramedics, members of the local Red Crescent Society, and French military medics. Later medical response included

U.S. Navy personnel from nearby U.S. Forces deployed in the area. The embassy was knocked out of action for some time, initially moving operations to the nearby British Embassy. CIA operations were hit the hardest with military training assistance also affected strongly. Review after the attack indicated that the embassy had been targeted by four previous attacks of some type. The information released to the public indicates that the use-of-force or screening actions taken by security personnel at the time of the attack could not be determined, and that the attack technique could not be pinpointed. No one could state whether it was a suicide bomber or whether the bomber had escaped by utilizing a covert approach and some type of delay fusing. From these sketchy facts, the following observations can be made:

a. Previous incidents had not caused an improvement in the surrounding physical barrier system, and seems not to have altered the guard deployment or use-of-force considerations.

b. An inconspicuous civilian vehicle was used for the attack.

c. 2,000 pounds of explosives should have overloaded the vehicle, reducing its maneuverability and tending to make it more conspicuous.

d. The circular drive approach made emplacement near the front of the building relatively easy, and the attack was directed against the center of the building along this easy approach.

e. Critical personnel were utilizing office space in the front, center portion of the building at the point where the easiest approach intersected with the building.

f. The embassy performed critical functions, but the facility itself was of little critical importance. The criticality was established by the presence of the key personnel.

g. 2,000 pounds of explosives should have produced a pressure wave capable of cracking reinforced concrete at a distance of approximately 100 feet. Car bombs, which were very common in Beirut at the time, would have produced a similar overpressure at a distance of approximately 50 feet (assuming use of the usual 200-300 pounds typical at the time). Consequently, the effect on the building should have been predictable and anticipated.

h. The response by local Paramedics was quick, but not controlled. The casualties were dispersed without record of who was removed or where they were taken. This created some initial difficulty for personnel accountability.

i. The rescue operation was relatively simple with response forces immediately present who were experienced in the response actions required.

j. The incident occurred in a setting where it was relatively common. This reduced the psychological impact and favored effective response.

CASE 2. AMERICAN EMBASSY ANNEX, BEIRUT, LEBANON, SEPTEMBER 20, 1985[2]

A van driven by a suicide bomber drove around concrete barriers outside the multistory Embassy Annex. It was fired upon by embassy security personnel and by members of the SAS who happened to be present due to the visit of a British official. The van detonated outside of the building, short of its apparent target, an underground parking garage. The detonation was rated at 3,000 pounds. It left a six-foot deep crater and killed 23 personnel including two servicemen. The pertinent observations of this incident are:

a. An inconspicuous vehicle was used.

b. The presence of security provisions, barriers, and armed guards did not prevent the attack from occurring. The barriers did force an obvious commitment to the attack which alerted the guards present to the attack and also extended the engagement time by slowing the vehicle approach speed.

c. Use of deadly force by highly trained personnel did not stop the attack; it only reduced its effectiveness by stopping it short of the best emplacement position.

d. A multiple-story building with an underground parking area is an excellent target. The enclosed area will increase the overpressure; the fact that the enclosed area was directly under the building stack could also have increased the effectiveness of the overall damage. Any initial structural damage is then subject to gravity which gives an effective secondary attack.

e. 3,000 pounds of explosives should put out a pressure wave capable of breaking reinforced concrete at a distance of approximately 110 feet. In spite of this, the building did not collapse.

    f. Previous incidents had obviously affected the security preparations and worked to reduce the attack. The security force was alert, recognized the attack, and was psychologically prepared to deal with it.

CASE 3. MARINE BLT HEADQUARTERS, BEIRUT, LEBANON, OCTOBER 23, 1983[3]

At 0622 in the morning, a yellow Mercedes stake bed truck, similar in appearance to ones operating in the airport area, drove along the road parallel to the U.S. Marine barracks and entered the public parking lot. After partially circling the lot, the vehicle accelerated, crashed through surrounding fences, swerved around embedded pipes, passed Marine sentries with unprepared rifles, and crashed through the sandbagged sergeant-of-the-guard post into the building. It penetrated to the interior of the ground floor and then detonated. Sentries attempting to engage the vehicle by fire had insufficient time to chamber a round and fire their rifles. The Sergeant of the Guard had time only to yell warnings and run for cover prior to detonation.

Survivors estimated that the truck attained a speed between 35 and 60 mph during penetration. The detonation was rated at 12,000 pounds of enhanced explosives; bottled gas canisters were used to enhance it. The explosion lifted and collapsed the four-story building when it detonated in the open central atrium area, breaking two reinforced concrete supports that were fifteen feet in circumference (4.7 feet diameter) and leaving an oblong crater that measured thirty-nine feet by twenty-nine feet by eight feet eight inches in depth below the seven-inch reinforced concrete floor. Two hundred forty-one servicemen, mostly U. S. Marines, were killed in the explosion. Some survivors of the blast would later relate experiences that seemed surrealistic to most people: blown out an upper story window 30 feet in the air, landing on your feet unharmed until struck by falling debris; riding the roof of the collapsing building down, feeling each floor falling with a jar before sliding into the center of the cracked roof and debris; trapped in narrow spaces in awkward positions awaiting rescue, praying or disassembling a folding cot for more space and something to do.

Virtually simultaneously, a French military headquarters was successfully attacked by another suicide truck bomber. That building also collapsed killing 58 soldiers. A photograph taken by an Iranian newsman seconds after the blast at the marine headquarters shows a cloud of smoke and dust that extends hundreds of feet into the air. People throughout the city had no doubt that a major attack had occurred or where it was.

The marines at the scene, however, were dodging falling debris, wandering through the thick choking dust with heads ringing, and rallying to defend against a further attack. Some started immediately to help but did not realize the scope of the problem. All internal and external communications were severed as a result of the attack. The battalion aid station was buried in the debris with most of the medics killed and the rest injured and trapped. The unit motor pool and equipment were also destroyed in the blast. Response was initiated by those personnel at the scene with what they had, but effective response only began with the arrival of outside help and a realization of the extent of the problem. Nearly all those in the immediate vicinity believed that their position had been hit by incoming indirect fire, and only discovered that their perception was wrong by checking the area. Those more distant could tell that a large scale explosion had occurred, suspecting a hit on ammunition or petroleum stocks, but could not pinpoint the exact location or cause.

The initial reports of the scope of the attack were made by three sources almost simultaneously. One was a marine in the building who initially tried to help others and then realized more assistance was needed. He ran barefooted to a nearby unit to report the situation, but those receiving the report could not initially accept what he was saying. His obvious injuries probably affected their judgment of his report. The second was the marine commander who responded to the blast by checking for damage to his building. Finding none, he looked further. Upon seeing that the BLT building was no longer visible, he realized the extent of the disaster and returned to his command center to activate the appropriate command channels. The third source was a command group from a nearby unit outside the immediate area. They arrived by vehicle in response to the event, audible and visible from their unit. Their response to the blast was a reconnaissance for information. Upon arrival at the site, the officer in charge remained on the scene and began organizing those present who seemed fixated on the sight in front of them. He dispatched the senior NCO with him to the nearby support unit to obtain heavy equipment. The medical officer in the team quickly checked a few walking wounded and then headed for the nearby unit's medical team to arrange for mass casualty treatment. He grabbed medical supplies and returned to the site with a team of medics to establish a triage point. The rescue and recovery action would take three days and involve considerable outside assistance of a variety of types.

The route of the attack into the ground floor and the layout of the ground floor are illustrated in Figures 26[4] and 27.[5]

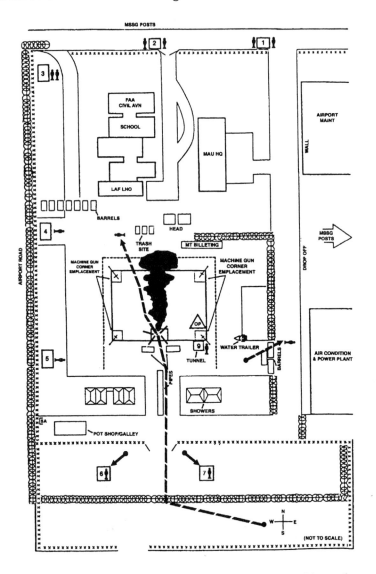

Figure 26. Route of attack on BLT headquarters and barracks.

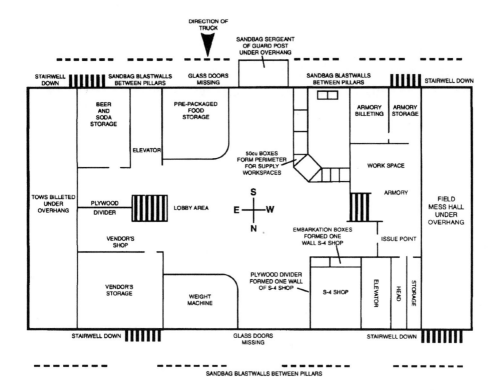

Figure 27. First floor, BLT headquarters and barracks.

Response tasks performed included dealing with the on-scene psychological "shock" to survivors and responders; clearing debris from the path for support vehicles to reach the site; alerting outside sources for support; triage of patients at the scene and evacuation sites; establishing tactical security around the blast site; establishing a command point; controlling routine and emergency traffic entering the blast site and medical sites; gathering or scavenging tools and heavy equipment from the area and from civilian contractors; cutting, lifting, or removing debris by various means; securing loose classified equipment, weapons, and personal effects; controlling looters and sightseers; locating hastily evacuated personnel; dealing with the news media and VIP visitors; talking to or assisting the trapped who were injured and dying; recovering dead bodies and parts of bodies, creating a temporary morgue and "matching" parts; identifying who was present, determining their status, and accounting for them to friends and relatives; and reestablishing the operations lost in the blast.

Several observations are pertinent from a study of this incident aside from the response tasks listed above:

a. The vehicle used was inconspicuous in the setting in which it was deployed. It was exactly like trucks being used to pick up cargo in the airport area. Many were typically seen on the approach road to the parking lot each day. The vehicle utilized a parallel approach for the initial deployment, and then a similar parallel approach (the parking lot) for launching the final attack. The attack from the parking lot was along a direct approach to the entrance and through the guard station, set up across the entrance, into the interior.

b. Examination of the defensive perimeter around the headquarters building shows that it was not designed to stop a truck or car bomb attack. The barriers in place along the perimeter were simple wire fences capable of impeding personnel, but not vehicles. Embedded posts which were on the attack route only slowed or diverted the attacking vehicle; they were not capable of stopping the vehicle. The sandbag emplacements around the buildings were capable of stopping fragmentation or bullets while providing only limited barriers against an attack. The truck, in fact, drove right over one such emplacement to penetrate the target. The perimeter had a number of armed personnel posts, so it is obvious that primary reliance was put upon sentry observation to detect any attack and neutralize it by firepower. When the sentries did not identify the truck movement as an attack during its approach to the perimeter, the defense design failed. When the sentries did detect an attack, they had insufficient engagement time left to respond.

c. The rules of engagement (Use-of-Deadly-Force instructions) issued to the guards prohibited loading a round into the chamber of the weapons of the sentries. This increased the amount of defensive time needed to engage the attacking vehicle by firepower. Sentries on the line of attack could not chamber and fire fast enough to actually shoot at the attacking vehicle. The short distance from the perimeter fences to the building prevented the sentries from even communicating a warning. The sole warning given, based on a thorough reading of the reference, was a verbal yell to "Hit the Deck" shouted by the Sergeant-of-the-Guard whose post was overrun by the attacking vehicle. Yet, even this simple warning probably saved at least two marines.

d. The internal and external communications were totally disrupted by the attack. The Sergeant-of-the-Guard post had multiple radios and phones; it was directly in the line-of-attack. Other points in the building which would typically have had communications were buried in the rubble.

e. The internal medical first aid capability of the unit was unavailable; the medics were all killed or injured and trapped in debris.

f. The scope of the disaster was not immediately clear to anyone; there was delayed perception by nearly everyone. Of primary significance is that two of the first three activations of the emergency response were made by officers with command and emergency medical experience and training. They knew precisely what had to be done and initiated it immediately upon recognition of the situation. These officers had all responded from outside the immediate attack area. This clearly indicates a need for "area" response planning rather than "site" or "facility" response planning.

g. Those present at the scene were basically military personnel who were trained to react to tactical emergencies. They were deployed in an operational area in which there were active attacks occurring almost daily. In spite of this mental preparation, many of the personnel experienced psychological difficulty dealing with the incident. Delayed response, reluctance to handle the dead, and rage at perceived inappropriate actions by others all caused difficulties for some and problems for those officials controlling the rescue and recovery operation.

h. Many casualties were burned as well as otherwise injured. This was a result of the enhancement of the explosive. The only significant secondary fire occurred in the vicinity of the unit ammunition storage area.

i. The last trapped casualty who survived was freed about six hours after the blast. Several others, still trapped, but alive, could not be freed in time to provide appropriate medical treatment; the entrapping debris was simply too extensive.

j. The pressure wave created by 12,000 pounds of explosive (Relative Effect) should have been capable of cracking reinforced concrete at over 180 feet from ground zero (The FBI lab estimated the vehicle bomb would have been capable of inflicting major damage to the building and significant casualties at 330 feet from ground zero). The containment of the explosion inside the building tended to increase the overpressure, magnifying the effect. The high level of pressure is clearly seen in the breaking of the two reinforced concrete columns which were the primary structure supports. They were nearly 5 feet in diameter but failed anyway. This visible support gave the impression to many that the construction of the building made it "impregnable", and may have affected the security planning.

k. Many survivors in the immediate area were initially buried under collapsed sandbag walls used in field fortifications or injured by heavy items stored overhead in living quarters.

l. One unusual reaction was that of engineer personnel at the immediate blast site. Their initial response was to begin clearing an access route into the site to allow other recovery actions. The training background was apparent in their response.

m. The entry to the scene quickly became clogged with vehicles. Even entry of emergency vehicles had to be controlled.

n. Casualty handling and evacuation experienced three significant problems. Not all casualties were processed through the triage point established immediately. Some were taken directly to civilian hospitals. This caused difficulty in tracking or accounting for personnel. There was also some indication that some of the casualties might not have received the quality of medical care that was needed, although this is not clear. The flow of casualties through the system was not smooth initially. The evacuation system was ready to clear casualties before they arrived, but initial sorting of casualties beyond the triage point evacuated the injured or the dead to the wrong points in the evacuation system. This was cured quickly. Traffic control to the evacuation points was not initially considered; it had to be implemented by security personnel when the problem surfaced.

The observations should conclude with a review of pertinent information, conclusions, and quotations from the official Department of Defense report.[6] It cited the perceptional differences and decision-making of authorities controlling the mission as a contributory factor, a clear intelligence failure which failed to recognize or correctly interpret the increasing threats or incidence of terrorist activity, and the use of two sets of Rules Of Engagement with strict enforcement, ostensibly to ensure the appearance of "neutrality" in the peacekeeping set-ting. The report specifically stated that this created a "mind set" against appropriate use of force to repel terrorist attack. Look at the report's conclusions and statements on some topics:

a. **Mission Assumptions**. The peacekeeping mission was formulated on four assumptions:

(1) The marine unit would not be in combat; it would be in a benign envi-ronment.

(2) Peacetime Rules of Engagement would be appropriate; any combat would be undertaken by other forces.

(3) The mission was of limited duration; the peacekeeping force would be extracted if hostilities escalated.

(4) The peacekeeping force would be evacuated rather than used to fight.

When the mission expanded outside this original view of its scope, these assumptions were no longer valid. The failure to recognize this and make appropriate adjustments contributed to the tactical outcome.

The environment into which the USMNF was inserted on 29 September 1982 was clearly permissive. The judgment that the USMNF was perceived as a neutral, stabilizing presence by most, if not all, factions in the Beirut area can be drawn from the general absence of hostile reactions in the initial months of their permissive environment. But, the environment proved to be dynamic, and became increasingly hostile to the USMNF component as the U.S. pres-ence stretched beyond the brief stay envisioned by the original exchange of notes.

The Commission believes that for any ROE to be effective, they should incorporate definitions of hostile intent and hostile action which correspond to the realities of the environment in which they are to be implemented. To be adequate, they must also provide the commander explicit authority to respond quickly to acts defined as hostile.[7]

In short, the experience of the United Nations Interim Force in Lebanon (UNIFIL) demonstrated that a peace-keeping force requires certain conditions to be present if it is to operate effectively.[8]

The Commission concludes that the "presence" mission was not interpreted the same by all levels of the chain of command and that perceptual differences regarding that mission, including the responsibility of the USMNF for the security of Beirut International Airport, should have been recognized and cor-rected by the chain of command.[9]

b. **Rules of Engagement**. The Rules of Engagement must be tailored to the setting and situation with a conscious understanding of the defense situation including both the actual terrain and the division of authority in the defense mission forces.

The MAU Commander explained that he made a conscious decision not to permit insertion of magazines in weapons on interior posts to preclude accidental discharge and possible injury to innocent civilians. This is indicative of the emphasis on prevention of harm to civilians, notwithstanding some degradation of security.[10]

The Commission concludes that a single set of ROE providing specific guidance for countering the type of vehicular terrorist attacks that destroyed the U.S. Embassy in 18 April 1983 and the BLT Headquarters building on 23 October 1983 had not been provided to, nor implemented by, the Marine Amphibious Unit Commander.[11]

c. **Nature of the terrorist threat**. The political/military situation in Lebanon is dominated by a host of diverse national, subnational and local political entities pursuing their own ends through an expedient but orchestrated process of negotiation and conflict. The spectrum of armed conflict in Lebanon is bounded by individual acts of terrorism on one end and formal conventional operations on three levels: conventional warfare, guerilla warfare and terrorism.[12]

Terrorism is warfare "on the cheap" and entails few risks. It permits small countries to attack U.S. interests in a manner, which if done openly, would constitute acts of war and justify a direct U.S. military response.

Combating terrorism requires an active policy. A reactive policy only forfeits the initiative to the terrorists.[13]

d. **Nature of the response**. Response must be commensurate with the threat and the value of the targets. Not everyone or everything can be fully protected. The object is not absolute security, but reduced vulnerability for the individuals and facilities, and diminished chances of success for the terrorist.[14]

e. **Nature of the problem**. The commission concludes that the U.S. Multi-National Force was not trained, organized, staffed or supported to deal effectively with the terrorist threat in Lebanon. The commission further concludes that much needs to be done to prepare U.S. military forces to defend against and counter terrorism.[15]

CASE 4. WORLD TRADE CENTER, NEW YORK CITY, NY, FEBRUARY 26, 1993[16]

A rental truck of typical commercial design was emplaced in a publicly-accessible, but improper parking area on a ramp in the B-2 level of the underground parking garage next to Tower One of the World Trade Center. The vehicle contained approximately 1,200 pounds of explosives enhanced with three bottles of hydrogen. The bomb was initiated by a simple burning fuse routed through surgical tubing to disguise the smoke from the burning fuse and extend the fuse burn-time. When the bomb detonated at 12:17, it destroyed five parking levels and affected six levels directly. The eleven inch thick concrete slab floor of level B-2 was left with a crater 200 feet by 150 feet; level B-1 had a crater about 80 feet by 59 feet. Damage extended through the floor of the Vista Hotel directly overhead. A steel diagonal beam between two of the vertical steel support columns of the tower building was torn from place and hurled across the garage. Vehicles 600 feet from ground zero were destroyed with many more left in flames. Six people were killed, 15 seriously injured, and over 1,000 were treated for inhalation of smoke which spread from the garage fires throughout the structure which exceeds 100 stories in height. One of the dead was killed when the pressure wave vented up the garage entry ramp into the street.

The first alarm from the explosion sounded immediately at a power station when approximately half of the major electrical lines to the structure overloaded. The second alarm was turned-in within seconds by an experienced firefighter some distance from the blast site who heard the blast, saw the flickering of lights in the Trade Center, the sudden rise of pigeons above the building, and assumed it was an electrical transformer exploding. He immediately initiated notification to the emergency dispatcher and began a response with the fire equipment under his control. Prior to arrival at the scene, the firefighter saw more smoke than he expected from a transformer fire and requested a second alarm. Familiar with the location, he feared that smoke might spread into the connected Vista Hotel. The next notification was a caller reporting an explosion in the underground parking garage, giving the exact location. The caller could not identify exactly what had caused it. At 12:29, the third call was received by the emergency communications center; it was from an individual who was injured and trapped in the affected area. At 12:36, the fourth call was received from a man on the 48th floor of the building reporting smoke coming from the vents. People attempting to leave the building had difficulty. Some were trapped in elevators; some were experiencing heavy smoke on the floors or in the stairwells.

The building did not collapse, but an assessment by the building architect three hours later showed two significant findings. First, the explosion had broken the seal into the ventilation and elevator shafts. This was significant since it meant that smoke from garage fires could circulate throughout the building. Most fire codes have requirements to prevent this situation since smoke inhalation causes the most deaths in fires. Second, the architect saw that the destruction presented no immediate danger of building collapse, but could easily lead to a future situation which would be critical. The weakened support for the side walls within the garage area could result in water seepage by osmotic pressure against the side walls. The steel frame that withstood the blast with little damage would sustain critical water damage that would drastically shorten the structure's useful life. Some bracing reduced the risk but illustrated how closely the blast had come to total destruction of the building. The rescue operation was over by the evening; the evidentiary operation by law enforcement would take much longer. The critical evidence, however, would be recovered in a matter of hours. Heavy steel parts of the vehicle had survived the blast, bent but intact. The strike directed at a building in which approximately 50,000 people were employed inflicted injuries of some type on over a thousand. The potential disruption and casualty count was much higher, but was not attained by this attack.

The pertinent observations to take from this account are as follows:

a. The vehicle used was an inconspicuous civilian van that matched those used in the area and routinely parked in the underground garage. It was emplaced in an area accessible to the public; no penetration of any perimeter security was required.

b. The pressure wave from 1,200 pounds of explosives would normally be capable of cracking reinforced concrete at approximately 85 feet. The enhancement with hydrogen and the general confinement inside the garage would have increased the overpressure.

c. The initial emergency report was made by an experienced observer who was trained in emergency response. Although not located at the blast site, he initiated notification and response without knowing exactly what the problem was. It was approximately 10 minutes after the blast before the extent of the problem was recognized and appropriate overall responses initiated even though this occurred in an urban area with a well-developed emergency communications system.

d. The explosion was almost entirely absorbed by and contained in the interior of one building. This prevented the pressure wave from significantly damaging surrounding structures in the urban area. The same blast outside the same location would have caused a large number of casualties in surrounding structures due to glass fragmentation impact without considering other casualty-producing possibilities.

e. Most casualties produced in this incident were minor and were the result of smoke inhalation from the secondary fires. This made the casualty handling portion of the incident easier to control. It is also significant to notice that the explosives caused few direct casualties; most casualties were the result of the secondary fires which were primarily caused by the enhancement of the explosives, the hydrogen cylinders which spread fire throughout the structure. This would take advantage of the existing flammable materials in the parking garage (the gasoline in the vehicles). This illustrates a natural disadvantage of parking areas; they will have a large quantity of flammable liquids on any given day. The casualty effect, however, resulted from the combination of the explosion and resulting fire. Normally, the building design would have prevented the spread of smoke from the garage throughout the building. The explosion destroyed the barrier that prevented this. Therefore, the large number of casualties was the result of a combined effect of an enhanced explosive device. It would not have occurred to this extent with either a vehicle bomb or an arson device used alone.

f. The assessment made by the building architect within three hours after the incident was excellent. It determined the continuing short-term and long-term risks to the structure. This was an example of excellent procedural response.

g. The steel beam and girder frame was mostly unaffected by the blast; only one diagonal brace was directly, seriously damaged.

h. The building was designed to assume great loads from the wind blowing against this tall structure. The strength of the design helped the building defeat the damage attempt. This is a clear indication that the basic building design theory is part of the equation in determining building survival during attack by a conventional weapon of mass destruction, and possibly the most important part.

i. The blast was set in an underground parking garage. One natural security feature of such structures is the restricted size of the entry point. Large vehicles are not able to enter. The limited size of the entry tends to screen out the largest potential vehicle bombs.

CASE 5. MURRAH FEDERAL BUILDING, OKLAHOMA CITY, OK, APRIL 19, 1995[17]

Shortly before 0900, a rental truck was parked parallel to the street curb near the Murrah Federal Building. The vehicle was left in the parking lane inset from northwest Fifth Street, approximately 15 feet from the structure. The vehicle had approximately 4,800 pounds of explosives with a time delay fuse which, according to trial testimony, may have been internally arranged within the truck to "focus" the explosion in a specific direction.[18] At 0902, the bomb detonated destroying three of the primary columns supporting that side of the precast concrete structure and one internal column. Approximately 30 percent of the nine-story building collapsed immediately. Seven other structures in the immediate area were heavily damaged, six received moderate damage. One hundred sixty-eight people were killed by the blast that left a crater approximately 30 feet in diameter by 8 feet deep.

Initial reports broadcast by news media indicated that the explosion was caused by natural gas. There was an initial reluctance to accept that it was a bomb. The rescue and recovery effort in this case was extensive. It lasted for weeks. Yet, the last living victim was recovered within hours of the initial blast. Shortly after it began, there was a stoppage caused by the possibility of a second bomb present at the scene. This proved to be an error but demonstrates control problems in the initial stages of the response. Although psychologically unprepared for an incident of this type, citizen response to provide assistance was strong. Medical, fire, and police personnel from a widearea responded to the scene without being summoned. Some persons attempting to provide assistance initially had to be restrained from entering areas that were not safe. Strong control had to be exercised to lessen risk to these citizens while continuing effective response. Problems in locating victims evacuated from the scene were encountered within a short time of the blast and took a few days to straighten out as did assembling a list of people believed to be in the building. The nature of the services provided in the building made this determination difficult.

As the recovery operation extended, firefighters and other rescue workers were frequently quoted as saying that the amount and small size of the debris was surprising. The extended time period required relief of rescue workers due to exhaustion. People with specialized skills had to be brought in from other localities to support the effort.

After the recovery was determined to be complete, the building was demolished as unsafe. The pertinent observations to take from this incident are as follows:

a. The attack was mounted by using a common vehicle, but one which was slightly conspicuous given the type of services provided in that building. The vehicle was emplaced on a parallel approach in a publicly-accessible area; it did not have to pass through any security screening to reach the emplacement point. The structure had no defense for this type of attack.

b. The pressure wave from a 4,800 pound standard ammonium-nitrate-mixture-based device would normally be capable of cracking precast concrete at a distance of in excess of 100 feet.[19] At the 15-foot emplacement distance, the precast concrete pillars of the exterior wall would have been subjected to an overpressure of several hundred pounds per square inch, enough to virtually pulverize the columns. In fact, the building design (specifically the combination of the precast construction technique, the slight overhang of the second floor above the sidewalk, and the inset parking lane) created an extreme vulnerability which made the structure an unusually favorable target for a vehicle bomb.

c. Sensitive assets (day care center) were assigned to office space at the primary point of attack. This is an indication of the level of psychological preparation for the incident. Security considerations were not being given importance since the probability of this type of attack was obviously considered to be low. However, security was a consideration in some placements within the structure. The assignment of the law enforcement agencies on the upper stories of the building was probably the result of vulnerability studies conducted during the time period when attacks on such agencies were made by small bombs. By locating the agencies on the upper stories, the assignment was intended to reduce the possibility of attack on those agencies and the building generally. Unfortunately, it caused the attack to escalate in size to reach the intended target and placed others directly in the line-of-fire. This is an example of failing to update defensive measures (placement within the structure) in a changing threat environment.

d. Access control to the scene was a clear problem in the early stages of the response. This is indication of the level of preparation for the problem both psychologically and actually.

e. The psychological preparation for the event was obviously low. Even the previous attack on the World Trade Center did not prepare the general population for a truck bombing of this magnitude. All previous incidents had been overseas and had been directed against official or military personnel (when Americans were targeted). Without concentrations of military or official power present in Oklahoma City, the Federal Building was not perceived as a target. Americans tend to view the sensitive locations, the power centers within the United States, as the nation's Capitol, Washington, D.C., and the world's Capitol, the United Nations building. Essentially, the perception was that any attack of this type would be directed against targets in Washington, D.C. and New York. The location of the event did not meet this assumption which controlled the psychological preparation for it. This perceptional misdirection enhanced their reactions. This showed in the strong desire to help, the extended recovery period at the scene, and the exceptionally emotional response to the presence of children. This caused a perception that children were deliberately targeted. This is an exceptionally clear example of strategic impact by a conventional weapon of mass destruction.

f. The attempt to internally design the bomb to focus shows a higher level of skill than many attacks. Assuming this were true, it would help explain the depth of the collapse which occurred when the internal column also collapsed. Such a design would extend the very high pressure area to a greater distance within the structure. The large amounts of glass in the structure would support this assumption since the glass surface areas would allow the high-pressure area to penetrate easily.

g. The design of the building was a critical factor in the collapse. The overhang of the second floor above the first floor sidewalk and the parallel parking inset, designed to be a drop-off point, allowed the vehicle with the bomb to be emplaced at a favorable point. The overhang would tend to trap the pressure wave moving upward from the blast increasing the effectiveness. A review of the basic construction design showed that the pillars at the ground level supported a beam which had a greater number of pillars resting on them. Consequently, the loss of one pillar at ground level would be magnified in stress at the second floor by the basic design of the building. This increased the effectiveness of any bomb emplaced at the ground level. See the emplacement diagram (Figure 28).

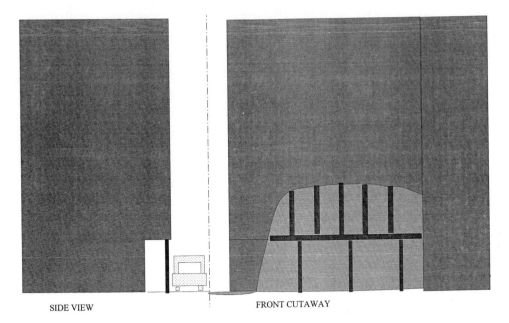

SIDE VIEW   FRONT CUTAWAY

Figure 28. Murrah Federal Building emplacement position.

h. The extent of the small rubble repeatedly encountered by the rescue workers was a sign of the pressure levels attained during the explosion. Minimum pressure displaces or reflects from the surface struck. As the pressure increases, the surface first distorts, then cracks, then shatters, and then, finally, pulverizes. The presence of extensive small rubble reveals that the areas were subjected to very high pressures. It is also an indication of lessened survival probability. Survival in a collapse is dependent on the creation of spaces within the debris that are large enough to "house" a person. As the size of the rubble decreases, the chance of such survival space being formed decreases. When this is added to the simple fact that survivors in such areas would have been subjected to the same high pressure as the building, increasing the likelihood of direct blast casualty effects (projectiles, displacement, lung rupture) on them, the probability of survival drops dramatically. In such circumstances, survivors are most likely to be found outside of the high pressure area formed by the blast. This usually means the side opposite the blast, the corners, and the upper stories. In both the Marine Headquarters incident and the Murrah Building incident, the last survivors were uncovered in a matter of hours. In the World Trade Center incident, the entire rescue was essentially over in a matter of hours. The only lone person recovered after that initial time period was known to have been in the area of high pressure, heavy smoke and heavy debris, a virtual guarantee of death. The debris created by a high pressure bomb is significantly different than that created by structures that collapse during earthquakes, tornados, hurricanes, or other natural actions. Planning for the rescue effort must take this into account.

CASE 6. KHOBAR TOWERS, DHAHRAN, KINGDOM OF SAUDI ARABIA, JUNE 25, 1996[20]

The Historical Background

In August 1991, U.S. military forces deployed to the Persian Gulf as part of a coalition to confront Iraqi forces in Kuwait. Among the problems facing military logisticians was billeting space. Making use of all facilities, the logisticians located and utilized Khobar Towers, an empty high-rise apartment complex located on the fringes of the city of Dhahran in the blue-collar suburban areas of Al-Khobar and Thuqbah. King Abdul Aziz Air Force Base is nearby. Use of part of the facility was approved by the Saudi Government and control was transferred by a verbal "handshake". The complex consisted of apartment buildings in three basic designs and heights with a few administrative buildings, parking garages, paved streets, utilities, and simple chain-link perimeter fences. The facility was used to the maximum during Desert Shield and Desert Storm. During this time period, every troop was armed with individual weapons and the perimeter was manned with fighting vehicles, snipers, and other overwatch positions. The primary concern was not ground attack but rocket attack. The facility was within SCUD range of Iraq. The warehouse in which many American soldiers died is just a short distance from the complex. In response to potential SCUD attack, glass windows were taped, shelters areas were identified, and both the local civil defense alarm system and internal systems were used to provide warning of incoming SCUDS. After the air and ground war, Khobar Towers was used as a reception point to process outward-bound troops from all services.

In June 1991, a relief-in-place was conducted with a large number of reserve personnel activated as individual replacements to allow deactivation or redeployment of personnel with extensive time in the theater. This relief was conducted over approximately a two-month period to allow continuity and a smooth transition of duties. At approximately this time period, the tactical risk was rated to be sufficiently low to allow reversion to "administrative" duties rather than "tactical" duties in the Dhahran area. In short, the individual weapons were turned in; most fighting vehicles had departed with combat formations or were scheduled to do so. Recognizing that this changed the risk factor for individual troops and compounds, the command restructured the billeting and security arrangements. Troops were centralized into selected compounds where defense was easier to perform than in the many scattered locations of varying vulnerability. These selected compounds were then assigned an armed security force to defend them. Low risks outside of the selected compounds were accepted unless an unusual risk factor was present (sensitive equipment and personnel or personnel concentrations). The largest facility created for U.S. personnel was Khobar Towers where, by July 1991, 20,000 unarmed American personnel were concentrated into an area of approximately one square kilometer, yet the Persian Gulf was still considered a hostile fire zone. Arriving in July 1991, I was assigned as the Army Provost Marshal, Khobar Towers and given control of the military police force which was controlling access and defending the largest sector. The mission was simple to state: In coordination with U.S. Air Force Security Police, Saudi Arabian Army Military Police, and local Saudi Criminal Police, defend the personnel in Khobar Towers against terrorist or special operations forces attacks.

I had the good fortune to be assigned to this duty with another excellent Military Police Officer, the Deputy Provost Marshal, as well as two additional excellent Military Police Officers already at work, and to work with an experienced Saudi Arabian Army Military Police Officer with previous counterterrorist experience. He served as the Liaison Officer and Commander of the Saudi MP Detachment. I also had the bad fortune to be replacing a Provost Marshal who was involved in a dispute with the Headquarters administering the facility. Complicating this situation further was an incomplete mission hand-off from the Rear Area Operations Center (RAOC) that had been handling base defense at Khobar Towers. Attempts to obtain a debriefing of its operation or to review its operations plan failed. Some carryover personnel familiar with the operations of the RAOC provided some information, but no complete plan could be located. Review of that plan was complicated by the simple fact that the RAOC had apparently confused part of the standard terminology or had implemented a defense which significantly differed from the joint doctrine implemented for Rear Battle in the years before the Persian Gulf deployment. The differing terminology confused the assignment of standard missions and responsibilities. When I was finally able to determine what they had apparently done, I saw that it was an error seen frequently in training exercises prior to the war. It was usually made by personnel who were unfamiliar with the doctrine. This problem was to continue to plague base defense operations. As the complete situation was reviewed, it became apparent that the defense of the base sectors was not completely integrated; in short, neither the Army nor the Air Force were using the joint doctrine developed for the situation. In at least one case, a senior officer seemed to be completely ignorant of the entire concept. This made implementing any defense more difficult. Attempts to more completely integrate the base defense were only partially successful. As part of the solution to this problem, an extensive vulnerability analysis of the base was undertaken as recommended prior to my arrival.

The in-depth vulnerability analysis produced several important findings, but no consensus. There were significant differences of professional opinion between the Air Force and the Army concerning the probability of certain actions and on the exact defensive measures needed. While these differences were being sorted out, the political and tactical situation shifted slightly, causing the redeployment of U.S. Army Air Defense Units equipped with the Patriot system for SCUD interception. This affected the risk profile and caused some changes. Without directly commenting on any disputes or differences of opinion, certain specific defense instructions were received directly from the Theater Commander (LTG Pagonis, at that point). Two will be mentioned; the primary risk to be considered was a truck bomb, and the secondary consideration was to be the political implications of an attack occurring during the peace conference which was to resolve the Kuwaiti-Iraqi dispute. Some other considerations placed limitations on the defense and response actions.

Khobar Towers was owned and operated by the government of Saudi Arabia. All unused portions were scheduled to be returned to their complete control. Consequently, all permanent changes had to be approved by the Saudi government. The planned phase-out of American troops indicated that the population at Khobar Towers would gradually decrease with the Army eventually turning American control of the facility over to the Air Force for sustained operations of indefinite, but temporary, length. The reduction in troop concentration at Khobar Towers would reduce both its attractiveness as a target and the number and type of resources available to defend or respond to any incident. Political implications had to be considered on all actions. United States military forces were present in a foreign country with significant social and cultural differences during a politically-sensitive period. Arrogant or excessive display and use of force might create problems. There was no formal Status of Forces Agreement such as those existing in Europe or South Korea where long-term stationing of U.S. military forces has occurred subject to certain treaties and international agreements. Almost all agreements between the United States and Saudi Arabia were informal, verbal agreements, those typical of friends cooperating in a joint venture. Unilateral action based solely upon tactical considerations was not possible, and might actually have been provocative and counterproductive in view of the existing political situation within Saudi Arabia and the Arab nations generally. Additional limitations were contained within the framework of the Charter and selected Resolutions of the United Nations. Foreign troops within another country at their request are required to comply with the limitations imposed upon them. Any deviation can be considered an "act of aggression" which gives legitimate, legal grounds under international law for local partisans to "rise up" against the "act of war." Aside from this requirement of international law, simple respect for the sovereign integrity of another nation and friend demands it. In addition to these considerations, cost-benefit analysis would be required on all physical defense measures, particularly in view of the limited time foreseen by existing instructions for the overall military mission.

The vulnerability analysis and a terrain analysis showed several pertinent points, only a few of which will be mentioned for continuing security reasons. The Eastern Province of Saudi Arabia was predominately populated by Shia Muslims rather than Sunni Muslims. In spite of this, the region was viewed as generally favorable to U.S. forces due to the economics involved in having a major income source located there. Additionally, the primary internal political actions within Saudi

Arabia occur at the political center, the capitol (Riyadh), and at the religious centers (Mecca and Medina). None are located in the Eastern Province, making U.S. Forces mostly "out-of-sight and out-of-mind." There were also operational reasons which made using the Eastern Province favorable. The eastern half of Khobar Towers was populated by refugees from the battle at Khafji, Saudi soldiers, and a few religious students or others receiving assistance from the Saudi government. That half was entirely controlled by the Saudis. Bordering the perimeter surrounding the complex were a public park, public roads, private business property, unowned publicly-accessible property, and a government controlled waste water facility. Within small-arms range of the perimeter were residential areas for civilians, civilian businesses, open areas, public parks, and structures specifically identified for protection under the Law of Land Warfare (a prayer tower, mosque, prison, and schools). Entry to the facility was restricted but still included the U.S. Forces, coalition force members, Saudi government official personnel from various agencies, and contractors providing services both to the physical facility and to the residents. Due to the limiting factors, creation of a completely protective stand-off distance for truck bomb explosion was not possible for a short time period. It would have required seizure of private property and significant disruption of both vehicle traffic flow and governmental or private business operations in the surrounding area.

There were several direct approaches to the perimeter as well as parallel approaches. The entrances to the complex were limited to two: one tightly restricted gate for the operating engineer (obstructed parallel approach) and one public gate for everything else (direct approach). The latter was a straight, direct road running from an intersection off a ramp from an interstate-style highway that was heavily traveled. Significant barrier emplacement was required to prevent truck penetration through the existing perimeter and to limit personnel penetration for internal staging. Analysis showed that it was critical to keep any truck bomb attack outside the perimeter. In addition to truck bomb attack, attack by small-arms fire, both direct and indirect, had to be included in planning. Mobile response capability had to be maintained both inside and outside the perimeter fence. Planning for response had to include a variety of organizations. During the course of implementing and operating this mission, several decisions were made which would have impact upon the later incident. These illustrate the impact of past planning decisions upon an event.

a. In mid-1991, the U.S. Air Force requested the use of a different facility to house its personnel for the sustained mission that they would operate for an indefinite period. This request was overruled by the Theater Commander. An analysis and comparison of the facilities showed that the requested facility had different security features which presented no net gain in overall security; the advantages and disadvantages seemed, subjectively, to balance out. Additionally, the other facility would require considerable renovations and repair to make it liveable for a long term. These problems had been acceptable (I should say simply endured) during the war but would not be acceptable under other circumstances. This decision left the U.S. Air Force personnel housed in Khobar Towers against its recommendation.

b. In the latter part of 1991, the U.S. Air Force assumed control of Khobar Towers from the Army. At the time it did so, the Air Force had the option to move into the buildings of its choice within the sector used by the U.S. Forces. The Air Force chose to remain deployed within the northern sector of Khobar Towers citing the length of the mission (they believed that they would be departing in a short time) and the improvements to the rooms and buildings. They preferred to avoid disruption of an established mission structure and to retain the "quality of life" improvements rather than move to buildings without them (Air Force personnel always seem to live better than Army personnel). The Air Force remained in the north section of Khobar Towers.

c. At the time of the Khobar Towers security mission hand-off to the Air Force Security Police, the close relationship developed by the U.S. Army Military Police and Saudi Arabian Army Military Police began to deteriorate. This close relationship had been extremely beneficial to American Forces although this was not widely recognized. This was due to two factors: the mission of the Saudi MPs in their army and their society, and the personal influence of the Saudi Army Officer serving as the Liaison Officer and MP Commander. The Air Force openly stated that they preferred to work through the Saudi Air Force Security Police to lessen their coordination problems.

d. When the security mission hand-off occurred at Khobar Towers, many of the barriers and other physical security provisions implemented by the Army were removed or altered by the Air Force. The defense "style" that they adopted was obviously based on the professional opinions developed by their vulnerability analysis and not by those developed in the Army vulnerability analysis. Stronger reliance was obviously placed upon intelligence sources. Shortly after this mission handoff (December 1991), the last Army General Officer left Saudi Arabia (June 1992) leaving the Air Force with the ranking officer present in the country.

e. The U.S. Air Force began staffing the sustainment mission as temporary duty. This meant that most of their personnel rotated through the assignment every four months. This affected the "institutional memory" of the organization concerning decisions, analysis, risks, etc. By July 1992 (my departure date from the area), I had seen four different Air Force Security Police Commanders for Khobar Towers in a one-year time period, two as a Provost Marshal at the facility and two as an Operations Officer at Headquarters, Army Forces Central Command (Forward). In that position, I had to help draft long-term rear area security plans and a set of Rules of Engagement for a temporary base defense force in Kuwait.

The Persian Gulf mission, foreseen as short-term in late 1991 and early 1992, was still in progress five years later, substantially unchanged. It appears that no definitive mission guidance was provided by the Commander-in-Chief or the Congress during that time period. The mission appears to have just continued with a constantly renewed short-term viewpoint. In November 1995, a car bomb was detonated in Riyadh near a building used jointly by U.S. military training personnel, Saudi military personnel, and civilians. The building was not specifically assigned to nor under the control of U.S. forces. The persons responsible were arrested, and four were executed in early 1996. This incident clearly altered the validity of the risk analysis for car or truck bomb attack in Saudi Arabia as completed by the Air Force in the 1991-1992 time frame. However, there appears to have been little change in the actual defense of Khobar Towers after this incident. The extended, short-term defensive concept used for Khobar Towers was about to be tested.

The Attack

Shortly before 2230 hours, 25 June 1996, a petroleum tanker truck approached the main entrance of the Khobar Towers apartment complex in Dhahran. The primary entrance at the southwest corner screened all persons and vehicles entering the facility. The tanker truck was denied entry; it departed. Air Force Mobile Security Patrols were dispatched to check further as the guards at the entry point were suspicious; there was no need for a petroleum tanker truck to enter a housing area at night. Moments later, the petroleum tanker truck pulled into a public parking area on the north side of the complex located between the prayer tower and the local prison. Just across the two streets were residential areas. It was emplaced outside the concrete barriers surrounding the facility, stopping about 100 feet from Building 131 which was used for personnel housing. The driver climbed out of the truck and got into a small white car driven by another man. It sped away. Air Force Security personnel manning observation points saw the suspicious activity. The mobile patrol moved to check the vehicle and security personnel began evacuating people from the nearby buildings. At approximately 2230 hours, the vehicle detonated with the force of approximately 3,000 pounds of RDX (4,800 pounds relative explosive power) leaving a crater 85 feet in diameter by 35 feet deep.

NineteenU.S. Air Force personnel were killed in the blast and approximately 270 Americans and 140 local people were injured. The building, of concrete pillar-and-slab style construction with masonry walls, did not collapse. The masonry walls closest to the blast site obviously came apart. Many other buildings in the complex and general area sustained damage. Media reports in the days after the blast were obviously tightly controlled but made some things clear. I was able to see that some parts of the planning we had made would clearly have worked and other parts would have failed. On the basis of my personal experience, I will make the following observations about this incident:

a. The planning decision of the Army Theater Commander in 1991, made for reasons that seem entirely valid, helped expose the Air Force personnel at the Khobar Towers facility to a risk in 1996 that would have been less likely to occur had the Air Force relocated to the other facility they recommended (This is a subjective evaluation).

b. The planning decision made by the Air Force Commander in late 1991 to remain in the northern section of Khobar Towers was a tactically-risky decision which may have been reasonably acceptable for a short period, but not for a long period. I felt that it was an error at the time it was made. Unfortunately, that personal assessment was correct. The southern sector being used by the Army at that time was sited on terrain that was more defensible against truck bomb attack. The actual attack mounted against the northern sector in 1996 would have produced less casualties if the same attack had been mounted against the southern sector.

c. The failure of the National Command Center to correctly forecast the long-term military mission requirements helped create a short-term viewpoint which encouraged assumption of a higher level of risk than was actually necessary. This has to be viewed as a command failure by the civilian leadership, but also a command failure at military headquarters as well. Based on past experience, military officers in these headquarters should have foreseen that the mission would obviously extend over a much longer time and initiated planning on that basis.

d. The failure of the Air Force to maintain very close relations with the Saudi Arabian Army Military Police was probably an error. While understandable from one point-of-view, it failed to recognize the actual strengths and weaknesses inherent in the host nation forces and correctly utilize them to the benefit of the U.S. forces. My own experience had shown that the Saudi MPs would frequently take care of problems that the Americans did not even know they had, and could be relied upon to provide support quickly when it was needed. Their mission assignment and role within the society gave them considerable clout. Only a close relationship made this obvious and made continued support dependable. The same statement was generally true of the Saudi Criminal Police as well. The short-term approach helped create this failure. This observation applies directly to any defense situation since all buildings which must be defended are always supported by area emergency response forces. A joint and close liaison to response forces in the area surrounding any facility is critical to achieve the level of prevention, defense, and response needed. This has to be viewed as an "area" task and not a "facility" task. The event of an attack is simply too overwhelming for a specific site to handle.

e. The failure of the truck bomb to penetrate the perimeter has to be viewed as a security success. It illustrates that part of the security provisions were working exactly as intended, but also illustrates a failure by the bombers. The selection of a tanker truck to penetrate this perimeter during a stealth attack was an error. This choice may have been needed to smuggle the explosive into Saudi Arabia from another country. The explosive reportedly used, RDX, is not a commonly available explosive. It is of exceptionally high relative power and would have been difficult to obtain undetected in the reported quantity inside Saudi Arabia. It is, therefore, also clear that part of the counterintelligence operations worked. But part of the vulnerability analysis clearly failed (These observations are made on the basis of news media reports and information not included here).

f. The emplacement of the truck bomb at approximately 100 feet from Building 131 would have subjected the masonry walls of the eleven-story building to a pressure wave which was capable of cracking masonry construction at approximately 140 feet. Extension of the barrier system only 50 feet further outward from the building might have lessened the pressure to a level that would have prevented masonry failure. This distance could easily have been attained in the area where the emplacement was made, but would have been more difficult in other areas of the northern sector perimeter. This extension outward would have required Saudi clearance. The failure to extend outward after the blast in Riyadh in late 1995 has to be viewed as an error.

g. The area in which the truck bomb was emplaced was difficult to reach quickly with mobile patrols responding from inside the billeting area of Khobar Towers due to the design of the defensive barrier system and the physical layout of the complex. Aggressive exterior mobile patrol was required in this setting, particularly when the risk escalated after the car bomb in Riyadh. The media reports indicate that during the truck bomb attack, Air Force Security personnel responded to the suspicious action and were checking the truck bomb when it detonated. While there is no way to know, it is reasonable to assume that an aggressive exterior patrol would be more likely to deter the second emplacement than a mobile patrol responding from the interior. There is no way to determine from the media reports where the mobile patrol was operated at the time this occurred. Consequently, no evaluation can be made of this portion of the defense.

h. Two Air Force security personnel were cited for bravery during this incident. Responding from their assigned observation posts, they were alerting personnel to evacuate from the area when the detonation occurred. This action would probably have been unnecessary had an internal alarm system been developed. Khobar Towers had its own switchboard. Consequently, it would have been possible to hardwire a complex-wide warning system for each building which was triggered from a central point. This should have been relatively simple and not very costly. This is an observation that seems clear in a civilian setting, but does not fit into the usual military setting very well. It is an effective technique which could have been used.

i. The final observation to make is that the Rear Battle doctrine and associated training utilized by the military services needs adjustment to effectively address the risk of truck bomb attack. There is considerable difference between defense of this type and the typical battlefield threat for which infantry, armor, artillery, or even military police units train. This doctrinal problem extends to certain equipment areas and was obvious and reported by me after the experience of operating a Military Police defense force in this setting. The same general observation applies to the civilian police training many of the individual reservists assigned with me in 1991 had previously received in their civilian jobs.

CASE 7. AMERICAN EMBASSIES IN AFRICA, 7 AUGUST 1998[21]

Nairobi, Kenya

At approximately 10:30 AM, a covered pickup truck passed through the checkpoint in front of the Cooperative Bank in the busy downtown of Nairobi, Kenya. Having passed the lane dividers which separate the busy Haile Selassie Avenue from direct vehicular access to the perimeter of the nearby American Embassy, the pickup truck halted outside of the basement garage entry to the embassy. This positioned it in the alley between the embassy and the Ufundi Cooperative House. Conflicting witness reports indicate that the guards on duty at the embassy checkpoint were suspicious and exchanged fire with the men in the pickup who may have been disguised as security employees. Both gunfire and grenade explosions were reported by the witnesses. Within seconds after the reported exchange, the pickup detonated with an estimated 800 kilograms (1760 pounds) of TNT, probably enhanced by compressed gas. The results were the most horrific attained by a vehicular bomb to that date, at least in terms of the total casualties.

The 5-story Ufundi Cooperative House, made of precast concrete, completely collapsed. Windows were stripped from both the 21-story Cooperative Bank and the 5-story American Embassy. Bomb doors on the embassy were blown inward and the building was obviously scorched, but it did not collapse. Buses and cars in the nearby busy street were instantly destroyed. Over the next week, the casualty total rose daily, eventually stabilizing at 247 dead and 5,500 wounded.

Local hospitals were overwhelmed with the wounded, many of whom arrived on foot or in the hands of other local citizens who had immediately swarmed over the collapsed building and the surrounding area to try to assist the injured and trapped. Initial American security response to limit entry to the danger zone would be criticized by local citizens as hampering the rescue efforts. Within hours, assistance was dispatched, primarily from Israel, Germany, and the United States. Security personnel, search and rescue equipment and personnel, investigative personnel, and medical personnel were in the first response. Additional resources followed over the next few days with some of the injured being evacuated from the country due to the overload of local medical facilities. Those people trapped in the collapsed building would be recovered over the next two to three days, but some who survived the blast and collapse would not survive long enough to be freed from the rubble. Within approximately a week, the rescue effort had ended and the investigation was intensifying. Arrests began within a few days.

Dar es Salaam, Tanzania

At approximately 10:35 AM, a water tank truck approached the entry checkpoint of the American Embassy located near the Nigerian Embassy in the outskirts of the capital city. As the embassy vehicle was being checked by security personnel, a car seen earlier in the nearby parking lot detonated outside of the security perimeter, approximately 12 feet from the gate. The explosion was estimated at approximately 500 pounds. It killed 10 people, injured 74, and collapsed a portion of the nearest wall of the American Embassy. Damage to the building overall was limited by the 2-foot thick concrete and metal perimeter wall which sustained considerable damage near the blast site. Response actions were minimal due to the rather limited effects of the bomb at that emplacement site. Investigation teams that arrived a short time later were very impressed with the protection of the crime scene by security personnel.

On August 20, 1998, the United States launched military strikes against terrorist camps in Afghanistan and a factory in Sudan. These actions were based on investigative information of the bombing supplemented by intelligence information. During explanations of the military action, the United States indicated a more aggressive counterterrorist policy, particularly against groups associated with a particular individual. Based on limited and incomplete information less than two weeks after the explosions, the following observations can be made which are pertinent:

a. The vehicles used in the two bombings appear to have been civilian-style vehicles which were mostly inconspicuous in the settings to which deployed. The failure of the covered pickup to penetrate the embassy garage may have been due, in part, to its appearance which contributed to alerting the guards. Both vehicles were using direct approaches to the buildings and were at or near the entry points at the time of detonation. Both attacks were under security observation at the time of detonation.

b. News reports indicate that the terrorists had approximately 800 kilograms (1760 pounds) of explosives available to them in Kenya and that approximately 500 pounds of explosives were used in Tanzania. A bomb of 1760 pounds would normally be capable of cracking precast concrete at a distance in excess of 100 feet.

Since this is distance that is 4-6 times the width of a two-lane roadway, it is reasonable to conclude that the bomb was not intended for use against the Ufundi Cooperative Society Building since that required considerably less quantity of explosives to damage it from that emplacement position. That building would have been subjected to pressures that exceeded 100 psi which explains its collapse. It is also reasonable to conclude that the bomb was intended for emplacement inside the embassy garage. Since its detonation was insufficient to destroy the embassy from the exterior, the terrorists either miscalculated in building the bomb or failed during the emplacement stage. The manner in which the attack was mounted indicates that some limited prestrike surveillance was done. It is, therefore, reasonable to conclude that the terrorists possessed some knowledge of the basic design and construction of the embassy. Since the suspect was reported to be an engineer, it would seem that the emplacement failed and that the collapse of the Ufundi Cooperative Society building was the result of the failed emplacement. This can also be viewed as a planning failure, a failure to analyze collateral damage which is a typical assessment in a military setting.

The 500-pound bomb used in Tanzania would normally be capable of cracking structures at a distance in excess of 60 feet. Since the bomb was reported to have detonated only 12 feet outside of the perimeter fence and attained only a partial collapse of one building wall, this is also a tactical failure during emplacement, assuming that the intention was to significantly damage the structure. Again, this indicates a lower skill level during the attack.

c. These nearly simultaneous detonations in the capital cities of two different countries present an interesting study in the differences of tactical, operational, and strategic results.

1. At the tactical level, these two incidents demonstrate a mixed result which is mostly a failure. Neither attack managed to penetrate into the embassy interiors. While the information is incomplete at the time of this analysis, both attacks were obviously reduced in their intended effects by the existing security provisions. The penetration of the initial entry point near the bank in Kenya is the sole, clear tactical success for the attackers in the operation. These tactical failures had significant strategic impact.

2. At the operational level, the attackers managed to build two large bombs and deploy them in the vicinity of two different

embassies approximately 450 miles apart, nearly simultaneously. While an indication of some skill in terrorist levels, the security level in both countries was so low that little effort should have been required to defeat the security. Yet, they failed to defeat the final layer of security in both attacks. This shows a profile of a mid-skill level group of terrorists, not the "highly-skilled" terrorist operation as pictured in many news reports. While some might be tempted to state that the very high number of casualties was indication of high skill, this is an incorrect analysis. The target population was not the population that sustained most of the injury and damage. In essence, both attacks essentially "missed" the targets at the tactical level while succeeding at the operational level. This mixed result at the tactical and operational levels affects the strategic outcome.

3. At the strategic level, use of these two bombs has become the worst strategic error in recent terrorist operations. The attack produced an unusually large number of casualties who were primarily local citizens unrelated to the stated dispute. The average citizen in Kenya had no reason to believe that he was endangered by a terrorist group disputing the policy of the United States. Since there were no known hostilities in Kenya (no declaration of war or previous hostilities) and since the attack was not proceeded by a specific bombardment notice, the government of Kenya can legitimately argue that the action clearly constitutes an act of war and a war crime even if mounted by "a group seeking self-determination." Kenya can seek action in the United Nations under the existing charter or in the international courts. Its standing to do so is quite strong. It was a neutral party to the claimed dispute. The fact that thousands were injured by one action makes the international policy of treating it as a criminal act absurd. What crime, typically, directly injures thousands? What member nation of the U.N. would take the stance that a single bomb which injuries thousands does *not* constitute an act of war which justifies self-defense action up to and including the declaration of war? This action opened the door to a dramatic, political shift in terrorist counteraction which was immediately taken by the United States. These actions were treated as an act or war and the response was made on that basis.

d. The vehicle bomb detonated in Kenya was in close proximity to two 5-story buildings of different design and construction.

Both would have been subjected to approximately the same over-pressure levels; one collapsed, the other didn't. The precast concrete building failure is significant; this construction method is proving to be very susceptible to collapse.

e. Many witnesses reported a "thud", then gunfire and then a detonation after a short delay. The sequence is very interesting. It may be interpreted in several ways:

1. It could indicate a sequential attack plan in which the final perimeter was to be breeched by simply killing the guards before emplacing the vehicle in the underground garage.

2. It could indicate defensive fire which halted the attack short of its emplacement point and possibly triggered the premature detonation of the device.

3. It could indicate the sequential triggering of separate parts of an enhanced explosive device.

4. It could indicate a mixture of the first three interpretations.

Final determination of the significance of the witness reports may not be possible due to the circumstances. The final point to make is that the reported sequence actually increased the injuries to a large number of people. The noise combined with the delay before detonation served to draw the curious into more exposed positions which increased the total number injured and the severity of their injuries. This was probably an unintended result, but the lesson should not be lost on those who work in and around target areas.

f. The shielding effect of the reinforced perimeter wall at the embassy in Tanzania should be reviewed closely for its overall effect on the outcome. It is an excellent example of effective barrier use. It appears to have affected both emplacement and the destruction by the pressure wave, the exact effect that should be sought by a barrier system. Only further study or more information would clarify the exact extent of the shielding.

g. The massive casualties in Kenya demonstrate two points very clearly:

1. Effective defense (or ineffective offense) may displace the attack in a manner which is actually more detrimental overall. Had the attacker successfully emplaced the vehicle bomb inside the embassy, it would likely have resulted in collapsing the embassy building. This, in turn, would likely have confined most of the damage and casualties to people in that building. The overall result

would have been a considerable increase in American casualties, but also an *extreme* decrease in Kenyan casualties. In short, accepting this attack in this setting would probably have injured and killed less people than defeating its entry to the garage did. The guards, however, would not be able to determine this while making decisions at the entry point.

2. The detonation caused a nearby building collapse and injured thousands in the proximity of the embassy. This was a predictable outcome which could have been partly reduced by emplacement of a deflector between the garage entrance and the nearby major avenue. It clearly illustrates the absolute necessity of "area" versus "point" planning. Security provisions around the embassy had to be coordinated with local authorities. American security personnel have no authority to control the local citizens on the street or in the nearby buildings; this is up to the local government and their officials. The outcome of any attack is the product of the actions by both governments and the attacker.

h. The swarming of the collapsed building and the immediate area of the blast is a natural reaction by concerned, but untrained citizens who do not realize the continuing risk from further collapse or secondary detonation. American security personnel who attempted to control entry in that situation had no authority to do so and were misinterpreted by the local citizens (also a typical reaction in emergencies and crowd control situations). Many local citizens complained afterward. Security planning must include consideration of the "public image" of the security actions as well as the necessity for the actions.

i. The CCTV at the embassy in Kenya was operating during the attack, but failed to record it. The CCTV was used only for live transmission to the guard checkpoints; it was not recorded. The evidence collection possibility was missed.

CASE 8. DETONATION OF SEMITRAILER DURING FIRE, KANSAS CITY, MISSOURI[22]

A fire unit was dispatched to a pickup truck fire near a construction site in the southeastern part of Kansas City, Missouri in the early morning hours. A new section of closed access highway was being constructed; the site was being used for equipment storage during the construction. As the pickup truck fire was being extinguished, a second fire was noticed inside the construction storage area. The second fire was a fully involved semitrailer, the result of arson. The security officers assigned to the site advised the firefighters that the trailer had fertilizer and diesel fuel in it. The firefighters proceeded to the semi-trailer fire, apparently unaware that the "fertilizer" was "ammonium nitrate." That term was not used by the security officer nor was its significance understood by him. Investigation after the fact indicated that approximately 25,000 pounds of ammonium nitrate was present. With no warning, the burning semitrailer detonated instantly killing six firefighters and destroying two fire trucks (stripped to the frame and drive train). It also damaged additional firefighting equipment, and knocked other firefighters to the ground. Both were more distant from the blast. Houses and business buildings several blocks to the west of the semi-isolated urban site received glass and some structural damage. At the time this occurred, I was wide awake, a night-shift security officer on my day off. My residence, a wood-frame, one-story house approximately nine miles northwest of the blast site, shook and rattled. A later visit to the site showed that a twenty to thirty-foot high, shear rock wall was along the east of the blast site. Houses and businesses to the east were shielded from the blast by the terrain while those to the west were damaged. The linear distance to the structures was the same to the east and to the west. The important observations are:

a. The semitrailer size blast, consisting of 25,000 pounds of confined ammonium nitrate, would have produced a relative explosive power of only approximately 10,500 pounds of TNT (it is a relatively low-grade explosive). The resulting pressure wave would be capable of cracking reinforced concrete at 170 feet and breaking glass at more than 300 feet from the blast site under normal circumstances. In this case, the wave was reflected immediately by the shear rock wall.

b. The reflected pressure wave traveled noticeably further than would be expected for a blast this size. The change in air pressure was noticeable at nine miles.

c. The terrain shield was remarkably effective in redirecting the pressure wave. It shielded structures to the east, but increased the damage area to the west.

CASE 9. DETONATION OF TRACTOR-TRAILER ON
INTERSTATE HIGHWAY[23]

A civilian DOD contractor driving a tractor-trailer for a Joplin, Missouri firm was hauling Class A explosives for the military along an interstate highway. The firm was involved in a labor dispute at the time. A pickup truck pulled nearby and one occupant fired at the tractor-trailer with a rifle, intending to intimidate the driver. The semi-trailer detonated. The driver was killed instantly, the semitrailer was destroyed, the occupants of the pickup were injured, and several other cars were affected. A crater approximately 200 feet long and 50 feet deep was left in the Interstate roadbed, completely removing one side of the dual roadway. The exact quantity of explosives was not released, but a semi-trailer of that size would be capable of carrying 40,000 pounds. The two important observations from this incident are:

> a. Explosives in transport can be detonated by simple gunfire. This has important ramifications for firing upon an attacking truck bomb.
> b. The pressure wave produced by 40,000 pounds of explosives would normally be capable of cracking reinforced concrete at approximately 270 feet. This amount of force would be likely to destroy or collapse most structures.

CASE 10. SELECTED OPERATIONAL TECHNIQUES[24]

Beirut, Lebanon area, early 1980s

a. A car bomb was infiltrated into the French Embassy by assembling it inside the car of an embassy employee who, apparently unwittingly, delivered it the next morning. Upon delivery, it was command-detonated, killing the employee. This is an example of stealth emplacement by a courier of a bomb which was specifically designed to bypass the existing security screening. It illustrates an off-site vulnerability which has to be considered, and the necessity of applying screening techniques equally against all vehicles entering the perimeter.

b. A car bomb emplaced outside of the Kuwait Embassy was command-detonated as a small U.S. military convoy passed nearby. This is a tactical ambush technique used extensively in Beirut. In some cases, the target was a specific individual; in others, the target was the military or security forces. Vehicle bombs do not have to be oriented against buildings. They may target personnel collectively or specifically based on job or simply on location at a certain time.

c. Two car bombs were emplaced in a marketplace area using delay fusing. After the first detonated, a crowd gathered to watch the response. The second car bomb detonated in the area being used by the crowd and responders, killing or injuring a large number. This is an example of a sequential attack and of deliberate targeting of response forces.

d. A truck bomb was emplaced outside of a French military unit by a driver who simply abandoned the vehicle in the street and then escaped by jumping into a nearby car that accompanied him. The detonation killed a sentry and wounded several others; it also killed about twenty noncombatants. The military building was shielded by earthen works, reducing the effectiveness of the bomb considerably. The first observation to make is that the personnel manning the security points will be the most frequent casualties during attacks. This raises important issues for screening of these personnel, and points out a transient security vulnerability. Right after the detonation, there is a breach in security which can be exploited by an attacker. The second observation is that the emplacement technique used, a drop-off with short delay, is virtually impossible to defend against. The size of the blast was simply increased, a truck bomb versus a car bomb, to overcome the disadvantage of emplacement outside of the established perimeter. The size increase turned out to be mostly ineffective in this case, the third observation. The defense works constructed by the defenders created a survival zone for the building and obviously reduced the military casualties.

American Embassy, Kuwait, December 12, 1983

e. A suicide bomber drove a truck bomb through the closed gate of the American Embassy. The bomb was of enhanced explosive construction; it had gas canisters surrounding the explosives. It detonated in the parking lot collapsing one building and extensively damaging others. Three embassy employees and two others were killed in addition to the driver. On the same day, five car bombs were also detonated in the vicinity using delay fusing techniques. The targets were the French Embassy, the airport control tower, an American residential area, a power station, and a petrochemical plant. A sixth was located and defused outside of a passport office. The detonations all occurred within a one hour time frame. The first point to notice is the delivery technique of simply ramming through the existing barrier. This is an effective technique under some circumstances. Its use in conjunction with an individual willing to sacrifice himself neutralizes many defense techniques. Use-of-force at this point in the attack would likely be ineffective, which has important implications for defense. The second observation is the sequential or nearly simultaneous detonation of other large devices against multiple targets. This type attack requires a lot more planning and coordination for both the attacker and defender; it would overload virtually any response force. It may also be intended to cause the response to occur in a certain order creating temporary security lapses in certain areas which may increase the effectiveness or the chance of success of other attacks. This is a typical tactical diversion or manipulation technique. It indicates a high level of training and experience from the attacker. Defense against attacks of this type may be a requirement; this determination is made during the assessment of the terrorist group and development of its operational profile.

Local Political Headquarters, Tokyo, Japan, 19 September 1984

f. A civilian cargo truck pulled up to the front of the Liberal Democratic Party Headquarters and parked with the front of the truck toward the building. A short time later, the vehicle ignited. A large-scale flame weapon had been installed in the rear cargo van with the nozzle over the cab of the truck. In effect, it acted as a giant flame thrower, setting the building afire. A short time later, a second time-delay device ignited inside the truck doing extensive damage. This is an example of two important techniques: the device was built to operate in a specific direction. This affected the emplacement requirement. Second, the use of incendiaries as the destructive mechanism presents a considerably different risk than a large explosion, and requires a much different response.

Rhein-Main AFB, Germany, August 1985

g. A car bomb detonated on the base near the U.S. Air Force head-quarters killing two and injuring seventeen. A letter received afterward claimed the attack on behalf of the Red Army Faction. Enclosed in the letter was the missing identification card of a serviceman found mur-dered off-base the night before the attack. The initial investigation indicated that he had last been seen with a woman in a local bar. He was found dead in an isolated wooded area. The RAF had several known female operatives. The conclusion reached was that the ser-viceman had been murdered by the terrorists for the sole purpose of obtaining his identification for use during the emplacement of the car bomb. The important points from this operation are the necessity to screen all identification closely, and the vulnerability of personnel in off-site areas. Even incidents which appear to be unrelated, that are typical activity for the area, but which involve personnel with access, must be monitored for potential security problems.

NATO Support Facility, Brussels, Belgium, January 1985

h. Two military police personnel observed a suspicious civilian vehi-cle improperly parallel-parked along the street by a wall surrounding a military compound. As they moved to check it, the vehicle explod-ed causing minor injuries to both MPs. The attack was later claimed by the Combatant Communist Cells. There are two observations to make here. Vehicle bomb emplacement may be disguised as routine parking, but frequently is parked where it is conspicuous, that is "out-of-place," to trained observers. Parking control can assist in identifying attacks, but does not prevent them. Second, security personnel must be taught the correct check out procedures.

Turkish Embassy, Ottawa, Canada, March 1985

i. A truck approached a security checkpoint at an entrance along the walled perimeter of the Turkish Embassy and rammed into it, killing the Canadian security guard on duty. Commandos for the Armenian Revolutionary Army then jumped from the vehicle and attacked the embassy, seizing it for a short time. They missed the ambassador who escaped through a back window using a prepared escape route. This is an example of a sequential attack in which the vehicle is used to penetrate the perimeter. It could easily be paired with a secondary vehicle bomb attack that utilizes the cleared route to reach the best emplacement point.

American University, Beirut, Lebanon, 1992

j. A car bomb detonated inside a university building at night causing considerable damage to the structure and killing two security guards. Investigation revealed that one guard had died of gunshot wounds prior to the detonation. That guard had been assigned to a security post at a vehicle entrance on the perimeter of the university. The obvious conclusion was that penetration of the perimeter was accomplished by simply assassinating the lone security official at a selected point, thereby overcoming the security provisions. This is an example of a sequential attack; one to penetrate and one to destroy the building. It also illustrates the vulnerability of checkpoints with one guard and limited support or overwatch procedures.

Omagh, Northern Ireland, August 15, 1998[25]

k. Local press officials received a phone call at about 2:30pm indicating that a car bomb had been emplaced outside of the local courthouse on the west side of town. Authorities reacted to the call by clearing a perimeter around the courthouse on High Street. Approximately 40 minutes after the call, a 500-pound car bomb detonated on Market Street east of the courthouse and outside of the security perimeter. Many people had been directed down this street by police to remove them from the danger zone. The result was the highest level of casualties in any bombing in Northern Ireland; 28 dead and 220 injured. Included among the casualties were citizens from both sides of the long-running dispute, three generations of one family and foreign tourists.

The bombing was immediately condemned by all parties involved in the current peace process, including the Sinn Fein which had supported the IRA bombings for decades. The result was widely perceived as a deliberate lure of citizens to the bombing area for the sole purpose of increasing the death count. This is an effective technique for ambush which had previously been used against security forces in the area. The terrorist group claiming credit for the bombing, "The Real IRA," denied that allegation claiming they had stated that the bomb was 300-400 yards from the courthouse. The bombers stated that the authorities had been given the exact location, and botched the security operation. Authorities effectively countered that charge. The "Real IRA" later issued an apology for the bombing. Shortly thereafter, five bombers were arrested and counterterrorist provisions were increased by agreement of all parties involved in the current peace process. The tactically effective lure-and-bomb technique resulted in a strategic failure with wide-sweeping counterterrorist changes that may totally destroy "The Real IRA."

SUMMARY AND CONCLUSIONS

Study of these and other incidents gives a generic profile of an attack. The sequence of events in any attack by a conventional weapon of mass destruction goes as follows:

Decision phase–Motivation development and attack selection.
Acquisition phase–Learning how to build the weapon, gathering the materials and surveilling the target.
Construction phase–Preparing the chemicals and assembling the device.
Transport phase–Moving the bomb to the target.
Emplacement phase–Actually placing the bomb at the selected location.
Detonation phase–The time period after emplacement before the actual explosion.

A tactical analysis of the phases can be used to develop preventive and defensive strategies. The generic attack and its result usually follow this profile:

The device is mounted in a common vehicle of civilian design using locally available materials.

The device is directed at the front center of the structure following the most frequently used approach to the building. In most cases, this is the main entrance from the street or parking area next to the building.

Most attacks occur when the most people are present in the building which is usually during the daytime.

Most devices are emplaced in the publicly-accessible areas around the structure with no attempt to enter any perimeter whether secured or not.

About half of the attacks are overt and half covert. The overt attacks may take the form of either a "suicide driver" or of a driver who is simply willing to assume a short, high risk.

When the attack occurs, security and communications will be disrupted; frequently, they will be completely destroyed. Accessability to building maintenance areas will be blocked and may be destroyed.

Building collapse only occurs in about one-fourth of the incidents with very close proximity or penetration of the structure increasing the chance of structure failure. Collapse or destruction of an exterior wall occurs in most incidents.

The side opposite the emplacement and the corners of the structure will be most likely to survive the attack.

Blending the sequence of events with the tactical observations made previously, the following tactical points concerning prevention and defense of generic attacks can be made:

Prevention efforts apply primarily to the Decision, Acquisition, Construction, and Transport Phases of the conventional weapon of mass destruction event sequence. Defense efforts should orient primarily on the Emplacement and Detonation Phases with secondary orientation on transportation.

Psychological preparation for the attack event is probably the critical tactical prevention action. There are clear differences in preparation requirements for the general public, the planners, the specific defenders, and the responders.

The building design factors will be the primary determinant of the results of the attack. It may work to deter or to attract the attacker. Of the design factors, the framework design is probably the most important followed by the construction materials and then the building shape.

The relative size of the explosive used in the conventional weapon of mass destruction can be adjusted to overcome the defensive barrier system. It is the second of the critical determinants of the overall result.

Placement of critical assets within the structure has the strongest impact on the casualty results and the overall effectiveness of the result. It is important to remember that the "target" is usually the people and their social organizations, not the structure itself. The building should be viewed as a part of the "weapon system" being deployed against the people or the terrain on which the engagement occurs. The structure is, simply, the kill zone of the conventional weapon of mass destruction deployed against people; occasionally, it is also the defender's equipment which is destroyed to reduce the defender's effectiveness as a military or political force.

The primary effectiveness of visible security forces is their "show-of-force" value. Their actual tactical effectiveness for defense is very low. The ability to prevent entry by covert methods is their primary defensive attribute; prevention of overt attack is primarily a function of the barrier system.

Parking controls have limited value as a preventive technique; they only help identify that an attack is in progress. The parking controls have virtually no value as a defense technique, and, in fact, may actually create vulnerability by freeing the approach to the structure of its usual traffic congestion. The time period for attack that is most favorable to the attacker coincides with the time period of most traffic congestion. Removing other vehicles actually removes part of the barriers which impede the attacker and which may partially shield the other people present from minor fragmentation.

The emplacement time period of an attacking vehicle bomb varies; covert attack is measured in days, hours, or minutes while overt attack is measured in minutes or seconds. The duration of the tactical engagement between the security force and the attack vehicle is measured in seconds making tactical firepower virtually ineffective for either type of attack. Even combat vehicle weapon systems would have difficulty effectively halting such an attack. They are designed primarily to engage other vehicles which makes them suitable to the basic tactical engagement task, vehicle destruction. However, most current vehicles are designed to engage at extended ranges rather than the short ranges typical of vehicle bombs which makes the engagement more difficult for these vehicles to accomplish. Additionally, the combat weapon systems would require 100 percent operational capability for extended periods. Individual or light crew-served weapons have insufficient power to reliably halt an attacking vehicle making their usefulness unreliable for the defense against conventional weapons of mass destruction. They are also subject to the 100 percent operational capability requirement for extended periods. This is difficult to attain. Even when these problems are resolved, firepower lacks the ability to accomplish the second of the tactical tasks, defusing the bomb. Firepower is incapable of doing this except by pure chance damage to the device mechanism. It can, however, frequently cause detonation of the device. The probability of detonation increases as the capability of the defending weapon increases. The three probable outcomes of such an engagement are the vehicle bomb emplaces successfully, the vehicle bomb is halted short of its emplacement point, or the vehicle bomb detonates when engaged. The common factor of the three outcomes is a high probability of detonation. The tactical disadvantages for the attacker can be overcome by simple dead-man or short-delay activation switches which require no further action by the vehicle driver at the time engaged. Therefore, the best possible outcome is halting the vehicle bomb short of the emplacement point which still requires time to defuse it. During the emplacement phase, the tactical advantage belongs to the attacker.

A terrain shield is the most effective defense against the conventional weapon of mass destruction. Creating an extended stand-off distance is the next most effective defense.

Preventing penetration of the structure or of the barrier system is the critical tactical task for the defender. The speed of the overt emplacement complicates the use of barriers as an "instant" defense. The mass of a barrier that is strong enough to halt a vehicle tends to make its quick deployment difficult. Consequently, barriers that require no deployment will be the most effective.

The defensive barrier system is the third of the critical determinants of the overall result. It can be used to create a shield or redirect the pressure wave. This is actually the barrier's secondary purpose that occurs over the largest linear frontage of the barriers. Its primary purpose is to channel the attack to a point where it is detected and where the blast can be "managed." In short, the barrier system should be designed to create a "trap zone" where the conventional weapon of mass destruction can be most favorably engaged along the emplacement approach likely to be used. The "trap zone" is designed to halt, engage, and, probably, detonate the weapon of mass destruction at the point of your choice.

Barriers will obstruct the defender and the responder affecting both tactical and emergency response. This must be considered by the planner in all phases.

The tactical implications of the various observations must be modified to the specific operational profile of the terrorist group involved and to the specific vulnerability of the site being defended. While these observations provide general guidance for the defender, it is important to remember that all tactics evolve, all tactical operators vary in capability, and all tactical advantages or disadvantages can be overcome. There are no absolute guarantees. The best possible tactic performed by highly-trained personnel at precisely the right time may fail; the worst tactic performed by untrained personnel at the wrong time may succeed far beyond anyone's expectations. The possible permutations of tactical possibilities is so high that it can not be reliably predicted at high probability levels. In the final analysis, you are left with the simple guidance: plan for the worst and hope for the best. I would reiterate this strongly. My own experience at Khobar Towers showed that there are basically two types of planners: those who consider what to do *if* something happens and those who consider what to do *when* something happens. The difference is in the basic assumption of the planner, and to some extent, in the planner's tactical experience; the difference between operating in the strategic environment where a lot of general information is available and errors of prediction allow extended reaction times and operating in the tactical environment where sparse information is available and errors of prediction allow little or no reaction times. One planner assumes that an event is possible but probably will not happen, the other assumes that any possible event probably will happen (*when* rather than *if*). The best planners for successful tactical operations are those who say "*When* this occurs..."

Notes

1. Primary sources: *The Root* by Eric Hammel, 1985, Harcourt, Brace, Jovanovich Publishers, San Diego, New York and London and "TVI Journal," Volume IV Number 4-6, published by Mark Monday, San Diego.

2. Primary sources: "TVI Journal," Volume 5, Number 3, Winter 1985 and *Terrorist Group Profiles* by U.S. Department of Defense, published by U.S. Government Printing Office, Washington, D.C.

3. Primary source: *The Root* by Eric Hammel, 1985, Harcourt, Brace, Jovanovich Publishers, San Diego, New York and London.

4. Figure 6-4, Page 98, "Report of the DOD Commission on Beirut International Airport Terrorist Act, October 23, 1983" dated 20 December 1983.

5. Figure 5-6, Page 79, "Report of the DOD Commission on Beirut International Airport Terrorist Act, October 23, 1983" dated 20 December 1983.

6. "Report of the DOD Commission on Beirut International Airport Terrorist Act, October 23, 1983" dated 20 December 1983.

7. Page 47.

8. Page 58.

9. Page 134.

10. Page 89.

11. Page 135.

12. Page 127.

13. Page 128.

14. Page 133.

15. "Report of the DOD Commission on Beirut International Airport Terrorist Act, October, 23, 1983" dated 20 December 1983.

16. Primary source: *Two Seconds Under the World*, by Jim Dwyer, David Kocieniewski, Deidre Murphy and Peg Tyre, 1994, Crown Publishers, Inc., New York.

17. Primary sources: "U.S. News and World Report", Volume 118, Number 17, May 1, 1995, published by U.S. News and World Report, Inc., Washington, D.C.; "Newsweek", Volume CXXV, Number 18, May 1, 1995, published by Newsweek, Inc., New York, NY; and "Time", Volume 145, Number 18, May 1, 1995, published by Time, Inc., New York, NY.

18. A visit made to the site approximately two and a half years after the detonation indicated that the relative explosive power of the blast was considerably larger than what would normally be produced by an ammonium nitrate bomb of the quantity listed here. The visible damage to the Journal Record Building (masonry construction) and the YMCA Building (concrete construction) could easily be viewed from the public streets. By examining this damage and cross-referencing the pressure ranges identified in nuclear tests at which such damage begins on these types of construction, a prediction of the pressure could be made at these two points which leads to further prediction. By making rough calculations of the distances from the approximate emplacement point, it was possible to cross reference the table of pressures produced by various quantities of explosives in the vulnerability assessment chapter and produce a rough guess of the relative explosive power. It would take approximately nine to ten times the quantity of ammonium nitrate mixture listed in the press to produce that type of pressure at those distances even considering the terrain effects on the pressure wave. Trial testimony indicated that nitromethane was used

to mix with the ammonium nitrate rather than diesel fuel. A nitromethane-ammonium nitrate mix would have a relative explosive factor of 1.196 rather than the .43 relative explosive factor of the diesel mix. This accounts for part of the difference. Trial testimony also indicated that explosives had been stolen from a construction site; the quantity or type stolen was not reported in the press. The addition of a quantity of dynamite, typically found at construction sites, would add a lot of explosive power and probably explains the remainder of the extra pressure. However, the facts printed in the news media and attributed to trial testimony do not account for the full explosive power damage demonstrated on the buildings. The relative explosive power had to be considerably higher to inflict this type of damage at that distance even considering the reflection of the pressure wave from the Murrah Building. The exact quantity of explosive used will probably not be known unless the bombers choose to release it.

19. If the 4,800 pounds listed by the media is the actual size and the RE Factor for ammonium nitrate is used, the explosive power becomes 2395 pounds which produces a pressure wave capable of cracking precast concrete at distances over 100 feet. At 15 feet, the over pressure would still exceed 300 pounds per square inch.

20. Primary sources: "Kansas City Star," Volume 116, Number 283, June 26, 1996 and Volume 116, Number 284, June 27, 1996 published by Kansas City Star Company, Kansas City, MO and a personal tour of duty as Provost Marshal, Khobar Towers during Cease-fire Phase of DESERT STORM.

21. Sources: *Terror Times Two* by Michael Elliott, Newsweek, Volume CXXXII, Number 17, August 17, 1998, Page 22; *Terror in Africa* by Johanna McGreary, Time, Volume 152, Number 7, August 17, 1998, Page 32; multiple articles from the "Kansas City Star," and multiple televised reports from various sources.

22. Primary sources: "Kansas City Star," January 23, 1997 and previous issues, local television reports, a site visit and personal experience the night of the explosion.

23. Primary source: Memory of news media reports at time of occurrence.

24. Primary sources: Multiple issues of "TVI Journal" published by Mark Monday, San Diego, CA; *Terrorist Group Profiles* by U.S. Department of Defense, published by the Superintendent of Documents, Washington, D.C. Additional instances rely upon memory from news media.

25. Multiple articles in "Kansas City Star" and multiple news reports in the electronic media.

Chapter 8

PREVENTIVE ACTIONS AGAINST THE
VEHICLE BOMB (CWMD)

Preventive actions consist of evaluations, preparatory legal analysis, and counterintelligence actions designed to deter the attack by the vehicle bomb (CWMD) or to aid the defense and response to that attack. It begins with the two parts of the risk analysis. First, the threat analysis develops the terrorist group operational profile and the vehicle bomb capability profile. Then, these are applied by the vulnerability analysis to develop the critical prevention, defense, and response tasks for a selected site. As the legal analysis begins, jurisdiction is identified in order to determine specific responsibilities and limitations. Among the primary considerations will be the authority of various governments or agencies; their arrest powers, emergency powers, and call-out or employment guidelines; their use-of-force statutes or policies; the local codes pertaining to structures and materials; and civil requirements for contracts and liabilities. Prevention continues by applying the information obtained and developing counteraction strategies. Part of these strategies will be implemented by various government administrative officials, part by counterintelligence forces, and part by defense forces.

In the evaluation phase of preventive actions, the necessity for further actions is determined. The evaluation begins with the simple determination that the overall situation demands an assessment of the possible risks and development of strategies to deal with whatever risks are found. This evaluation process is generally referred to as risk analysis. It may be composed of many parts, but the two usual ones are the threat analysis of whatever risk is perceived to be present and the vulnerability analysis of whatever operations, facilities, or forces

186

are perceived to be potentially affected by the threat. The details of the threat analysis for a terrorist action were summarized earlier. That analysis produces the threat definition, the terrorist group operational and vehicle bomb (CWMD) capability profiles. The vulnerability analysis was also covered in detail earlier. That analysis produces a listing of specific potential problems and identifies the critical locations, activities, personnel, etc. which must be protected. Once this has been accomplished, the prevention phase begins to develop the implementation of the critical tasks. It does this by examining the viability of various strategies to prevent, to respond, or to otherwise counter the risks involved. This phase may end with theoretical analysis of possible strategies and development of initial courses of action for further study. The courses of action are then examined in detail to determine their applicability, effectiveness, or viability in terms of available resources. The study of the potential courses of action is a decision-making process for the responsible official. It usually begins with the preparatory legal analysis, a study of the legal authority and consequences of the risks and possible counteractions identified.

The preparatory legal analysis begins with a complete review of the jurisdiction applicable to various aspects of the situation. This gets complicated quickly. Beginning at the physical level, the site may be owned either privately or publicly. If the site is under private ownership, actual control of any activity on the property will require the cooperation of the owner and a specific delegation of authority to the security and response forces involved. Some of their activities will require exercise of the business or property owner rights. Consequently, their authority must be clear. This issue will be more complicated when the property is accessible to the public; public officers usually have restricted authority on private property while private security officers usually have restricted authority on public property. Such a division of authority can be exploited by the attacker using a vehicle bomb. Similar problems occur when a private security officer has been contracted to provide security on public property and vice versa. When the ownership of the site and any surrounding locations likely to be affected has been determined, then the application of local codes can be reviewed.

Most planners would not examine local codes initially, as it would seem unrelated to the issue at hand. However, local codes affect three important areas: structural standards, access (ingress and egress), and business operations. Most localities within the United States have implemented building codes. This is exceptionally important as the structural codes applied to the building will give a strong indication of the building's basic ability to withstand a vehicular bombing. Examination of past incidents shows that certain types of structural design requirements are very significant. The low-yield nuclear blasts in Japan at the end of World War II produced blast waves that exceeded the force of one produced by a vehicle bomb. The results are applicable to this topic. Some buildings survived the blast wave, damaged but standing, while those around them were destroyed. A review by American Army officers conducted during the occupation showed that these buildings had been built to survive earthquakes. The difference in building specifications caused them to sufficiently withstand the blast wave produced by the nuclear explosion to prevent collapse. The same significant result can be seen in the World Trade Center blast. The building, due to its unusual height, had been specifically designed to withstand stress from wind acting against its entire height. This design enabled it to withstand the blast wave of the car bomb, damaged, but not collapsing. From these two incidents, it can obviously be concluded that buildings which have been designed to withstand certain natural phenomenon will survive a vehicular bombing without collapsing.

The significant civilian code specifications would be those used for hurricanes, tornados, and earthquakes. The first two are natural phenomenon which utilize the same physical mechanisms to produce damage, air movement (wind), and pressure change. The significance of earthquake specifications is that the structure is designed to prevent collapse as a result of sudden building movement. A pressure wave causes sudden building movement but not in exactly the same manner as an earthquake. Nevertheless, the earthquake standards should be effective in limiting collapse. This will work to reduce possible injuries. The use of such structural standards is an indication of building survivability.

Mechanical and electrical standards are of some importance, but are unlikely to directly affect a building's survivability. They will be more likely to affect the overall number of casualties since these systems deal with ventilation and operation of emergency equipment such as lighting, elevators, or fire suppression systems. To a lesser extent, these specifications may also affect the internal communications or warning system in use inside the structure. These are also addressed by the fire codes which are the next most significant local codes to examine.

Fire codes contain a number of provisions that will directly affect both the defense against and the response to a vehicular bombing. These codes usually contain specifications for "Fire Lanes" and "Fire Exits". This specification of accessibility to a structure by fire equipment will place strong limitations on defensive barrier systems in many locations. Likewise, the evacuation routes required in these codes will affect the ability to limit access for prevention, but may help accessibility of certain interior portions of the structure during a response to any incident. Other sections of the fire code may specify alarm or communication systems, ventilation systems, fire walls, or storage locations for various materials.

The fire alarm systems which are common in public structures are designed to detect problems by heat, smoke, water flow, or deliberate personal activation. As such, the design parameters are not focused on the specific mechanism of damage in the vehicular bombing incident. Consequently, their effectiveness will be limited, particularly when you consider that the system integrity is likely to be disrupted instantly by the blast. Fire detection systems frequently require a relatively long time period to detect and transmit the alarm to either an external central monitoring station or an internal monitoring and relay point. Given the speed of the damaging force in a vehicular bombing, the fire alarm system may fail since it is not specifically designed for survivability in these circumstances. When it does function as intended, it will transmit and sound as a fire alarm. This will result in the initial response of those hearing or receiving the alarm to be focused on fire rather than on the type problem that has occurred.

Ventilation systems may be required by fire codes (or mechanical codes) to have positive pressures to protect certain areas from smoke. Such systems may be damaged by the pressures in the blast as well as having their structural integrity affected by the force. This could allow the protected areas to be filled with smoke from any secondary fires or with other fumes and contaminants. Firewall location and composition will tend to shield certain parts of the structure from damage, possibly limiting collapse or localizing the blast damage. Internal storage locations for hazardous materials may be controlled by the fire code. This raises the possibility that they may be put into exterior, publicly-accessible areas where they may be used to enhance an attack; it will, quite probably, cause their presence to be identifiable to any attacker, regardless of where they are located. Other codes may apply to a site.

State or local traffic codes will quite likely contain parking, standing, turning, or other requirements which will affect entry control. Public health codes may apply in some limited circumstances, and environmental laws in other situations. Certainly, the federal Americans with Disabilities Act and similar state or local laws will strongly affect emplacement of barriers. ADA contains specific provisions for accessibility to public buildings; yet, preventing or limiting access is exactly what is required to prevent or defend against the vehicle bomb. This means that these laws directly conflict with the basic defense purpose. Any defensive action, might actually be illegal under various provisions. Finally, there are various codes, statutes, and regulations which pertain to hazardous materials. These may apply to manufacture, possession, transportation, storage, or usage. The variety of agencies involved here can be quite large in scope. Many of these issues are subject to federal, state, and local control with clear overlap of duties and responsibilities. Determining the requirements contained within these will give some indication of the viability of various courses of action. These codes and statutes may place limitations upon the preventive or defensive courses of action. At the very least, the codes will tend to define the problem areas and to also indicate the resources required for the solutions.

The next preparatory legal area of consideration is the emergency powers of various levels of government. Most states, and some cities, have enacted various emergency powers statutes for use in natural disasters or civil disobedience situations. These statutes typically require a request or declaration of some type by certain officials prior to implementing their provisions. This limits their usefulness in the vehicular bombing situation. There is unlikely to be time to declare an emergency prior to warning of or actual incidence of such an attack. Consequently, the provisions of the statutes may need to be modified. Typically, these statutes contain provisions for call-out of the militia (activation of the National Guard), ability to restrict entry or travel into certain areas, ability to establish curfews in affected areas, authority to utilize state or local resources for immediate private benefit, and specific command and control or support arrangements. States typically designate certain state agencies to command operations in certain circumstances or establish mutual aid compacts applicable between cities or between themselves and other states. This sorts out the finances, authority questions, and similar problems in advance. The actual statutes and codes will have part of the answers, but the administrative procedures in effect will also need to be examined.

These may be the official regulations published by the agency involved or they may be the internal procedures which simply outline how official duties will be performed by an agency. All of these will help outline the necessary procedures for various counteractions. This portion of the legal preparation is intended to identify what the existing arrangements are, what limitations this places upon counteractions, and what changes or additional statutes, codes or contingency contracts (a business or support arrangement that is only used during a disaster or similar incident) may be needed. At this point, it should be clear that any vehicle bomb incident is going to require multijurisdictional counteraction. The scope of the impact of a vehicular bombing literally forces multijurisdictional actions. Consequently, the authority guidelines for civilian versus military operations, public versus private operations, and local versus state or federal operations must be completely considered. Planning can not be done in isolation; it must be joint. The sheer variety of problems that occur can only be addressed by a joint operation. No single governmental organization, no single level of government and no single private party, regardless of size or structure, will possess the authority or assets to deal with the problem. The next area of preparatory legal consideration will be the use of force requirements.

Lawful use of force is typically found in state statutes. The federal government has not legislated use of force by specific statutory law. The federal agencies that utilize deadly force do so based upon executive authority, not specific codes. State and local agencies typically have implementing policies which are based upon the state statutes and upon case law considerations, both criminal and civil. While this makes the situation slightly different in each locality, there are certain similarities which will be the same everywhere. Most states define deadly force as action likely to cause death or serious bodily injury to a person, and limit its use to certain circumstances. The usual circumstances are in defense of a person or, in most states, in defense of a dwelling, defined as a place where a person normally lives. Use of deadly force under other circumstances is mostly prohibited, but may be permissible in some locations. This approach has serious tactical limitations for the engagement of a vehicle bomb by firearms.

The first problem that arises is the simple fact that most of the high-risk locations are either public buildings or gatherings. These locations do not meet the definition of a dwelling. Consequently, an attack on such a location must meet the defense of a person standard in order for the use of force to be lawful under the typical state statute. This forces a delayed decision which is likely to cause tactical engagement failure for the defender. The rules of engagement must vary for each set of circumstances in order to be tactically effective. Accomplishing this will require adjustment. At the very least, a broader spectrum of lawful defense must become incorporated within existing statutes, either formally or informally, to meet the tactical reality. One method of making this adjustment is through the modified use of emergency powers. The third point that arises is the need for statutes which address group actions. As incidents of deliberate resistance to arrest have recurred and escalated, the existence of the gray zone of decision-making is more frequent. Consequently, the need for more clearly drawn policy and statutes has become apparent.

In some of these incidents, there is a clear question whether the boundary between open warfare and criminal conduct has been crossed. The current self-defense and arrest use-of-force statutes do not deal with this issue which is intermingled with the inherent question of the internationally recognized right of self-determination and self-defense against alien domination. Finally, the civil liability law is currently framed in a manner to deal effectively with individual self-defense, but not against attack by vehicle bomb. The theories of self-defense law are based upon conflict between two persons. When the issue becomes conflict between or defense of a collection of individuals, these laws and precedents become cumbersome and inapplicable quickly. Immunity from liability, collective reinsurance, etc. may be necessary to relieve this problem.

Actually, the entire balance of equal individual rights is skewed in the attack by the vehicle bomb. This is clearly illustrated by the Oklahoma City attack where one man was convicted for the murder of over one hundred individuals. The law charged each individual death as a separate count. It did not view the single attack as a collective murder, but rather as the simultaneous occurrence of multiple, individual murders. The criminal law, therefore, views the right of self-defense as exactly the same, simultaneously and repetitively, for each individual attacked. It does not recognize a differing collective right of self-defense for the individual victims that would alter the tactical balance to favor risking the rights of one attacker rather than the rights of the many defenders. The current legalistic balance, therefore, favors the attacker of the many. It allows the attacker to more easily infringe upon the rights of the many, collectively, by use of a vehicle bomb or other weapon of mass destruction in a way that would not be possible by attacking them individually with other weapons. This approach actually tends to deny the right of self-defense to collections of individuals within the United States, requiring them to surrender their rights due simply to the presence of others.

Effective defense against the vehicle bomb (CWMD) requires statutory recognition inside the United States of the collective right of self-defense, and definition of the circumstances where the collective right outweighs the individual right in the self-defense encounter. Under current precedence and statutes, the tactical actions necessary for effective self-defense against the vehicle bomb within the United States would probably qualify as a civil rights violation of the attacker. In the past, the collective right of self-defense was exercised by going to war. The official policy, however, defines terrorism as criminal conduct, not warfare. When a terrorist action is defined as an act of criminality rather than an act of war, the defender surrenders the collective right of self-defense under the current legal system. This surrender of the collective right of self-defense has not been addressed by the implementation of statutes which address that collective right, the common defense, even though it is described by the Constitution as one of the fundamental purposes of the union. This problem has to be addressed in the prevention stage in order to effectively defend against any vehicle bomb within the United States.

Counterintelligence activities are the last of the actions usually implemented during the prevention phase. There are three primary means by which intelligence agencies or police agencies may interrupt the phases of a vehicle bomb attack. The first means is denial of the supply sources. This means may be used during the decision, acquisition, construction, transport, and, possibly, the emplacement phases. In the decision phase, this requires restriction of technical information pertaining to the acquisition or construction of the vehicle bomb. This is difficult, particularly in a democracy that has free access to information including technical information useful for a vehicle bomb (CWMD). Many of the materials necessary to construct the vehicle bomb are easily available, and the manufacturing process is also rather simple. Both require some knowledge, but not a high level of skill. Further, the knowledge is available in a wide variety of sources since many of the acquisition and construction skills are also applicable to other, routine activities within the society. As the quality (relative effectiveness) of the explosive desired for the vehicular bombing increases, the skill needed to acquire and manufacture it increases. This encourages acquisition by illegal means in order to overcome both the access restriction and the skill problem. Regardless of how acquired, once the knowledge has been acquired and the decision made to proceed, physical acquisition and construction begin. The same technique of restricting availability can be applied to the acquisition and construction phases as was applied to the decision phase, but more easily.

In this situation, the society has accepted that regulation of hazardous materials is necessary. Consequently, restricting access to materials usable for a vehicle bomb becomes easier. Licensing, permits, registration, or other purchase and use controls create a screening system which can be utilized by both intelligence or police agencies. This requires that the agencies perform the appropriate coordination with the people who normally perform the regulatory function. This is usually not a law enforcement agency, but an administrator or a private citizen in some type of related business. The primary benefit of such coordination is that it orients the regulator or citizen involved on the necessity of attentiveness during the normal process. Since these individuals are required to monitor or be present during the process, they are the people most likely to detect unusual activity. This coordination is not, however, going to be easy. The sheer quantity of regulatory agencies tends to complicate the task. Fortunately, many of the materials usable for a vehicle bomb are routinely monitored by existing agencies such as BATF which perform such coordination as part of their daily activities.

The second primary means is countersurveillance at the probable targets. The purpose here is to limit the amount of information available to a possible attacker. This is applied generally to all information, but specifically to both the site and the personnel usually employed there. Site technical information such as blueprints or floor plans would be of tremendous benefit in planning an attack with a vehicle bomb. Consequently, access to such information should be controlled as tightly as possible. This is not easy since code administrators, architects, utilities personnel, etc. will all need this information for legitimate activities. Additionally, due to the destructiveness of a vehicle bomb, it will be critical to store such information off-site for effective response to an incident. Limiting of personnel information is also important due to the manner in which it can be exploited. Whether or where certain individuals work in a building may affect the specific emplacement in some circumstances. Also, background information on employees may be used to determine who might be sympathetic to the "cause" and therefore provide assistance of some type. Alternately, such information can be used to determine an exploitable human weakness of certain employees which can be used to assist the attack. Obviously, such activities apply to the decision, acquisition, emplacement and, occasionally, to the construction and transport phases. The third primary means for counterintelligence prevention, monitoring of groups or individuals, is controlled quite closely by a variety of existing laws within the United States. A short review of the basic limitations and division of responsibilities is helpful before examining the type activities.

U.S. Armed Forces are prohibited from routinely gathering information on civilians within the United States. The Central Intelligence Agency is also restricted on performing operations within the United States, but there is a wider range of lawful exceptions to the restrictions than there is for the military. The Federal Bureau of Investigation is delegated the task of counterintelligence activities within the United States, but even they have limitations which control their activities. The foreign intelligence service act[1] and the federal wiretapping[2] provisions contain the most important limitations placed on them. While the provisions are broadly prohibitory in nature, they do provide for national defense exceptions as does the Federal Fair Credit Reporting Act.[3] These are applied in limited circumstances after review by either a special legal panel or other governmental officials. All police agencies would generally be bound by the same restrictions with some state or local agencies having restricting state or local requirements as well. Recognizing the legal limitations, a short discussion of the possible forms of group monitoring follows.

Communications monitoring is the first form of group monitoring. It can take basically three forms without any regard to the type of communication we are monitoring. The first form is communications traffic pattern analysis. In this type, the point is to identify the stations, organizations or people that routinely communicate with each other, the circumstances in which they do so, or the type of communications used. From this, an organizational diagram or sociometric diagram of some type is created. The resulting diagram is then analyzed to check for patterns such as likely authority or supervision, taskings, etc. This analysis is aided by using the second form, format analysis. In this form, the purpose is to reach conclusions about the type of communication. Analysis of this type is based on the simple fact that people tend to communicate in accepted patterns. Two examples would be the format of the standard letter (date, address, salutation, body, and signature) or a simple order (date, buyer, seller, quantity, item description, price, shipping instructions). Various formats for either the word content or the electronic transmission data are in use and can be identified and utilized to help determine both the nature of the relationship between the sender and receiver and the probable content of the communication. This brings us to the final form, content analysis. The purpose of content analysis is to actually read, hear, display, etc. the text of the message and determine what it means. This may be simple or incredibly complex dependent upon whether the message is clear, scrambled, encoded, encrypted, etc. The three forms of communication analysis can be applied individually or in concert to provide a broad spectrum of information and some internal cross-checking of validity.

The next form of group monitoring is infiltration of activities. This is usually done by use of informants or undercover agents, but recruiting or subversion of existing members is also a possibility. The degree of complexity and effectiveness, along with the legality, will vary widely in this monitoring approach. Sometimes this can be accomplished easily using publicly accessible information or opportunities.

Facility identification is the next form of monitoring. This process involves the simple presumption that certain types of social activity must occur or will most probably occur at certain locations. A person staying overnight in a strange city, for example, will most likely be found in a motel, campground, or residence of a friend or relative. By following a similar line of reasoning, certain facilities can be identified as the probable location for collecting information, for purchasing, for transporting, etc. In short, each phase of the vehicular bombing has critical facilities which can be monitored to identify an attack in its early phases and allow counteraction to prevent it.

The same concept can be applied to various supporters of the group. Use of group members at various locations can facilitate operations. By relying upon group members to perform certain activities, the overall activity can be disguised. As an example, the purchase of 100 pounds of dynamite by one individual would be conspicuous while 20 purchases of 5 pounds scattered over a large area would be far less suspicious. Likewise, the arrival of a particular individual is less obvious at a local residence than at a local motel. A group can avoid detection by making its activities appear routine or inconspicuous. The only counter to this is total group identification and monitoring which is very time consuming and expensive in terms of resources. Creating a likely task organization by use of a sociometric diagram can help identify key points in any group which are likely to provide a tip off or warning of vehicle bomb activity.

The final typical means of group monitoring is examination of financial data. Identifying the sources of income or watching the transactions made is a specific form of communication analysis which has broader implications. Not only does it assist in identifying the group structure, it helps identify its facilities, its access to critical materials, and may help determine its capability to act at any given time. Some groups rely upon cash transactions simply to avoid this type monitoring, but this can backfire, making them obvious in some settings or unable to act at a critical time and place. Access to credit or transaction data is limited under the Federal Fair Credit Reporting Act with stronger restrictions on law enforcement than on the private sector. This is one area where cooperation between the two sectors is of immense assistance. A recent change allows access for national defense under limited circumstances with review procedures.

This brings us to the final preventive measure, the defense of a site. Once everything has been gathered and analyzed, it is used to create defense for possible attack sites. While defense serves a preventive purpose, it is more appropriately addressed in a separate section due to its complexity and the finality of its preventive effectiveness. Defense primarily addresses the emplacement phase and secondarily the detonation phase while response orients on the last phase, detonation.

Prevention of a vehicle bomb attack is, for local police forces, primarily an analysis, preparation, and planning activity. The ability of local police forces or private agencies to conduct extensive counterintelligence operations is rather limited. Therefore, local police should concentrate on coordination with appropriate state or federal agencies for overall group monitoring and analysis while concentrating local activities on community contacts for identifying and monitoring critical locations and resources for the attacker and the vehicle bomb. Preparing the defense of local sites and the response to attacks on local sites is the primary area of concern. In short, do not overlook counterintelligence input opportunities, but remember that defense and response actions are the most critical for local agencies. The private sector lacks the authority and impetus to conduct area planning, while the state and federal agencies have higher priorities and an overload of localities. If the local police agency doesn't do the defense and response planning, it probably won't get done.

Notes

1. Foreign Intelligence Surveillance Act of 1978 50 USC 1801.
2. 18 USC 2511.
3. 15 USC 1681.

Chapter 9

DEFENSIVE ACTIONS AGAINST THE
VEHICLE BOMB (CWMD)

A well-planned defense at the site of possible attack is both the final preventive action and the initial response action. As the final measure in prevention, the defensive actions may serve to completely deter the attack by vehicle bomb using various perimeter barriers, access controls, detection devices, and emergency response considerations. However, when the prevention measures fail, the defensive actions become the first part of the response to the attack. In this capacity, it serves to minimize the attack effects to whatever extent is instantly possible. Accomplishing this requires an in-depth understanding of the tasks, their importance, application, and limitations.

The defensive task analysis begins by defining the counteraction to the nature of the attack, the vehicle bomb. There are two parts to the counteraction at the site during the attack: halting the emplacement of the vehicle and deactivating the bomb. Halting the emplacement short of the intended target will work to reduce the effectiveness of the attack, but the bomb must also be deactivated to be completely successful. This is a difficult task combination which is, frankly, unlikely to completely succeed. Consequently, two critical elements of application to a site should be clearly stated as the realistic goal of the defender. These two critical, realistic goals of defense are as follows:

Prevent penetration of the actual building (and possibly selected other areas);
Create survival zones for the building and the people likely to be present.

In this context, a survival zone is defined as an area within which the building remains standing after a detonation. Damage may be extensive, but the structure does not immediately collapse even if so seriously damaged that it must eventually be demolished. For a person, a survival zone is an area in which the person is likely to remain alive after a detonation even if seriously, but not usually fatally, injured. Based on these goal statements, important supporting tasks for defense can be stated:

• Monitor the site and surrounding area for reconnaissance (pre-strike surveillance) by the attacker.

• Establish a denial perimeter by use of barriers and access control procedures which creates both survival zones and safety zones (In this context, a safety zone is an area where the building or any people are likely to receive only minor damage or injuries).

• Establish specific use of force procedures for the individual site that are designed to halt the attack or to detonate it at the most favorable location for the defender.

These three defense tasks constitute the initial mission statement for the defensive action. The final task of these three is actually the first task for response. Goals of the response will be examined further in the next section. Thorough analysis of defensive actions requires an in-depth examination of the various defensive barrier techniques and firepower techniques that may be employed against a vehicle bomb.

TECHNICAL EXAMINATION OF VEHICLE BOMB BARRIER DEFENSE TECHNIQUES

A review of the threat assessment of vehicles and the mobility factors chart just prior to reading this section will be of benefit. The technical components and terminology of a barrier defense system that apply to a vehicular bombing are detailed below in alphabetical order. Some terrain description terms are also included along with commentary on the usage of the barriers.

Barrier Components

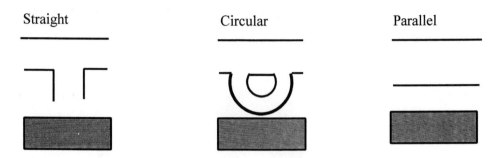

Figure 29. Type entry or approach.

Approach (Figure 29). Generally, the approach is simply the common path, aisle, or route that can be used by the vehicle to arrive at the specific site being defended. A straight approach is one where the vehicle is traveling directly toward the site in a straight line. It is usually perpendicular to the defensive perimeter and frequently ends in a parking lot. A circular approach is one where the vehicle is traveling on a curved line toward the site. Curved approaches usually have a parallel pass by an entrance to the building or a drop-off point before recurving back to the original nearby roadway. A parallel approach is one where the vehicle is traveling toward the site on a route that takes it past on a line that is parallel with the wall of the building. Parallel approaches are predominant in urban areas and frequently pass directly by the entrance to the site. A steep approach is one that has an increasing grade on the roadway (it is uphill). The term can also be used for a sharp angle at the entry point which causes the front of the vehicle to dig into the roadway, slowing or halting it, but this is usually referred to as a steep or sharp approach angle at a specific point to differentiate the term from the overall grade.

Baffle. A screen, of louvered or grid design, or a staggered series of objects that slow, redirect, or breakup a pressure wave to reduce its effectiveness.

Berm. Originally, this technical term referred to the footpath area between the rampart and the escarp (back side of the ditch) in castle defenses of several centuries ago.[1] Now, it is normally used to describe any earthen embankment that is raised above the level of the surrounding terrain. Its common usages are to shield the interior from direct fire or to deter, prevent, or delay attack by vehicle. Berms can be very effective against the vehicular bombing if properly designed and maintained. The materials' cost is usually low while the construction cost is usually high. Berms can channel, halt or slow vehicles and can serve to halt, or deflect the pressure wave.

Figure 30. Sharp breakover.

Breakover (Figure 30). This is any sharp angular surface, over which a vehicle passes, that will normally cause the vehicle to rotate around its center of gravity (usually end-to-end, but could be side-to-side) as it passes over it. Breakovers may be incorporated into berms, roadways, ramps, etc. A high or sharp breakover tends to cause wheeled vehicles to "high center" (hang up on the frame midway between the axles). Tracked vehicles handle a breakover better, but expose their weak-armor bottoms as they climb over them. Breakovers can be defeated by higher speeds which cause the front wheels to leave the ground momentarily, but this can be countered by combining them with other components of the barrier system. High speed also has certain disadvantages for the attacker as the resulting return to earth can damage the bomb components causing it to fail or causing it to simply detonate on impact before it emplaces.

Checkpoint. The physical location of the guard or security station that screens personnel or vehicles entering the area.

Clearance barriers. See width restrictions and overhead barriers.

Crossarm or crash bar (Figure 31). A crossarm or crash bar is simply a pole, pipe, plank, rail, etc. that is installed perpendicular to the roadway so that it can be lowered to a blocking position or raised for entry. It usually is counterweighted and pivots around a point at the side of the roadway. Simple models are typically operated by the security personnel physically or may have electrical or hydraulic controls. Crossarms are most effective in low traffic areas where they can be left down most of the time. Crossarms are usually installed so that the arm is at windshield height for the vehicle. This is done to interfere with driver action rather than to actually halt the vehicle. Halting a moving vehicle with a crossarm requires a massive crossarm which makes it difficult to operate or causes it to operate so slowly that it cannot be deployed in the defensive reaction time available.

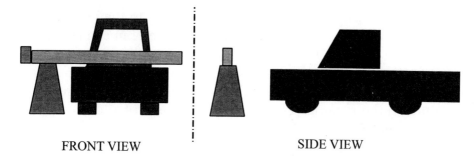

FRONT VIEW   SIDE VIEW

Figure 31. Crossarm or crash bar. Crossarms are installed at
windshield height to deter driver.

Curb (Figure 32). The slight rise at the edge of a roadway which serves to define the edge, channel water, and redirect vehicles back onto the roadway. A curb of one-third the vehicle wheel height will interfere with the steering while a curb of one-half the wheel height will interfere with the axle.

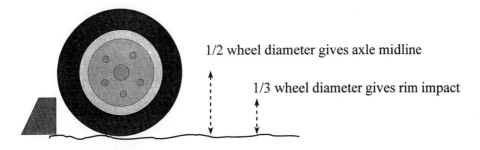

1/2 wheel diameter gives axle midline

1/3 wheel diameter gives rim impact

Figure 32. Curb and wheel interaction. One-half wheel diameter causes axle impact;
one-third wheel diameter gives rim impact.

Decision point. A physical location or a procedural step that requires an attacker or defender to make a tactical choice of alternative courses of action.

Deflector. A surface or object which is intended to redirect a pressure wave. Deflectors are normally integrated into other portions of the barrier system such as a berm.

Dip. A small ditch or depression in an approach normally used in reference to a sudden perpendicular fall and rise in the roadway elevation.

Ditch. An excavation in front of the rampart (berm).[2] In current usage, any trench that is along or in the approach to the defense site. A ditch is very effective in halting wheeled vehicles, but can be defeated by higher speeds. It must be wide enough to prevent jumping at higher speeds or it must be integrated with other measures to be effective. Ditches are much more easily defeated by tracked vehicles. Depending on the material used, ditches may require a lot of maintenance, particularly in certain weather conditions.

Dividers (Figure 33). A pole, rail, etc. used to separate one lane of travel from another. A "Jersey Barrier" is a divider; it was originally designed to prevent vehicles from crossing the medial area of superhighways by turning them back into their lane of travel. This means that a Jersey barrier was originally intended to be emplaced parallel to the approach, not perpendicular to it. A Jersey barrier is highly effective at turning a vehicle back into its parallel lane of travel but much less effective at dealing with a perpendicular force hit. It will typically fall over or rotate when struck in this way. If it falls over, it has the advantage of being high enough to prevent vehicles from driving over it, but will still need to be reset into an upright position. This problem and the rotation problem can be partially overcome by fastening the barrier firmly in place. Most locations using these barriers for vehicle bomb defense have not done this.

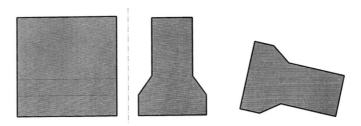

Figure 33. Jersey barrier. Concrete dividers are easily emplaced, but should be fastened together. An overturned barrier still has sufficient height to stop most vehicles.

Drop barrier *or* ***Deadfall*** (Figure 34). A gate, roadway section, etc. that is designed to fall or collapse when activated.

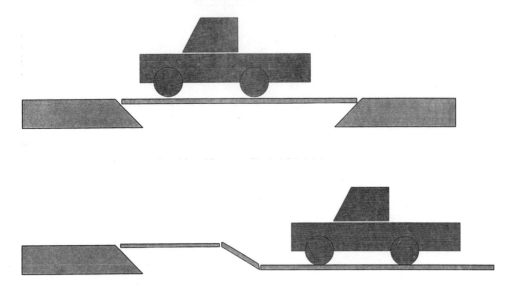

Figure 34. Vehicle deadfall. Weight or entry speed limit is set so that deadfall collapses when predetermined force limit is exceeded.

Glacis. "An elevated mound of earth on the country side of the ditch, ... , so that an enemy attacking the ditch must move up it and thus be exposed to fire from the parapet."[3] A glacis is basically a slope on the approach to the site. It is clearly advantageous to force the attacker to drive uphill as this limits the ability to accelerate easily giving the defense more response time. As you can see from the definition, a glacis was integrated with the ditch in castle defense. This is a concept worth remembering.

Guardrails. A series of upright posts or poles along the edge of a roadway to which has been fastened a long pole, plank or beam. It is intended to prevent the vehicle from going off of the roadway at that point. It is actually a vehicle fence. In the United States, they are typically made of metal posts to which are fastened formed, essentially flat, long metal plates.

Hedgehogs (Figure 35). A military vehicle obstacle formed by three large beams or rails that are fastened together at the centers to form a tripod. When viewed from a distance, it usually appears to be a large "X." Easily constructed, installed, and moved (with lifting equipment), they may be set in concrete for larger vehicles. Highly effective, it is capable of stopping both wheeled and tracked vehicles. However, it is rather ugly in appearance for urban applications.

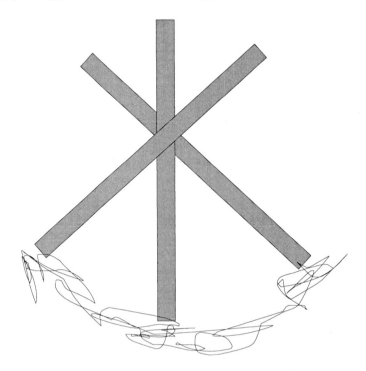

Figure 35. Hedgehog. Manufactured locally. Size determines defensive capability.

Load limit. The total weight or force that a vehicle exerts downward on the roadway or approach. The entry route can be designed with a load limit that slows a vehicle approaching (such as loose sand) or a collapsing section that simply falls or otherwise activates when too much force is applied to it.

Overhead barrier (Figure 36). A height restriction that prevents entry of vehicles that are too tall. Very effective against trucks, this is the easiest method of screening out trucks while accepting cars. Extremely effective when paired with a sharp breakover surface.

Overwatch position (Figure 37). The physical location of the guard or security position that monitors or backs up the checkpoint. It is usually the location of the heavy firepower of the defense. This modern terminology refers to the same defensive concept applied in castle defenses from the parapet.

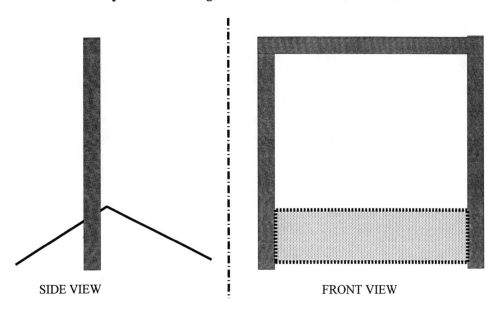

SIDE VIEW   FRONT VIEW

Figure 36. Sharp breakover with overhead barrier.

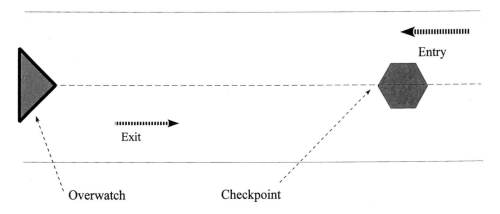

Figure 37. Overwatch and checkpoint relationship. Arriving vehicles halt at checkpoint for entry clearance; armed officer in overwatch covers vehicle.

Parapet. A bank of earth over which a soldier may fire. In permanent works, it crowns the rampart. Also known as a breastwork.[4] Included primarily for terminology use. A parapet is not recommended for several reasons; the primary one is exposure of the defender during firing over the top. The DePuy method of firing around cover rather than over it should be implemented if possible. However, the parapet's placement in the old castle defenses is significant and gives a clue to appropriate anti-wheeled vehicle combat.

Posts. Sometimes referred to as pickets or palisades in special usages, the simple post can be used to supplement the primary barrier line. The post should be of a solid material such as metal, reinforced concrete, or a hollow pipe filled with concrete. The minimum size is approximately four inches in diameter with a height above the frame level of the vehicle to be halted. Above the required frame level, additional height will add visibility of the barrier which will be important to prevent unnecessary damage to the barriers or vehicles routinely operating in the area. Can be made with lifting handles or rings to allow the barriers to be removed for emergency access such as into firefighting lanes mandated in urban settings.

Rampart. A bank of earth behind a ditch.[5] This term is not typically in use and has been replaced with "berm." The defensive concept is the same regardless of the term.

Reverse banking (Figure 38). In roadway construction, the surface of the curves are usually sloped toward the inside of the turn (the portion of the roadway with the smaller radius). This is done to help keep the vehicle on the roadway; it takes advantage of the centrifugal force being exerted outward by the vehicle. In reverse banking, the surface is sloped toward the outside of the curve. This causes the vehicle to have more tendency to go off the roadway or overturn as the vehicle speed increases. This will effectively reduce the attack speed which extends the time available for defensive response. One clear advantage of reverse banking is that it requires no further action by the security force in order to operate. Certain adverse weather conditions can cause serious problems for this barrier.

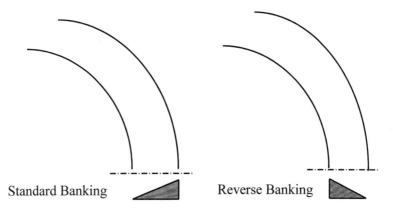

Standard Banking   Reverse Banking

Figure 38. Reverse banking. Standard slope toward center of curve assists turning at higher speeds. Reverse banking tends to throw vehicle out of control.

Sally port (Figure 39). Originally, an opening cut in the glacis at the faces of the reentering places of arms and at the branches of the covered way to allow raiding parties to leave the work and regain it.[6] Now the term is used to refer to a controlled entry point which has a series of obstacles, usually gates, through which anyone entering must pass sequentially. Normally, one gate or barrier must close or bar the way before the next can be opened. This slows the entry process to allow the defender a lot of control.

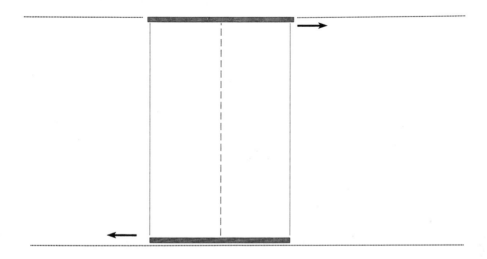

Figure 39. Sally port entry. Barriers block vehicle entry and are sequentially opened after the first closes.

Slalom (Figure 40). A series of obstacles placed on a roadway that cause a vehicle to turn left and right in order to "weave" its way through. A slalom prevents a straight run on a direct approach and tends to reduce vehicle speed which increases the available defensive response time. Effective in this one respect, this system has serious problems in operation. A slalom which effectively slows a car down completely halts larger vehicles. A slalom which works well for truck entry is easily negotiated by a car. Most important, a slalom actually blocks a large portion of the field of fire during an attack. This is a serious drawback. Slalom placement and design are the most frequent error made in this type of barrier defense, but it is usually the first type of barrier defenders think about using. In actual operation, slaloms require a lot of maintenance as they are typically being sideswiped and moved out of position by large vehicles or just hit and broken. The best usage of a slalom is on the approach to the initial checkpoint, not between the checkpoint and the overwatch point.

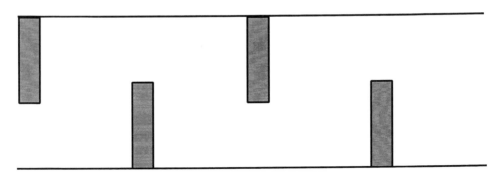

Figure 40. Slalom. Typically emplaced on existing entry points, but may interfere with defensive fire. Proper placement and spacing is critical.

Speed bump (Figure 41). A deliberate, sharp rise in the elevation of the roadway, usually a small ridge in design. It is intended to cause the vehicle to bounce noticeably and convince the driver to slow down. In normal usage for safety, speed bumps are installed perpendicular to the direction of travel. For vehicle bomb defense, they should be installed at an angle greater than 90 degrees to the direction of travel (the closest end of the speed bump to the direction of the vehicle approach is the apex of the angle). This causes the vehicle wheels to strike it at slightly different times which tends to turn the vehicle. By integrating this with another defensive measure, at higher speeds the vehicle can be turned in a way that will tend to cause it to crash. The advantage of speed bumps in this application is that they do not require operation by the defense force and that they tend to jar the vehicle sufficiently to cause failure of the bomb construction or detonation at that point.

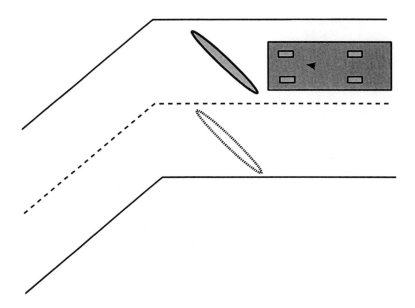

Figure 41. Speed bumps and dips. Bumps and dips are angled from, not perpendicular to, the vehicle line of travel. Placing near curve is very effective.

Spikes. Spike barriers are simply pointed objects that protrude upward from the roadway or outward from the walls. They come in a wide variety of forms from the simple caltrop to complex hydraulic or air-activated systems that pop up out of the roadway. Spike barriers are of limited effectiveness against a vehicle bomb. First, they are hard to emplace in front of an attacking vehicle. While this can be overcome with certain mechanical, hydraulic or electrical systems, the installation and maintenance cost is high and it does not overcome the primary problem. Second, all that a spike barrier can accomplish under favorable circumstances is to blow out the vehicle tires. This reduces its maneuverability, but does not stop it. The attacking vehicle can keeping moving to the intended emplacement point, especially if it has "run-flat" tires which are now common in many parts of the world.

Standoff distance or range (Figure 42). The distance at which you are outside of the range of effectiveness of the opponent's weapon system.

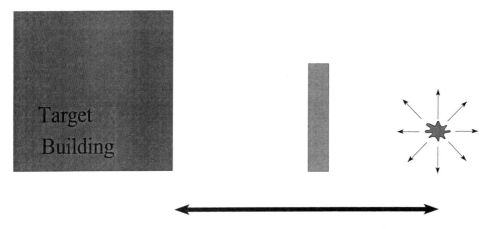

Figure 42. Standoff range. The distance at which a target is no longer affected by the opposing weapon. In this case, a conventional weapon of mass destruction with an intermediate barrier.

Terrain shield. A natural part of the geographic area such as a hill, embankment, slope, forest, etc. which is located where it actually shelters the defended site from the onset or the effects of an attack.

Tetrahedron (Figure 43). A framed or solid object formed by joining the edges of four equilateral triangular surfaces. Sometimes called "dragon's teeth." They are made of joined steel beams or solid concrete in varying sizes. Easily constructed, emplaced, or moved, they are effective in halting various sizes of vehicles by entangling the axles or frame as the vehicle tries to run over them. Obviously, the larger the size, the larger the vehicle that they will halt and the larger the lifting equipment needed to move them.

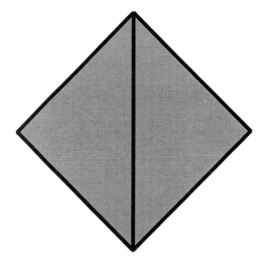

Figure 43. Tetrahedron. Sometimes called "Dragon's Teeth." Manufactured locally; used in depth. Retains same height when knocked over.

Trap zone. An area where the barrier system is designed to halt a vehicle bomb for engagement by fire, deactivation, or detonation. It may also be referred to as a kill zone, tactical engagement area, fire sack, etc. As used in this setting, it is intended to serve the purposes of both a tactical engagement area and an entry sally port.

Turning restriction (Figure 44). A curve on the entry route with a short inner radius that prevents long wheelbase vehicles from turning while remaining on the roadway. This is an excellent way to screen out larger vehicles while allowing small vehicles easy access.

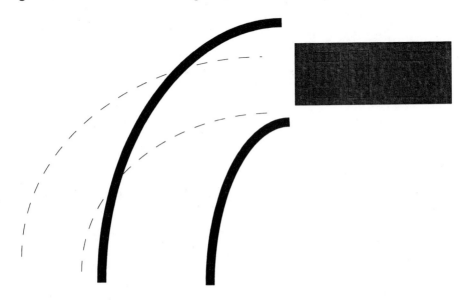

Figure 44. Turning restriction. The vehicle turning radius (dotted line) is larger than the radius of the curve (solid line).

Vent pit (Figure 45). A depressed or embanked area along the vehicle entry route where the constructed barrier system or the natural terrain shields the defended site when a vehicle bomb detonates. The pressure wave is deflected or redirected, usually upward, or in another direction that causes minimal damage.

SIDE VIEW CUTAWAY

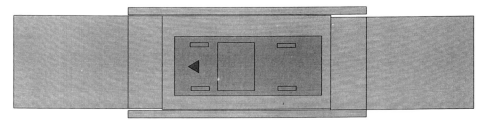

TOP VIEW

Figure 45. Vent pit. Vehicle pulls into an explosive ventilation pit and waits for clearance to procee.

Walls. A narrow, vertical berm. For use against vehicles, they represent the ultimate in a sharp approach angle. Walls can shield a site from the effects of a blast, but are usually not designed to do so. Consequently, they will frequently fail in this regard. Depending upon their material and design, they may not be strong enough to prevent a vehicle from penetrating them. Most walls are designed to restrict movement of people, not vehicles. In some cases, the wall may actually increase damage rather than decrease it dependent upon a variety of factors.

Width restriction. A point along the normal entry route for vehicles which is narrow enough to prevent a large vehicle from passing. An excellent way to screen large vehicles while allowing small vehicles to enter.

TECHNICAL EXAMINATION OF VEHICLE BOMB DEFENSIVE FIRE

The second portion of the technical aspects of defensive action is an examination of the use of typical police firearms against a vehicle bomb. Police officers and security officers within the United States are typically armed with small caliber, personal firearms and some limited explosive devices. Here is a rundown of the firearms, ammunition, and firing techniques typically available, and an analysis of their effectiveness against this type attack.

Types of Firearms

Handguns. Most police officers, many private security officers, and occasional national guard personnel will have handguns available for defensive use. Realistically speaking, a handgun can seldom be effectively employed against a vehicle. First, only well-trained officers will be able to reliably hit the necessary aiming points on the vehicles at distances of 25 yards or less. Actually, most officers need distances of 10 yards or less to be reliable. The second problem is that most handgun calibers have difficulty penetrating parts of a vehicle, particularly with the hollowpoint rounds typically found in police use at the current time. Due to these considerations, the only aiming point of any usefulness is the vehicle driver who is typically obscured by various body parts from the angle of a ground level firer, particularly in a truck after it has passed the checkpoint. The effectiveness of handguns in this application can be increased by use of armor-piercing rounds and larger calibers. Armor piercing rounds will be illegal for private security officers and are rarely actually available to police officers. National Guard personnel can easily obtain and use armor-piercing rounds but usually are not issued them when assigned to law enforcement duties.

Shotguns. Many police officers, an occasional private security officer, and very few national guard personnel will have shotguns available for defensive use. Most officers issued shotguns can effectively engage a vehicle at 25 yards, and possibly out to 50 yards. Shotguns have the advantage that a wide range of ammunition is typically available for them. Buckshot is highly effective when the aiming point is a vehicle's tires but less effective against the other aiming areas on a vehicle. Buckshot ballistic capability drops significantly at longer ranges (25 - 50 yards). However, shotguns also have rifled slugs available. Slugs are reliable for penetrating body parts of most vehicles. Consequently, they are the best choice for this type of engagement.

Rifles. A few police officers, almost no private security officers, and virtually all National Guard personnel will have rifles available to them. Most rifle firers can reliably engage vehicular targets at ranges out to 100 yards. Rifles have the advantage that almost all typical calibers have sufficient muzzle energy to reliably penetrate the average vehicle body making them useful against most trucks without regard to angle of fire. Smaller caliber rifles may need to rely upon armor-piercing or full metal jacket rounds to accomplish penetration. Use of rifles against vehicle bombs is recommended where the choice can be implemented. The power and range of the rifle round will need to be part of the planning as detailed later.

Carbines. Police agencies have been implementing the use of "pistol-caliber" carbines (a short-barreled rifle which is chambered to fire a cartridge normally used only in handguns). This is an attempt by police agencies to overcome the spread or unpredictability of the pellet pattern with buckshot, the likely overpenetration problems found with shotgun slugs in many settings, and the strong recoil of the typical 12-gauge shotgun in use by most agencies. It is also an attempt to overcome the strong penetration of the usual rifle round. This is of primary concern to urban agencies where maximum ranges frequently do not exceed 100 yards due to the surrounding buildings. Availability of carbines will be similar to that found for rifles among police officers and very rare among private security officers or National Guard personnel. Carbines with legal length barrels (16" or greater) will probably perform reliably through vehicle bodies, but carbines with shorter barrels may fail to penetrate depending upon the cartridge caliber, load and bullet chosen. Police departments using pistol-caliber carbines may wish to test penetration before using in this type of defensive setting.

Automatic weapons. Firearms capable of automatic fire are occasionally available to police officers, particularly tactical teams, seldom available to private security officers, and almost always available to National Guard personnel. They are recommended in this type of engagement with full automatic rather than burst control probably being a better selection in most circumstances.

Military crew-served weapons. A number of military weapons are available to the National Guard personnel that will probably not be available to police officers or private security officers. These systems should be utilized where feasible since they are designed to engage vehicles in combat circumstances. The effectiveness of these systems varies by type and by the particular circumstances at the defense site.

Many would not be feasible for employment in civilian urban settings where a vehicle bomb is most likely to be used. Many combat vehicles might actually have difficulty trying to engage a truck under these circumstances due to the exact design characteristics of the combat weapon system and the typical short engagement range in this setting.

Ammunition

Ammunition selected for use against vehicle bombs should be full metal jacket with armor-piercing capability being an advantage under most circumstances. Hollowpoint rounds should be avoided whenever possible due to their poor penetration capability and the possible legal ramifications. Pointed or round-nose bullets are preferred due to their superior penetrating capability. Jacketed flat-nose rounds are usually acceptable, but not preferred. Heavy grain (weight) bullets will probably outperform lighter bullets in this usage.

Explosive Devices

Some police officers and National Guard personnel will have explosive devices available. Most of these will have little effect since hand-thrown devices would most likely need to be inside the vehicle to be effective, particularly those flash-bang devices usually available to police officers. While they may provide a distraction that affects the driver, the overall performance would be expected to be low. In some settings, command detonated land mines would be feasible for National Guard personnel, but their installation would most likely be viewed very negatively in a civilian, public setting. There is some potential for effective use of explosives against the exterior of the vehicle in all settings. Their use requires an automatic timing device in order to insure proper timing against the attack, but should include sequential arming steps with command detonation as one step for overall safety.

Aiming Points

There are four aiming points for firearms usage against the usual wheeled vehicle that can potentially halt it. They are:

Fuel tank. A hit of the fuel tank can cause a loss of fuel which will eventually stop the engine. The amount of time necessary for this to occur makes this aiming point of no use for defense against vehicle bombs.

Radiator or engine area. A hit of the radiator in a water-cooled system will eventually cause the engine to overheat and lock up if it continues operation. Hits on various other engine components could conceivably cause engine stoppage, but the probability of hitting these parts effectively with a firearm is very low. Many of the engine component hits, including the radiator hits, would be of no value since the amount of time necessary to halt the engine due to the damage would be too long to prevent emplacement of the vehicle bomb. Certain antiarmor weapons can effectively be employed against the engine, but these are not available to police officers and private security officers. National Guard personnel have these weapons available but may not be able to utilize them for a variety of reasons.

Tires. A hit on the tires slows the vehicle and affects its maneuverability, but firearms hits on the tires are unlikely to halt the vehicle unless the driving surface is soft and the wheel now digs into the surface. On hard surfaces, the vehicle can continue to move for long distances on the wheel rims. The tires themselves are more difficult to hit from the front of the vehicle than from the side due to their natural profile and size, but the side shot hit probability on the tires will be degraded by the vehicle movement while the front shot would retain the relatively static target during movement. Additionally, "run-flat" tires with internal stiffeners that keep a flat tire up are commonly available. This degrades the effectiveness of hitting them with gunfire at all. The final problem is that tire shots are frequently blocked by portions of the barrier system in use such as improperly positioned slaloms. Tire shots, consequently, are of very little usefulness in defending against an attack by a vehicle bomb.

Driver. The driver is the most effective aiming point for quickly disabling the vehicle bomb. Aside from the legal and moral considerations involved, there are two tactical problems with use of this aiming point. First, killing the driver does not halt the vehicle; it only stops his control. The vehicle will continue to move until it strikes something solid, overturns, stalls, or is shutdown by the security force. In short, the vehicle could conceivably emplace itself even with a dead driver. Second, the attacker may have been dedicated enough to plan for this possibility. The usual such plan is to utilize a "dead man" switch (a fail-safe) of various designs which will activate the bomb at the time the driver dies or shortly thereafter. Consequently, while the driver is the most effective aiming point for disabling the vehicle, even this does not necessarily accomplish the first defensive subtask, halting the emplacement of the vehicle.

Vehicle cargo area. The final aiming point, the cargo area, is the most effective in one respect. Targeting the cargo area is based upon certain assumptions. First, this assumes that the actual explosive device is in this area. Second, it assumes that the gunfire will cause the device to activate, a possibility whenever the vehicle is taken under fire regardless of aiming point. In this case, that is the intention. The third assumption is that we have a specific location where we prefer to have the bomb detonate. This technique definitely prevents emplacement, but does so by accepting actual damage at a more favorable location for the defender. Even so, this technique may fail since there is always the possibility that repeated gunfire into the explosive may not cause it to detonate.

Aspect of Fire

The aspect of fire is the angular relationship of the firer to the target; in this case, the police officer to the attacking vehicle. There are a couple of observations which need to be made. For reference purposes, consider the front of the vehicle as the 12 o'clock position for both horizontal and vertical axis with 3 o'clock being to the vehicle's right in the horizontal axis and directly above the vehicle in the vertical axis. During the comments below, it will be assumed that the firer and the vehicle are on flat terrain with the firer engaging the target from a standing position.

Moving vehicle. A moving vehicle presents a relatively static target from the 12 and 6 o'clock positions, making engagement most favorable from those positions with oblique shots between 11 to 1 and 5 to 7 o'clock (moving clockwise) retaining much of this advantage for the firer. This is commonly understood. What is usually missed is the favorable angles for certain aiming points on the horizontal axis and any consideration of the vertical axis at all.

Shielding effects. Certain portions of automotive vehicles will normally stop gunfire or at least slow or deflect it. The portions that usually stop bullets are engine block, transmission, differential or axles, wheels, frame, and most door pillars. Parts that may stop bullets are internal door safety beams, window operating mechanisms, bumpers, and some heavy truck cargo floors or sides.

Aiming point—Fuel tank and engine. Not considered since they are completely ineffective for defensive engagement with firearms against the vehicle bomb.

Aiming point—Tires. In the horizontal axis, the tires can be engaged from any angle with engagements from 2 to 4 or 8 to 10 o'clock, exposing larger surfaces of the tires. In the vertical axis, the tires can only be directly engaged from 7 to 11 o'clock angles.

Aiming point—Driver; horizontal axis. On a left hand drive vehicle (U.S. Style) the driver can be engaged from virtually any angle in a standard car but will have intervening obstacles from certain positions. The engine and transmission (assuming the most frequent front engine design) tend to shield the driver somewhat from the 11 to 1 o'clock firing positions; door pillars will provide shielding from various positions (changing with the car design); and door safety beams or window mechanisms provide some protection from the 8 to 10 o'clock and 2 to 4 o'clock positions. On a truck, notice that the driver can only be seen from the positions of about 9 clockwise to 2 o'clock and that the cargo body provides some shielding from the 4 to 9 o'clock positions. The truck driver has the same basic shielding advantage from the engine, transmission, etc as a car driver.

Aiming point—Driver; vertical axis. Notice that the shielding effects of the engine in a car occur between 10 to 12 o'clock while the standing firer is typically engaging from the 1 o'clock angle. The window and door pillars shield between 12 to 2 o'clock and 8 to 2 o'clock respectively. Door components shield at about the 12 o'clock position. This changes dramatically on a truck; the cab usually sets much higher from the ground. A truck driver is still shielded by the engine from the 10 to 12 o'clock positions, but the standing firer is typically engaging from the 11 o'clock angle. The window and door pillars shield the truck driver from the 12 to 2 o'clock and 8 to 2 o'clock respectively which moves the window pillars out of the line of fire from the 11 o'clock position. The internal window mechanisms shield from about 11 to 12 o'clock positions; larger trucks do not have door safety beams as the side collision impacts occur lower on the vehicle so less passenger protection is needed. The cargo bed of the truck tends to shield from the 11 o'clock to 3 o'clock positions. The truck frame tends to shield from the 10 o'clock firing position.

Aiming point–Cargo area; horizontal axis. The cargo area is screened by the engine in the 11 to 1 o'clock firing positions. Occasional shielding by door pillars, internal door side beams, etc. will mostly occur through the same arc. The shielding will be basically the same for cars and trucks, but trucks will have better cargo area exposure even from the 11 to 1 o'clock position.

Aiming point–Cargo area; vertical axis. The cargo area of a car is normally in the 4 to 6 o'clock range but is generally accessible throughout the 12 to 7 o'clock range. This will hold true for trucks as well. The primary difference will be the angle of the firer's position which will remain about 1 o'clock for firing at cars and 11 o'clock for firing at trucks.

A summary of the critical parts of this discussion and diagrams on aspect of firing is as follows:

A standing firer has a tactical advantage when firing at a car that he loses when firing at a truck. That advantage is the downward aspect of his fire which clears the parts of the vehicle that would normally shield the driver or cargo area.

A firer who engages directly from the front or the rear gains a relatively static target, an advantage which he does not have when firing from the sides of the moving vehicle. The latter requires "leading" the target in order to hit it. This reduces hit probability.

Firing at tires is impractical from any firing position excpect prone, and is of little tactical value in most settings anyway. Consequently, tire attack should be left to spike barriers which deploy from the ground upward or disregarded entirely.

The most favorable horizontal firing positions are from 11 to 1 o'clock and 5 to 7 o'clock due to the moving target (Figure 46), but the frontal vertical limiting shield of the engine (11-1) must be considered. Firing from other positions may work, but they have lesser hit probability.

The most favorable vertical firing positions are from 1 to 2 o'clock or 4 to 5 o'clock (Figure 47). Firing positions from 2 to 4 o'clock would work, but are difficult to obtain in this defensive setting. This angle is recommended due to its clearance of the natural shields of the vehicle components. *The critical point to note is that defensive fire against the vehicle front (11-1 horizontal) must be made from a high angle (1-2 vertical) to clear the shielding effect of the engine.*

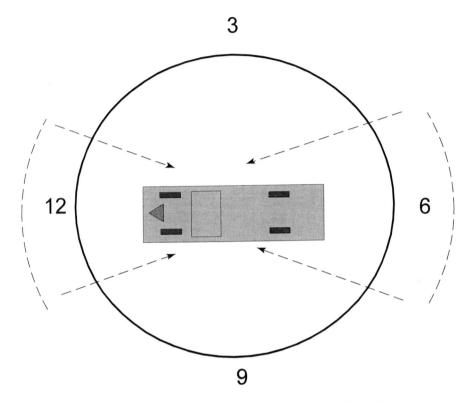

Figure 46. Horizontal axis. Favorable firing angles are indicated by arrows.

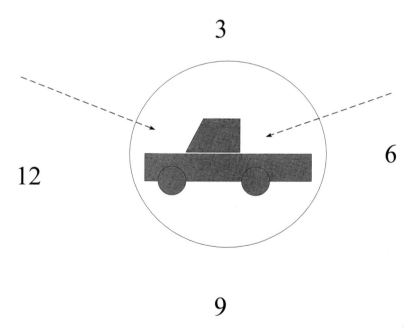

Figure 47. Vertical axis. Favorable firing angles are indicated by arrows.

Legal Decisions for Use of Deadly Force Against the Vehicle Bomb

The decision to fire at a vehicle bomb in a civilian setting by the police officer, private security officer, or National Guard personnel will be determined under the laws of the state in which the incident occurs unless martial law has been declared in the area being defended or an act of war has or is occurring. Having addressed the difficulties with this issue in an earlier chapter, martial law and acts of war will be disregarded for simplicity in this chapter. The assumption will be that this vehicle bomb attack is a criminal act and defense and response is made to it on that basis. The first consideration in the decision is the imminent danger standard and its application at the specific time and place.

Imminent danger. Most state use of force law specifies that deadly force may be used to defend when there is an imminent danger of death or serious bodily injury to a person. A vehicle bomb becomes an apparent danger at the point when it is assembled as a workable explosive, called a destructive device under current law. This occurs when the fuse, initiating charge, and main charge are together. It reaches the status of imminent danger when it has the present capability to detonate. The present capability to detonate can be achieved in two ways: a person of criminal intent is in its proximity or a person of criminal intent has activated a fusing mechanism which no longer requires his presence to detonate the bomb. Notice that the key difference between its apparent danger state and its imminent danger state is its capability to activate on command. That command is fulfilled either by a person directly controlling it or by a person activating an automatic feature no longer requiring personal control. To simplify it, use the term "activated" to mean either command or delay detonation in use of force instructions as the basis for determining imminent danger.

Defense of a person. Imminent danger exists when a vehicle bomb is both activated and any person is within the destructive range of the explosion that could result when it detonates. This means that deadly force can be directed against a car or truck bomb at any point between its assembly site and its emplacement site. (Ridiculous as it seems, the presence of the mad bomber in the driver seat of the truck bomb fulfills the second element of the legal requirement.)

Defense of a dwelling. Many states have statutes which allow use of deadly force when there is imminent danger to a dwelling (a place where a person lives). Imminent danger exists when a vehicle bomb is both activated and any personal dwelling is within the destructive range of the explosion that could result when it detonates. It may not matter whether the dwelling is actually occupied at the exact instant of imminent danger, only that it typically is. This differentiation is placed in statutes primarily for civil liability issues relating to demonstrating that deadly force by an aggressor was targeted at a specific person in a dwelling. In some states, however, it may matter whether the defender uses the dwelling himself.

Defense of property other than a dwelling. Most state statutes prohibit the use of deadly force in defense of property that is not a dwelling.

> It is important to point out several observations at this juncture in the discussion:
>
> The key element in imminent danger for a vehicle bomb is its activation potential.
>
> A government building, or business building, seldom qualifies as a dwelling. Consequently, a vehicle bomb directed against a government building must meet the legal test of endangering a person before use of deadly force is justified under state laws.[8]
>
> Notice that the current situation in state statutes allows one person in his own home a greater justification in the use of force than several hundred assembled at a public place. This points out a legal weakness in our current self-defense and use of force laws when applied to vehicle bombs.
>
> The classification of buildings as dwellings or not is mostly immaterial in the case of the vehicle bomb. Their destructive range is so large that they will almost always be endangering a person without regard to how the building classifies.
>
> Finally, notice that the security official engaging the target is usually within the destructive range of the vehicle bomb. His presence alone establishes the second element of the legal requirement of imminent danger.

Having stated all of that, it should be obvious to those familiar with self-defense and use of force statutes that there is no difference in the legal right to use deadly force against a vehicle bomb for a police officer, a private security officer, or a National Guard member deployed by the state. While police officers typically have a greater right to use deadly force under most state statutes than a private security officer or other private citizen, there is seldom any difference in the right to defend when a person is in imminent danger. A National Guard member deployed by the state almost always has the legal authority of a police officer of the state. This is usually established by statutes but is sometimes established by executive regulation or proclamation. The difference in the justification of these three categories of personnel in this decision will not be found in the right to use force as determined by statutory elements of various state laws but rather in their legal responsibility for their decision to use deadly force as developed in case precedents on the statutory elements of those various state laws.

Objective reasonableness. In reviewing the shooting decisions of police officers, the courts have established and relied upon the test of "objective reasonableness" to determine whether an officer's decision to fire was justified. This test is stated in Graham vs Connors:[9] "The question is whether the officers' actions are 'objectively reasonable' in the light of the facts and circumstances confronting them ..." The point in question was whether a police officer was justified in firing when the officer's belief of what was occurring proved to be wrong. Working from the common reasonable belief doctrine, the court ruled that the decision was supportable if it was reasonable at the time the decision had to be made. When it proved to be based on an inaccurate assessment by the officer, the error was viewed as one a reasonable man would make in those circumstances. Consequently, the test of justification is to be based on what the officer knew at the time of the shooting decision.

Applying this court precedent, objective reasonableness, to a vehicle bomb (CWMD), the legal question is not whether an imminent danger exists but when a reasonable man could tell that it was a present capability. Like a firearm, a vehicle bomb constitutes a deadly weapon under all but unusual circumstances. Unlike a firearm, an officer looking at a vehicle bomb cannot necessarily tell that it is a weapon. This is similar to a concealed firearm situation. The firearm is a deadly weapon while concealed, but an officer is taught to fire only when he can determine that the firearm is present and about to be used. This same concept applies directly to the vehicle bomb. It is a concealed weapon when its assembly as a destructive device is complete. It is an imminent danger the moment it is activated since the unlawful intent is present. The officer tasked to defend a specific site, however, only becomes objectively aware of the imminent danger at the point where he can identify the specific car or truck as a moving bomb rather than an ordinary form of transportation. Consequently, the officer's judgment training to engage a vehicle bomb, the site deadly force instructions, and the overall site defense measures must orient on the identification of the weapon. In short, the defensive barrier and procedures must create a decision point where the vehicle bomb self-identifies as a weapon rather than a simple vehicle; the attacker is forced to attack in a way that identifies him as an aggressor. The officer's judgment decision then changes from *whether there is danger to when it is present.* The physical security procedures and design of the decision point must force a tactical decision to commit to the attack, clearly demonstrating the presence of danger while simultaneously providing notice and opportunity for those of innocent intent to demonstrate the absence of danger (The latter part of that statement is a higher legal standard than typically demanded of an ordinary citizen in this country). This identification decision is so difficult to make that it should not be left solely to the officer's individual ability. The barrier system and entry procedures must be designed to make it obvious and the use of deadly force instructions must be specific to the site design.

In creating this integrated defense, the official responsible must remember that the target will be moving, the engagement time frame is very short, and the losing encounter will be exceptionally expensive in terms of casualties. Remember, "accidental" deaths from bad judgment, excessive rounds, or overpenetration will have to be repeated an enormous number of times to equal the number of deaths in one successful vehicular bombing. A typical pattern in past defense settings is for the responsible administrative official to place too much restriction on the use of deadly force usually citing either the danger to the innocent public, specifically, or the political, moral, or legal implications, generally. The excessive restriction actually removes any chance of successful defense by use of deadly force, but the official does not confront that possibility either deliberately or through ignorance of the tactical reality. When this occurs, the official leading the defense force must respond to the administrative official's inappropriate actions, explaining the tactical reality in clear terms. It must be made clear to the administrative official that this "tactical" decision is actually a "strategic" decision which foreordains loss of the defense encounter.[10] The results of a vehicular bombing are so devastating that failing to stand against inappropriate use of deadly force instructions or similar blunders easily constitutes negligence in the performance of your duties. By taking a stand, you force the administrator to confront the real issue, not the safety of one isolated person, but the safety of a much larger group that will be affected by the vehicular bombing. In short, the administrator must make the tactical decision (actually strategic decision) of whether it is better to risk killing one person or ten, twenty, fifty, one hundred, etc. Notice that killing no one is not one of the options in that statement. The administrator needs to realize that, not only for the tactical reality but for the legal reality involved with either acting or with failing to act, what the lawyers like to call an act of commission or an act of omission. Private security officials will quickly recognize this as a restatement of the business liability standard, "reasonably foreseeable circumstances".

Reasonably foreseeable circumstance. Private businesses have had the reasonable man doctrine applied to their operations by the courts ruling on civil liability cases.[11] Issues involving the possible negligence of the business in customer safety during their public operations have been the basis of these liability suits. Basically, the courts have ruled that the customer is entitled to expect safety in the business operations or at least notification of any possible risk. The concept is that a business can predict what will probably happen in the existing conditions and circumstances. This concept applies to businesses dealing with the possibility of a vehicle bomb, but it also applies to the government officials who are involved. A vehicular bombing is so devastating that it will affect nearby operations without regard to whether they are public or private. This is easily predictable, and therefore, is a reasonably foreseeable circumstance. The business or government operation involved, therefore, assumes a responsibility under this doctrine to deal with the foreseeable circumstance. Failing to deal with a possible vehicle bomb attack is just as likely to result in civil liability as dealing with it improperly or even dealing with it properly. While there is no way to avoid civil liability risk in these circumstances, the risk is offset somewhat by the court rulings that a business is not the guarantor of the safety of the individual particularly from criminal conduct.

The courts have traditionally held that a business has limited capability to control criminal conduct by members of the public, and, consequently, has limited liability for criminal conduct occurring on their property. Additionally, the courts have also traditionally held that a government agency has no clear responsibility to defend a particular individual; rather, the agency provides protection collectively to all the individuals in its jurisdiction. This legal doctrine of business absolution for criminal conduct on its property could apply to the vehicular bombing, but is weak in application since an *individual* is seldom targeted by a vehicle bomb or other weapon of mass destruction. Further, an individual seldom has the resources to effectively defend against such an attack. Therefore, it is reasonable to conclude that this responsibility has to be assumed by the business or government agency involved as an implementation of the "common defense" rather than defense of an individual. This favors a legal interpretation which relies overwhelmingly on the "reasonably foreseeable circumstance" doctrine and its assessment of business responsibility since the individual will not be individually targeted and the individual will not have the resources to respond. The target is the business or public agency, not the individual. Reason argues, therefore, that it will be better to stand in front of a court having attempted to act responsibly and failed than to stand in front of it having knowingly acted improperly. This is exactly the liability decision that is inherent in confronting the defense against and the use of deadly force against the vehicle bomb. Consequently, the tactical engagement must be planned in a thorough and responsible manner.

TACTICAL ENGAGEMENT OF THE VEHICLE BOMB (CWMD)

The starting point for an examination of the tactical engagement of the vehicle bomb begins with a look at the theory of increasing, usually concentric, defense levels that prevail in the military, police, and security doctrines that typically are used. A further review of the task analysis, historical observations, and technical observations will then lead to the integration of the defense.

The recent U.S. joint military doctrine for armed conflict on land includes a portion referred to as Rear Battle, the protection of the logistics and other assets not directly engaged in actual combat. As outlined in joint doctrine, an installation (or base) in the rear has three defense zones: the close defense area, the main defense area, and the screening force area (Figure 48). As envisioned in this doctrine, the close defense area includes the critical asset (for illustration, let's say it is a headquarters building) and the immediate area around it. The main defense area would typically be the perimeter fence around the installation on which the headquarters building sits, and the screening force area would be the land surrounding the perimeter from which a ground attack could be immediately mounted. The important point to note is that the three areas roughly conform to the responsibilities assigned to various defending forces. The close defense area is primarily assigned to the occupants and any security forces assigned to that particular building. The main defense area is typically assigned to a base defense force formed by all occupants of the base or, occasionally, a military or security police force specifically assigned to the base; the latter typically occurs only at critical installations. The screening force area is usually defended by a military police force or civilian police force with secondary reliance upon a tactical combat force when needed.

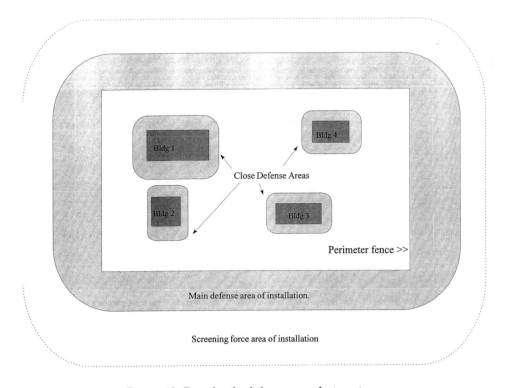

Figure 48. Rear battle defense area designations.

The same concept of increasing security levels is found in the industrial security specifications used for secure areas related to national defense operations, and is also found in the correctional setting (Figure 49). The most secure level in the industrial setting is identified as the exclusion zone; it contains the asset to be protected. Access in this area

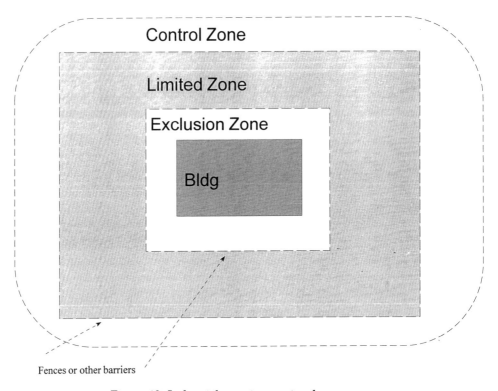

Figure 49. Industrial security restricted access zones.

is restricted to a very select group. Surrounding the exclusion zone is a limited zone. Entry to the limited zone has some requirements, but they are not as strict as those for the exclusion zone. Surrounding the limited zone is the control zone. Entry into this area is not restricted, but is monitored. In the corrections setting, these terms are replaced by the conceptual terms maximum, medium, and minimum security with the access restrictions being applied for both movement into and out of the areas. This similarity of increasingly restricted access can be directly applied to the defense of a site against the vehicular bombing. In applying these concepts to site defense, it seems most beneficial to apply the military Rear Battle doctrine to defense of a group of buildings while applying the industrial security concepts to a specific building. In this fashion the two concepts will work together to form an integrated defensive approach since the first orients primarily upon security force organization and mission for the defense while the second orients strongly upon the right of access to property and, consequently, the jurisdiction of the defense forces. Both tend to match the defensive goals stated above and the tasks identified in the site vulnerability assessment previously stated.

Blending these security doctrines and their terminology with previous defense goals to align the concepts and tasks produces this description or definition of the vehicle bomb defense zones (Figure 50):

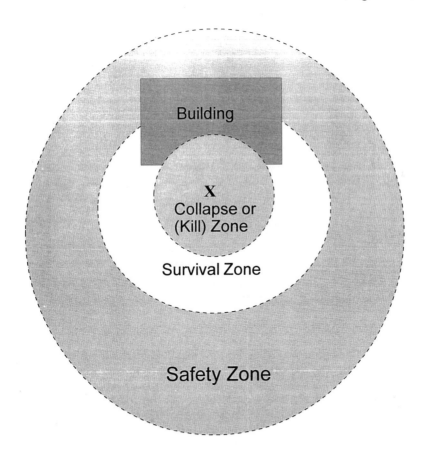

Figure 50. Building CWMD Defense zones.

The building "exclusion zone" (Kill or Collapse zone) is the area where a vehicle bomb detonation would cause immediate collapse. People in this area would most likely be fatally injured.

The building "limited zone" (survival zone) is the area where a vehicle bomb detonation would cause the building to receive significant damage, but it would not immediately collapse even if so seriously damaged that it would eventually be torn down. People in this zone might be seriously injured, but would be expected to survive.

The building "control zone" (safety zone) is the area where a vehicle bomb detonation would cause the building to receive damage which would be repairable. Persons in the safety zone might be injured, but the injuries would be relatively minor.

Using these definitions, we can restate the defense action tasks and subtasks as follows:

Critical Defense Tasks

Prevent penetration of the building exclusion zone (kill zone) by a vehicle bomb;

Create a limited zone (survival zones for the building and the people likely to be present) and reduce the possibility of penetration by the vehicle bomb into the limited zone.

Priority Defense Subtasks

Monitor the site control zones or screening force area for reconnaissance (prestrike surveillance) by the attacker;

Establish a denial perimeter by use of barriers and access control procedures which performs the critical tasks and the priority subtasks;

Establish specific use of force procedures for the individual site that are designed to halt the attack by a vehicle bomb for deactivation or to detonate it at the planned locations which are favorable for the defender.

These defense tasks and subtasks must be applied in terms of the practical realities learned during past incidents. First, the ability to obtain the appropriate standoff distance for a vehicle bomb with a barrier system will be limited. Second, the use of force is unlikely to halt an actual attack but is somewhat likely to cause detonation. With these two limitations, it makes sense to design the defense to help overcome them to the maximum extent possible in the setting. In short, one plans the engagement to favor the defender.

Recognizing that the emplacement of the vehicle bomb will occur with tactical surprise and within a very short time frame, the barrier system must be designed to channel the vehicle. First, the barriers must push the attack outward from the building to as close to standoff range (outside the building safety zone) as possible in the setting and, second, the barrier system must design the entry point to force a tactical engagement where both firepower and detonation are manageable. Historically, most defensive measures at entry points have been designed to *exclude* attack, to halt it at the barrier line or checkpoint; any use of force in this approach is normally planned to fire outward from the barrier line or checkpoint. Basically, this is the application of firepower to overwhelm the opponent, the typical use of mass and fire on a battlefield. This application, however, is not on a battlefield; it is in a "peacetime" or "peacekeeping" setting. This battlefield approach can work where there are large areas empty of civilians and friendly forces, but it does not work where there are large concentrations of civilians and friendly forces surrounding the building. Consequently, the defense should be laid to accept the attack, channeling it into a trap zone which allows controlled engagement by firepower, with relative safety to nearby civilians, and controlled detonation in a way that achieves the same basic relative safety. *The point is to maneuver the mobile attack to a favorable location before it is engaged by fire, deactivated, or detonated.* This is accomplished by integrating the barrier system, the access control procedures, the use of force and other response procedures. Methods of accomplishing this are the final portion of the discussion on defensive actions.

INTEGRATION OF THE DEFENSE

Integrating the defensive measures starts with recognition that the barrier system and checkpoint constitute a decision point in the physical terrain for the defender and the attacker. At the barrier line or checkpoint, the attacker must commit to the attack or abandon it while the defender must detect and engage it or accept the consequences of the attack. Consequently, we can accurately predict that it is at the decision point that use of force or detonation of the vehicle bomb is most likely to occur. Effective barrier and checkpoint design should consider this. What is not typically recognized is that the decision point is both tactical and strategic for the individual building. In the past, primarily at existing facilities, defense has been based on three primary assumptions which have typically been implemented without question. These three assumptions are, frankly, tactical errors (in the form of omission from or incompleteness of the assumptions) which need to be understood in order to effectively design a defense. Here are the three typical assumptions:

1. The barrier system must be designed to stop an attacking vehicle.
2. The checkpoint will be located at the entry point or points through the barrier system.
3. The use of deadly force to stop an attack will be exercised from the checkpoint or interior of the barrier system toward the attacking vehicle which is outside of or coming through the barrier system or past the checkpoint.

These three assumptions need to be restated to illustrate and to overcome the tactical deficiencies in the thinking behind them:

1. The barrier system must be designed to detect or stop an attacking vehicle bomb and to block, deflect or otherwise reduce a pressure wave from a detonation.

2. The checkpoint must be located forward of the primary defense line of the barrier system and sited to accomplish three purposes:

*Provide **public notice** of the instant use of deadly force for non-compliance beyond a certain point **and** of search and seizure. In a civilian setting, the siting of the checkpoint must also provide the **opportunity for voluntary compliance** or avoidance of the risk. **The enforcement by deadly force without further warning must be clear to the public!***

The siting of the checkpoint must channel the attacking vehicle bomb to a "trap zone" or similar area where it can be deactivated or detonated with minimal damage to the assets being protected.

The siting of the checkpoint must allow engagement by planned deadly force in a manner and location which prevents or reduces the possibility of friendly fire casualties either inside of or outside of the barrier system.

3. The use of deadly force will be exercised from the checkpoint and an overwatch point into a designated "trap zone" or channeled area of the approach that is designed to absorb stray bullets that miss the vehicle when it is engaged while simultaneously permitting 'venting' or similar blast protection.

These defensive objectives are accomplished by applying certain tactical principles in coordination with the building defense zones previously identified to achieve the integrated defense.

Ideally, both the primary barrier line and the approach to the entry checkpoint are located outside of the safety zone for the building. Placing them outside of the survival zone of the building is acceptable in restricted terrain but is not the preferable placement. In the approach to the checkpoint, two primary things should be accomplished. Approaching vehicles must be slowed down to allow the defense to react, and the driver must be given the appropriate notices and opportunity for either entry compliance or entry avoidance. Notices of mobility restrictions such as breakovers, width, height, or turning restrictions must be posted at a point which allows vehicles that cannot meet the minimums to halt or turn out so the entry point will not become blocked. Notices that provide warning of the search and seizure provisions and the immediate use of deadly force must be clear. A wide variety of barriers which slow down the approach speed are acceptable. The point is to alert the defense force that someone is approaching and give them appropriate reaction time. At the checkpoint, the vehicle receives preliminary clearance to enter using the access criteria. Depending upon the exact design of the system and other factors, the vehicle may be subject to search outside of the checkpoint or just past the checkpoint inside the trap zone. There are advantages and disadvantages with either approach. Once the vehicle passes the checkpoint, it enters into the trap zone where engagement, deactivation, or detonation is designed to occur. In this zone, barriers to slow the vehicle may be used, but only those that are built into the roadway itself such as speed bumps, dips, reverse banking, sharp turns, breakovers, etc. Barriers extending above the roadway surface, such as slaloms, should not be used since they will shield the vehicle from deadly force. In some cases, it may be advantageous to raise the overwatch point above the surface of the roadway to assist in gaining the favorable attack aspect for firing. The trap zone may have few movement restrictions or a variety of restrictions, but it is critical for it to have defensive measures which will serve as backstops for deadly force and as effective deflection, ventilation, etc of any pressure wave from detonation. At the end of the trap zone is the overwatch point where final clearance for entry is given. This point is at the line of the primary barrier system which is, preferably, outside of the safety zone for the building. With this general understanding of the integrated defense against a vehicular bombing, let us examine certain aspects of the integrated system to attain a greater depth of understanding.

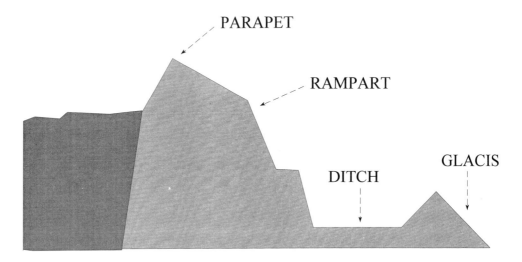

Figure 51. Elements of castle defense.

The first aspect to notice is how elements of ancient castle defense worked together to attain the overall purpose of the defense. In Figure 51, some basic elements of a castle defense are illustrated to show their relationship. A typical defense method began with a glacis or series of glacis with various forms of spike barriers in between them. The glacis was originally sloped uphill toward the castle to slow down the attacker's approach and to force the attacker to expose himself to defensive fire at the top of the slope. It can serve these same purposes in defense of a building against vehicular bombing, but it can also serve to deflect the pressure wave above a critical point of the building. In the same figure, the ditch appears next. Sometimes it was filled with water (making it a moat) or various spike barriers, and contained design features on the rear wall (the escarp) to prevent attacker's from crawling out. The purpose of the ditch was to halt forward progress of mounted or foot troops and any siege towers in use. It also was intended to be at a lower elevation so that attacker's would themselves be subject to defensive attack from above. The rampart was behind the ditch. Its height prevented both easy scaling and attack on the castle wall or its foundations (a technique called undermining) while constantly subjecting the trapped troops to fire from above. The ditch can serve the same purpose in the defense against the vehicle bomb; it prevents forward progress and inhibits further attack by subjecting the attacker to overhead fire. The rampart behind the ditch extended the slope of the escarp and served the same purpose. It served to deflect any attack directly upon the castle. The rampart can serve to deflect a pressure wave of any detonation caused when a vehicle bomb is entangled in the ditch. Working in combination with the ditch, it serves as a giant "vent pit" in which an explosion's force can be redirected upward to prevent damage to the primary structure. Finally, the parapet served as a place where defending troops could fire down on the attackers. This was the "overwatch" concept, using the modern term. Looking at this illustration of concepts from castle defense, some important observations can be made.

Figure 52. Glacis and ditch. Arrow shows direction of vehicle approach.

First, notice that a glacis and ditch can easily be formed into a sharp breakover which would cause a vehicle to hang up on the frame or to rollover (Figure 52). In order to defeat it, high speed could be used, but this results in the vehicle going head first into the ditch which acts as a "vent pit" in either circumstance. Second, a breakover followed by a rampart, with or without a ditch, stops the vehicle while also providing deflection of any pressure wave (Figure 53). The rampart (deflector) could be topped with a parapet for overhead defense; in this case, the parapet becomes a baffle to breakup the pressure wave (Figure 54). These concepts offer ideas for successful defense against a vehicle bomb. Here are some possibilities:

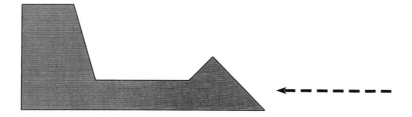

Figure 53. Glacis, ditch and rempart. Arrow shows direction of vehicle approach.

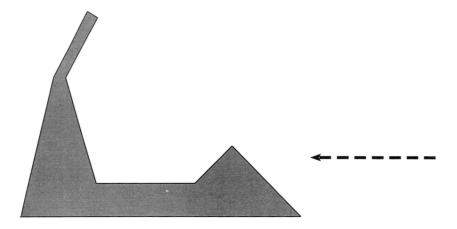

Figure 54. Glacis, ditch rampart and modified parapet. By reversing the slope of
the parapet, it can become a baffle. This adaptation serves the same defensive purpose;
it directly counters the attackers action.

CWMD Anti-Emplacement Barrier (Figure 55). The barrier can
serve the same purpose as a Jersey barrier, halting a vehicle, while
also serving to deflect the pressure wave. By designing it with a
face that transmits the force through the center of gravity, the barrier is likely to remain in place when hit with a pressure wave leaving the barrier defense line essentially intact. This is a clear advantage in the event of sequentially attack by multiple car bombs. The
height can be varied as needed as long as the essential relationship
of force transmission and wave deflection are maintained. It is possible to reduce the shipment weight by designing a hard metal or
ballistic plastic shell which can be quickly assembled and filled
with concrete at the emplacement site. By having internal stiffeners from front to back, the shells could be stacked during transport.
The hard surfaces would hold up better to the crushing force of the
overpressure than the typical concrete surface.

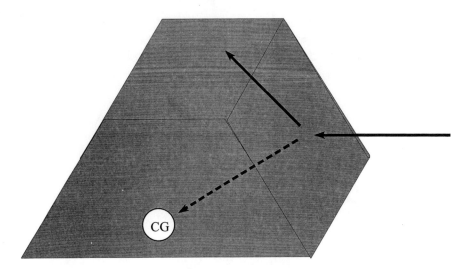

Figure 55. Anti-emplacement CWMD barrier. Pressure wave strikes face and deflects upward. Barrier is pushed downward, through the center of gravity, remaining in place. Barrier acts as a sharp breakover to block vehicle emplacement by rollover or high-centering of the attacking vehicle.

CWMD Baffle Wall Barrier (Figure 56). A baffle wall can be created with variable height to fit the defensive situation. The baffle or top deflector can be either part of the wall barrier or a separate barrier device behind the Wall Barrier. The essential point is that the wall is angled to deflect the pressure wave and is of sufficient strength to halt a vehicle. Obviously, it would be an advantage to retain the force transmission through center-of-gravity concept explained for the CWMD barrier above. The problem will be the relationship between the weight, the anchored mass of the barrier and its structural strength versus the upward force of the pressure wave. At some point, the upward force exerted on the top baffle will exceed the total anchored weight and the barrier will displace or come apart. The exact threat in combination with the exact defense requirements of the site will be important. It would appear that the wall barrier would probably be feasible against package and car bombs but probably not against truck bombs. The baffle would probably have to be a separate structure for the last, if it could be used at all. Part of the solution may be extending the distance above the expected height of detonation (2' - 7' above the roadway surface based on the standard height of cargo areas of current vehicles) to reduce the overpressure to a manageable level. Likewise, part of the solution might be to arrange the baffles to alternately deflect in differing directions creating an offsetting force situation when hit by the pressure wave.

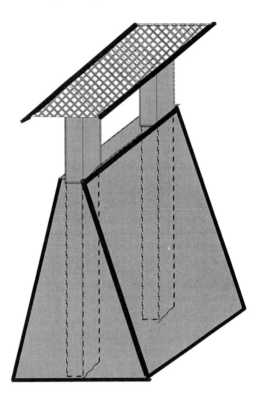

Figure 56. CWMD baffle-wall barrier. Top baffle vents alternate in direction to stabilize barrier during blast. Baffle legs are anchored or jointed with breakaway of baffle at predetermined pressure to prevent wall displacement.

The Angled Wall (Figure 57). A reinforced wall can simply be constructed and angled to deflect a pressure wave above the building. The offset distance will be of importance.

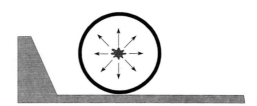

Figure 57. Building CWMD defensive measures #1. A simple sloped wall (rampart) will stop vehicles while deflecting a pressure wave above the building.

A Sharp Breakover with An Angled Wall (Glacis and Rampart) (Figure 58). This forms an effective defensive combination.

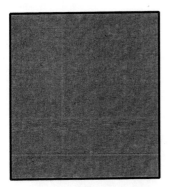
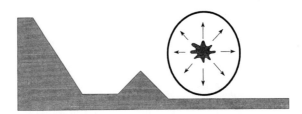

Figure 58. Building CWMD defensive measures #2. A sharp breakover with ditch will halt a vehicle and deflect the pressure wave above the building. Notice that the glacis leading to the breakover serves as an additional deflector when the denotation occurs outside the barrier system rather that in the ditch.

A Sharp Breakover, Ditch and Wall (Glacis, Ditch and Rampart) (Figure 59). This forms an exceptionally effective defensive combination.

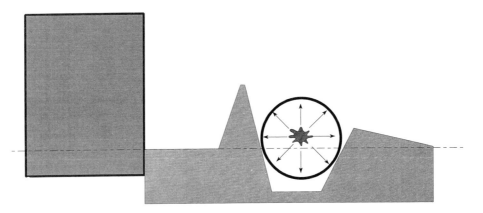

Figure 59. Building CWMD defensive measures #3. A gently sloping glacis leading to a sharp breakover and ditch with a modified rampart angled to deflect the pressure wave over the top line of the building. This is an adaption of the ancient castle defense system.

A Sharp Breakover, Ditch, Wall and Baffle (Glacis, Ditch, Rampart and Parapet) (Figure 60).

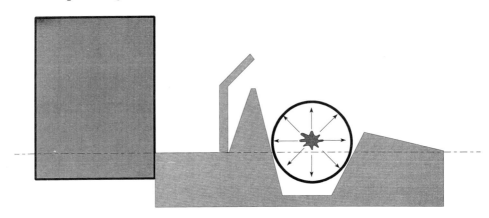

Figure 60. Building CWMD defensive measures #4. Addition of a baffle (modified parapet) shows a complete adaptation of the ancient castle defense to the modern threat.

More defensive combinations could be devised rather easily; the point is to notice that they integrate the two functions of halting the vehicular movement to emplace while simultaneously dealing with the highly probable detonation. This is the first part of the integration combination. The next part is to integrate the defensive fire as well.

The defensive fire (use of deadly force) is integrated by designing the specific shoot and no-shoot instructions for the individual site and each of its entry points. Basically, the instructions are written to align the use of force with the three zones of the site defense. In the controlled zone, the use of force is very restricted. It is limited to defending a person against the usual imminent danger of deadly attack such as aggravated assault, aggravated robbery, etc. The use of deadly force against a vehicle bomb would not normally occur since the area is outside of the critical risk to the building (that is, it is outside of the safety zone) and the risk of detonation by gunfire might endanger surrounding locations. In the limited zone, the use of deadly force is aggressive, occurring instantly whenever an imminent danger of vehicular bombing exists. This imminent danger is defined by an attack profile consisting of the probable operational profile of a terrorist and by the specific vulnerabilities of the site or by the failure to comply with specified security measures for that site and entry point. In short, actions that indicate an attack by vehicle bomb (high speed approach, attempts to breach the barrier system, obvious evasive actions, etc.). This use of deadly force occurs in the area where the defense is designed to engage the vehicle bomb and manage the stray fire and possible detonation. In the exclusion zone, the use of deadly force against a vehicle bomb is restricted to absolutely critical points where further penetration will increase the likelihood of collapse of the building. If the vehicle bomb is in the exclusion zone, the defense has basically failed. The strategy at this point should not be to engage the vehicle, but to engage the driver before he can activate the device. In this setting, the detonation will kill (collapse) the building so we will not engage by fire unless a clear shot of the driver is available. Do not use deadly force to assist the bomber in completing his self-proclaimed mission. Detonation caused by gunfire is an acceptable risk in the limited zone, but is not an acceptable risk in the exclusion zone. The question, then, is how do you fit these concepts together.

Figure 61 and 62 show examples of a building's security zones designed with a "Z Approach" for integrated defense (Figures 61 and 62). The Z Approach is designed to fit into the limited zone of the site being defended. The initial part of the approach is uphill with various barriers to further slow any vehicle and notices of security and use of deadly force posted on signs or barriers. The checkpoint is at the identified beginning of the survival zone; it has an aerodynamic design that

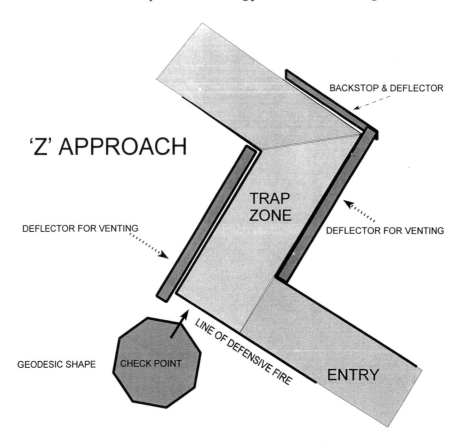

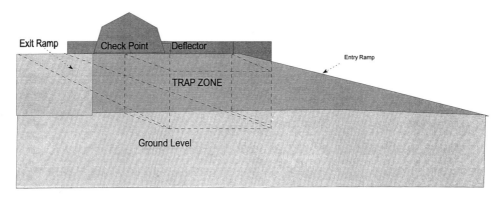

Figure 61a and 61b. The "Z" approach. Top and side views. An intergrated, single guard-site defense point for high risk, low-medium volume applications.

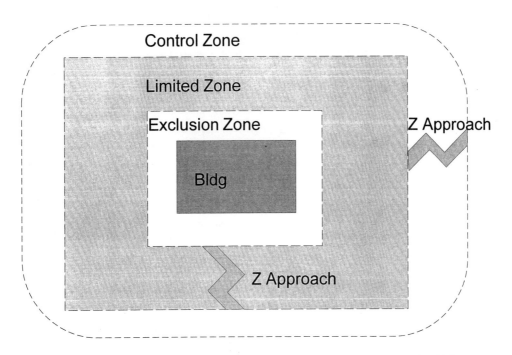

Figure 62. The "Z" approach relationship to industrial security zones. The "Z" on the right is in the control zone, the preferred siting. The "Z" on the bottom is in the limited zone, acceptable siting in some circumstances.

improves its survivability during a detonation. The vehicle halts here for clearance to proceed. When the vehicle proceeds, it goes downhill into a Trap Zone with deflectors built into the sides. The downward aspect gives a security officer at the checkpoint a favorable engagement angle for firing. The deflector on the final leg of the Z serves as a backstop for the bullets which will be striking it at a nearly perpendicular angle. This reduces the possibility of ricochet and virtually eliminates the possibility of stray fire going into friendly areas. The deflectors also channel any resulting explosion in a direction that causes the least damage.

The Trap Zone is a combined sally port, enclosed firing range and bomb disposal pit. In the Trap Zone, speed bumps, dips, spike barriers, drop barriers, or similar barriers which slow or halt vehicle movement but do not block the line of fire may be used. There are possibilities here for automatic devices such as hydraulic front or side rams, electrical charges which fry the vehicle electrical system, and so forth. Bomb detection equipment or various sensing devices for alarms could also be installed in this area. When the vehicle turns onto the final leg, the checkpoint will have a flank shot toward the driver while it is still inside a vent pit. The vehicle approaches the final barrier going uphill over a sharp breakover. Since the final barrier is controlled automatically from the original checkpoint, the barrier remains in place until activated by the security officer. This barrier is at the dividing line between the limited zone and the exclusion zone. Notice that the design allows the option for the final barrier to be controlled by an overwatch point sited at the exit from the final leg of the Z. This would provide two points of firepower for engagement with interlocking fields of fire against the attacking vehicle. This is implemented in the more fully-developed entry called the **"Diamond Approach"** (Figure 63).

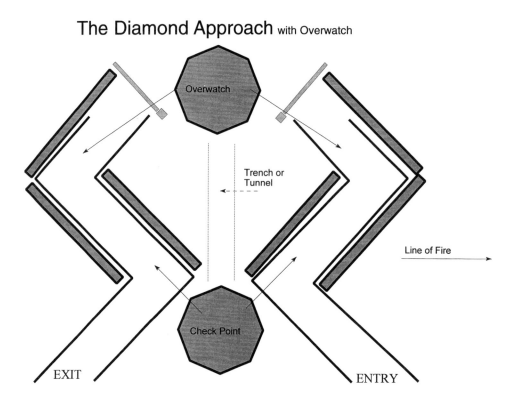

Figure 63. The diamond appoach. Formed of a "Z" approach and a reverse image "Z," the Diamond Approach can be highly effective defensive position. It is shown here with crossarm barriers, tunnels interconnecting the Checkpoint and OverWatch, and interlocking fields of fire into the dual Trap Zones which serve as vent pits and firing backstops. This is a highly intergrated defensive entrance capable of high volume flow and strong control.

The Diamond Approach is composed of two Z Approaches; the second is in reverse image along the same line of approach. This creates an approach with the same advantages of the single Z Approach plus an increased capability to handle traffic flow and supporting, interlocking fields of engagement for use of deadly force from the checkpoint and the overwatch point. With the addition of access tunnels or ditches, security officers in the two points can directly reinforce each other without exposure or they can move to vehicle search or screening points in the trap zones. Again, the overall purpose of the design is to provide a barrier to limit vehicles while simultaneously providing a point for controlled detonation.

Obviously, the Diamond Approach is placed in the defense zones in the same manner as the Z Approach, and, obviously, requires a lot of physical space to lay out effectively. In some applications, it will not be possible to implement it due to space limitations. In others, the space limitation can be overcome by such techniques as sinking the trap zone downward into the existing terrain or siting the overwatch point in the second story of the building. The manner of integration is not as important as the total concept of integrating the barrier system with an engagement zone and bomb disposal point.

Most current building defense against vehicular bombing has involved modification of existing facilities which seriously limits some of the possible tactical solutions. However, the integration of the defense can be incorporated in a variety of ways, even in limited settings. Most existing facilities are typified by limited surrounding space which prevents defense barrier designs that achieves stand-off range. In these cases, alternatives can be considered. The primary problem of venting an explosion is simply one manner of redirecting the pressure wave. It may be possible to engineer other methods of redirecting or dealing with the overpressure produced. Use of "elastic" barriers that give may be one method.

Recognizing that a pressure wave is primarily a sudden, pushing force of gas, it may be possible to attach barriers to hydraulic systems that spread the force through various methods. A simple illustration of this concept is the use of protective traffic barriers in front of highway dividers at turn-offs. When a car fails to make the turn and strikes the barrier, the force of the collision is transmitted to the liquid which is forced upward or outward from the barrier. This works to soften the blow, to lessen the total force exerted against the car or hard barrier.

It does this by extending the time period of the collision to lower the peak load (via its elasticity) and by redirecting part of the force where it produces little significant damage. This same approach can be utilized for bomb detonations. It may be possible to design liquid or gas pressure barriers that can trigger when struck by the incoming pressure wave from a detonation thereby destroying or redirecting part of its force. A liquid barrier can absorb the incoming pressure wave and simply disperse it or lower its pressure to a nondestructive level. Elasticity can also be achieved using mechanical means.

We are all familiar with the heavy-bottom dummy that stands back up after you hit it. A barrier can be mechanically loaded by various means to accomplish the same thing. Springs, hinges, or hydraulics can all be used to cause a barrier to give and then return to its original position; this lessens the peak load against the barrier and gives it better survivability. By using hydraulics, the force can actually be redirected to counter the pushing force so that it tends to work against itself. The concept of countering a pressure wave in this fashion has already been addressed by the military in a limited fashion, the development of reactive armor for tanks. Reactive armor actually is the triggering of a countering explosion by an incoming warhead. This interferes with the explosive design of the attacking warhead reducing its effectiveness. The same principle can be applied to an incoming pressure wave from a vehicle bomb by use of sensors which trigger release of a liquid or gas barrier which works against the incoming force causing reduction of its effectiveness. This seems possible but may not be feasible; only an engineer or architect would be able to make that determination. The possibilities are rather endless. Consequently, it is more important to grasp the fundamental principles behind the concepts.

CONCLUSIONS

When prevention of an attack fails, the best defense is always one that is coordinated and integrated. The initial defense goals of preventing penetration of the building and identifying and protecting the building survival zone are accomplished by a fully coordinated, integrated defense. Against the vehicle bomb, the integrated defense is composed of three parts:

1. Use of a barrier system to deny entry to the building kill zone while creating and controlling entry to the building survival and safety zones.

2. Use of a barrier system which controls the pressure wave of a detonation.

3. Use of engagement channels for defensive fire which limit the collateral damage potential of the engagement.

This synthesis of the initial, realistic defense missions with the various considerations and issues raised in the discussion produces a final statement of the realistic defense goals in three parts. In effect, these three statements constitute what the U.S. Army would call the commander's intent in this tactical setting. When these three defense goals are fully integrated, a successful defense against vehicle bomb attack at a vulnerable location is possible. When integration fails, one of the two defensive tasks, halting the emplacement or controlling the detonation, will fail with disastrous results for the defender. Integration of these three intentions to achieve the two defensive tasks is the key to successful site defense against the conventional weapon of mass destruction.

Notes

1. See *Fortress: A History of Military Defence* by Ian V. Hogg, 1975, St. Martin's Press, Inc., New York.

2. See *Fortress: A History of Military Defence* by Ian V. Hogg, 1975, St. Martin's Press, Inc., New York.

3. See *Fortress: A History of Military Defence* by Ian V. Hogg, 1975, St. Martin's Press, Inc., New York.

4. See *Fortress: A History of Military Defence* by Ian V. Hogg, 1975, St. Martin's Press, Inc., New York.

5. See *Fortress: A History of Military Defence* by Ian V. Hogg, 1975, St. Martins Press, Inc., New York.

6. See *Fortress: A History of Military Defence* by Ian V. Hogg, 1975, St. Martin's Press, Inc., New York

7. A four-pointed design of spikes joined at a common center so that when deployed a triangle of points is always down and a single spike straight up.

8. Notice that the legal test does not consider how many people are in the building or what their status is. Consider four of the case histories: Khobar Towers, Marine Headquarters, World Trade Center, and Murrah Federal Building. Khobar Towers Building 131, next to the bomb emplacement site, was the sleeping quarters for Air Force personnel. This qualified it as a dwelling. Under the state statutory standards cited above, such a situation would have justified the use of deadly force even

though the bomb was not directed at a specific person in the structure. The truck bomb driven into the Marine Headquarters Building in Lebanon entered a building that contained a mixture of offices and sleeping quarters for Marine personnel. This met the qualification of state statutes for a dwelling, and deadly force would be justified in a similar circumstance. At the World Trade Center, however, the building contained a vast number of people (several thousand) who worked at the building, but none that lived there. Consequently, it did not automatically qualify as a dwelling, and threat to a person who have to be demonstrated in order to use deadly force in similar circumstances. It could be argued, however, that it was a dwelling since the car bomb affected parts of the Vista Hotel which contains sleeping rooms that would qualify as the temporary dwelling place of a much smaller number of people. The final case, the Murrah Federal Building, is also mixed. It basically contained the work sites of a large number of people and public sites visited by a larger number of people on a typical day. This does not qualify it as a dwelling even though hundreds of person were present. What might qualify it as a dwelling was the day care center. The legal test used to establish a person's dwelling is typically where does he sleep. Using this legal criteria, you could argue that young children typically nap (sleep) during their stay at a day care center. Consequently, the Murrah Federal Building could conceivably qualify as their daytime dwelling place.

9. Graham vs Connors, 490 US 386, (1989).

10. When the administrative official turns red in the face, froths at the mouth and begins screaming orders you have four possible responses:

A. Quote President Truman, "The buck stops here."

B. Quote President Truman, "If you can't take the heat, get out of the kitchen".

C. Quote this author, "Those who get paid the big bucks are required to assume the big responsibility each and every time. If you want me to assume the big responsibility, start paying me the big bucks. Then you can shut up and go home."

D. Shut your own mouth and go home.

The correct response is A, B and C. As a person who has had to confront this exact problem in a real tactical setting and has studied the results of similar tactical situations, I can unequivocally state that this is the time and place to sound off. I not only believe that firmly, I practice it. To those who might doubt my veracity, I quote to you from an officer efficiency report filled out in the mid-1970s to evaluate my performance as a military police lieutenant: "LT Ellis can in no way be described as a yes man." - (In the time period after the prosecution of LT Calley, "Yes Men" were abhorrent.) The lieutenant colonel was absolutely right and I have both the military and civilian law enforcement career path to prove it.

11. It is defined as: "An injury is foreseeable if a person of ordinary prudence would have foreseen that such an injury might and probably would result from the act of negligence."

12. This example assumes that there is limited space and that the controlled zone is the safety zone. Obviously, where there is more space, the approach should be placed so that the checkpoint is at the initial edge of the safety zone rather than at the initial edge of the survival zone.

Chapter 10

RESPONSE ACTIONS TO THE VEHICLE BOMB (CWMD)

Response actions to the vehicle bomb (CWMD) begin, generally, as part of the assessment phase and continue through all preparatory activities to the specific site response as part of the defense. Response actions will generally follow a response critical path sequence and may be based upon certain planning assumptions. Neither this critical path sequence nor the planning assumptions are unique to the vehicular bombing, but the problems that may be encountered at each critical point on the path are somewhat different than standard emergency services response within the United States. Examining these assumptions will give clues as to the necessary response tasks and organization for those tasks.

PLANNING ASSUMPTIONS

The first planning assumption should be recognition of the sequential nature of the response that will be needed. Mentioned above, the critical response path can be stated as: recognition of the problem, identification of its specifics, isolation of the affected area or people, assessment of response requirements, organization of response assets, activation of the response force, and control of the response. The first four phases of the sequence (recognition, identification, isolation, and assessment) occur within minutes and can be referred to as the initial stage of response. The second stage of response, the formation stage, occurs within a matter of hours and includes the organization, activation, and control phases of the sequence, but only the initiation of the

251

control phase. The final stage of response, the stabilized stage, occurs over a period of days. It covers the extended part of response control and then repeats the response sequence with an eye toward the long-term requirements and not the emergency requirements.

The second planning assumption is to recognize the basically circular pattern of damage and injuries with its concentric rings of lessening severity that will result from the detonation of a vehicle bomb. This pattern affects a number of planning considerations. For example, movement typically becomes increasingly difficult as you move toward the center of the circular pattern of damage. In some cases, a path may actually have to be cleared to allow entry. Other planning areas may be affected in a similar fashion.

The third planning assumption is that the affected zone will be so large that area planning and response will be necessary rather than simple site response. This applies both to the attack site itself and to the geographic locality which surrounds it. The destruction caused by a vehicle bomb will typically encompass a varied number of both public and private facilities. Consequently, planning may not be limited just to the probable target; it must be coordinated with the other facilities in the probable affected area. Similarly, the government of the locality surrounding the site must coordinate with other governments in the geographic region. This complicates the planning task considerably and raises clear command problems. The inclusion of both private and public domains and various governments on both the same and different governmental levels also complicates it. When you add in the possibility that military forces may be required in some settings, the command problem becomes even more complex.

The fourth planning assumption is the recognition of probable overload. This will take a variety of forms. The sheer number of casualties, for example, will require more emergency treatment and transportation than is immediately available in most areas of the United States. This will apply to the number of ambulances, the EMTs or crews in the ambulances, the rescue personnel available to extricate people from damaged locations, the number of hospitals, the number of doctors or nurses staffing them, and so forth. Area activation plans for mutual aid personnel and prepositioned stocks of medical supplies or equipment may be required.

The final planning assumption is that a vehicle bomb detonation will present response requirements for personnel with specialized training and for specialized equipment. Even if immediately available, these specialized personnel or the specialized equipment are unlikely to be present in sufficient quantity to fulfill the total need for the duration of the response.

RECOGNITION OF THE VEHICLE BOMBING EVENT

Recognizing these planning assumptions, appropriate response can be developed by examination of a typical event and its requirements. This will be done by following the critical event path, making observations, and then projecting these observations on existing emergency service organizations to develop the tasking, organization, training and equipment needed for the response. The first critical path event to be examined will be the recognition of the problem, the manner in which the vehicle bomb will be brought to the attention of the usual emergency agencies. This recognition may occur when the defense force detects or engages the attack or it may occur when the vehicle bomb actually detonates. In this examination, then, response actions will be viewed from the time of recognition of successful emplacement of the vehicle bomb at a site.

It is important to notice initially that there are two basic notification calls for assistance: the passive call regarding a suspicious, emplaced vehicle or similar circumstance and the active call of a detonation which has just occurred. It is reasonable to assume that the initial notification to an emergency communication center will not be received from a caller who specifically states that a vehicle bomb is located at a specific site or that a vehicle bomb has just detonated. The initial calls for assistance will be similar to other events, and the communications and initial response personnel will have to make a determination that the reported situation involves a vehicle bomb. From this observation, we can forecast the need for preparation and training of personnel in two areas: identification of vehicle bomb-related events and initiation of specialized dispatch procedures based on that evaluation. The passive call will be examined first.

The primary directive espoused by bomb disposal personnel is usually: "Don't touch it. Don't move it. Just secure it for expert examination." The basic underlying strategy behind this statement is that the risk entailed by moving or examining the device is not justified since it may cause detonation of a device that might otherwise be deactivated without detonation. This basic strategy is understandable, but you must recognize that it is based upon certain assumptions which may not be valid for larger devices.

First, with most explosive devices, the effective kill zone is so small that moving the people out of the kill zone is relatively simple. As the size of the kill zone of the explosive device increases, eventually a point is reached where evacuation of the kill zone is a practical impossibility, particularly in a limited time frame. Exactly when and where that point is reached will vary with each set of defensive circumstances and potential vehicle bomb size. It is important to keep in mind that buildings tend to shield people from some effects of a blast until the building failure point is reached, then remaining in the building increases the danger. Additionally, the evacuation routes through which or assembly areas to which groups might move may be inside the kill zone of the large device. This creates the possibility that evacuation of the people will actually increase their risk in some situations. Consequently, the first decision in the passive call is determining whether an evacuation should occur and whether the evacuation should be of the people in the affected area or of the vehicle bomb from the affected area. This requires a thorough risk analysis in advance and formulation of specific instructions. A simple example determination might be the following: car bombs–evacuate personnel and deactivate in place; truck bombs–place personnel in immediate survival areas and relocate truck to a disposal area to deactivate. As one can see, a passive call strategy uses a preplanned response based on assessed risk of injury and damage at varying explosive pressure levels.

When the passive call is received, the emergency communications center activates the preplanned assessment procedure by a command unit and then activates further response based on the initial evaluation of the command unit. Obviously, the command personnel involved must understand the risk assessment process, must be familiar with the site evacuation plan, and must actually evaluate the situation in some manner, usually by a physical or technical inspection. Once the evaluation has been made by the command personnel, the site is evacuated according to preplanned routes, modified as necessary for the particular situation.

When the evaluation calls for evacuation of the area, first the vehicle bomb should be isolated by barriers or shielding material to the extent possible in the time available, then move the people, completely outside the area whenever possible, or to identified survival or safety zones in and around the site when that isn't possible. There may also be requirements to shut down utilities, move certain hazardous or critical materials, or isolate the suspicious device with baffles or other protective barriers. The situation is then turned over to the bomb experts for deactivation.

The command unit sets up the necessary inner and outer perimeters, traffic and crowd control, and standby emergency equipment as deemed necessary. In this case, the outer perimeter is intended to be the outer edge of the safety zone; the outer edge of the survival zone may be used in extreme circumstances but should be avoided whenever possible due to the increased risk. The command post, equipment staging areas, triage point, and other designated control points are set up outside of or along the outer perimeter. The inner perimeter is totally under control of the bomb disposal team. The procedures used in this type of passive call are similar to what is typically used for any bomb situation. The primary difference is the need for blast shielding material which is larger and stronger than normal. In the second form of passive call, however, the procedures differ somewhat.

When the evaluation indicates that the suspicious device should be evacuated rather than the people, the actions change somewhat. Any people in the area are alerted to move into immediate survival or safety zones within the structures, assuming that there is time to do this. In this type of evaluation, the decision to move is based upon the fact that it is a greater risk to leave it in place rather than move it to a controlled point. Due to the type of decision, there may not be time to implement any warnings prior to the move. This is a command decision, again, based upon an understanding of risk assessment including a very thorough understanding of the technical aspects of the threat. In this situation, the command person has opted to assume a higher risk for a short time period in order to assume a significantly lesser overall risk for the longer time period. Such a decision requires advance preparation.

There must be a designated disposal area identified during the vulnerability analysis of the site. There must also be the means to move the suspected device into the disposal area; temporary shielding material would also be of benefit during the move. Once the device is in the designated disposal area, then this passive call proceeds according to the planning used in the first type of call. Obviously, procedures have to be implemented to sort out the hoaxes from the legitimate call and to reduce erroneous evaluations. Basically, the passive call is a preplanned, automatic response to a threat that has been identified in advance. The procedures are simply activated by the emergency communications center and the appropriate command personnel. In the active call, classifying the event is the first task.

Recognition of the vehicle bomb-related event requires that the emergency communications monitoring system recognize a pattern of calls or it requires installation of special detectors at selected locations near probable targets. The patterns that have emerged from past vehicular bombings should consistently be present in most future events as well. Typically, the site of the blast in a populated area experiences some type of alarm activation. The form of the alarm activation will vary by site. Usually the actual location may trigger a distant, not local, alarm caused by electrical power loss or some other utility fluctuation. In many locations it will take the form of line interruption for fire or burglar alarms. These will typically be interpreted by the receiving central monitoring station as a standard alarm event rather than a vehicle bomb-related event. Complicating the interpretation is the simple fact that most of these alarms will be monitored at a location that is not part of the emergency communications monitoring system operated by a public agency. Utilities companies will tend to respond to these alarms as though they are the loss of the utilities monitored while alarm service companies will tend to treat it as the fire or burglary indicated by the type of alarm. This recognition gap will have to be addressed through the risk analysis process, and appropriate actions implemented in coordination with the private businesses involved.

Some sites, however, will not trigger any alarms from the site itself either due to the lack of an alarm system or due to the rapid destruction of the alarm system during the actual blast. In these instances, the second possible alarm pattern will be seen: The alarms will be generated at locations surrounding the attack site. These are most likely to be burglar alarms of various types due to glass breakage or motion detection of falling objects but may appear as fire alarms due to sprinkler activation caused by the pressure wave vibrations or by actual water line breaks. One tip-off that it is a vehicular bombing will be alarm activation in a roughly circular area surrounding the attack site. This leads to the probability that the affected area could be identified in advance, and this pre-identified pattern can be used as part of an attack profile by the emergency communications center or the alarm service companies.

The best method of identifying this event by alarm systems is the installation of pressure detectors in locations around, but not on, the actual site. Such a detector should trigger an alarm directly to the emergency communications center rather than to alarm service companies for faster response. Reliance upon alarm service companies will complicate the planning but may be necessary and is effective if planned well.

Varied approaches can be taken for using pressure sensitive devices. By installing them at known distances from the probable attack site with a minimum overpressure setting for initiation, a rough picture of the affected area can be identified by determining which sensors activated. This would be of considerable assistance in forming the initial emergency response. A second approach is to install a sensor which measures the overpressure near the attack site. By cross-referencing the overpressure reading with a prepared chart, prepared area diagram or similar prepared material, the affected area could be determined quickly. This shortcut would allow efficient initial dispatch of resources.

Aside from the alarm patterns, a similar two part pattern of voice calls will probably occur. The actual site of the blast will most likely have its phone service disrupted to the extent that calls from the actual attack site or its immediate vicinity may be completely eliminated. If calls from the attack site do occur, the callers are likely to be unclear on what has happened. Some may have trouble hearing, which will enormously complicate the communications attempt. Some will have trouble seeing since the center of the blast is typically obscured with smoke or dust in the first few minutes after a detonation. Some will be unable to tell you where they are either due to disorientation effects of the shock wave or simple unfamiliarity with the public locations. Others may be trapped in strange locations or simply be unable to recognize the altered structure. These calls will provide some indication of the center of the affected zone, but may not be of much assistance in initially determining the overall problem. The best overall determinations will come from outside the immediate blast site.

Emergency calls being received from the surrounding areas will typically report an explosion, a large cloud of smoke or dust, or simply damage at their location. These types of calls are of tremendous value in the first few minutes if worked properly. By determining the caller's location and either the direction to the explosion or smoke or by the type of damage at their location, the emergency communications center can pinpoint the center of the explosion and the size of the affected area. This is critical information for initiating the appropriate first response. If the callers cannot provide this information immediately, then the initial response is to dispatch emergency units to the general area to make these determinations. In the initial response phase, these first units must identify the event as a vehicular bombing, its approximate detonation point, the size of the affected area, the extent of casualties, and the amount of damage. First responder units must concentrate on these determinations rather than stopping to provide initial assistance to particular persons or locations. At this point, it should be clear that the opening step in the response to a vehicular bombing requires close coordination between the emergency communications center and first responders; the actions of these two must be interwoven.

The emergency communications center begins by identifying a possible vehicle bomb event and communicating that to emergency units in the affected area. In turn, these emergency units must advise the communications center of their observations beginning with their own visual observations and their estimate of its probable location or their location and the direction to the observed problem for map or zone plotting in the communications center. As the units respond into the affected area, the recognition phase of response begins to phase into the next task, the identification of the affected area.

IDENTIFICATION OF THE SPECIFIC RESPONSE
AREA AND ZONES

Responding units must focus on accomplishing the identification objectives in furtherance of overall response. The quality of this task performance will dramatically affect the quality of the initial response as a whole. The first unit into the area should be tasked to determine the exact location of the event and make the determination, based on the type and extent of the apparent local damage, that it is in fact a vehicular bombing. The immediate following units should identify the approximate safety zones, survival zones and kill zones of the detonation. This will be accomplished quickly by a simple view of three key indicators: glass breakage, obvious structural damage, and structural collapse.

Repetitive glass breakage indicates the outer edge of the safety zone and should be used as a guide to establish the outer perimeter for traffic and entry control into the affected area. An intermediate perimeter should be identified and marked where structural damage, but not collapse, has occurred. This perimeter serves to alert emergency personnel that this is the area of survivors with serious injury and greater probability of continuing hazards than found in the safety zone. The inner perimeter should be set at the points where structural collapse has occurred. Entry beyond this point should be tightly controlled. As soon as these first responding units identify these zones, they shift to an assessment of the extent of casualties and continuing hazards present in each zone. At this point in the response, the emergency communications center, in conjunction with police, fire, or emergency service command units, determines that the event is a vehicular bombing and initiates several actions which are based upon prepared plans. This is the beginning of the isolation phase of the response.

ISOLATION OF THE AFFECTED AREA OR PEOPLE

First, the command center isolates the area by establishing three perimeters (outer, intermediate, and inner) which coincide with the circumferences of the safety zone, survival zone, and kill zone of the detonation site. Civilian traffic inside the outer perimeter is eliminated and emergency vehicles are tightly controlled to prevent traffic jams caused by the accumulation of emergency vehicles. An event of this size will draw enough emergency vehicles to cause traffic problems inside the outer perimeter unless this is done. Simultaneously, an inner perimeter is established to preserve evidence and establish scene security at the detonation site. Entry into this area is tightly controlled by police officials; even other emergency workers are initially restricted.

This is done to preserve evidence, to allow the scene to be checked for unexploded bomb material, and to allow stabilization of the debris at the scene.

This restriction is not a natural reaction for most people or for most emergency workers; the tendency is to gravitate to the worst-looking area on the assumption that the people most in need of immediate help will be found there. This is not the case in large bombings. The restriction must be enforced even when some people might object to the restriction; it is actually based upon sound reasoning and application of emergency principles. The high pressures and consequent small debris size in the kill zone make it very unlikely that survivors are present. Those who are present will probably be difficult to locate, stabilize, and evacuate.

The intermediate perimeter is loosely established to identify the area of increasing hazard and injury. In the opening stages of emergency response, the seriously injured are most likely to be easily found in the survival zone of the explosion site, the area between the inner and intermediate perimeters. Using emergency medical triage principles, these casualties should be addressed first as they are most likely to be located, stabilized, and evacuated relatively easily while having the most serious injuries that are likely to be successfully treatable. Inside the survival and safety zones, priority is given to searching from the inner perimeter (circumference of the kill zone) outward to the outer perimeter (circumference of the safety zone) as the lessening damage will probably coincide with less critical injuries. The secondary zone for casualties will be inside the inner perimeter with the final zone being beyond the outer perimeter.

Second, the communications center and command personnel initiate a utilities shutdown. As the initial reaction, all gas, electric, and water utilities inside the inner perimeter are cutoff. Phone lines are left operative if possible. Between the inner and intermediate perimeters, electric and gas utilities are cutoff with water and phone lines being left on initially. If a water problem appears in this zone, it may be cutoff for a specific site. All utilities are left on in the area between the intermediate perimeter and outer perimeter unless a specific location has a specific hazard. That location is then shut down. These initial response actions are intended to reduce secondary risks caused by damaged utilities.

Third, the command personnel establish the location of triage sites, command post locations, entry and exit points, evacuation routes, equipment staging sites, and collection points for evidence, hazardous material control, and information. The siting of each is made on the basis of open space available, access routes, and proximity to the specific problems or emergency facilities.

Fourth, the command initiates certain response plans prepared for the event. This last is typically done by the emergency communications center based on the command evaluation and directives. Having isolated the area, the response now enters the assessment phase. This requires that the responding personnel conduct a detailed examination of the exact emergency problems present in each sector of the affected area.

INITIAL ASSESSMENT OF RESPONSE REQUIREMENTS

Assessment is primarily a command function within the emergency services, but in this instance, the work overload will require formation of a team or teams to complete the initial work-up in the short time frame needed. The typical problems found within the three perimeters will be as follows:

Inner perimeter (Kill zone): Structural collapse, disrupted utilities, some possibility of fire, movement nearly completely blocked, some hazardous materials, possibility of secondary explosives, most of the dead, a few trapped survivors, little initial activity, evidence of the criminal act, limited initial visibility, and inoperative site communications.

Intermediate perimeter (Survival zone): Structural damage, some utilities damage, occasional fires, serious movement problems, some hazardous materials, some possibility of secondary explosives, a large number of injured (mostly seriously), some trapped survivors, some dead, responding emergency personnel, some responding citizens, some evidence of the criminal act, some visibility reduction initially, and some site communications inoperative.

Outer perimeter (Safety zone): A large amount of glass breakage, occasional utilities damage, occasional movement restrictions, occasional hazardous material, a large number of injured persons (mostly minor), responding emergency personnel, a large number of responding citizens and press, initial confusion and fear, possibility of evidence of the criminal act, and occasional communications interruption.

Assessment may be organized by zone, or may be organized by functional skill which crosses the zones. Whichever form is used, the personnel selected for the task should be as experienced and as advanced in training as possible. Mid-level-command personnel are usually the best selection as they are psychologically prepared in three ways: they are used to assigning others to perform tasks rather than doing the tasks themselves, they have usually experienced previous scenes of death and destruction, and they have had to make risk-balancing decisions prior to this. All three experiences will better prepare them for the environment that confronts them at the time of assessment.

The assessment area will be cluttered with all types of debris and filled with a variety of hazards that need immediate attention. It will be populated with people who need immediate help and expect to get it from public safety personnel. It will be a scene obscured by smoke and dust, lit here and there by crackling flames and sparking utilities. Faceless voices of humanity will be crying out in despair while nameless members of humanity will be crawling from under debris so covered with dust, blood, and ashes that they will be unrecognizable to their own friends and relatives. Dead bodies in grotesque positions and barely recognizable parts of bodies will be scattered among the debris. It is a scene more fitting to a battlefield than to daily life. In this instant, the civilian official assessing the scene has more in common with the soldiers of countless conflicts than do many soldiers who served but never fought. It is an overwhelming scene of mankind's inhumanity, but it cannot be permitted to overwhelm the emotions. An effective response requires action, not emotional collapse. It takes an iron will to walk past a crying, injured child, but it must be done when the decisions for continued action will affect the survival of a hundred others. In this setting, the assessing official is confronted with the same conflict confronting the battlefield commander: "Who do I risk? What do I gain by risking them?" The assessments and decisions for priorities are made on this simple basis. Rephrased it may be stated in slightly different form which goes to the heart of the decision-making process involved here: "Where is the greatest need?" "What provides the greatest good for the greatest number of those in need in the shortest amount of time?"

These decisions are not easy, and they are not clear. The situation demands decisiveness; it absolutely requires experienced people with the right training and the psychological mind set to endure the horror and serve the public under the most difficult of circumstances. With that in mind, let us further examine the forms of assessment teams.

In the first form, personnel with skills in assessment of all anticipated problem areas are assigned to the assessment teams and work throughout the kill, survival, or safety zone to which assigned. The team takes note of the various problems and classifies their level of emergency response action as urgent, priority, or routine. The three lists are consolidated as quickly as possible to form one complete listing of response actions required and their emergency classification. The command group then makes a determination of the resources required and activates them.

In the second form of assessment, the teams are organized along the standard functional lines of the public service departments with each team conducting a separate assessment beginning at the center of the affected area and working outward. Each functional department then determines what its priorities are, begins work on its list, and reports it to the overall command group, requesting the resources required that exceed its response capacity. The command group resolves conflicts or rearranges priorities as required.

Each form of assessment team organization has advantages and disadvantages. The first, the integrated assessment team, requires a better prepared assessment team than the second and is capable of resolving most priority conflicts at the team level due to the integration of the emergency evaluations being made. The second type of team is more quickly deployed without advance preparation and training but has the advantage of better evaluation in the individual response areas. It is capable of more in-depth analysis but less capable of integrating the priorities and taskings at the team level. In some circumstances, both types of assessments may be used, the functional type being used immediately and the integrated type being used as a backup procedure as the initial responses are being activated. Regardless of which type is used, the personnel assigned need to possess certain skills to perform assessment effectively.

The first point to understand is that more effective long-term response is obtained by completing the assessment and initiating all of the necessary responses, before stopping to render aid, direct responders or control bystanders. This goes against the grain of standard behavior but is critical to maximize overall response effectiveness. The second point is to assign personnel with the necessary skills to perform the evaluations needed for incident assessment. Based on the above outline of the typical problems encompassed within the three perimeters, a short list of the training or experience background requirements for both the assessment team and the responding forces can be forecast:

> *Inner perimeter:* architectural or construction expertise, bomb and hazardous material experience, utilities expertise, rescue techniques training, emergency medical evaluation ability, and evidence handling experience.
> *Intermediate perimeter:* some architectural or construction expertise, utilities expertise, hazardous materials expertise, traffic or crowd control expertise, emergency medical triage capability, medical evacuation capability, and evidence handling.
> *Outer perimeter:* traffic and crowd control expertise, emergency medical training, and press or public relations capability.

Once the assessment is complete, the assessment teams are positioned to organize and assume control of the responding emergency assets.

ORGANIZATION OF RESPONSE ASSETS

Response assets may also be organized by integrated units assigned to zones or by functional units based on the usual duties of each public department which are assigned to the entirety of the affected area. Either procedure is operable, but, again, they have different advantages and disadvantages which are quite similar to those previously mentioned for the assessment teams. In the integrated unit response, each unit is task organized with the type of functional assets that are needed to accomplish the tasks identified in a particular zone. The functional assets simply report to the assessment teams for each zone for task assignment. Notice that each zone varies in the type of tasks that will be required and their priorities. As a simple guide, the most critical tasks in the three zones can be summarized as follows:

Inner perimeter (Kill zone): Tactical stabilization; that is reducing the continuing risk. The secondary risk may come from a planned, sequential attack or unplanned second detonation, hazardous materials or disrupted utilities. This is primarily a police tactical unit, bomb squad and HAZMAT squad job.

Intermediate perimeter (Survival zone): Medical stabilization and evacuation. This is primarily a medical task supplemented by rescue squads and traffic control teams.

Outer perimeter (Safety zone): Isolation. This is primarily a police task supplemented by civilian command and administrative personnel for public liaison.

Integrated response orients on the types and priorities within the particular zone; coordination problems are minimal. Functional response, on the other hand, orients on the typical functional tasks and priorities throughout the three zones. This has inherent coordination problems since priorities will differ between functional departments at a particular location and time. At this point, a complete task analysis by typical functional departments will probably assist the discussion.

The typical tasks that each functional department can expect to perform at the scene of a vehicular bombing are listed below:

Police Department
> Tactical security
> Bomb search and disposal
> Traffic control
> Crowd control
> Witness location and interview
> Property owner identification and notification
> Crime scene processing
> Location and identification of victims
> Incident assessment
> Public relations
> Response command

Fire Department
> Firefighting
> Hazardous material control
> Location of victims

Rescue operations and medical assistance
Incident assessment
Response command

Medical Services
Triage
Some casualty extrication
Immediate emergency care
Evacuation of victims
Public health evaluation
Coroner/Medical Examiner services
Incident assessment
Response command

Communications Services
Incident notification
Dispatch services
Some recording of events

Public Utilities Departments or Private Companies
Emergency shutdown of services by area or point
Restoration of services
Incident assessment
Response command

Public Streets Departments or Private Construction Companies
Heavy lift equipment provision and operation
Heavy cutting, welding or similar salvage equipment provision
    and operation
Debris removal

Public Administration
Proclamations or exercise of emergency powers
Recording of events
Public and press relations
Liaison to supporting agencies
Architects, engineers and building codes inspectors or similar
    personnel
Legal advice or services

Contracting of support services
Overall command

Various Departments or Sources
Coordination with private businesses, organizations, property
    owners, etc
Disaster services
Chaplains, Counselors, Psychiatrists, etc

The typical task list is based on the most frequent large-to-medium city structures. In smaller urban areas, the departments will tend to be more generalist than specialized. Consequently, they can be expected to perform better in a zone organization while larger cities will probably perform better by use of functional organizations during the initial, critical stage of response. Additionally, functional organization will be favored where prior planning has not been accomplished or is incomplete. Integrated response forces require the proper preparation and training to reach highly cooperative performance levels. Regardless of the size or exact level of preparation, the response force is organized by command personnel according to the perceived strengths and weaknesses after analyzing the task list, the structures of the various departments, and their training or preparation. The various organizations are then activated and given instructions to report to the responsible command point.

ACTIVATION OF THE RESPONSE FORCE

Activation of a response force of this size and complexity requires a lot of work and can contribute to the communications overload if not handled correctly. All response forces being activated need to be told the nature of the problem, the exact point to which to report, the exact person to whom to report, and the emergency priority for reporting. In some cases, they will also need to be advised of the expected duration and of any unusual equipment or supply requirements. The manner of notification can vary, but the content should be clear. The emergency communications center should be relieved of as much of the notification requirements as possible.

Emergency response assignments of on-duty personnel should be the primary responsibility for the communications center; secondary notifications which provide additional support should be directed to personnel who are not immediately providing emergency assistance. These notifications can be made by administrative personnel who are pulled from routine duties to back up the communications center. Using prepared lists from plans, these administrative personnel make calls for mutual support resources, recall off-duty personnel, handle routine reassignment of equipment to cover larger response areas for other emergencies, and activation of all previously identified public agency nonemergency personnel or private service contract personnel. Calls to certain mutual assistance points or other agencies may need to be made by command personnel due to the provisions of either emergency powers or mutual aid agreements and statutes. Where this is a consideration, the notification plan can specify this in advance. When the notification is complete, a core of administrative personnel is retained to perform additional support functions.

During this notification period, the communications system will be stretched to the limits. The emergency phone systems will probably be jammed with reports and inquiries from the public. At the same time, the communication center will be trying to determine that the event is a vehicle bomb detonation, assigning command personnel for assessment, and activating whatever notification and dispatch procedures are ordered by either standing procedures or command directive from the site. Unpublished command phone lines will be a necessity, but usage of supplemental phone communications by responding personnel will be a limited option since phones in the affected area are likely to be inoperative or inaccessible. Consequently, modified radio communications procedures will have to be invoked.

Certain types of communications may be prohibited or restricted to prevent conflict with emergency traffic from the affected zone. Command nets will have to be established. The response organizations, integrated or functional, should have separate channels as well. These communications should be separated from the normal emergency communications traffic which will continue in the surrounding areas. Computer networks, e-mail, teletypes, or similar communications may be of considerable assistance during the event, and should be used whenever possible. Communications problems can be anticipated and rearranged, as planned in advance, but other command and control functions will also be affected. Some of these will be unpredictable, but others can be minimized by planning and controlling the arrival of emergency units at the affected area. This formation stage of the response is reaching completion as the control phase is beginning. Command problems will surface during the initial and extended portions of the response control phase in a variety of ways.

CONTROL OF THE RESPONSE TO THE
VEHICULAR BOMBING

The key to control of the response in the initial stage is isolation of the affected site as soon as possible. As envisioned throughout this discussion, the initial response task is to identify the event as a vehicular bombing at a specific site, and then determine the affected area. When the affected area is determined, the next step is isolation followed by assessment of the affected area. These two should be completed or at least be in-progress before emergency personnel are assigned to other tasks. With the outer perimeter in place, arriving emergency equipment and personnel can be directed to specific control points established by the assessment or command personnel. At these control points, various tasks can be consolidated for easy command.

After entry control has been initiated along the outer perimeter, the most critical control points to establish in the initial minutes will be triage points. These should be sited along the intermediate perimeter near clear entry routes. This placement avoids most of the expected movement problems allowing easier entry by medical personnel and quicker evacuation of the patients. It also centralizes triage in the middle of the areas where most of the immediately accessible and treatable casualties will be found. Multiple points may be needed if the area is large, movement around the perimeter is difficult, or the patient load is very high. A smaller, secondary triage point may be located along the inner perimeter if it appears feasible with the available resources. Open space will be required for the triage points as well as easy entry and exit. This will allow patients to be seated or laid prone for treatment using available emergency ambulances or other shelters. However, it is very important not to clog this site or its entry route with parked emergency vehicles. Doing so hampers evacuation and inhibits further response to the overall scene. This raises the second internal control procedure, equipment staging points.

Initially, many personnel will be responding from many locations in a variety of emergency vehicles. On arrival, some of these emergency vehicles are used for various emergency tasks, but a significant number will simply be parked while their occupants perform various duties. The available space can quickly become clogged if traffic control is not emphasized from the beginning. Establishment of equipment staging points helps address this problem. Initially, three points should be established; one in the vicinity of the inner perimeter, one in the proximity of the triage point, and one along the outer perimeter. All vehicles should be left unlocked with keys either in the ignition or available under the control of an equipment staging area manager. Obviously, some minimal security of the equipment will be required to prevent possible theft but also to simply keep track of its location if it is suddenly needed for an emergency response after it has been pressed into use for a lower priority task. The size, number, and location of the staging areas will vary as the response continues into the stabilized stage and requirements vary.

There are three police control points that require initial placement. The first is the entry control point which handles the outer perimeter and the evacuation routes. This may be placed at the primary entry point along the outer perimeter but may be co-located with the triage point if that appears to be a better solution at the scene. Primary duties at this location will be entry traffic control, evacuation route control, and equipment staging management. The second police control point will be the crime scene control point. This is placed near the inner perimeter. It orients on tactical security of the site, bomb disposal operations, investigation, and evidence identification and collection. Certain firefighting operations may be co-located as noted later. The third police control point is an information center. Initially located along the outer perimeter, it can easily be moved or established at other locations with little loss of effectiveness. This control point provides the following information: personnel and equipment assignments; lists of the dead or missing; patient evacuation reports; official emergency proclamations; curfews; determinations of unsafe buildings, areas, or total damage; and expected recovery information. Additional police control points may be required as the response advances, but this would vary from response to response.

Two firefighting control points are needed initially. The first is established near the inner perimeter and may be co-located with the police crime scene control point. Fire operations at this control point orient on hazardous material response and rescue operations in the collapsed structure. Neither are easily assessed nor instantly performed. Consequently, personnel at this control point must orient on longer-term operations. The second firefighting control point is established to deal with whatever fires are present. The locations of these cannot be reliably predicted but will predominately be inside the intermediate perimeter and concentrated in the survival zone in most circumstances. The exact location for the control point cannot be forecast but should be at the point most favorable to fight the fires. Additional firefighting control points may be established if multiple rescue operations are required in various parts of the affected zone. These are the critical police, medical, and firefighting control points needed in the initial and formation stages of the emergency response to the vehicular bombing. As the response moves into the stabilized stage, control must begin to focus on extended operations.

A stabilized operation requires the establishment of a complete emergency management team which is frequently referred to as a crisis management team in many federal planning references. As envisioned in those references, the team is structured, and in this instance adapted, to cover the following areas or responsibilities that would typically arise in a vehicular bombing:

Command: Overall control and recording.

Personnel: Personnel reinforcement or replacement, financial support, public affairs, legal, chaplain services.

Information: Plans, reference information, liaison to outside resources and private agencies.

Operations: Communications, police services, firefighting services, and medical services. This includes security of site/resources, rescue operations, evidence collection, explosive ordinance disposal and hazardous material control.

Logistics: Utilities services, provision of supplies, repair of equipment, engineer or architectural technical advice, clearing of entry routes, initial removal of debris.

As seen by the structure, the command and the operation is clearly intended to be integrated at some level. The primary difference in various response structures is the exact level at which the command structure is integrated across functional department or agency lines. This is an unavoidable situation due to the sheer size and scope of the operation. Consequently, the impact of integrated command must be considered during organization of the assets.

Integrated response has one inherent command problem: some of its functional units must work for a supervisor or commander that is not part of their typical structure. This unfamiliarity will cause some conflict which will be unpredictable in its forms. It is important to reduce the potential by training in advance.

The priority conflicts inherent in functional operations across the entire affected area will also be unpredictable in their forms. These unpredictable conflicts must be addressed by the command structure at the level where integrated command occurs. Keep in mind that the integrated command will not only control public assets but also private assets and volunteers. The structure must have the appropriate authority and capability to do this.

The stabilized response will vary considerably from incident to incident. Typically, this is where problems of additional resources surface. The primary government controlling the response will discover that it lacks certain equipment, skilled personnel, supplies, etc. These must be obtained and must be financed somehow to continue the response. This is also where questions about missing persons, identification of victims, etc. will surface. Public or political pressure may be intense and must be managed. Due to its emotional basis, it will be somewhat unpredictable in form. Having considered the response by its sequential nature, it will now be of benefit to examine it by functional area and make certain observations concerning the preparation and tasking of each area.

Police response to a vehicular bombing is, in many ways, a secondary or ancillary response to the emergency requirements presented. It must be recognized at the outset that the only police tasks that are truly emergency in nature are those which provide further security (tactical coverage and bomb disposal) and those which facilitate the firefighting and medical response. All other police tasks are the type that can be delayed without immediately endangering life. Since one of the anticipated problems in any event is a shortage of skilled personnel, it makes sense to plan for police to assume most of the non-emergency taskings. This allows the firefighters and medical personnel, whose skills will be in short supply, to be utilized to the maximum. Command tasks, information tasks, equipment control points, liaison jobs, patient information lists, etc. fit into this category. Anywhere that technical skill of a particular type is not essential, police or volunteer personnel can be assigned to allow concentration of the best personnel on the emergency tasks. Following this general observation, the police will probably have the following problems surface:

- The scope of the crime scene will exceed immediate processing resources.
- The responding officers will probably have limited bombing investigation experience.
- The police agency will probably have limited dog and other search equipment to locate bombs or trapped persons.
- Police officers will be controlling disoriented, emotional members of the public.

Medical response will probably have the following problems surface:

- The immediate medical treatment requirement will exceed the immediate capability at the scene, of the transport from the scene and at the hospitals or clinics.
- The strategic theory behind emergency medical response, stabilize and transport for further detailed treatment, may fail partially or completely.
- The medical overload at the scene may require doctors at the scene; a response that is not normally planned.
- Patient tracking or administrative processing will be inadequate.
- Extreme or unusual medical treatment may have to be provided to trapped victims with minimal facilities.
- Medical supplies at the scene will be exhausted quickly with no standard supporting plan for immediate resupply.

Fire and rescue operations will experience the following problems at the scene:

- Heavy rescue equipment will not be heavy enough for the tasks confronting the rescuers.

• Construction skills and equipment will be required but unavailable immediately.

• Search equipment for detection of people will be required but unavailable in sufficient quantity.

• Light rescue requirements will overload the available personnel and equipment.

• Hazardous material response has probably not been practiced in conjunction with either explosive ordinance disposal or ongoing rescue operations.

Local government administrators will have the following problems surface:

• Lack of experience in direct command of operations and emergencies in general.

• Lack of appropriate emergency powers or experience in invoking them.

• Public pressures for services not normally provided.

• Lack of procedures for emergency purchases or contracting.

• Financial shortages to cover emergency purchases or contracting of equipment, supplies and services; reimbursement of mutual support personnel or equipment; and extended, unplanned payroll of city personnel.

• No procedures for ongoing liaison to other governmental agencies, nonprofit groups, and volunteers or private companies involved in the operation.

• Work overload in virtually every area of services provided by the local government.

Private companies will have the following problems surface:

• Emergency restrictions on business operations and access.

• Damage or other loss which exceeds the anticipated business risk.

• Required participation or support of the emergency operations which had not been previously planned by the business.

• Indefinite legal status in regard to control and liability of their business activities.

These are the typical problems which can easily be forecast. General solutions are easily suggested but would need to be adapted to the particular locality in recognition of their specific structures. In any case, the problems would be expected to vary slightly from vehicular bombing event to vehicular bombing event.

At this point in the planning, detailed operational planning is usually passed to the appropriate functional commanders, businesses, or consultants to identify the specific response task lists. This eventually leads to procurement of any specialized equipment which is not immediately available and to development of the necessary personnel training to utilize it. Once the necessary individuals and equipment components of the organization are in place, unified response training can begin to complete the formula for effective response.

The key in response formulation at the integrated command level is to focus upon the breadth and scope of the problem and not become mired in operational details that are best addressed in subordinate operational procedures. Focus on the big picture and upon those facets that will be unusual from other forms of emergency response. This will allow the emergency response planner to properly develop the overall command plan and to orient the subordinate functions upon the task planning that will be necessary at their functional level. The most difficult portion of the planning will probably be addressing the inherent problems in the overall dimension of the disaster. The overlapping impact upon a variety of public and private entities and the inherent conflicts between them can be expected to create a coordination problem of unbelievable proportions. Some planners will have difficulty adjusting their thinking to this scope and to adjusting to the differing parameters between the public and private sector operations or the differing functional operations. Skill in such an area may prove to be a limited and valuable asset.

In review, the Initial Stage of response consists of recognition of the problem, identification of its specifics, isolation of the affected area or people, and assessment of requirements. In the Formation Stage of response, the response force is organized, then activated, and then subject to initial control. This leads to the Stabilized Stage in which extended control of the response force occurs with repetition of the sequential steps in a more detailed manner. By applying this identified sequential nature of response (the response critical path) to a vehicle bomb event, planners can project the probable patterns and develop the necessary detailed procedures to deal with the vehicle bomb. Analysis clearly shows that integrated response between the public and private sector, between the various levels of government, and between the various functional areas of emergency response is critical to effectively handling any vehicular bombing. The nature of the event and its response requirements are so overwhelming that it will probably surpass any previous emergency response and hinder success unless the system is thoroughly prepared to respond. Ad hoc arrangements may work, but will impose costs of a type that both the public and the responders will abhor. The nature of the event is so strong in its psychological impact that preparation is needed simply to counter the feeling of devastation created by the detonation of a vehicle bomb if not the actual destruction caused by the event. In the final analysis, the psychological preparation for response may be of more importance than the actual preparation for response. The human element *is* the critical component of the response.

Chapter 11

CONCLUSIONS AND COMMENTS

Fourscore and seven years ago, our fathers brought forth on this continent a new nation, conceived in liberty and dedicated to the proposition that all men are created equal. Now we are engaged in a great civil war testing whether that nation or any nation so conceived and so dedicated can long endure. We are met on a great battlefield of that war. ..."

These words of President Abraham Lincoln, delivered in 1863 during a time of civil war within the United States, reflected the state of the country at the time. However, his words have proven to be more than a dedication; they have proven to be prophetic. They forecast the recurring question about the American society: can it long endure? The text of the speech embodies the essential "feel" of an internal conflict in a democratic society as well as the recurring process by which it is resolved. An attack upon the interior of the United States, whether mounted by domestic terrorists or transnational terrorists, has essentially this same feel of internal conflict to the society. Consequently, the introductory words of the Gettysburg address serve as a good starting point for the conclusions and commentary on the possible use of vehicle bombs or other weapons of mass destruction inside the United States.

It is important, in one respect, to view the threats discussed as a pending battle: the interior of the cities, towns, and buildings of the United States as the battlefield and the police, private security, and National Guard as the common defense forces. Yet, as President Lincoln also clearly understood, it is important to remember in application that "a house divided against itself can not stand." Vehicle bombs in the hands of terrorists have the potential to test the nation as never before, and amplify existing divisions. As in 1863, the point of the "testing" is whether "a nation conceived in liberty and dedicated to the proposition that all men are created equal can long endure." It is critical to remember that any action to counter the threats must retain the social balance necessary for a free society. The strategic decisions must be effective both tactically and socially. All tactical action within the United States has immediate societal impact. That impact must support "the government of the people, by the people and for the people." Success in this tactical setting is a two-part, interwoven process, prevailing upon the field of battle and prevailing upon the field of honor as set by the societal standards of a democracy.

Whether the attacker is a domestic terrorist, a transnational terrorist, or a state-sponsored agent, the motive of the attacker will be to influence the free people of the nation. The attacker's purposes and ultimate goals will vary somewhat, but the impact on the target will not. The questions at this point are as follows: What changes and actions will be needed to counter this threat as it increases, and how will these changes impact upon the society? The answers, in short form, are the preparations that must be made by the society and its defense forces.

POLICY PREPARATION FOR BATTLE

The international policy advocated by the United States and most other nations is to treat terrorists as criminals rather than as warriors engaged in battle. The validity of this policy will increasingly come under question as the battle moves into the interior of the United States, regardless of the origins of the groups involved. As Clausewitz observed in commenting on warfare shortly after the French revolution:[1]

> ... This policy had called forth other means and other powers, by which it became possible to conduct War with a degree of energy which could not have been thought of otherwise.
>
> Therefore, the actual changes in the Art of War are a consequence of alterations in policy; and, so far from being an argument for the possible separation of the two, they are, on the contrary, very strong evidence of the intimacy of their connexion.

Therefore, once more: War is an instrument of policy; it must necessarily bear its character, it must measure with its scale: the conduct of War, in its great features, is therefore policy itself, which takes up the sword in place of the pen, but does not on that account cease to think according to its own laws.

Some dispute the theoretical relationship of war and policy advanced by Clausewitz and its application to politics on several basis. I prefer to make the simple observation that this quotation is only one way of stating that people react to the world around them, altering their behavior to attain or continue life within their viewpoint. Viewing war as a means of social change is nothing new or unusual. Rejecting the concept requires that you reject the foundational basis of sociology and a great deal of history. But most important here may be the final line of the quotation, the statement that people think according to their own laws. Applying this observation, the first point of discussion is to examine the role of the United Nations and its impact on the situation.

The United Nations formed nearly five decades ago in response to worldwide war. The Charter opens by stating that the framers are "... determined to save succeeding generations from the scourge of war ...." The framers of the Charter had seen, firsthand, the results of war in both the urban and rural environments and in industrially-developed, developing, and undeveloped nations on a broad scale twice within thirty years. But, it is important to remember, they had experienced these wars with certain social expectations of both people, generally, and war, specifically.

At the time of World War II, many international agreements concerning the conduct of war existed; most of the Law of Warfare was already developed. Inherent in these laws is the "chivalrous" viewpoint that battle is conducted between the armed forces of nations; the general population is not targeted. This viewpoint, the historical validity of which is questionable, was severely stretched by many of the actions which occurred during that war, but the general belief and influence remained. In one respect, one could state that the Charter represented the desire of mankind to return to "chivalrous" conduct during war.

The framers of the Charter of the United Nations structured the entire document on the basis that it was an agreement between member nations, that war was fought between nations, that limiting it to the military forces would reduce the civilian suffering, that respecting the sovereign integrity of each nation fosters respect between nations, and that the dual thrust of granting respect and eliminating war would create peace. No formal consideration was given to the possibility that war could be conducted by anyone other than a nation, that a nation could practice war while not calling it by its rightful name, that the era of massive civil wars had mostly passed, that the technology of war had increased to a point where confining it was nearly impossible, that non-violent confrontation could be used on a massive scale, or that simple respect is based on shared values and experiences. The framers were implementing the historical and ethnocentric viewpoint of both mankind and nations. It is simultaneously rosy in spite of experience and unimaginative in its prediction of the future. It fails to acknowledge that the world changes and that it stays the same.

People respond to any regulation of conduct. Sociology, history, and simple daily observations teach us that people typically adjust their conduct to fit it into the unregulated sphere. The world's populations and the nations did that in response to the Charter of the United Nations. In this case, war simply shifted to the unregulated sphere. It is now frequently fought, not by nations, but by groups "seeking self-determination." Nations do not now engage in wars; they engage in "police actions," "low-intensity conflict," "interventions" and 'peace-keeping' under a variety of international treaties, resolutions, flags, justifications, excuses, etc. Nations dealing with conflict have abandoned the label of war since it is prohibited conduct, but haven't necessarily abandoned war fighting. This social pretense allows resolving conflict by arms while retaining compliance with the Charter of the United Nations, giving a social illusion of peace. The reality, of course, is that a war by any other rosy name leaves the nation's soldiers just as dead, its populace just as ravaged, and its social perception just as skewed. The reality of abandoning pretense ravages more than just the dead; it ravages social values as well. Abandoning social value in one area of daily life encourages abandoning social values in other areas. Having abandoned the reality of war for the pretense of "peace-keeping," the nations and the groups seeking self-determination also abandoned the war-fighting forces as the intended targets. One long-term effect of the Charter of the United Nations has been a tendency to shift the target of warfare from the war-fighting forces of a nation to the population of a nation. The history of conflict worldwide since World War II overwhelmingly shows this effect. But another trend is also discernable over the same period.

At about the time that the Charter of the United Nations was written, Mahatmas Ghandi began a successful demonstration of the massive use of nonviolent confrontation to achieve social and political ends. This means of confrontation has continued in other countries by other social movements for varied purposes. The results have been mixed. Most of the proponents of this form of conflict resolution cite the essay of Henry David Thoreau, "On Civil Disobedience," as the source of the idea. Others refer to the works of Ghandi, the "Letter from a Birmingham Jail" by Martin Luther King or political essays by John Locke. Their source of inspiration is mostly immaterial. What matters is that the belief in such confrontation now widely exists and has been widely practiced inside the United States by various groups. Some of these groups understand the ideological thrust of this approach and the tactics that support it and some don't. Even nonviolent movements produce violent subgroups, and frequently engage in pretense, masquerading as something they are not. The basic problem, however, is that those who advocate and have previously used the nonviolent tactics have done so in limited environments that have not clearly illustrated the tactical and strategic limitations of nonviolent confrontation. Their experience causes them to apply nonviolence in situations where its use will fail; a man applies what he knows to any task. Since the collective knowledge of the many becomes a social norm, the collective experience of this group causes them to also demand that others practice this "norm" of confrontation, even in situations where it will fail. Having engaged in battle only upon the streets of a democratic battlefield themselves, they fail to understand the violence of the true battlefield in a variety of ways. Nonviolent confrontation has clear limitations; this was clearly illustrated at both Mount Carmel and Tiananmen Square. It takes two to tango, two to negotiate, and two to confront. Where one side retains unrealistic expectations or advances unrealistic demands, violent confrontation becomes inevitable. Where both sides retain the unwillingness to act violently, nothing violent occurs.

The basic problem for governments, of course, is that they have a duty to act on behalf of citizens. Where one group of citizens makes demands that conflict with another group, the government is caught between and will fail to support the people, at least from one group's viewpoint. The encounter will then turn to violent confrontation; the level of violence being determined by the combined actions of the participants. In the end, nonviolent confrontation can only stop bullets in two ways: by convincing the holder of the weapon not to fire or by absorbing the bullet with its own body. Some would argue that the latter is the ultimate purpose. Those who do so never grasped the real thrust of Thoreau's work or the dual meaning of its title which indicates both the manner and the target of nonviolence. Nonviolence fails when it orients on and forces its will on other citizens by targeting the individual; it becomes, then, only a form of persecution. Both the so-called "peace" movement of the 1960s and the antiabortion forces of the 1990s failed to grasp this. Both have engaged in persecution of individual citizens whose beliefs differed from theirs. Neither group shows any signs of altering its opinion of the necessity for such actions. Both groups have created long-term opposition groups as a result of that persecution of individuals.

Yet, nonviolence retains a powerful, if limited, potential. Who can forget the photo of the lone Chinese man who halted a tank column? Even more remarkable was an incident in the Philippines during the period of civil upheaval in the years of the rise and fall of the Aquino government. One Filipino military force was sent to take control of a military compound where the local military unit had announced it would no longer be bound by instructions from the central government. Following its instructions, the central government military force arrived in the area prepared to attack the rebellious unit in the next town. It was instead confronted by a crowd of local citizens lead by religious figures. They positioned themselves between the two military forces and refused to move. Neither military force would initiate attack through the citizens. It was the single most courageous use of massive, nonviolent confrontation witnessed in decades, if not centuries, citizens freely interposing themselves between two military forces. Yet, it went largely unnoticed by most of the world. The nonviolence succeeded because it established the common ground between the two forces; both sought to act for the benefit of the citizens. Both were persuaded to withhold force; the bullet was not fired.

These two events clearly illustrate both the power and the limitations of nonviolence. Even military forces may be deterred by courageous citizens reminding them of their humanity, but ultimately, the success of nonviolent confrontation depends upon a decision to act humanely. Terrorists using vehicle bombs have already decided to act inhumanely. Consequently, nonviolent tactics against terrorists are virtually guaranteed to fail at the point of attack. Immediate, armed tactical defense is a necessity at that point. Nonviolence must orient upon the decision to act inhumanely. It cannot do so when the government is supporting acts of inhumanity. Domestic terrorism inside the United States is, at the current time, escalating mostly on the belief that the government is supporting acts of inhumanity or inequity. These observations raise certain political implications affecting both policy and strategy, which is the reason for making them.

To understand our policy and the strategy that must flow out of it, we must focus on the social purpose. The comments above suggest the necessity to reassess and possibly amend the Charter of the United Nations. As the number, frequency, and complexity of peacekeeping missions escalates, the disparity between the Charter's goals and the world's means will grow. It may be time to validate a return to limited warfare between nations as a means of reducing the effect of war on the general population by focusing it on the war-fighting forces. It is clearly time to examine whether or how the Charter of the United Nations will be applied to internal conflicts within a nation. The original framers included strong recognition for sovereign nations and an inclination to avoid interference in internal matters. Worldwide peacekeeping missions are tending to cross over into that sphere. While these questions are pertinent to the discussion, they go beyond the scope of this text and the discussion of vehicle bombs. Unfortunately, these issues are unlikely to be addressed and unlikely to deter the continued attack by terrorists for some years if they were addressed by the international community. Social change frequently comes slowly, and is always dependent upon perceptional shift.

The current internal policy of the United States requires that vehicle bombs be treated as weapons of crime and the terrorists utilizing them as criminals. As raised in various parts of the preceding chapters, the following problems arise when applying this current policy inside the United States:

    • A violent group acting inside the United States can claim the right of self-determination, shifting their action from criminal conduct to war under international law.
    • The Constitution of the United States requires that war be conducted by the federal government; states do not have the authority to conduct it except in immediate self-defense. Such immediate

self-defense falls to the state's partisans or its legal militia. Federal troops are unlikely to be immediately available.

• The legally-defined militia is not on-duty in the United States. It must be "called forth"; summoned, first by the state, and then by the nation.

• Local or state police forces are on duty, but they are not part of the military forces of either the federal or state government; therefore, they have legal limitations in their ability to conduct war. They also have tactical limitations.

• Federal police forces can legally engage in war under the Constitution (a disputable legal point) but are not normally expected to do so nor usually prepared to do so. Their ability to do so is severely limited by number, deployment, training, and equipment.

• Private security forces can qualify as partisans in warfare but have very strong limitations on their tactical ability to conduct war or to simply enforce the law. They are seldom trained to confront this type of threat and prohibited from having the type of tactical equipment that is required to perform it with tactical effectiveness.

• Federal military forces have limited authority to engage in law enforcement; the Posse Comitatus Act directly prohibits it, and portions of the federal code tightly control the limited employment that is allowed.

In short, those who have the tactical capability and authority to conduct war are not available; those who are available lack the authority and tactical capability to conduct war against terrorists effectively. This is a succinct definition of the term "vulnerability." But, this problem with the internal policy does not apply just to groups seeking self-determination. There is no difference in the tactical limitations of the defense forces when vehicle bombs are used for an act of criminality rather than an act of war. You are, therefore, forced to the realization that the internal policy cannot be successfully implemented in an increasing risk environment. Changes in the policy and the supporting legal statutes are required. The tactical limitations just noted indicate the strategic policy that is needed.

Currently, the employment of vehicle bombs by terrorists affects the population of a nation regardless of whether the weapons are targeted at government buildings, at its military forces, or at the general population. Even the effects of the simple car bomb are so large that they usually kill civilians surrounding whatever military forces may be targeted. Frequently, the civilians are the intended target. This means that the strategy to prevent, defend, or respond to such attacks must be oriented on defense of the whole population and not just on the defense of the military forces or the particular governmental site. This vastly increases the scope of the internal defense measures that are necessary and is the opposite of the current trend in military operations. The latter are tending to focus on high mobility with orientation on the opposing forces rather than on positional defense. By its very nature, internal defense of the governmental structure and the population it serves virtually demands positional defenses. Mobile defense against vehicle bombs, as currently used by terrorists, will mostly fail as the risk escalates. Static defense forces will be required. These forces must be prepared for the battle but so must the population.

The preparation for battle by the population has begun inside the United States. The World Trade Center attack began the psychological preparation as no other event had, but the Murrah Federal Building attack really drove home the consequences to the general public in a way that no other incident had. More Americans died in the attack on the Marine BLT Headquarters, but they were Marines and soldiers on a foreign battlefield. Battlefield losses are expected; the losses in Oklahoma City weren't. The general population of the United States had to confront the reality of the attack, unnecessarily prolonged by the current propensity of the pop culture for emotional hand-wringing in a variety of manners. This psychological response to a stark confrontation with reality was not an unusual one by those involved. Those experienced with crime victims are familiar with the usual crime victim behavioral response sequence. We have seen it operating on a massive scale in relation to the Oklahoma City bombing. A similar response sequence occurs on the battlefield. After the blast, there was the initial phase of disbelief, an unwillingness to recognize and accept the reality, followed by the anger phase. Most of the population is still in the next phase, dealing with what occurred and attempting to understand it. Eventually, most will pass to the final phase; some won't.

Unfortunately, psychological preparation has a tendency to be transitory. If the incident or the danger is not repeated, people will tend to adjust to the new, lower threat level. The bombing at Khobar Towers, as an example, produced nowhere near the public reaction that the Oklahoma City incident did. The tendency to relax, to return to normal is very strong. Few people can maintain the psychological level of readiness needed to handle events of this type. Response personnel must. That is the reason that part of the material included in this text contains expositions that put the reader into the event or otherwise force a confrontation with the reality of the event. That is the first step in dealing with it: confronting the reality. The next step is understanding it in depth and then learning to act upon the understanding. Once the psychological decision to act has been made, then the policy forms and the legal preparation begins. The preparation must orient on forming, organizing, and assigning the static defense forces to the necessary tasks.

LEGAL PREPARATION FOR BATTLE

The international laws pertaining to warfare must be reviewed for implementation inside the United States in a way that will probably exceed all previous internal security actions, even those of World War II. Some of the actions that may be required will be controversial and many will be hard for the average American citizen to accept. As this discussion proceeds, let me unequivocally state that I am assuming that appropriate political debate will occur, that measures will only be implemented when needed, and that the rights of citizens will be protected. Some of these legal changes raise serious questions and serious concerns of a type seldom considered in this country. It is critical that the government *of* the people remain clearly *for* the people *by* acceptance of its purpose by the people. At all times, in all considerations, the policy-makers must orient upon the purpose in the Preamble of the Constitution:

> ... to form a more perfect Union, establish Justice, insure domestic Tranquility, provide for the common defense, promote the general Welfare, and secure the Blessings of Liberty to ourselves and our Posterity, ...

The considerations that follow simply *demand* such a focus; it is unusually important for the decision-makers to retain that patriotic center in order to make the correct decisions.

The Law of Warfare was written to apply primarily to conflict between nations. In this instance, it will be primarily applied to groups claiming the right of self-determination and not to nations. The United States has obligated itself to voluntary compliance with these provisions of international law. While it could be argued that the obligations pertain only to conduct between nations, such an argument raises moral questions about the government. That is a moral stance that is unacceptable to a democratic society and detrimental to successful response. The common defense against groups claiming self-determination requires clear delineation of the boundary between war and crime and clear delineation of both the authority and responsibility to conduct war or to enforce the law. There simply must be no question of who is responsible for acting, what their exact authority and obligation to act are, and what the response will be. Nor can there be any question as to whether a specific response is law enforcement or war. The current vulnerability exists due to gaps between the ability of the judicial and defense systems of both the state and federal governments to respond effectively. This requires adjustments to the existing legal codes and statutes of the United States based on an announced, clearly-known policy.

The first adjustment will be announced policy provisions at all governmental levels which clearly define the boundary between war and crime. Any acts must have clear points at which they cross the boundary or halt short of it. The limits may be tied to specific triggering events, specific means, or simply specific times. Here are some examples of policy possibilities which take this approach and address current policy and tactical deficiencies:

1. *The federal government might announce a policy that the possession of a nuclear weapon inside the United States without the permission of the federal government would be considered an act of war regardless of the motive of the group.* Under current law, possession of a nuclear weapon is a criminal act and other factors are necessary to determine whether the motive constitutes an act of war. With this policy alteration, the nation's defense forces would instantly respond with military force. No arrests, no negotiations, no diplomacy delays, just military action conducted under the law of war. Obviously, such a policy would need to recognize permission implied from certain treaties with friendly military forces.

2. *The federal government might announce a policy that an internal group declaring "self-determination" is effectively renouncing its U.S. citi-*

zenship. This immediately invokes certain existing firearms laws, immigration laws, trade laws, etc. which may be enforced against the group. If the group wants to claim they are and to act like they are a sovereign nation, then hit them with the full load of nation-state responsibilities and all of the attendant consequences. At the current time, groups are using this claim as a device to evade legal obligations. Counter by increasing the legal obligations, then the advantage fades and only the groups who actually are seeking self-determination will claim it. Obviously, the Constitutional limitation on exile of citizens would have to be examined.

3. *Place automatic lockouts on the duration of arrests of armed groups.* The stand-offs by armed groups such as the Republic of Texas, Montana Freemen, Branch Davidians, etc. have gone on for weeks. The police tactics used in those incidents were originally developed to deal with nonviolent groups that were more interested either in political statements or in portraying the government as repressive by prompting overreaction. Now the groups are more heavily armed and more inclined to actually forcibly resist. The police tactics must shift in recognition of this difference. By establishing a specific time deadline, the groups must either surrender to legal authority or clearly engage in an act of war. Under international law, an armed group that holds a portion of the interior meets the legal test of an invasion. The United States government is entitled to respond to it as an act of war under international law at some point. By announcing the event or time limits at which this response occurs, the incentive for the group to resolve the situation short of that point is increased while the procrastination factor of the political decision-makers is overcome. They must act when the matter reaches that point. The political discussion on the merits of the actions need not occur during the event, the necessary decisions have already been made in advance of need.

4. *Redefine the legal militia.* The primary response problem is that there are limited numbers of military personnel to respond daily to any act of war while the available police or private security personnel have limited authority to respond to an act of war. This can be rectified by a formal legal definition that includes the police or private security officers within the militia. This could be done at the federal level or state level and possibly at the local level as well. Obviously, many problems are raised by this approach,

but it overcomes the primary force deficiency and directly counters the strategy of the groups attempting to hide under a banner of self-determination.

Having examined some examples of policy changes, let us examine in more detail specific areas of the law that will need attention. The exact changes taken will be dependent upon the policy selected. There are five general areas previously examined: materials control, codes, emergency powers, militia and use of force. At this point, the fact that changes will be needed is clear in some of these general areas while the exact form of the changes is not yet developed or is dependent, as stated, on the policy chosen.

Materials Control

Controls on critical materials pertaining to nuclear weapons are already in place, and seem to be working reasonably well in accomplishing the goals. The same statement applies generally to the control of explosives. The one clear problem in the explosive control area is the widespread mixing of chemicals to make explosives on the spot rather than meet the stringent storage requirements of high-grade explosives. This is an example of an unintended societal response to regulation. Some changes may be needed in the storage requirements of either the high-grade explosives (making the provisions easier to implement) or of the precursor components of binary or other site-mixed explosives. That will be difficult due to the dual use problem with most of the chemicals.

Other chemicals are being monitored in a number of ways, particularly where they are in the workplace or in transport. The primary problem developing in regard to chemicals is the wide-spread release of information currently being required as a result of the worker and community right-to-know programs. This approach will need to be reviewed as it identifies to the disgruntled the exact locations, content, etc. of harmful material which can be diverted or immediately utilized. Policy will have to be developed to balance the two requirements. Worker safety can be jeopardized by too much information as well as too little information. The primary control measures concerning critical materials that is showing a weakness are those pertaining to biological warfare agents. This area needs attention but will be unusually difficult to impact in any meaningful way. The nature of the materials, their common usage, and the fact that they appear in the course of daily life rather than being manufactured makes the possibility of control rather limited. Defensive action may be the only option since prevention will be more difficult.

Codes

The vulnerability assessment techniques reviewed in earlier chapters highlighted some of the potential problem areas in various codes pertaining to structures and their access. The necessity to defend against an attack of this type was not foreseen as a realistic possibility when most building codes and zoning ordinances were developed. Federal buildings have been subject to certain security standards for several years as a result of previous targeting, mostly during the 1960s and 1970s. It appears that local and state codes may need to adopt security standards for various public buildings based on the type of utilization of the structure. Architects and urban planners will have to integrate civil defense considerations into their evaluations and standards. In effect, they must become familiar with urban combat damage and transform into civil defense planners.

Local zoning ordinances and planning may need to isolate those governmental structures subject to attack. This can be done first by separating the agencies most likely to be targeted from other governmental services. This reduces the direct risk to the other governmental services and the indirect risk to the population that they serve. In most instances, the agencies most likely to be targeted typically service a very small number of the general population making physical isolation an effective means of reducing the casualty count. Isolation can also be accomplished by establishing site setback requirements, effectively creating isolation zones around the probable targets. These zones will allow defensive space for preventing or engaging the attack and will also tend to reduce the effects of any successful attack on surrounding civilian businesses. Nearby structures may also have certain requirements added to them in recognition of their presence in a secondary risk zone. Some of these requirements may be intended to protect the individual business and its customers; others may serve a defense or response function for the point of attack. Structural strengthening would be an example of the first while a preplanned first aid station would be an example of the second.

Utility routes into the government site may need to be covered or disguised to make them inaccessible or less vulnerable to attack. Off-site emergency shutdown points may be needed to allow quick isolation of a government site. Likewise, drainage from certain sites subject to chemical attack may have to be considered due to the likelihood of spreading contamination beyond the point of attack. Catch basins to control outflow or soil filtration systems designed to protect leeching into nearby water sources may be required. A little work here may save considerable effort at a later date.

Traffic flow into a site must be considered both as an element of the defense and of the response. The site internal approaches and available external routes will have strong impact on both defense and response that cannot be easily adjusted when a situation develops. Finally, locations may have landscaping requirements added as a means of limiting damage. Both vegetation and grading may be covered in these. In short, urban planners are going to have to plan for site defense and battle damage caused by a weapon of mass destruction as part of the site development. This is a significant departure in thinking for urban planners and zoning commissions which will require both a perceptional change for priorities and supporting changes in the training of people performing zoning analysis and enforcement.

Next, the buildings themselves must be designed to withstand the attack. Certain overall design shapes may have to be restricted or specified due to their increased or decreased vulnerability to attack. Building codes may have to adopt requirements for construction techniques, reinforced joints, shielding, multiple exterior walls, or material restrictions to deal with the structural damage threat posed by vehicle bombs. Pressurized, divertable, and filtered ventilation systems may become a standard requirement in government buildings. Requirements for specific internal shelter areas of varied types and locations may be necessary. Electrical systems may have to incorporate extensive emergency backup systems tied directly to critical systems such as ventilation, filtration, or detection alarms. All utilities may require internal shutdown or access points to allow limited internal control by those who are temporarily trapped during an event.

Building security systems may have to change significantly, incorporating pressure detection, radiation detection, chemical agent detection, or biological agent detection and warning devices. Local meteorological data sites which give wind speed and direction along with atmospheric pressure readings may become a standard feature both on and off-site. Systems may be required to activate internal defense mechanisms automatically or may enable them for local activation by site personnel in a two-step process. Central monitoring stations may incorporate city-wide monitoring sites to allow emergency communications centers to instantly identify an event and to predict the probable affected area. Varied warning signals or systems may be needed to separately identify the type of emergency situation.

Building fire codes will need review to adjust egress requirements from structures in recognition of the type of damage or contamination that may be present. Internal contamination from a chemical or biological attack will occur much differently than the toxic products of combustion created during a fire. Pressurized or ventilated stairways or elevator shafts may need additional protections in order to maintain their life-saving functions. Strict ingress requirements for fire equipment access will need to be reviewed against the building defensive system requirements. Rigid compliance may no longer be feasible in view of the changing risk to life that is presented. Fire codes must adapt to the physical setting and balance the risks.

The Americans with Disabilities Act will need serious attention. The easy access specifications intended to assist the disabled with daily living contains requirements that directly counter the defensive needs of a governmental structure in this threat situation. These are the primary buildings that are required to enact all of the provisions. Compromises will have to be made; these will result in some lessened access for the disabled. At the current time, there is no obvious way to avoid this clash of needs. It will be a very difficult area in which to make adjustments fairly. Conscientious people on both sides of the issues will be at a premium.

Finally, local civil defense codes will need to be developed and applied. These must specify the marking of protected structures under the appropriate international Law of Warfare. Similar markings must be identified and applied for protected personnel and equipment. New categories may be needed for utility workers, vital in the modern urban area. Their status should be similar to that foreseen for merchant marine, aircraft crews, and other transportation workers whose duties frequently bring them into hostile-fire zones as noncombatants. Shelters and first aid stations must be identified, marked, stocked, and manned as needed in the locality of primary targets. Obviously, training sessions for the public may become a requirement in certain locations or in general. The local officials must decide what is needed and be prepared to respond with it. They can do nothing without the necessary legal structure. With this observation we have reached the consideration of governmental emergency powers.

Emergency Powers

A discussion of emergency powers always makes Americans uncomfortable. This is a natural reaction for a democracy, especially one that arose partly in defiance to emergency powers enacted to enforce orders from a monarch. There are two keys to dealing with the topic. Retaining the focus on the democratic purpose is the first and the second is viewing the laws as a form of social contract written to obtain that purpose. Emergency powers are provisions intended to allow the elected official concerned to achieve that democratic purpose at a time and place where the usual democratic government operation is unable to do so. Such powers always have the potential for abuse of the electorate; the secret to preventing that abuse lies in the quality of the elected officials. That quality is in the hands of the electorate. It must be enforced, routinely and constantly by the electorate each and every election, each and every time there is a performance failure by an official. In that way, when emergency powers are needed, the state and local officials involved will have the appropriate tempering to wield them on behalf of the democracy.

States and some local governments have identified emergency powers already in their legal structure. Typically, these statutes focus on the organization and activation of the state militia and the evacuation or control of areas affected by natural disasters and civil disorders such as riots. There is also some planning pertaining to nuclear wars evident in the typical statutes which provide for continuation of the government. An overview indicates that these emergency powers are deficient in certain areas pertaining to vehicular bombings and require changes.

The state militia structures will probably undergo significant changes in response to the threat of vehicle bombs. This will prompt a need to alter the means of ordering the militia into active service by the state. It may be necessary to authorize local officials to activate portions on request or in certain circumstances. More than any other threat, the vehicular bombing will easily overcome local resources. This forces the need for a local planning and response structure. Consequently, the county and city-level disaster and planning agencies will become more important with interjurisdictional planning becoming critical. This may lead to reimposition of the draft in altered form or to some form of mandatory service or training of the general population.

Legal liability will surface as a major issue and will require significant alterations in current doctrine. Exactly how the response forces are structured or authorized may, in the final analysis, be influenced primarily by the liability risk involved. Immunities or limitations of liability will be necessary.

Legal authority to order entry into private property, condemnation of private property or other control measures over private property will have to be strengthened in order to deal with the risks inherent in the vehicle bomb attack. This applies first to the various local codes that apply to buildings. Business and occupational licensing requirements may be affected as well. The state may have to specify the adoption of certain security measures in zoning or building codes as a means of protecting the public or of solving interjurisdictional disputes. State training requirements for selected occupations or officials may become necessary.

City and state officials will be required to enact emergency powers in a way that has not been considered in a modern democracy for decades. Cities and states must prepare their ordinances and statutes as needed to fit their own situation, the projected emergencies based on past experience, and simple area or terrain analysis, and the state and federal requirements that pertain to them.

Militia

Constitution of the United States

Article I Section 8 (Powers of Congress). The Congress shall have power to:
Paragraph 14. To make rules for the government and regulation of the

land and naval forces.

Paragraph 15. To provide for calling forth the militia to exercise the laws of the Union, suppress insurrections, and repel invasions.

Paragraph 16. To provide for organizing, arming, and disciplining the militia, and for governing such part of them as may be employed in the service of the United States, reserving to the states respectively the appointment of the officers, and the authority of training the militia according to the discipline prescribed by the Congress.

Article I Section 10 (States prohibited from the exercise of certain powers.)

Paragraph 3. No state shall, without the consent of Congress ... keep troops or ships of war in time of peace, ... or engage in war, unless actually invaded, or in such imminent danger as will not admit of delay.

The basic parameters for the militia are established in the Constitution and implemented by a variety of federal codes and regulations. Depending upon the policy implemented and the strategy chosen, changes will be required in certain portions of the federal codes and state statutes. Those pertaining to the legally-defined militia will probably be reviewed first. When these changes are made, there are two key points to remember.

The cumulative effect of the provisions listed above is a specific control procedure for the militia. Certain tasks are reserved to Congress and certain tasks reserved to the states. Any adjustments must recognize and retain this procedure or a constitutional amendment will be necessary. Notice, also, that the states retain the right of maintaining troops and engaging in war when they are "in such imminent danger as will not admit of delay." The threat posed by terrorist use of vehicle bombs probably meets the legal test inherent in that phrase. Assuming that legal interpretation is correct, states have the option of taking action without direct congressional authorization *if* such action meets the regulation specified by Congress for the militia. With these comments in mind, the following are the most likely considerations to adjusting the militia codes and statutes:

Definition. Currently, the legal definition of the militia recognizes the organized militia and the unorganized militia. The basic question will be whether to include police agencies, fire departments, private security officers, and other emergency workers into the existing definition and into which category. Creation of new categories may be needed at either the federal or state levels. Formation of both federal and local militias, as opposed to state militias, may also be needed.

Arms and Equipment. There are two basic questions here. First, is how the necessary defense equipment will be provided to any members of the legally-defined militias and what the exact specifications of the equipment will be. The second consideration will be directly influenced by the first decision. If the firearms or other equipment provided are normally restricted by various other laws, then some adjustments will have to be made to the necessary laws involved (The M16A2 Rifle currently authorized for military use is both an automatic weapon and an "assault rifle" under existing federal guns laws which prohibit their possession and use by private citizens). There may even have to be some reconsideration of the Second Amendment; it is likely to be prominent in any discussions or considerations pertaining to the issues.

Activation. The current laws require that activation of the militia or of federal troops be based on a request for assistance from the local officials. The state then confirms the need and either acts or forwards the request to the federal government. This procedure has two problems in relation to the vehicle bomb. First, a vehicle bomb is likely to be targeted against government operations and may, consequently, destroy part of the operation necessary to activate or respond to the request. Second, this type of attack requires a response speed which is faster than that which the current activation procedure is capable of attaining. Changes to make this essentially a local decision and response will be necessary.

Authority. The primary question will be when or under what circumstances the militia will operate, and whether they do so as soldiers or as law enforcers. Secondary consideration will be the level at which control is retained (local, state, or federal).

As will be discussed further below, the principal organizational requirement is for a paramilitary police organization, one that has both the authority and the capability to conduct either law enforcement operations or military operations (fight crime or fight a war). It must be both responsive and flexible while retaining the appropriate level of training and discipline necessary to retain the integrity of the force and the integrity of the state.

Use of Force

As reviewed in Chapter 9, the use-of-force statutes found in most states have a tactical limitation when applied to attack by vehicle bombs. The basic problem is that the usual self-defense statutes are designed to control confrontations between two individuals. They are not designed to deal with attacks against groups, particularly large groups. Effective defense against the vehicle bomb requires statutory recognition inside the United States of the collective right of self-defense, and definition of the circumstances where the collective right outweighs the individual right in the self-defense encounter. Revised use-of-force statutes must accomplish certain objectives as outlined here:

Group defense. The concept of imminent danger must be expanded to allow a broader interpretation for group defense situations than for individual defense situations.

Government buildings and assembly places. The defense of dwelling standard must be applied to government buildings and assembly places as a means of obtaining the group defense needed. Use-of-deadly force must be authorized on the basis of an "attack profile" or on the basis of "non-compliance with stated or posted instructions." This is to overcome the tactical disadvantage inherent in the situational interpretation of imminent danger and the related objective reasonableness standard.

Defense zones. The use of force must be altered to allow the local or state officials to establish building or site defense zones inside of which instant use of deadly force is authorized without further warning. This is best accomplished by passing enabling legislation at the federal level which must be activated or applied by the state or local government as needed. This approach maintains the appropriate balance of power arrangements while standardizing the duties and responsibilities. The nationwide standard is important due to the responsibility or citizen duty imposed on the public by this approach. Each citizen must understand the risk involved and where it applies.

Public notification. The establishment of defense zones must be accomplished by clear public notification. Each defense zone must be marked so that any citizen unfamiliar with the area is obviously forewarned that he is entering a defense zone. The use-of-force approach taken places an assumed risk on each citizen entering the defense zone. Each citizen must understand that risk and have the opportunity to avoid it if they choose to do so.

There will be many who will object to this approach to defense of groups. Each citizen must understand the tactical risk and the choice that it forces. One must either accept the risk inherent in this type of defensive approach or accept the consequences of any attack by a vehicle bomb. There is no middle ground. Saying "*No*" to this defense approach is equivalent to saying "*Yes*" to the consequences of a truck bomb. The decision-makers and the citizens voting for them must understand that this is the choice. That is the only way that the approach can be made to work.

Civil Liability

Liability for any action is a fact of life in the United States. In the government setting, it is applied differently than in the private setting. The defense against vehicle bombs raises a number of liability issues which will have to resolved in the authority and classification of the common defense forces. The following is a short rundown of the issues and possible actions.

Military forces. Military forces are exempt from individual liability under our current legal structure. If a military force causes damage to a citizen or his property in peacetime, then the citizen is entitled to file a claim under the U.S. Government tort claim system. In a wartime setting, this system may or may not be viable. Militias, when acting under the control of the Department of Defense, will be included in this exemption from individual liability.

Police forces. Police forces, as part of a government operation, usually have limited immunity. The exact amount of immunity from liability varies from state to state depending upon their local statutes. In addition, police officers are traditionally entitled to what the courts term "a good faith error" which acknowledges that officers can be in error while acting reasonably with good intent. However, individual police officers retain individual liability for acting outside of their authority under various civil rights provisions and court precedents. If police forces are redefined as militias, then this liability situation will be altered since military forces have individual immunity. Such a change may be necessary to deal with the defense situation against vehicle bombs. The level of defensive force required against an attack by a vehicle bomb is likely to produce a higher than normal rate of mistakes. This needs to be recognized and the individual officer will need liability protection in this setting. Failure to provide it may cause hesitancy to fire which will be adverse to the public defense. If police forces are not made into militias for this defensive mission, then adjustment to the individual liability will be needed.

Private security forces. Under the standards for citizen arrest and use of force, a private security officer has complete individual liability for errors without regard to the reasonableness of the error. In addition, the business must meet the "reasonable care doctrine." The result is that a private security force which defends against vehicle bombs has no way to avoid liability, only a choice of whether to accept it for successful defense or unsuccessful defense against an attack. If private security officers are to provide the defense, then the situation will require adjustment. Creating a "militia" category of private security officer is one way to do it. When a private security officer becomes a member of the militia, he assumes the civil liability immunity of military forces. Otherwise, the civil liability exposure must be adjusted by the state laws in recognition of the risks and tactical factors involved. This is the only way that a private business could reasonably afford to perform this defense task. The scope of a vehicular bombing will simply exceed the insurance or loss resources of most businesses. If private security is involved in the defense against vehicle bombs, it is likely to prompt federal or state regulation of the private security industry to an extent never before seen in the United States.

Defense zones. The creation of building or site defense zones will have some impact on the liability risk in the area surrounding the defense zone. This may increase the insurance requirement or premium for businesses operating in those areas. The amount of increase may be so large that government action to assist will be required in order for the business operations surrounding a government building or other probable attack site to remain open.

Private citizens. Many insurance policies contain provisions which exempt acts of war. This needs to be adjusted in some manner as the loss which can be expected by a vehicular bombing can easily overwhelm the total assets of a private citizen or even an insurance company. The classification of a vehicular bombing as either a crime or an act of war makes considerable difference in insurance coverage and its costs. This will need to be considered and possibly adjusted. To some extent, the difference is already covered in provisions found in the "disaster zone" proclamation process at both state and federal levels, but more attention may be needed to clarify the requirements for application to a vehicle bomb.

Civil liability is a problem which is partly addressed by the legal status of the defense force organization. It must be part of the discussion when making the policy decisions and must be addressed in advance. If a private citizen or private business is required to accept the loss risk, they need to know that in advance to have the opportunity to make the best decisions.

ORGANIZATION FOR BATTLE

The organization of the common defense forces to prepare for any attack by a vehicle bomb will be dependent upon the overall strategy chosen. It is a task that can be accomplished in a variety of ways. This examination will review the current missions of various organizations and comment on the advantages or disadvantages with the certain approaches or choices of agencies. The primary requirement for any organization is the authority and capability to both enforce the law and to fight the war. The primary analysis of each will be based upon this dual role which can be stated simply as its capability to perform as a "paramilitary police force." This can be fulfilled by a police force performing military duties or a military force performing police duties. At the current time, there are very few organizations that can meet this test. These are some federal law enforcement agencies and the National Guard. Starting at that point, and assuming that uniformed operations will be required, the following is an analysis of the current organizations which could be used.[3]

Federal Organizations

Department of Justice.

The Department of Justice is an executive department of the federal government. As such, it possesses the same constitutional war-fighting authority as the Department of Defense and could conceivably be tasked to exercise it by presidential directive. Such an approach has some problems. The first is the Attorney General.

Attorney General. The key to recognizing the essential problem here is to ask a simple question. Why is the Department of Justice run by the Attorney General? Or to phrase it in a manner which makes the problem more obvious, why is the Department of Justice always run by an attorney? At the time that the Cabinet was originally formed, the only educated people in what is now the criminal justice system were attorneys. This was still mostly true into the mid-1900s. Now it is no longer true. Now the criminal justice system has a corps of professionals with advanced degrees in public administration, criminal justice, behavioral sciences, education, etc. Many of these have experience in running prisons, courts, and law enforcement agencies which makes them more knowledgeable concerning many of the problems in the criminal justice system than attorneys are. Yet, these professionals are not considered for the top federal job. Attorneys, by contrast, usually have little experience running anything other than a law firm. Most law firms are considerably smaller in numbers of personnel and tend to be isolated from a number of other factors or situations that arise in managing public agencies. Does this influence the result? Well, look at the current DOJ mission statement:[4]

> As the largest law firm in the Nation, the Department of Justice serves as counsel for its citizens. It represents them in enforcing the law in the public interest. Through its thousands of lawyers, investigators and agents, the Department plays the key role in protection against criminals and subversion, in ensuring healthy competition of business in our free enterprise system, in safeguarding the consumer, and in enforcing drug, immigration and naturalization laws. The Department also plays a significant role in protecting citizens through its efforts for effective law enforcement, crime prevention, crime detection, and prosecution and rehabilitation of offenders.
>
> Moreover, the Department conducts all suits in the Supreme Court in which the United States is concerned. It represents the Government in legal matters generally, rendering legal advice and opinions, upon request, to the president

and to the heads of the executive departments. The Attorney General supervises and directs these activities, as well as those of the U.S. Attorneys and U.S.
Marshals in the various judicial districts around the country. (28 USC 501, 503,
509)

If the idea that the criminal justice system is run by a "law firm" is new
to you, you're not alone. The perspective which generated this mission
statement is important.

Attorneys constitute a limited social group within the American
society. As a subgroup, they bring a limited social perspective, a limited range of education, and a limited range of experience to the position of Attorney General. The threat posed by vehicle bombs will
require a different range of management skills within the Department
of Justice which attorneys as a group are unlikely to have. Other supporting points, which do not pertain to vehicle bombs, can also be
raised.

The recent history of conflict between the Presidency and the
Congress has resulted in the repetitive appointment of special prosecutors. The conflict presented by having an Attorney General who
works for the person being investigated has been resolved by the
appointment of special prosecutors. This is clearly demonstrating a
conflict of legal needs between the Office of the President, the occupant of that office, the Executive Branch generally, and the public in
particular. One attorney cannot effectively represent all the competing
interests. It seems to be clear indication that the legal representation of
the country (essentially the Department of Justice) should be restructured. As one of those changes, the position of Attorney General needs
to be separated from that of the Agency Head. Opening the top job to
a wider range of backgrounds will be beneficial. There are times when
the nation is best served by having an attorney manage the
Department of Justice, but there are also times when it would be best
served by a warden, a police chief, a sheriff, a court administrator, a
state police director, a city administrator, a governor, a crime victim,
or even a reformed bandit. From a practical viewpoint, it doesn't make
sense to automatically exclude all others from consideration. The
broad range of the management responsibility requires a broader perspective than possessed by the typical attorney. Limiting the top job to
attorneys tends to limit the perspective, the management experience,
and the management potential. The rise of vehicular bombings and

the possible assignment of war-fighting duties to the Department of Justice will probably prove to be the final step in demonstrating that a restructuring is overdue.

Federal Bureau of Investigation. The current mission statement of the FBI is as follows:

> The Federal Bureau of Investigation is the principal investigative arm of the United States Department of Justice. ... Its jurisdiction includes a wide range of responsibilities in the criminal, civil and security fields. Priority has been assigned to the five areas that affect society the most: organized crime/drugs, counterterrorism, white-collar crime, foreign counterintelligence and violent crime.[5]

The FBI presents a mixed picture of advantages and disadvantages as a paramilitary police force. Traditionally, most of their personnel are drawn from sources that rely heavily upon academic backgrounds rather than experience backgrounds. This has altered somewhat over the last two decades, but the influence is still present. Some personnel are drawn from the military and some from police agencies, but, overall, the FBI does not have a core of people who are experienced with uniformed operations. Their primary mission continues to be investigations and other operations which orient upon plainclothes activities that are significantly different from uniformed operations. The hostage rescue unit is an exception to these overall comments, but it constitutes a very small percentage of the agency's operations and missions.

Assigning a uniformed police operation to the agency also assigned the counterintelligence mission has some unity of command advantages but has clear balance of power disadvantages. Such a centralization of authority will probably make citizens nervous. Intelligence agencies typically operate in a gray zone of legality which will raise questions about the lawfulness of the overall operation. The gray zone has to be avoided in this setting. In addition, intelligence agents frequently are overly secretive and have difficulty translating their evaluations into real operational terms. They frequently miss or misinterpret intelligence that is important for operations while simultaneously placing too much emphasis on collection activities or too much reliance upon covert counteractions. By positioning the tactical arm in a different agency, the counterintelligence operatives will be forced to "make their case" and to openly disclose their operations and analysis to those who do not have a vested interest in either from a performance viewpoint. In the long run, this approach will probably be most beneficial to a democracy in this situation.

The FBI has a reputation for hostility to local law enforcement, particularly in some areas of the country and during certain time periods. This is caused, in part, by their mission to enforce ethics in government and civil rights, but is also attributable to their operational style as well. A Deputy U.S. Marshal once observed to the author that the FBI never makes small arrests, only big ones. They are frequently perceived as simply "using" other agencies to obtain their own ends. But, this is partly due to their agent locations. The deployment of the FBI, as with most other federal agencies, is primarily in urban areas. It is difficult for them to concentrate agents anywhere, particularly in rural areas. This means that there must be heavy reliance upon local police officials in order to succeed in a paramilitary environment. This situation will handicap them. Finally, what reputation it does have in tactics is preceded, or perhaps overcome, by its negotiation philosophy, its definition of success. Any operation is considered a success if it results in no loss of life.

This is a statement of both strategic and tactical limitation. A force that is so concentrated on keeping people alive has a strategic credibility problem; the opposition will be inclined to think that it won't consider use of force, or will, at least, delay it. Tactically, the concentration upon any one tactic, in this case, negotiation, eventually leads to the development of effective countertactics by the opposition. This is part of the current problem. The overconcentration upon the negotiation approach and its application when it is ineffective is lessening the chances of successfully using the tactic when it is appropriate and lessening the chances of tactical success when it isn't appropriate. If the FBI is assigned the paramilitary mission, it will have to alter its mind-set and develop a flexible range of tactics to meet a variety of situations.

Last, the FBI has no direct mission for defense of buildings or property. Its counterintelligence mission does require it to be familiar with security standards and vulnerability analysis generally, but it is not required to implement the actual defense. This is a skill that would have to be more fully developed.

United States Marshal Service. The Marshal Service performs a variety of tasks primarily related to the courts. The appropriate extracts of its current mission statement for this discussion are:

Providing support and protection for the federal courts, including security for over 700 judicial facilities ...; apprehending most federal fugitives; operating the federal witness security program, ... responding to emergency circumstances, including civil disturbances, terrorist incidents and other crisis situations ...[6]

The U.S. Marshal Service also presents a rather mixed profile for consideration as a paramilitary police force. The oldest federal law enforcement agency, it has repeatedly been bypassed when new missions were identified for permanent law enforcement expansion. This is primarily due to its history of political appointees; all positions were appointed until the 1970s. Now, only the Director and the U.S. Marshal for each court district are political appointees. This handicap, which in the past has been seen as an impediment to professionalization, provides an effective mechanism for local control, an effective balance of power arrangement which may be an advantage in this setting.

Marshals have traditionally been drawn from the ranks of local politics, local agencies, and the military. They have much stronger ties to local agencies due to this and to their frequent contact with various sheriffs, jails, and prisons in both process service and prisoner handling roles. This type of duty, however, has caused them to be considered a lower skill agency within the Department of Justice. Consequently, the USMS has traditionally been treated as an ugly duckling, and its employees have been held at lower pay levels than the major investigative agencies over the years. This has contributed to its difficulty in attracting and holding high-quality employees. Its reputation for mismanagement and abuse of its employees has also held it back. In spite of this, the USMS has both the broadest law enforcement authority of any agency and a history of having performed virtually every job there is at some time.

Its current mission to protect federal courts gives it direct experience in vulnerability analysis and defense of a building. This skill base would need to be broadened over the full-range of the threat. Its Special Operations Group has been assigned a broad range of tactical response over the years; so it does possess some paramilitary capability. The breadth of tactical action would need to be expanded. While it possesses these two attributes which partially qualify it for the paramilitary police mission, it has previously declined the opportunity to take on a uniformed branch (turned down mission of guarding all government buildings) and has the same deployment problem as the FBI. It would have difficulty assembling a force in any location, particularly in rural areas.

Drug Enforcement Administration[7]

> The Administration enforces the provisions of the controlled substances and chemical diversion and trafficking laws and regulations of the United States, and operates on a worldwide basis. ...regulations governing the legal manufacture distribution and dispensing or controlled substances ... manages the El Paso Intelligence Center (EPIC).

DEA was consolidated with the FBI in the 1980s. Its current mission gives it some crossover capability to paramilitary missions, but, overall, it would not be a good selection for the job. Its personnel are typically drawn from local and state agencies with which they have a lot of continuing contact. However, their typical operation is completely plainclothes; there is virtually no long-term experience in operating uniform response. What tactical experience its agents have is focused on raid or entry response which is a very narrow range of tactical expertise. The limited authority is also too narrow to be of value. Its expertise in the area of chemicals and clandestine laboratories is of considerable value in evaluating possible manufacture of either chemical or biological agents. Like the other members of the federal law enforcement community, it would have difficulty assembling a team at any location within the United States.

Immigration and Naturalization Service[8]

> The service carries out its mission through operational programs in adjudications and nationality, inspections, investigations, and detention and deportation, as well as the U.S. Border Patrol.
> ...preventing improper entry and the granting of benefits to those not legally entitled to them;
> ...apprehending and removing those aliens who enter or remain illegally in the United States and/or whose stay is not in the public interest; ...

The Border Patrol performs a limited law enforcement mission, but tends to organize and operate more like a military force during its operations. Its limited authority and numbers of personnel as well as its deployment would prevent it from being effectively utilized without a major change in size and mission.

Department of Defense[9]

The Department of Defense is responsible for providing the military forces needed to deter war and protect the security of our country (10 USC 111).

Its ability to provide security internally is limited by the Posse Comitatus Act (18 USC 1385) which prohibits use of the armed forces for law enforcement.

Department of the Army[10]

The mission of the Department of Defense is to organize, train and equip active duty and reserve forces for the preservation of peace, security and the defense of our Nation. As part of our national military team, the Army focuses on land operations; its soldiers must be trained with modern arms and equipment and be ready to respond quickly. The Army also administers programs aimed at protecting the environment, improving waterway navigation, flood and beach erosion control, and water resource development. It provides military assistance to Federal, State and local government agencies, including natural disaster relief assistance. (10 USC 3012, 3062).

Ground defense of the interior of the United States is technically tasked to the United States Army; the mission is assigned to its Army Area Headquarters through Headquarters, Forces Command. The basic defense would be performed primarily through the units of the National Guard of the various states. Under the current structure, the National Guard is the organized militia. It is not part of the active force until called forth by the federal government, so it is not bound by the limitations in the Posse Comitatus Act. In most states, the National Guard is granted state law enforcement officer status when called into service by the governor of the state. This gives it the basic authority necessary to perform either mission. The National Guard possesses basic and advanced tactical training which exceeds most law enforcement agencies. However, National Guard units are organized and trained primarily for combat missions, not for law enforcement missions. The tactical training they have may not be appropriate to the mission.

The primary problem with use of the National Guard is its daily availability. The members are scattered throughout the various communities of each state but are not engaged in Guard duties. Additionally, when called into state service, there will be an insufficient number to actually perform the duties required over an extended time period. Some reorganization will be required, but this force already has an excellent balance of power arrangement.

Also within the Department of Defense are two additional forces which can be considered for paramilitary police use. These are the Special Operations Command and the military police or security police units of the Army or Air Force respectively. As active units, these organizations are bound by the limitations of Posse Comitatus. This will limit their deployment or require alteration of that law. SOCOM has a wide range of tactical capability but comes with a reputation that may raise questions during its use for law enforcement. The tactical training that it does have is not oriented to law enforcement; it may require retraining on the judgment portion of the firing process to meet the legal standards for law enforcement.

Military police units, on the other hand, are trained in both facets of use-of-force from the beginning, constantly changing from law enforcement to military operations. This makes them unusually suited to the role requirement, but they lack the authority necessary to perform it. Realistically, they also lack the necessary resources and the local contacts. MP/SP units typically are very limited in number and have limited contact with local authorities except in the immediate vicinity of military bases. Once released to perform the paramilitary mission, they would have to be replaced at the military bases where they are performing law enforcement duties. These units would have difficulty assembling at most locations due to the limited number. For the most part, this effectively eliminates them as a viable force for paramilitary police use.

Department of the Treasury[11]

The Department of the Treasury is an executive department of the federal government so it also possesses the same basic war-fighting authority as the other departments. Its structure makes it less prepared than even the Department of Justice. While it is not suffering from a similar limitation with its top job, its law enforcement agencies have little in the way of tactical capability.

> The Department of the Treasury performs four basic functions: formulating and recommending economic, financial, tax, and fiscal policies; serving as financial agent for the US Government; enforcing the law; and manufacturing coins and currency. (31 USC 301).

Bureau of Alcohol Tobacco and Firearms[12]

> The Bureau is responsible for enforcing and administering firearms and explosives laws, as well as those covering the production, taxation, and distribution of alcohol and tobacco products. ... Ensure that storage facilities for explosives are safe, secure and properly stored to avoid presenting a hazard to the public; (Treasury Order 120-1) ...

BATF is assigned extensive regulatory duties and law enforcement duties. It has formed some regional tactical teams, but these are oriented toward raid or entry operations which makes them limited in scope. The mission to regulate explosives and investigate bombings provides BATF with a strong base for conducting vulnerability analysis in regard to vehicle bombs, but this mission is not put into practical use by them to actually guard vulnerable sites. It simply provides it to other agencies. BATF frequently has contact with local agencies through arson investigation and frequently draws personnel from local agencies. Due to the nature of its investigations, however, it has limited experience in long-term uniform operations. That limitation, paired with its limited authority make it of limited usefulness for a paramilitary police force. Like the other federal agencies, it would have difficulty trying to assemble a force at any point due to its limited numbers.

United States Secret Service[13]

> Protect the President ... Protect the White House, temporary residence of the Vice President and foreign diplomatic missions in Washington, DC ...

The Secret Service possesses a very strong reputation due primarily to its role in personal protection. In this role, it has experience making vulnerability analysis for buildings and other sites as well as implementing them. Within the last two decades it has also acquired a small uniformed force to augment its corps of plainclothes investigators. The investigative role assigned to the Secret Service gives them some contact with local agencies as does the site coordination role for presidential visits. However, it does not draw most of its personnel from law enforcement ranks. Traditionally, most Secret Service agents come from outside of law enforcement and are trained as investigators. This background and its duties give a focus which is not consistent with tactical operations even though it operates a uniformed force of limited jurisdiction. The limited duty of the agency makes it unsuited for use as a paramilitary police force. It also has the same assembly problem seen in the other federal agencies.

Department of Transportation[14]

> The U.S. Department of Transportation establishes the Nation's overall transportation policy. Under its umbrella there are 10 administrations whose jurisdictions include highway planning, development and construction; urban mass transit; railroads; aviation; and the safety of waterways, ports, highways, and oil and gas pipelines. ... (49 USC 102)

The Transportation Department originally developed hazardous material transportation regulations. These lead to the development of hazardous materials teams all over the United States. This will continue to be a means of regulating the access to the necessary materials for vehicle bombs. This department also controls the Coast Guard which already serves as a paramilitary police force.

United States Coast Guard[15]

> The Coast Guard is a Branch of the Armed Forces of the United States at all times and is a service within the Department of Transportation except when operating as part of the Navy in time of War or when the president directs. (14 USC 1).
>   Maritime Law Enforcement. The Coast Guard is the primary law enforcement agency for the United States. It enforces or assists in the enforcement of applicable Federal laws and treaties and other international agreements to which the United States is party, on, over and under the high seas and waters subject to the jurisdiction of the United States, and may conduct investigations into suspected violations of such laws and international agreements. The Coast Guard works with other federal agencies in the enforcement of such laws as

they pertain to the protection of living and nonliving resources and in the suppression of smuggling and illicit drug trafficking.

The U.S. Coast Guard performs effectively as paramilitary police force, but the possibility of expanding it is limited by the nature of its mission. Consequently, it can not be considered for an additional ground defense mission, although attachment of an amphibious or Marine paramilitary police force may be worth considering for limited applications.

General Services Administration[16]

The General Services Administration establishes policy for and provides economical and efficient management of Government property and records; including construction and operation of buildings; ... (40 USC 751)

The General Services Administration is not an executive department of the federal government, so it does not have authority equivalent to the Department of Defense. It is not clear, however, that this would limit its ability to control a war-fighting force since it is still part of the federal government. Its mission to provide construction management of government buildings gives it considerable experience in developing security standards based on vulnerability studies. Past standards may have to be altered to meet the new threat. GSA supervises the Federal Protective Service which provides security to the majority of federal buildings. Consequently, GSA brings some experience supervising a uniformed police force. These forces possess limited tactical capability. While they do have response forces, these forces are seldom put into operation.

Office of the Federal Protective Service[17]

... The FPS coordinates with appropriate Federal Emergency Management Agency representatives for security and law enforcement requirements. It gathers protective intelligence information pertaining to demonstrations, bomb threats, and other criminal activities. The office provides centralized communications, alarm monitoring, and coordination for state and federal officials regarding Federal facilities. It develops a nationwide physical security protection program and coordinates a nationwide Occupant Emergency Program.

The Federal Protective Service provides security services to the majority of federal buildings. In this position, they develop defense plans to the buildings and have daily or frequent contact with local authorities. FPS is providing many of the services that will be required to conduct effective site defense. However, FPS has limited experience in operating in other uniformed operations which would limit it effectiveness if deployed in a tactical role as a paramilitary police force. Like the other federal agencies, it has limited ability to assemble a response force at any point in the country.

State Organizations

Most states have established state police organizations which could be tasked to perform a paramilitary police function. In some states, the investigative arm is separated from the uniformed patrol function while others maintain integrated state police organizations. Most of these state police organizations provide on-call tactical teams in some form. Contact with local officials in most state police organizations is a daily occurrence, and they frequently draw recruits from the local police and sheriff agencies of the state. The experience operating uniformed patrol over extended periods of time is an asset as is the variety of response problems typically tasked to state police organizations. The primary difficulties faced by state police organizations center in three areas.

The investigative arm of the state police usually handles the undercover and intelligence functions for the state. In organizations where these functions are integrated with uniform patrol, there will be a lessened balance of power which may be inappropriate to the task of paramilitary operations. Tasking paramilitary operations to an investigative agency should be avoided wherever possible. In uniformed agencies, the individual troopers frequently work very independently and are frequently scattered in isolated posts around the state. While providing better local contact, this hinders easy assembly of a large group for action. The final problem area is equipment. State police organizations are usually not equipped with the type of individual weapons or vehicles that may be needed for the type of operations required.

Each state already has a National Guard headquarters with the appropriate authority for paramilitary police operations. In most cases, it will be easier to build on this existing organization for response than to create other capabilities. The problem, as mentioned before, is that they are not typically available on a daily basis. It takes time to notify, assemble, and deploy them for a response unless they are already activated. This suggests that a multilevel response approach must be implemented for overall effectiveness.

Local Organizations

At the local level (city and county), the police and sheriff's departments are typically the only official organization capable of paramilitary police response. No city currently keeps troops organized into any militia; they simply rely on state organizations which are requested as needed. Small police organizations would find that the threat posed by vehicle bombs exceeds their resources due to the size of the response. Fortunately, at the current time, the threat is greatest in urban areas where larger departments are typically found. These larger organizations may also be overwhelmed, something which many of them would not expect if asked to evaluate their capability prior to an in-depth analysis.

Police departments are seldom equipped with the type of firearms needed to defend a site, the personal protective equipment needed to respond, or the command and tactical equipment needed to engage an opposing force under the Law of Warfare. Many have personnel with military experience, but most departments would not know how to make the shift to a combat operation rather than an enforcement operation. They have simply not planned for it, even those that have well-developed tactical response teams. The training scenarios for those teams seldom envision the type of response that might be necessary. At the current time, reliance upon the federal or state resources is almost mandatory for local agencies.

Private Organizations

Many cities and some states license private security officers in varying categories. Applying the partisan test outlined in an earlier chapter, these organizations could conceivably be used as part of the defensive structure at a local level. This approach is enormously complicated due to the legal structure currently in place. Overall, the private security organizations lack the training, experience, and equipment necessary to tackle the assignment of paramilitary police duties. However, their daily availability and experience with site defense operations (usually called by other names in this setting) make them a better selection for site defense than most police organizations. In some settings, the best choice may be to utilize the private security organizations for paramilitary operations. This will obviously require significant authority or legal status adjustments to accomplish.

The only other possibility that will be mentioned is the private citizen in general and specifically, those that belong to informal militias. Private citizens as a whole are not organized, trained, equipped, or mentally prepared to defend sites. This task goes beyond the realm of personal defense. While their daily availability and certainly their motivation is high, the extent of the legal authority necessary is lacking. Their ability for instant call out varies considerably as does their personal skill in the various areas. This approach can not be considered without significant adjustments in the structure.

Finally, let us address the possibility of organized groups of private citizens in two forms, those that call themselves militias and the rest of them. These groups of private citizens all face the same primary problem mentioned for individual private citizens. Regardless of motive, they do not possess the legal authority necessary under our current structure to engage in paramilitary police operations. Those that claim to be "militias" cannot pass the constitutional test for militias, although some individuals within some of these groups can individually pass the statutory militia member test.[18] This approach should not be considered anywhere. If private citizens are needed to expand the capability, they must be brought into the existing legal structures in order to properly sort out all of the authority and liability questions involved.

Having briefly looked at the various possibilities for organizing a paramilitary police force, the examination will conclude with a short review of other federal agencies that perform missions that relate to the response to weapons of mass destruction.

Other Federal Organizations with Response Missions

Department of State[19]

Advises the President in the formulation and execution of foreign policy. ... Primary objective in the conduct of foreign relations is to promote the long-range security and well-being of the United States. ...

The Department of State controls counterterrorist policy overseas and coordinates with foreign governments on related matters. It receives input which will be pertinent to other agencies.

Department of the Interior[20]

The Department of the Interior has some site defense missions due to its responsibility for historic sites. While these are probably not primary targets under the current threat, they are potential targets. This mission is performed primarily through the National Park Service.

The mission of the Department of the Interior is to protect and provide access to our nation's natural and cultural heritage and honor our trust responsibilities to tribes. This includes fostering sound use of our land and water resources; assessing and protecting our fish, wildlife and biological diversity; preserving the environmental and cultural values of our national parks and historical places; and providing for the enjoyment of life through outdoor recreation. (43 USC 1451).

National Park Service[21]

The National Park Service is dedicated to conserving unimpaired the natural and cultural resources and values of the National Park System for the enjoyment, education and inspiration of this and future generations. ... The National Park Service has a Service Center in Denver that provides planning, architectural, engineering, and other professional services. ...

Department of Labor[22] (15 USC 1501)

The Labor Department controls OSHA which regulates worker safety. The notification requirements and access to hazardous materials are directed by this agency.

Occupational Safety and Health Administration.[23] The regulatory authority exercised here can be beneficial in some investigative circumstances.

> ... develops and promulgates occupational safety and health standards; .. conducts investigations and inspections to determine compliance with safety and health standards and regulations; and issues citations ... (29 USC 651).

Federal Emergency Management Agency[24]

FEMA was recently restructured to assume a broader range of duties than had previously been assigned to it. It can be expected to be the central point for coordination in training and response to all forms of weapons of mass destruction. The key is that it orients on response and not defense.

> The Federal Emergency Management Agency is the central agency within the Federal Government for emergency planning, preparedness, mitigation, response, and recovery. Working closely with State and local governments, the Agency funds emergency programs, offers technical guidance and training, and deploys Federal resources in times of catastrophic disaster. These coordinated activities ensure a broad-based program to protect life and property and provide recovery assistance after a disaster. (Exec Order 12127)

Central Intelligence Agency[25]

> ...under direction of the President or the National Security Council:
> makes recommendations to the NSC for the coordination of intelligence activities ...
> correlates and evaluates intelligence relating to the NSC and provides for the appropriate dissemination of such intelligence within the government;
> collects, produces, and disseminates counterintelligence and foreign intelligence, including information not otherwise obtainable. The collection of counterintelligence or foreign intelligence within the United States shall be coordinated with the Federal Bureau of Investigation (FBI) as required by procedures agreed upon by the Director of Central Intelligence and the Attorney General;
> collects, produces, and disseminates intelligence on foreign aspects of narcotics production and trafficking;
> conducts counterintelligence activities outside the United States and, without assuming or performing any internal security functions, conducts counterintelligence activities within the United States in coordination with the FBI as required by procedures agreed upon by the Director of Central Intelligence and the Attorney General;

> Protects the security of its installations, activities, information, property, and employees by appropriate means, including such investigations of applicants, employees, contractors, and other persons with similar associations with the Agency, as are necessary;
> The agency has no police, subpoena, or law enforcement powers or internal security functions. ...

Without police powers, the CIA is strongly limited in its ability to perform any actions within the United States but is involved in providing information and retains the protection of its own facilities, even those inside the United States.

The multitude of departments and agencies with missions related to prevention of, defense against, or response to weapons of mass destruction within the United States is quite large and tends to be confusing to the uninitiated. Within the last two years, the Department of Defense has initiated actions to form special response teams at the national level and recently announced that the National Guard will be tasked to perform portions of this mission. The full extent of the plans has not been released to the public. Within the last year, training of urban emergency responders has begun in sessions offered by DOD and FEMA. This training is expected to continue for the immediate future.

The Department of Justice has initiated changes since the major incidents at Waco and Ruby Ridge. There was a restructuring of the police tactical teams that existed in the various DOJ agencies and alteration of their responsibilities. More cooperation between agencies was initiated with clear guidelines on when mission hand-off would occur during an incident and which agency was responsible for what duties. The use-of-force guidelines were reviewed and altered. The full extent of the changes in the use-of-force policy has not been released to the public. Examination of the official report on Waco and review of other public sources[26] shows that tactical considerations have been integrated into the use-of-force instructions. They no longer depend entirely on a solely legalistic viewpoint of the engagement. There is indication that DOJ and other federal agencies have shifted their use-of-force policy to become more like the rules of engagement used by military forces. This is an improvement and a necessity in view of the extreme amount of attention being focused on the details of such engagements. It is also effective response to the perceived threat.

While the complete government strategy being implemented has not been publicly stated, the examination above indicates that strategy should focus on three levels of implementation which should be primarily based on timeliness and availability of forces. The instant level of response (defined as available within minutes of a threat or an attack–initial stage of response) has to be provided at the local level. Different techniques can be used, but it has to be locally controlled forces. The immediate level of response (defined as available within minutes to hours of a threat or an attack–formation stage of response), has to depend on multijurisdictional response. This indicates that it should be controlled by the various states rather than a local agency. This leaves the reinforcement level of response (defined as either available within days or as specialized in nature - stabilized stage of response). Due to its nature, it is probably best addressed at the national level, but may be manageable at the state level. The primary strategy being enacted here is based upon certain assumptions which can be stated as follows:

Prevention is tasked primarily to the level of government with intelligence assets and broad authority due to the mobile nature of the threat. This means that prevention belongs primarily to the federal government and secondarily to the state governments.

Defense is tasked primarily to the level of government with instantly available assets and authority to control the defense site. This means that defense belongs primarily to the local government supported by state assets or federal assets where state or federal sites are involved. The overall control structure can be at the state level, but must be implemented at the local level to be effective.

Response is tasked primarily to the level of government with instantly available assets and multijurisdictional authority. This means that response belongs primarily to the local government directly supported by state assets. State response can be used, but must be implemented at the local level to be effective.

Analysis of the material in the previous chapters leads to these conclusions which fit the currently available information on policy. It is the logical strategy to the threat posed. The analysis also gives strong indication of the changes that are needed in police organizations.

EQUIPPING FOR BATTLE

The equipment requirements for defending against weapons of mass destruction will vary depending upon the strategy undertaken and implemented. Some equipment deficiencies have already been recognized, the most obvious example being the developmental work underway in the detection of both explosives and chemical or biological agents. Other equipment needs will become more obvious as the defense situation progresses. As a result of the discussion in the previous chapters, there is a clear need for certain defense equipment. The following paragraphs provide a brief examination of these identified requirements.

Alarm Systems. Standard security alarm systems will need some reconfiguration to address the problems raised here. Pressure detectors will be critical as will radiation detectors. These already exist and can easily be attached to existing systems. The primary problem will be the necessity to install these at off-site locations as well as on-site locations. Detection of chemical and biological agents in a reliable, low-cost package is already an identified future goal. The primary area of deficiency which will require additional work is the shifting of security alarm systems to integrated defense systems.

Alarms are just the first step in activating defensive response. Integrated systems will need provisions for triggering various building defense response from simple warnings to activation of filter systems, pressure systems, ventilation systems, etc. This is much more complex and much more site specific. It requires integrating the alarm systems with other building control systems (temperature, elevators, water, etc.). The speed of the attack may require virtually automatic defensive response in order to successfully defend. Aside from the technical problems, this also raises personnel evaluation, training, and legal issues.

Ammunition. The potential legal problem noted with current police use of hollowpoint ammunition is likely to create a demand for fully-jacketed ammunition that complies with the Law of Warfare. The typical law enforcement defense situation will undergo some changes which will alter the ballistic profile of effective ammunition somewhat, but the demand for low penetration in crowded environments will continue for most defensive applications. The competing demands will lead to a compromise in which police ammunition, primarily for handguns, will be required to be fully-jacketed while not penetrating beyond the first person struck by the bullet. It is quite probable that, with some testing, a flat-nose jacketed bullet which meets this specification can be developed. The answer lies in creating the demand to the industry. It can respond when there is a financial reward and a clear need.

Barriers. The need for barrier development was discussed in the defense analysis of vehicle bombs (CWMD). The CWMD Anti-Emplacement Barrier (Figure 55) and the CWMD Baffle Wall Barrier (Figure 56) can be developed with some minor technical work or determined to be of little value with a good technical examination. Simple forms to allow fabrication by mold-pouring or filling at a deployment site will significantly reduce the logistics requirements for deployment. Alternately, by producing an exterior shell of ballistic, hardened, or dense material and filling the interior with concrete or a similar material, a barrier which can withstand the pressures without cracking or dislocating should be attainable at reasonable cost.

Examination of other barrier elements mentioned will be mostly technical in nature for the architects, engineers, and construction personnel. The Angled Wall (figure 57); A Sharp Breakover with An Angled Wall (Glacis and Rampart) (Figure 58); A Sharp Breakover, Ditch and Wall (Glacis, Ditch and Rampart) (Figure 59); or A Sharp Breakover, Ditch, Wall and Baffle (Glacis, Ditch, Rampart and Parapet) (Figure 60) will be site construction components that should be examined for incorporation with other security, landscaping, and access features. They are not equipment items but concepts which can be applied in a variety of ways.

Checkpoints or Entry Buildings. One problem which is virtually unacknowledged is the need to design checkpoint buildings for the entry point. When planning to defend against vehicle bombs, you need to consider the probable effects on the guard force. In order to maintain a prepared and motivated defense force, the individuals need to have a reasonable chance of survival. Currently, entry point buildings are designed to simply be shelters from the weather. Reinforced structures with aerodynamic designs will be more appropriate. It is quite probable that the geodesic dome, with the lower part below ground level, may prove to be an effective design due to its angles and relative structural strength. Regardless of the overall design, the structures will need to be multipurpose. Guards will need to operate from it daily and to activate various alarms and defense mechanisms. A basic design should be developed to replace the usual "shack" that predominates now. This type structure is actually worse than having the individual simply standing in the open.

Firearms. As examined in Chapter 1, the unorganized militia has no equipment, no organization, and virtually no training. If they are called forth, as envisioned by the Constitution of the United States, Article I, Section 8, to help provide the common defense, they will need equipment. The statutory conflict created by the restrictions within Title 18 and Title 32 of the United States Code (firearms provisions versus militia provisions) will have to be resolved. If the private sector is to provide the necessary site defense, the law will have to be altered to allow possession of appropriate firearms by private persons. Changes to the existing firearms laws will be required in order to provide the effective defense as discussed in Chapter 9.

If the necessary site defense is to be provided by calling forth the unorganized militia as part of the governmental structure, then the same change may be required. Traditionally, the unorganized militia has been required to provide its own equipment. The state has the option, of course, to provide the firearms, but this raises different problems. The firearms must be procured (manufactured, purchased, and distributed), they must be stored, and they must be provided to a group that has limited training in their use. This cannot be accomplished in a short time period due to the significant deterioration of the manufacturing and distribution base in the firearms industry as well as the training base shortage in the general population. Overall, this is a significant problem which clearly illustrates that the federal government has been enacting policy without properly balancing all of the effects. In short, the current situation exists due to legislative and executive incompetence. That is a problem which has to be cured by the voters.

Medical Centers and Supplies. The strategic medical approach being used is likely to fail. At the current time, there are few cities which maintain sufficient resources to provide large quantities of medical equipment and supplies. Mobile sources of medical supplies are simply unavailable. Supplies are usually stocked at hospitals or warehouses and are not intended to be delivered to the scene of a problem. Yet, this would be advantageous in mass casualty situations.

Prestocked vehicles or packs may be the easiest solution, but the current stabilization and evacuation strategy does not provide for this. Some urban areas have been closing hospitals in the urban core area due to declining usage. Retaining some of these in limited use may be part of the solution. Various approaches are possible, but further examination is needed to determine the best method for implementation.

Meteorological Stations. Simple weather data stations capable of providing wind speed and direction will be critical in forecasting the initial response stages. Use of pressure detection with these stations will help provide the necessary detection and identification of the vehicular bombing. Once installed, these stations can collect historical data for input to refine planning for other weapons of mass destruction. The technology for this is already available. The stations simply need to be packaged in the form needed and hooked to the appropriate alarm or data systems.

Modeling Resources. Some governmental agencies and some private contractors have various data and analysis programs which pertain to vehicular bombings. A simple vulnerability analysis computer program which can forecast basic effects of explosions on surfaces and shapes needs to be developed and made available to local police agencies and planners. These will be of particular value in the special weapons vulnerability assessment. The analysis requirements will probably increase as the threat increases.

Negative Pressure. Since the damage mechanism in a vehicle bomb is the pressure wave, development of negative pressure systems for defense is a logical counteraction. The concept may be applied in various ways. Installation of pressure tanks along the probable avenue of approach, in the vent pit, etc., allows an immediate defense. Activating them during a blast will reduce the total pressure achieved which tends to lower the damage. Such devices do not need to be used just at static defense locations. There is nothing that prevents the use of mobile tank trucks which can move into threatened area for a short time. Such systems need developmental exploration.

Palletized Bomb Containers. The Department of Defense has fielded a palletized loading system for supply transportation. Essentially, this is a large truck which has the ability to off-load a container without any other materials handling equipment. Applying this concept to the risk of vehicle bombs is possible. A portable ventilation shield can be developed for fast emplacement around suspected car bombs using palletized systems. This concept can also be concurrently developed for immediate use in most cities by relying upon the fleets of trash trucks that are currently available.

The trash truck fleets in most urban areas have two types of lift capability. The first is the front lift capability; it has two forks that simply slide into a container and lift it over the cab for dumping into the rear bed. The trucks could be used to emplace two-piece shields that interlock around the suspected bomb. The same trucks could be modified to carry the containers for emplacement or could have bomb disposal containers in the back allowing bombs or dispersal units to be scoop-lifted and dumped into the rear. The second type of trash truck is one that emplaces a 20- or 40-foot container using a system somewhat similar to the DOD palletized system. A 20-foot container is large enough to surround a car, van, or pickup so emplacement as a shield is possible. Obviously, there is some risk to using the technique, but it has the potential to lower the overall risk.

As with all equipment evaluations, cost factors and political decisions will come into play. Officials should not overlook the identification and application of existing equipment. Trash trucks, street sweepers, tank trucks, cranes, forklifts, etc. all have application to vehicular bombing response. The planning official must identify what is typically available and how to apply it before he begins creating requirements for other specialized equipment. The availability of the various equipment cited above will assist the prevention, defense, and response to weapons of mass destruction but will not guarantee the success of any particular approach. That is simply the nature of risk analysis and the technical solutions that it produces. The final determinant will be the level of vulnerability that the individual site has and the willingness to assume that level of risk.

COMMENTS ON FUTURE POLICE OPERATIONS

Certain trends and effects on police operations should have become evident based on the issues raised throughout the text. There are four general areas in which changes should be implemented or should be planned for future implementation. These areas are the authority and mission of police, the public image of police, the administration and training of police agencies, and the equipment of the typical department. The discussion in Chapter 1 laid the foundation for some of the observations that follow.

Authority and Mission

The authority of police agencies to deal with acts of war is likely to be modified in some form. There are several possibilities as previously discussed, but they all have the common factor that police agencies are likely to be involved in site defense in some manner. The legal authority will change in some fashion as this defense mission is added. From this simple common factor, we can predict that the police role in the community will be changing. Further, it will be changing in a manner that requires a close examination of police-community relations. The public is exceptionally conscious of use-of-force issues at the current time. In terms of the anticipated mission change, this means that there will be an unusually high visibility of the differences in the use-of-force against criminal acts as opposed to use-of-force against acts of war, at least in the initial phases of the transition to a "war" situation. This will also extend to the differences in arrest and imprisonment versus capture and detention. The distinctions will be important, and the public will need to understand the differences in order to support the police and military action. Assignment of a military mission will place new strains on the police agency and its relationship to the community.

Public Image

The professionalization of police agencies over the past two to three decades has been accompanied by unanticipated side effects. One is the increase in the public expectation of that performance. It has reached unrealistic levels in many areas. This is due to a combination of factors including an inflation of the perception of personal risk to officers and a resulting overemphasis on police survival training. These influences must be countered by the police agencies in order to maintain public support. Community education will be required to reverse that trend. It is time for police agencies to educate the public in the realities of the use-of-force and the realities of citizen responsibility in encounters with police. Agencies will not be able to do this alone. Other public officials must help. It is also time to put officer survival in appropriate personal context. There simply are times when an officer has to assume risk on behalf of society. The social impact of officer survival actions must be put into the self-defense and use-of-force training. Officers who object to assuming risk may need to be released from the job.

The primary community perception problem will be a clear definition of the dividing line between police actions and military actions. This requires a complete review of the appearance of officers performing a variety of duties. Police uniforms, particularly for tactical or entry teams, have had a tendency to move away from the traditional police uniform to a more military uniform and appearance. It will be exceptionally important to counter this trend. Many officers will argue against it for a variety of reasons, but it must be done. The visible image is exceptionally important. Since there is a difference in the authority and use-of-force between the police and military roles, the officer and the agency must "knock and announce identity and purpose" from the beginning of any encounter with a citizen. This means that current police tactical units and entry teams must discard the camouflage uniforms, subdued insignia, and similar accouterments that tend to blur the dividing line. Police officers must clearly look like police officers and soldiers must clearly look like soldiers. This military attire for police tactical teams is, quite frankly, mostly a police social fad anyway. The usefulness of most this attire is exceptionally limited in a police operation, particularly one in an urban area. A return to high visibility for police officers is mandatory in a democracy facing this type of problem.

Administration and Training

Police administrators will be confronted with a variety of problems for which most have limited experience or preparation. Administrators will need to seek training in policy development for military versus police operations. Use-of-force policy and instructions will change significantly. Planners will need to acquire threat and vulnerability analysis skills along with prediction skills for the full range of weapons of mass destruction. Management of personal exposure to hazardous materials will increase dramatically requiring administrators to increase knowledge in worker safety and similar areas to which police departments have traditionally been exempt. Command channels will change significantly affecting a variety of related subtasks such as communications, records, and personnel actions. Selection criteria for some personnel will change significantly as the mission changes.

Police tactical training and use-of-force training will undergo major shifts. Police academies have traditionally been weak in teaching basic tactics. When tactical skills are included, they have tended to focus on individual actions and practical performance with little emphasis on understanding basic principles. Group actions and application of principles in a variety of ways to fit the situation are critical elements in successful military operations. Individual protective skills against the hazards of special weapons of mass destruction will have to be included, particularly since the percentage of military veterans in police departments and the general population has dropped. Use-of-force training will have to expand from simple self-defense and arrest situations to include site defense and capture of military forces. Additional weapons training of a variety of types is likely to be necessary as well. Police training is likely to become more like basic military training. Some of these changes will apply to selected personnel while others will be more general in nature. The exact changes will be dependent upon the strategy implemented and the resulting authority and mission changes.

Equipment

Police agencies are likely to require equipment which they do not have. The threat posed by some weapons of mass destruction will require procurement of personal protective equipment for officers, monitoring and detection equipment, and firearms of different types. If the agency is assigned a military mission, the latter will quite likely be specified by type, model or caliber. There will be a clear trend toward uniformity in all types of equipment. Agencies may have to stock or control equipment issued to local militias, private security forces, or other organizations depending upon the type of strategy undertaken. Additional or specialized communications requirements may appear. Some of this equipment will be available as excess from recent Department of Defense downsizing or modernization, but much of it won't be. Budgets will be strained by procurement needs, but also by maintenance needs. Some of this equipment will require calibration or maintenance that is not typically available in the department or even in the community.

In addition to the defense forces themselves, police agencies may become the custodians of a variety of emergency supplies needed for the public. Chemical and biological agents require drugs or medicines to counteract them. Some of these are included on controlled substance lists. There will be security requirements for these as well which may increase the guard force mission. The variety of equipment and support requirements may create the need for additional support facilities and personnel.

COMMENTS ON FUTURE EMERGENCY OPERATIONS

The review in this textbook suggests that weaknesses exist in other areas of emergency response and the following these will need correction if the threat continues to develop.

Medical Operations. Medical operations at both the hospital and ambulance levels will probably be forced to assume a more regional approach to some emergency services. States have typically avoided becoming too involved in this area of the private sector but may have to act to fill certain voids. Some hospitals may have to be subsidized or operated by the state simply to maintain the specialized treatment facilities necessary to handle mass casualty cases or contaminated patients. Medical storehouses with specific stockpiled vaccines or drugs may also be necessary.

Ambulance operations have typically relied upon mutual support in order to increase capability in times of overload. Mass casualty situations of this type, particularly contaminated patients, will overload the system beyond the capability of mutual support for extended periods of time. It may be necessary for urban areas or states to create reserve fleets that can be put into service when needed for this type of incident.

Firefighting Operations. Firefighting operations have also relied upon mutual support to increase capability in times of overload. This type of incident, particularly where there is contamination, is likely to overload even the mutual support system. Urban areas or states may need to create reserve fleets of fire equipment to handle response to contaminated areas.

The specialized equipment needed to perform rescue or decontamination operations in collapsed structures and contaminated areas will quickly overload the capability of even the best prepared rescue or HAZMAT squads. The cost and the requirements will easily exceed the ability of most local departments. Regional or state approaches to these projected needs will be needed if this threat continues to develop. Specialized search, detection, and monitoring equipment; personal protective equipment; and decontamination materials will probably need to be stockpiled at reserve equipment points.

Communications Equipment. If this threat develops, the need to communicate between local, state and federal agencies will develop. This has been addressed to some extent in mutual aid frequencies. These frequencies will easily overload. Two other problems may easily occur. If the target is a government building, the local emergency communications center may be damaged. Planning at a state or regional level will need to include quick replacement of a modern emergency communications center. There will also be a need to communicate between military and civilian agencies. This crossover communication capability is somewhat limited at the current time. It will need to be addressed. Again, a state may need to create equipment stockpiles in this area.

Consolidation of Jurisdictions. The pressure put on emergency agencies in these types of incidents will be extreme. Areas which have consolidated agencies or jurisdictions will be able to respond more effectively. Consolidated departments of public safety which perform more than one of the three basic emergency services will find that the benefits of integration pay off in this type of incident. The crossover skills in both management and operational levels will increase performance overall. Areas which have consolidated jurisdictions for response will also experience the same benefit. This threat may prove to be a spur for more integration or consolidation of services.

States are mandated to have disaster planning operations. The recent increase in the occurrence of natural disasters has already focused more attention on these operations. The further development of this threat will increase the need for emergency planning, adding other planning and skill areas for those involved. Overall, the systems currently in place will need to integrate an approach which is more oriented on civil defense than on natural disasters.

PERSONAL COMMENTS

It is impossible to accurately predict whether or to what extent the threat posed by vehicle bombs will develop in the United States. Much of the information currently floating around in the accessible media tends to overstate the nature of the threat. In writing this text, I have taken, essentially, the worst case approach in order to demonstrate the nature of the threat more clearly and both the complexity and nature of effective response to the threat. In closing, I want to add comments on my personal experience at Khobar Towers and a few comments in the political spectrum which relate to both the development of the threat and the solutions being proposed.

The mission handed to me at Khobar Towers was a legitimate threat situation. I drew it by chance on the basis of my military rank and branch qualification. In terms of population, it was essentially equivalent to guarding a small city or providing security to an entire Army division of troops. I went into the assignment with an educational and experience background that I felt had prepared me pretty well for the assignment. I walked away from the assignment satisfied that I had performed in the satisfactory to good range overall. The mission performance was clearly not flawless and experienced a number of problems. My experience left me with a number of conclusions which have only been strengthened by my further study of the topic and the writing of this text. There are certain things which I want to strongly emphasize.

Policy-Makers and Administrators. Policy-makers and administrators often seem to want to implement use-of-force restrictions which are inappropriate to the tactical setting. They become excessively concerned about the public perception and issue orders for use-of-force which actually prevent successful defense. *As the person in charge of the defense force, it is absolutely critical that you clearly and unequivocally inform them when the policy is tactically inappropriate.* The policy-makers and administrators must understand that the decision they are making is to accept the consequences of attack by vehicle bombs rather than to risk the consequences of bad public perceptions. It is imperative that the nature of the decision is communicated to them in terms that they can understand.

The Public. The population that is using the facility and resides or works in the surrounding areas will present you with a number of problems. Even in the controlled environment of a military population, the defense force was repeatedly subjected to verbal abuse and various forms of refusal to comply with instructions. These came from a wide variety of people with varying status and ranks. The public must be clearly informed of the security procedures and both the public and the defense force must be dealt with appropriately and decisively in each and every confrontation incident.

Skill of the Defense Force. Most police chiefs or military commanders who are tasked with this mission will pay little attention to the skill level of the defense force. Most will assume that it is a one-size-fits all police or military job. The task of defending a site against a vehicle bomb requires police personnel in the average to high skill range. I observed this mission being performed by infantry personnel, military police personnel, and military personnel from a variety of other branches. Military police personnel are the best fit. The infantrymen had difficulty adjusting their thinking to the limited firepower concept and the judgment decision inherent in police use-of-force. They also demonstrated their "exceptional people skills" when interacting with the public. Soldiers from various supply, clerical, artillery, and maintenance backgrounds presented a rather mixed performance. They were able to grab the limited firepower concept easier than infantry, but usually did not have as much weapons skills as either the infantry or the military police personnel. Their people skills also generally fell between the skills of these two groups. This type of duty requires screening of the personnel. The five general areas of screening are weapons skill, use-of-force judgment capability, understanding of the legal parameters, public interaction capability, and psychological capability to withstand stress and to make quick, accurate decisions. This is a tough combination to find.

Stress. It is virtually impossible to adequately describe the level of stress in this type of defense position. The defense mission at Khobar

Towers was large enough for me to see the whole range of problems for a police official, but small enough that I was part of the mobile response force on a daily basis. On occasions, I substituted at the static defense positions for a short time period. The reality of psychologically confronting the fact that the lives of hundreds or thousands of people directly depends upon your instant performance is quite strong. The position requires you to decide whether you are willing to shoot at or to ram an attacking car bomb while you are in the kill zone; you can not avoid the psychological confrontation. It is quite a stark contrast to everyday life.

The position also requires you to make repetitive life-threatening evaluations literally hundreds of times each day. The simple act of screening identification of hundreds of people in vehicles puts you in a danger position and imposes repetitive physical actions which will give you sore muscles, or even periods of disorientation and vertigo.

Finally, it is also important for both the administrator and the tactical commander to grasp the simple fact that the defense force has to take pride in what it does in order to maintain performance. Imposing tactically inappropriate use-of-force restrictions tends to be viewed as insulting to a professional police officer. The higher the professionalism, the greater the insult to the officer. Such a policy tends to sap the morale over a long term, lowering performance. The verbal abuse also tends to do the same. The defense force has to be supported; the attitude that "the customer is always right" simply doesn't work in this environment. Decisions on public interaction problems must be fair. When the public is wrong, the defense force has to be supported. When the defense force is wrong, it must be disciplined. High standards are necessary.

Over the years I have performed a variety of military, law enforcement, and security duties. These included being under fire in combat, providing personal protection to federal witnesses in high risk situations, handling a wide variety of dangerous federal prisoners, and handling a variety of street emergencies, arrests and disturbances. None of these duties approached the level of stress inherent in controlling a military police force performing as a defense force against truck bombs. The stress factor applies to the supervisors, commanders and administrators as well as to the police officers filling the security posts.

When vehicle bombs are involved, the appropriate policy and skills are the foundation for successful prevention, defense and response, but both the public and the stress are significant factors which can overcome the first two factors. Success depends on the right combination.

Political Comments on the Threat

The final section of this text is the most difficult; it must have the right balance to it. This chapter began by quoting the opening lines of Lincoln's Gettysburg Address. The influence of his words have been quite strong on me over the years. At the age of about twelve, I joined several cousins in a family gathering hosted by an aunt living in Pennsylvania. The activities included visits to former residences of earlier generations of the family and a lengthy visit to the Gettysburg battlefield. Nearly forty years later, I can clearly recall standing there. I am not sure why the memory is so vivid or what influenced me the most. It may have been the scope of the battlefield and its elements, both vast and miniature. It may have been the clear portrayal of the conflict on a terrain map with lights for units. It may have been the talent I discovered while playing the board game of the battle purchased that summer. It may have been the discovery of my own name listed on a Union marker as "killed in action." It may have been the discovery of an unconfirmed family connection to a Union general killed at Gettysburg. It may have been the effects of reading the words of Lincoln as I stood in the midst of the battlefield and beginning to understand them. It may have been the combined effect of all these things. I know only that the Gettysburg battlefield calls to me at times. I sometimes feel destined to stand there; that I have some purpose yet to fulfill, some lesson yet to learn. This feeling has persisted over the years, recalled strongly while studying the role of Joshua Chamberlain in the battle as a reserve officer in the Command and General Staff Officer Course, and recalled again while viewing the PBS series on the Civil War. It has again become strong as I prepared this text. I have had to sort through a number of sources, references, memories, and experience to assemble it, and now some feelings to end it.

For several years, I have had the uncomfortable feeling that the country is again on the road to Gettysburg but doesn't realize it. One of the developing threats for the use of vehicle bombs inside the United States is coming from a segment of the American society with which I have a lot in common. I have occasionally encountered members of the informal militias as well as a variety of federal prisoners who belonged to various violent groups, many of which would be described as terrorist or hate groups by large portions of society. I find that I understand what a lot of them are saying while not particularly agreeing with them. What really astounds me is that the rest of the society does not seem to comprehend them at all. The informal militias are filled with an assorted array of popinjays, idiot savants, cranks, cuckoos, pretentious bandits, and occasionally misdirected, but otherwise, rational citizens. In short, they are socially equivalent to the so-called "Peace" movement of the 1960s. But, there are important differences between the movements and between the informal militias and other citizens.

The so-called "peace" movement espoused a belief of nonviolence while producing a number of factions that bombed, burned, robbed, and persecuted in the name of "peace." A tactical analysis of the people engaged in the bombing, burning, robbing, and persecuting shows that they really weren't all that skilled at it as individuals. Their backgrounds were deficient in the military arts, and they gloried in their self-selected role of being anti-government while trying to influence government. The informal militia is espousing either separatism or super-patriotism while producing factions that bomb, burn, rob, or persecute to attain those ends. They glory in their role of rejecting the current government, but are varying between trying to leave it and trying to influence it. They differ from the "peaceniks" in their individual skill. They possess people who actually know how to bomb, burn, rob, and persecute somewhat effectively although not nearly as effectively as they believe. The members of the informal militias differ from the average citizen in that they clearly recognize the vulnerability of the society to "sovereign nations," groups seeking "self-determination" and to vehicle bombs or similar weapons of mass destruction. The fascinating part of this equation is that the politicians who trace their support to the social groups who supported the so-called "peace" movement are themselves now moving toward open war with the informal militias. The same groups that advocated changing the government to absorb the protestors into the society in the 1960s are now advocating noncompromise with the opposing group and enacting various means to repress their speech, actions, and beliefs. The group in power is continuing to advocate "advancement" down the road they have selected without any regard to whether that road leads to the battlefield. It appears that the road to hell is paved with good intentions.

If the threat of vehicle bombs continues to develop, the police and military agencies of the United States will be confronted with the necessity for clear and decisive speech and clear and decisive action. The politicians are unlikely to support either. As a military police officer who has had to confront the actual threat of weapons of mass destruction in a civilian "peacetime" setting, I will leave you with this final guidance for the difficult decisions that you may have to face [The first speaker is Thomas Paine commenting on the willingness of some to blindly follow the monarchy]:

> ... However it is needless to spend much time in exposing the folly of hereditary right, if there are any so weak as to believe it, let them promiscuously worship the ass and lion, and welcome. I will neither copy their humility, nor disturb their devotion.[27]
>
> We, the people of the United States, in order to form a more perfect union, establish justice, insure domestic tranquility, provide for the common defence, promote the general welfare, and secure the blessings of liberty to ourselves and our posterity, do ordain and establish this Constitution of the United States.[28]

The purpose of the Constitution is clear even when the society isn't. Therefore, remember the words of Lincoln:

> ... It is for us the living, rather, to be dedicated here to the unfinished work which they who fought here have thus far so nobly advanced. It is rather for us to here be dedicated to the great task remaining before us...[29]

The great task remaining before us is to prevent, defend or respond to the use of vehicle bombs. The bombs at the World Trade Center and the Murrah Federal Building clearly demonstrate that the threat is increasing. How fast and how much it increases is difficult to predict. The politicians and the citizens may yet choose a different road than the one that leads to Gettysburg. If they do not, then the police and military officers of the country will find themselves on the Battlefield at Gettysburg.

Those who stand guard and those who stand behind them must always be prepared. Hopefully, this text has helped prepare those who stand guard and those who stand behind them, whenever and wherever they must stand against vehicle bombs.

Notes

1. Page 409-410, *On War* by Carl Von Clausewitz, edited by Anatol Rapoport, Penguin Books, 1968, Middlesex, England.

2. This is envisioned as a private security officer who is funded by the business, but must meet certain selection and training standards set by the state militia structure. Such an officer would have greater authority than a typical private security officer and would receive appropriate training through a state police or military training center.

3. The analysis and commentary presented in this section is based primarily upon personal observations and experience and does not reflect any extensive research into personnel practices or agency records. It should be treated as personal opinion of an educated and experienced observer.

4. Page 329, The United States Government Manual, 1996/1997, Office of the Federal Register, National Archives and Records Administration.

5. Page 349, The United States Government Manual, 1996/1997, Office of the Federal Register, National Archives and Records Administration.

6. Page 351, The United States Government Manual, 1996/1997, Office of the Federal Register, National Archives and Records Administration.

7. Page 353, The United States Government Manual, 1996/1997, Office of the Federal Register, National Archives and Records Administration.

8. Page 352, The United States Government Manual, 1996/1997, Office of the Federal Register, National Archives and Records Administration.

9. Page 174, The United States Government Manual, 1996/1997, Office of the Federal Register, National Archives and Records Administration.

10. Page 197, The United States Government Manual, 1996/1997, Office of the Federal Register, National Archives and Records Administration.

11. Page 446, The United States Government Manual, 1996/1997, Office of the Federal Register, National Archives and Records Administration.

12. Page 451, The United States Government Manual, 1996/1997, Office of the Federal Register, National Archives and Records Administration.

13. Page 460, The United States Government Manual, 1996/1997, Office of the Federal Register, National Archives and Records Administration.

14. Page 411, The United States Government Manual, 1996/1997, Office of the Federal Register, National Archives and Records Administration.

15. Page 215, The United States Government Manual, 1996/1997, Office of the Federal Register, National Archives and Records Administration.

16. Page 565, The United States Government Manual, 1996/1997, Office of the Federal Register, National Archives and Records Administration.

17. Page 573, The United States Government Manual, 1996/1997, Office of the Federal Register, National Archives and Records Administration.

18. The Constitutional test of the group is twofold: Is it controlled by the state, and does its equipment, arms, training and discipline meet the standards specified by the Congress? If either answer is no, the group can not legitimately be a militia under the United States Constitution. I know of no group which meets these tests or is interested in trying to meet them. The individual test for militia membership is current membership in the military forces of the United States including the National Guard or an able-bodied male, 17-45 years of age.

19. Page 389, The United States Government Manual, 1996/1997, Office of the Federal Register, National Archives and Records Administration.

20. Page 309, The United States Government Manual, 1996/1997, Office of the Federal Register, National Archives and Records Administration.

21. Page 316, The United States Government Manual, 1996/1997, Office of the Federal Register, National Archives and Records Administration.

22. Page 370, The United States Government Manual, 1996/1997, Office of the Federal Register, National Archives and Records Administration.

23. Page 382, The United States Government Manual, 1996/1997, Office of the Federal Register, National Archives and Records Administration.

24. Page 533, The United States Government Manual, 1996/1997, Office of the Federal Register, National Archives and Records Administration.

25. Page 490, The United States Government Manual, 1996/1997, Office of the Federal Register, National Archives and Records Administration.

26. This conclusion is based on articles in the FBI Law Enforcement Bulletin which show a shift in police use of force training. The articles are: "FBI Training on the New Federal Deadly Force Policy" by John C. Hall, J.D., April 1996, Page 25; "Integrated Use-of-Force Training Program" by Brian R. Arnspiger and Gordon A. Bowers, M.A., November 1996, Page 1; and "Improving Deadly Force Decision Making" by Dean T. Olson, February 1998, Page 1. The content and selection of the articles for printing indicates a shift in police thinking to a more tactical viewpoint than has been prevalent in traditional training.

27. Page 78, *Common Sense* by Thomas Paine, 1976, Penguin Books, Middlesex, England

28. Preamble, Constitution of the United States.

29. From the Gettysburg Address of Abraham Lincoln delivered November 19, 1863.

Appendix A

PREPARING THE CSS BASE FOR REAR BATTLE[1]

CAPTAIN JOHN W. ELLIS

The Army's rear battle doctrine is outlined in FM 90-14[2], Rear Battle. However, this manual does not address the process that should be followed in preparing combat service support (CSS) units for rear battle. After dealing with this mission at various levels, I have gained some insights into the problems, solutions, and tricks-of-the-trade of rear-battle planning. Some of the lessons learned about preparing for rear battle should benefit commanders of CSS units assigned to command a CSS base or base cluster.

The rear-battle mission includes two primary planning areas (rear-area security and area damage control) and two primary contingencies (evacuation or destruction of a CSS base). The keys to successfully accomplishing the rear battle mission are *thorough preparation, strong coordination, flexible integration, and imaginative adaptation.*

Thorough preparation begins when a unit assembles the necessary reference library of manuals, regulations, forms, and files. After key personnel understand the doctrine, rear-battle mission requirements should be compared to the unit's Army training and evaluation program (ARTEP) tasks. The two lists of tasks will overlap, though not completely. By matching rear-battle and ARTEP tasks, the unit develops a rear-battle task listing that aligns the unit's rear-battle and CSS functions.

During the analysis of tasks, it will probably become apparent that the unit's field standing operating procedure needs to be rewritten, or at least reorganized. All pertinent areas must be consolidated in the procedure to ensure proper coordination whenever the unit is assigned to command a base or base cluster. Commanders should expect to identify areas that need further attention. Evacuation and destruction procedures, command and control requirements, lateral coordination requirements, area damage control procedures, fire control procedures, and rules of engagement are typically weak or nonexistent in field standing operating procedures. The final stage of preparation is training under the new procedure and in any new tasks identified as a result of the rear-battle mission analysis.

Rear-battle doctrine stresses the need for *strong coordination.* The commander who faces the task of rear-battle command at any level will be confronted with the chal-

---

1. Army Logistician. January-February 1998. Professional Bulletin of United States Army Logistician. Reprinted by permission.
2. This manual has been replaced by a series of Rear Battle manuals.

337

lenge of coordinating a bewildering array of units. The variety of CSS branches defies unity of command. The task of determining what resources are available for rear battle is a formidable one filled with traps for the unwary.

The commander must coordinate units that are not designed for tactical operations. He must correctly assess the rear-battle capabilities of available units, looking for limitations that will become apparent only after analysis. These limitations can create total mission failure. However, there can also be offsetting capabilities that are not immediately evident. Be alert to all possibilities.

An excellent starting point for attacking the coordination problem is FM 101-10-2, Staff Officers' Field Manual: Organizational, Technical, and Logistical Data Extracts of Nondivisional Tables of Organization and Equipment. The standard missions, capabilities, and equipment of units can be determined from this manual. Using these data, staff planners can work through the personnel, intelligence, operations, logistics, and operations security estimates found in appendix E of FM 101-5, Staff Organization and Operations (estimates modified for the rear-battle mission). The commander can then create a rear-battle operations order modified from the example presented in appendix G of FM 101-5. A synopsis of the estimates that the planner should make follows.

Personnel estimate. Start with the authorized strength of the units assigned to the base, determine their assigned strength, and compute their available strength. An accurate count of available strength requires the planner to subtract those troops not available for rear-battle operations because of mission strength reduction or noncombatant status. Mission strength reduction occurs when a unit, such as a transportation unit, is assigned a mission that is performed away from the CSS base. Consequently, those troops are available for base defense only when they are not performing their primary missions.

Noncombatant strength includes personnel in medical units and temporary noncombatants, such as patients recovering from wounds, prisoners in custody, replacement personnel not yet issued equipment, and persons working or present in areas where weapons are prohibited. Besides reducing the combatant strength of the base, noncombatants may also create personnel concentrations that are highly attractive to attackers.

After determining available strength, identify base defense personnel requirements and seek soldiers with skills to match. Create a list of critical skills and survey units for them. CSS units typically have senior personnel with experience in other branches. Identify personnel with combat skills and use them to organize or train for base defense. Do not forget civilian skills such as proficiency in foreign languages. When available strength and needed skills are accurately determined, the personnel estimate is complete.

Intelligence estimate. This estimate may be the most difficult to make for two reasons. First, a CSS base is expected to defend primarily against Level-I threats (terrorism, sabotage by enemy sympathizers, and activity by enemy-controlled agents). However, this type of threat is difficult to assess. The targets and purposes differ from the usual military attack. It is also difficult to assess the organization, intentions, and capabilities of the threatening force because of the high level of operational security it exercises. This is where the intelligence deficiency of the CSS unit comes to the forefront. Defending against kidnaping, assassination of key personnel, or sabotage of utilities requires different techniques than defending a position against a conventional assault. The commander should not overlook the secondary skills of base personnel to assist in making the intelligence estimate.

The second difficulty comes in the intelligence preparation of the potential battlefield around the base area. The intelligence preparation is critical since it forms the basis of the command and control or fire control procedures that will be developed. The most common error is to assume that the base will be located in a passive environment. The potential complications offered by the base's surroundings are seldom considered. The rear area will be filled with friendly units, civilians, structures protected under the Law of Land Warfare, and such temporary elements as convoys or friendly air lanes. All must be identified because they create dead zones for fire that can be exploited by attackers. The base and its operations—ammunition points; petroleum, oils, and lubricants points; barracks; and transportation routes—can also create internal and external dead zones that can affect weapons employment both on and off the base.

These dead zones must be recognized during the intelligence preparation, specifically plotted on map overlays, and identified by type of limitation. The graphics must be complete and precise. Failure to identify dead zones can create the potential for destruction of friendly personnel or supplies. Be sure to include a transportation route analysis for both internal and external nets since speed of movement and route capability are important in emergencies.

Operations estimate. There are often two failures in making this estimate. The first is the assumption that resources in the area will be available to the CSS base when needed. For example, CSS bases often plan on receiving medical support from a nearby medical unit, or area damage control or firefighting from an engineer unit. Little consideration is given to what the base elements should do while awaiting support from these units or what the base should do when help is delayed.

The second failure is incomplete development of counteractions to overcome the vulnerabilities identified in the intelligence estimate. Since rear battle response typically involves personnel from several units, arrangements must be made in advance to ensure smooth operation.

The operations estimate should result in a defensive concept of operation that uses the base's capabilities to overcome vulnerabilities. A tasking list is developed with command and control procedures describing the chain-of-command, fire control procedures, notification and warning systems, area responsibilities, coordination provisions, and communications structure.

Logistics estimate. Errors in the logistics estimate for rear battle are usually those of omission. Resupply requirements and methods during rear battle operations must be determined and responsibilities assigned. Fortification and barrier requirements may be significant. Dispersion of personnel and material must be assessed for their vulnerability to attack and their importance to mission accomplishment. A critical equipment listing must be made. Operators for the equipment must be identified and their availability determined. Available area damage control resources must be identified and matched against the most probable area damage situations.

Finally, the commander must prepare for the evacuation or destruction of the CSS base under adverse tactical circumstances. The priorities to be implemented, the methods to be used, the authority to order actions, the material required, the sequence of events to be followed—all must be considered in planning for evacuation or destruction of the base. Failure to plan adequately can create enormous complications.

Operations security (OPSEC) estimate. This may be the most important estimate for a CSS base because effective OPSEC enhances the base's mission. OPSEC is passive defense and thus frees more resources for CSS operations than other modes of defense. In this way, effective OPSEC will help the CSS base counter one of the goals of a threatening force–reducing the base's ability to provide forward support to our forces. Because of its importance, the commander should resist the temptation to include OPSEC considerations under either the operations or logistics estimates. Such a consolidation, or the omission of an OPSEC estimate, is the most frequent OPSEC planning mistake.

The OPSEC estimate must include a review of the intelligence estimate of the local threat; the techniques used by threatening forces; the rules of engagement that will be used to comply with the Law of Land Warfare; camouflage, deception, information security, and physical security requirements; electronic warfare counter-techniques; and civil-military contacts. An effective OPSEC estimate directly assesses the Level-I threat and develops strong passive and some active counters to that threat.

While other estimates may be needed in some situations, the ones listed above should be considered critical for effective rear-battle planning.

Flexible integration is the most difficult, and perhaps the most critical, aspect of rear battle. The overall battlefield situation will be fluid and available resources will change as units arrive, depart, pass through, alter missions, sustain losses, and refit. The changes, combined with the variety of units initially deployed at the base, will require firm control. The rear-battle chain-of-command must be clearly established and must strongly function.

Areas of responsibility must be firmly established, communicated to all units, and adhered to strictly. The commander of the base should contact each unit within 1 hour of arrival and provide initial reports and requirements. This orientation must be followed by an in-depth assessment interview within 24 hours. Use of a survey, with sections for vulnerability, preparation, personnel, equipment, and team structures, is strongly recommended. Having made a valid assessment, the commander must determine the appropriate command and control provisions.

The most common error in effective rear-battle integration is the tendency to approach rear battle as a combined-arms operation conducted in a different setting with inadequate equipment. Rear battle encompasses much more. In some respects, a CSS base readied for rear battle operates more like an American city government than a combined arms organization. A CSS base requires police, ambulance and medical, firefighting, utility, street, disaster, and warning services. When the difference between a CSS base and a combined arms force is understood, effective integration of CSS operations becomes more likely.

The key to integration is tailoring the base's response to the incident being handled. A rear battle response depends on the proximity of the incident, the time available to respond, and the authority, capability, and size of the responding force. Since these factors create a critical operations path that varies from incident to incident, rear-battle integration must remain flexible.

At this point, the need for *imaginative adaptation* should be clear. Imaginative adaptation stresses countering a threat by using available resources in ways other than those for which they are intended. The timing, proximity, and nature of an incident frequently force the CSS base to resort to available resources, regardless of their type or effectiveness. The ability to effectively employ available resources requires imagination, planning, and on-the-spot adaptation.

Some examples can demonstrate the value of creatively using what is at hand. With proper use of their booms and cables, cranes and wreckers can be set up as barriers to temporarily deny access to the base. Landing zones or perimeters can be defended in this fashion. Forklifts can provide portable observation posts that can be used from protected positions. Portable loading ramps can quickly bridge an area covered with aerially dispersed mines while the base awaits explosive ordnance disposal specialists. Water trailers and shower and laundry equipment can be used for firefighting and decontamination.

Even CSS personnel can be "adapted" in an emergency. A track mechanic, tank turret mechanic, and ammunition handler can be placed under an officer or noncommissioned officer and, with little cross-training, function as a tank crew. Many such adaptations are possible in ordnance and supply units—only a little advance planning and training are required. The effectiveness of the adaptation is limited only by the imagination, preparation, and adaptive skill of the user.

The final stage of planning for rear battle is anticipating problems and integrating solutions into the plan. Experience shows that most units are unfamiliar with, do not understand, or cannot implement rear-battle doctrine. Rear-area operation centers (RAOC's) and headquarters assigned rear-battle missions can create enormous coordination problems by failing to adequately define areas of responsibility, fire limitations, and similar control measures. The poor results are then typically blamed on poor performance by subordinate units.

Another problem is the tendency of subordinate units to "run and gun," based on the belief that an armed reaction force that immediately responds to firing is performing effective rear battle. This type of thinking leaves many rear battle tasks undone, often to the tactical advantage of the attacker.

Other problems are caused by the rear-battle "blindness" of the units involved. This is a tunnel vision that results when units focus on their own missions and experiences. RAOC's frequently try to micro manage all things tactical in the belief that CSS personnel do not understand tactical operations. This usually creates a work overload at several levels. RAOC personnel are often unfamiliar with the organization and operations of CSS units and thus fail to see the enormous rear-battle potential of the materials-handling equipment, wreckers, cranes, bulldozers, and other items in the CSS units.

Another example of blindness is the weakness of CSS headquarters units in intelligence analysis, particularly in intelligence summaries. Level-I threat information is almost universally ignored. Military police units focus on Level-II threats and frequently do a poor job of integrating Level-I threat responses into their plans. (Level-II threats include diversionary or sabotage operations by unconventional forces; raid, ambush, and reconnaissance operations by combat units; and special or unconventional warfare missions.) Command and control may become a touchy issue in some military police units.

Medical units are often left out of rear-battle planning because of their noncombatant status. Unfortunately, this omission ignores the vulnerability of medical units to nuclear-biological-chemical and Level-I threats. It also ignores the fact that threatening forces will not recognize the noncombatant status of medical units. Medical units have a critical role in area damage control and must be integrated into the rear-battle structure without being assigned battle control responsibilities or battle missions.

CSS units have three weaknesses in rear-battle response. First, they fail to adapt standard CSS safety regulations to the existing tactical situation, thus failing to achieve their safety objective while leaving themselves vulnerable to attack. Second, units handling critical assets tend to overrate their own importance, assuming that they will be defended by military police forces under all circumstances and refusing to plan for other possibilities. These units typically fail to integrate their defense with assigned military police units and have no plan for action inside their unit storage areas.

The final CSS weakness is caused by battle inexperience and is not limited to CSS units. Lack of experience leads to unrealistic defense plans and response. CSS troops tend to overreact in tactical confrontations. The lack of tactical discipline of CSS troops must be addressed by training and strong fire control procedures or rules of engagement.

Rear battle is more than an infantry operation relocated to the rear area. It is a combination of many branch operations. It is the CSS equivalent of combined arms operations in the Air Land Battle. Effective rear battle relies on thorough preparation and strong coordination to achieve flexible integration through the imaginative adaptation of available resources. The ability to identify, obtain, unify, and use all the ingredients on hand is the mark of the rear-battle professional.

Appendix B

CHART 1
COMMAND EVALUATION AND
DECISION SEQUENCE
CRIMINAL ACT VERSUS ACT OF WAR

Criminal Act   **Evaluation Criteria**   **Act of War**

Act of Aggression - General and Specific Tests
    (General test)
Use of armed force by a state...against another state
    (Specific Tests)
Invasion/Attack on territory of a nation
Bombardment of territory of a nation
Blockade of ports or coasts of a nation
Attack on military forces of a nation
Use of armed forces within territory of another without agreement
Allowing territory of a nation to be used for act of aggression
Sending armed bands, groups, irregulars, mercenaries by a nation

YES
\/
\/

Declaration of Intent
    Self-Determination   War
    \/   \/
    \/   \/
    \/ >>>>   Action between Nations
    \/   YES>>>>   ACT OF WAR
    \/   NO
    \/   \/
    \/   \/

Group Exercising Right of Self-Determination
Freeing self from external interference
Forcibly deprived of right by colonial, racist or alien forces
Pursuing economic, social or cultural development
CRIMINAL   <<<<NO   YES
ACT   \/
                                                  \/

Group Meets Partisan Test
Commander responsible for subordinates
Recognizable insignia or uniform
Carrying arms openly
CRIMINAL   <<<<NO   YES
ACT   \/
                                                  \/
          Acts in accord with law of warfare
                                                  \/
                                                  \/

Law of Warfare Determination
Group Attacking Legitimate Targets
Bombardment notice given to noncombatants
Protected structures spared unless site defended
CRIMINAL   <<<<NO   YES
ACT   \/
                                                  \/
Weapons Appropriate Under Law of Warfare
No nuclear use
No chemical agent use
No biological agent use
No flame weapons
No unmarked mines
No multiple projectiles in anti-personnel light weapons
No explosive projectiles in anti-personnel light weapons
No frangible projectiles in anti-personnel light weapons
CRIMINAL   <<<<NO   YES>>>>   ACT OF WAR
ACT

COMMAND RESPONSE TO EVALUATION

Criminal Act   **Act of War**

Refer to appropriate law enforcement officers   Refer to Federal Military
                                                  Forces through State Adjutant;
                                                  State Forces may respond to
                                                  defend

Activate local emergency forces

Utilize current local legal structure
Refer to international tribunal if appropriate

Prepare to receive LEO and local emergency
forces

Activate local emergency forces

Defend with state, local &
partisan citizen forces pending
handoff of responsibility

Expand Use of Force Laws to
Wartime Rules of Engagement
for Low-Intensity Conflict

Check local equipment for
compliance with Law of Warfare

Prepare for hand-off of
responsibility to federal forces

TABLE I.
PHYSICAL CAPACITY OF COMMON TRANSPORT DEVICES
[Assumes use of high grade plastic explosive with low weight/high RE to
maximum physical space capacity]

CONTAINER	CUBIC FEET	POUNDS EXPLOSIVE
Briefcase	.4	43
5 gallon Can	.99	107
medium Backpack	1.3	140
55 gallon Drum	8.74	944
trunk of small Car	10	1080 (exceeds weight limit)
small trash Dumpster	68	7,344 (exceeds lift limit)
Van/Pickup w/shell	128	13,824 (exceeds weight limit)
2 ton cargo Truck	159	17,172 (exceeds weight limit)
1200 gallon tank Truck	160	17,280 (exceeds weight limit)
5000 gallon tank Truck	668	72,144 (exceeds weight limit)
20' trash Dumpster	1800	194,400 (exceeds lift limit)
40' Semi-trailer van	2100	226,800 (exceeds weight limit)

TABLE II.
PRACTICAL PLANNING LIMITATIONS
[Assumes high RE factor to maximum space or typical weight-carrying capacity
(whichever is smaller)]
[Survival zone assumes person is shielded from direct impact damage by
projectile or displacement by blast wave, and accepts minor pressure injuries
such as eardrum rupture. Safety zone assumes person is exposed to blast wave.]

CONTAINER	QUANTITY	SURVIVAL ZONE	SAFETY ZONE
Briefcase	50 pounds	35 feet	1,200 feet
5 gallon Can	110 pounds	45 feet	1,600 feet
Backpack	140 pounds	50 feet	1,800 feet

CONTAINER	QUANTITY	SURVIVAL ZONE	SAFETY ZONE
55 gallon Drum	500 pounds	65 feet	3,400 feet
Dumpster	2,000 pounds	115 feet	4,300 feet
Car	800 pounds	85 feet	3,200 feet
Pickup/Van	1,200 pounds	95 feet	3,700 feet
2 Ton cargo/ tank Truck	5,000 pounds	155 feet	5,900 feet
Tank Semi-trailer	52,500 pounds	340 feet	11,300 feet
Van Semi-Trailer	120,000 pounds	460 feet	17,000 feet

TABLE III.
STANDARD SAFETY DISTANCE COMPUTATION
[Multiple result by RE factor for more precise estimate. Assumes open ground between explosion and personnel.]

Safe distance from overpressure effects (feet) = 300 3√Pounds of Explosive

Safe distance from fragmentation effects (feet) = 600 3√Pounds of Explosive

PLANNING AND ANALYSIS REFERENCES

1. "The Effects of Nuclear Weapons" is available through the U.S. Government book stores. Using figure 3.72 (Peak overpressure in a 1-kiloton free air burst for sea-level ambient conditions), Table 5.145 (Conditions of failure of overpressure-sensitive elements), Table 12.38 (Tentative criteria for direct blast effects in man from fast-rising, long-duration pressure pulses) and equations found in paragraph 3.62, chart data can be produced for quick reference during analysis. Example:

	Pounds of explosive			
	A	B	C	D
Pressure				
W	d	d	d	d
X	d	d	d	d
Y	d(p)	d(p)	d(p)	d(p)
Z	d(s)	d(s)	d(s)	d(s)

Where W-Z equals pressures obtained from Figure 3.72, A-D may be worked into the equations to produce the distance (d) at which that pressure occurs in the lesser explosion. By selecting pressures which are equivalent to the damage levels found in tables 5.145 and 12.38, distances at which structures (s) are damaged or persons (p) are injured can be identified in the chart. The charts can be refined by supplementary information (Fatality probability by overpressure and Injury by impact with hard surface following displacement of person by pressure wave) from part 1 of "Medical Aspects of Nuclear Weapons and Their Effects on Medical Operations".

2. "Medical Aspects of Nuclear Weapons and Their Effects on Medical Operations" is usually available in local libraries that are designated as government repositories. It contains explanations of chemical, biological and radiological hazard prediction as

well as exposure guidance for personnel. Other military manuals may be used as well as information from FEMA, OSHA, NIOSH, CDC, or HHS.

3. "Technology Against Terrorism: The Federal Effort" contains a summary of bomb detection technology capabilities. It does not cover the use of bomb dogs.

Notes

1. "The Effects of Nuclear Weapons" compiled and edited by Samuel Glasstone and Philip J. Dolan, published by the United States Department of Defense and the Energy Research and Development Administration, third edition, 1977, U.S. Government Printing Office, Washington, D.C.

2. "Medical Aspects of Nuclear Weapons and Their Effects on Medical Operations," Subcourse MED447, by Academy of Health Sciences, U.S. Army, June 1990, Fort Sam Houston, TX.

3. "Technology Against Terrorism: The Federal Effort" by the Office of Technology Assessment, Congress of the United States, 1991, U.S. Government Printing Office, Washington, D.C.

BIBLIOGRAPHY

Books

Antokol, Norman and Nudell, Mayer; *The Handbook for Effective Emergency and Crisis Management*; Lexington, MA; Lexington Books; 1988.

Antoniou, Chris T. and Reisman, W. Michael; *The Law of War*; New York; Vintage Books; 1994.

Brown, Anthony Cave; *Bodyguard of Lies*; New York; Harper Collins Publishers, Inc.; 1975.

Brown, Anthony Cave, editor; *The Secret War Report of the OSS: Declassified*; New York; Berkley Publishing Corp.; 1976.

Clausewitz, Carl Von; *On War*; Middlesex, England; Penguin Books; 1968.

Commission on Beirut International Airport Terrorist Act, *Report of the DOD Commission on Beirut International Airport Terrorist Act, October 23, 1983*; 20 December 1983.

Dennis, Edward S.G., Jr., Department of Justice; *Evaluation of the Handling of the Branch Davidian Stand-off in Waco, Texas February 28 to April 19, 1993, Redacted Version*; Washington, D.C.; U.S. Government Printing Office; October 8, 1993.

Department of the Army; *Field Manual 90-12 Base Defense*; Washington, D.C.; October 1989.

Department of the Army; *Training Circular 19-16, Countering Terrorism on US Army Installations*; Washington, D.C.; April 1983.

Department of the Army; *Field Manual 5-250 Explosives and Demolitions*; Washington, D.C.; June 1992.

Department of the Army; *Field Manual 5-15 Field Fortifications*; Washington, D.C.; June 1972.

Department of the Army; *Field Manual 27-10 The Law of Land Warfare*; Washington, D.C.; July 1956.

Department of the Army; *Field Manual 19-30 Physical Security*; Washington, D.C.; March 1979.

Departments of the Army, Navy and Air Force; *Field Manual 3-9 Potential Military Chemical/Biological Agents and Compounds*; Washington, D.C.; 12 December 1990.

Department of the Army; *Field Manual 90-23 Rear Security Operations*; Washington, D.C.; November 1989.

Department of Defense; *Terrorist Group Profiles*; Washington, D.C.; Superintendent of Documents;

Department of Justice; *Recommendations of Experts for Improvements in Federal Law Enforcement After Waco*; Washington, D.C.; U.S. Government Printing Office; 1993.

Department of Justice; *Report to the Deputy Attorney General on the Events at Waco, Texas February 28 to April 19, 1993, Redacted version*; Washington, D.C.; U.S. Government Printing Office; October 1993.

Department of Justice, United States Marshal Service; *Vulnerability Assessment of Federal Facilities*; Washington, D.C.; U.S. Government Printing Office; June, 1995.

Department of the Treasury, Bureau of Alcohol, Tobacco and Firearms; *Bomb Threats and Physical Security Planning*; Washington, D.C.; U.S. Government Printing Office.

Dewar, Michael; *Weapons & Equipment of Counter-Terrorism*; London; Arms and Armour Press; 1987.

Dobson, Christopher and Payne, Ronald; *The Terrorists: Their Weapons, Leaders and Tactics, Revised edition*; New York; Facts on File, Inc.; 1982.

Compiled by Dolan, Phillip J. and Glasston, Samuel; *The Effects of Nuclear Weapons*; 3rd edition; Department of Defense and the Energy Research and Development Administration; Washington, D.C.; U.S. Government Printing Office; 1977.

Dwyer, Jim; Kocieniewski, David; Murphy, Diedre and Tyre, Peg; *Two Seconds Under the World*; New York; Crown Publishers, Inc.; 1994.

Compiled by Glasston, Samuel; and Dolan, Phillip J.; *The Effects of Nuclear Weapons*; 3rd edition; Department of Defense and the Energy Research and Development Administration; Washington, D.C.; U.S. Government Printing Office; 1977.

Hammel, Eric; *The Root*; San Diego, New York and London; Harcourt, Brace, Jovanovich Publishers; 1985.

Heyman, Philip B., Deputy Attorney General, Department of Justice; *Lessons of Waco: Proposed Changes in Federal Law Enforcement*; Washington, D.C.; U.S. Government Printing Office; October, 1993.

Hogg, Ian V.; *Fortress: A History of Military Defence*; New York; St. Martin's Press, Inc.; 1975.

Kocieniewski, David; Dwyer, Jim; Murphy, Diedre and Tyre, Peg; *Two Seconds Under the World*; New York; Crown Publishers, Inc.; 1994.

Lenz, Robert R.; *Explosives and Bomb Disposal Guide*; Springfield, IL; Thomas; 1976.

Motley, James B.; *US Strategy to Counter Domestic Political Terrorism*; Washington, D.C.; National Defense University Press; 1983.

Murphy, Diedre; Tyre, Peg; Dwyer, Jim; and Kocieniewski, David; *Two Seconds Under the World*; New York; Crown Publishers, Inc.; 1994.

Nudell, Mayer and Antokol, Norman; *The Handbook for Effective Emergency and Crisis Management*; Lexington, MA; Lexington Books; 1988.

Office of the Federal Register; *The United States Government Manual, 1996/1997*; National Archives and Records Administration.

Office of Technology Assessment, Congress of the United States; *Technology Against Terrorism: The Federal Effort*; US Government Printing Office; July 1991.

Paine, Thomas; *Common Sense*; 1976, Penguin Books, Middlesex, England.

Payne, Ronald and Dobson, Christopher; *The Terrorists: Their Weapons, Leaders and Tactics, Revised edition*; New York; Facts on File, Inc.; 1982.

Reaves, Dick J.; *The Ashes of Waco*; New York; Simon and Schuester; 1995.

Reisman, W. Michael and Antoniou, Chris T.; *The Law of War*, New York; Vintage Books; 1994.

Stoffel, Joseph, Major AUS (Ret.); *Explosives and Homemade Bombs*, Springfield, IL; Thomas; 1977.

Szasz, Thomas S., M.D.; *The Manufacture of Madness*, New York; Dell Publishing Co, Inc.; 1970.

Tyre, Peg; Dwyer, Jim; Kocieniewski, David; and Murphy, Diedre; *Two Seconds Under the World*, New York; Crown Publishers, Inc.; 1994.

Documents

Charter of the United Nations, 1949.

Constitution of the State of Kansas, 1861.

Constitution of the United States of America, 1789.

Declaration of Independence, 1776.

Executive Order 12960; *Amendments to the Manual for Courts-Martial, United States, 1984*; Office of the President of the United States; 12 May 1995.

Executive Order 12656; *Assignment of Emergency Preparedness Responsibilities*, Office of the President of the United States; 18 November 1988.

Periodicals

Arnspiger, Brian R. and Bowers, Gordon A., M.A.; *Integrated Use-of-Force Training Program*;" FBI Law Enforcement Bulletin, November 1996, Page 1.

Associated Press; *Officials Find the First Clue in Bombing Investigation*, The Kansas City Star, June 29, 1996. *Saudis Allow New Barrier for U.S. Complex*, The Kansas City Star, July 1, 1996. *Perry Draws Fire from Congressmen Over Bombing*, The Kansas City Star, July 2, 1996. *FBI Chief Visiting Dhahran*, The Kansas City Star, July 4, 1996. *Man Believed Dead in Saudi Bombing is Alive in Hospital*, The Kansas City Star, July 4, 1996. *Pentagon Looks to Move Riyadh-Based Troops*, The Kansas City Star, July 5, 1996. *Saudi Officials Restrict FBI Investigation of Truck-Bomb Attack*, The Kansas City Star, July 14, 1996. *Troop Move Opposed*, The Kansas City Star, 15 July 1996. *40 Shiites Held in Bombing, Sources Say*, The Colorado Springs Gazette Telegraph, September 6, 1996. *Security Revision Ordered in Effort to Protect Troops*, The Kansas City Star, September 14, 1996. *Saudi Man to give Leads on Bombing*, The Kansas City Star, June 18, 1997. *Saudi Tied to Khobar Bomb is Charged in Another Case*, The Kansas City Star, June 19, 1997.

Beck, Melinda; *'Get Me Out of Here!'*, Newsweek, Volume CXXV, Number 18, May 1, 1995; Page 40.

Bowers, Gordon A., M.A. and Arnspiger, Brian R.; *Integrated Use-of-Force Training Program*, FBI Law Enforcement Bulletin November 1996, Page 1.

Carpenter, Dave C., The Associated Press; *Embassy Suspect Bypasses U.S. Questioning*, The Kansas City Star, August 17, 1998.

Claibourne, William; The Washington Post; *'War Zone' in the Streets: Terror Strikes Two Capitals in East Africa*; The Kansas City Star; August 8, 1998.

Clarity, James F., New York Times News Service; *Bomb-Torn Ulster Town in Mourning;* The Kansas City Star, August 17, 1998.

Davies, Karin, The Associated Press; *Kenyan Bombing Victims Buried;* The Kansas City Star, August 16, 1998.

Dellios, Hugh, Chicago Tribune; *Suspects are Arrested in Kenya;* The Kansas City Star; August 13, 1998.

Duffy, Brian; *Terror in the Heartlands;* U.S. News and World Report, Volume 118, Number 17, May 1, 1995; Page 28.

Elliott, Michael; *Terror Times Two;* Newsweek; Volume CXXXII, Number 17, August 17, 1998; Page 22.

Ellis, John W.; *Preparing the CSS Base for Rear Battle;* Army Logistician; January-February 1988; Page 31.

Gazlay, Kristin, The Associated Press; *Apology to Bomb Victims;* The Kansas City Star, August 19, 1998.

Gellman, Barton; The Washington Post; *Squad Launches Global Manhunt for Terrorists;* The Kansas City Star, August 8, 1998.

Gibbs, Nancy; Oklahoma City: *Blood of Innocents;* Time, Volume 145, Number 18, May 1, 1995; Page 56.

Gleick, Elizabeth; *The Suspects: A Confederacy of Extremists;* Time, Volume 145, Number 18, May 1, 1995; Page 44.

Hall, John C., J.D.; *FBI Training on the New Federal Deadly Force Policy;* FBI Law Enforcement Bulletin, April 1996, Page 25.

Hillier, Timothy; *Bomb Attacks in City Centers;* FBI Law Enforcement Bulletin, September 1994; Page 13.

Hughes, Candice, Associated Press Writer; *No Confessions, FBI Says;* The Kansas City Star, August 18, 1998.

Ibrahim, Youssef M., New York Times; *Saudi Militants Blamed in Bombing of Barracks;* The Kansas City Star, August 15, 1996.

Jackman, Tom; *Witnesses Say They Warned KC Firefighters;* The Kansas City Star, January 23, 1997.

Klein, Joe; *The Nervous '90s;* Newsweek, Volume CXXV, Number 18, May 1, 1995; Page 58.

Knight-Ridder Newspapers; *Defense Secretary Shoulders Blame in 19 Deaths;* The Kansas City Star, September 19, 1996. *Pentagon Blamed in Bombing;* The Colorado Springs Gazette Telegraph, September 13, 1996. *FBI Hopes Engine has Clues to Blasts;* The Kansas City Star, August 12, 1998.

Knutson, Lawrence L., The Associated Press; *Ready for Grim Task, Team from U.S. Heads to Blast Site;* The Kansas City Star, August 9, 1998.

Lacayo, Richard; *Security: How Safe is Safe?;* Time, Volume 145, Number 18, May 1, 1995; Page 68.

Lavery, Robert; *Car Bombs: They Are Not a Lemon in the Terrorist Arsenal;* TVI Journal; Volume III, Number 1, Page 3.

Lederer, Edit M., The Associated Press; *Death Count Rises Past 200;* The Kansas City Star, August 10, 1998.

Levinson, Eric; *For a High Risk Office: Concrete Suggestions on 'Target Hardening,'* TVI Journal; Volume I, Number 6, Page 2.

Leland, John; *Why the Children?*, Newsweek, Volume CXXV, Number 18, May 1, 1995; Page 48.

Masland, Tom; *Life in the Bull's Eye*, Newsweek, Volume CXXV, Number 18, May 1, 1995; Page 56.

Mbitriu, Chege, The Associated Press; *FBI Raids Nairobi Hotel on Tip From Suspect*, The Kansas City Star, August 19, 1998.

McGeary, Johanna; *Terror in Africa*, Time, Volume 152, Number 7, August 17, 1998; Page 32.

McGraw, Dan and Walsh, Kenneth T.; *A Strike at the Very Heart of America*, U.S. News and World Report, Volume 118, Number 17, May 1, 1995; Page 51.

Miller, Alan C. and Murphy, Dean E., Los Angeles Times; *Investigators Question Role of Water Truck*, The Kansas City Star, August 14, 1998.

Miller, Marjorie and Murphy, Dean E., Los Angeles Times; *Toll Mounts in Twin Blasts*, The Kansas City Star, August 9, 1998.

Monday, Mark, editor; *A Growth in Terror: Low-Tech in High-Rise is Deadly*, TVI Journal; Volume IV, Number 7-9, Page 2.

Montgomery, Lori, Knight Ridder Newspapers; *U.S. Agents Work Slowly, Steadily to Gather Evidence at Tanzania Site*, The Kansas City Star, August 17, 1998.

Murphy, Dean E. and Miller, Alan C., Los Angeles Times; *Investigators Question Role of Water Truck*, The Kansas City Star, August 14, 1998.

Murphy, Dean E. and Miller, Marjorie, Los Angeles Times; *Toll Mounts in Twin Blasts*, The Kansas City Star, August 9, 1998.

Nydale, Ann; *Practice: Designing for Terrorism and Other Aggression*; TVI Journal; Volume 7, Number 1, Page 12.

Olson, Dean T.; *Improving Deadly Force Decision Making*, FBI Law Enforcement Bulletin; February 1998, Page 1.

Penn, Steve; *Trial Draws near in Explosion Death of Firefighters*, the Kansas City Star, November 24, 1994.

Pogatchnik, Shawn, The Associated Press; *Police Arrest 5 in Connection with Northern Ireland Bomb*, The Kansas City Star, August 18, 1998.

Royce, Knut, Newsday; *Bombing Suspect Names Associates*, The Kansas City Star, August 20, 1998.

Staff; *This Doesn't Happen Here*, Newsweek, Volume CXXV, Number 18, May 1, 1995; Page 24.

Staff; *When the Terror Comes from Within*; Time, Volume 145, Number 18, May 1, 1995; Page 36.

Staff; *Bomb Threats: When the Phone Rings It's Too Late to Plan*; TVI Journal; Volume IV Number 1-3, Page 3. *A Chronology of: Euroterrorist Actions 1984-April 1985*, TVI Journal; Volume 5, Number 4, Page 18.

Staff; *Update*, TVI Journal; Volume IV Number 4-6, 7-9 and 10-12; Volume V Number 3 and 4.

Star News Services; *Bomb Kills Americans in Saudi Capital*, The Kansas City Star, November 14, 1995. *Americans Die in Blast*, The Kansas City Star, Volume 116, Number 283, June 26, 1996. *$2.7 Million Reward Set in Fatal Blast*, The Kansas City Star, Volume 116, Number 284, June 27, 1996. *Site of Saudi Bombing Yields*

No Clues Yet, The Kansas City Star, Volume 116, Number 285, June 28, 1996.

Saudis Ignored U.S. Pleas, The Kansas City Star, Volume 116, Number 287, June 30, 1996. *Hope Remains for Rescue Efforts*, The Kansas City Star, August 11, 1998. *Car Bomb Explodes in Northern Ireland*, The Kansas City Star, August 16, 1998.

Tucker, Neely, Knight-Ridder Newspapers; *Egyptian Group is Bombing Suspect*, The Kansas City Star, August 15, 1998.

Walsh, Kenneth T. and McGraw, Dan; *A Strike at the Very Heart of America*, U.S. News and World Report, Volume 118, Number 17, May 1, 1995; Page 51.

The Washington Post; *Terror Threat Misjudged Perry Says*, The Kansas City Star, July 10, 1996.

INDEX